CHANCIN

Charles Montgomery

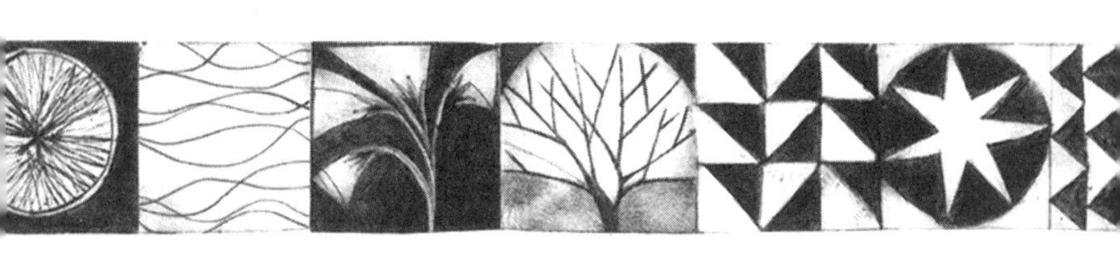

CHANCING THE LIGHT

POEMS

Charles Montgomery

NYMETWOOD BOOKS

First published in 2017 by Nymetwood Books

ISBN 978-1-9997169-0-5

Available from good bookshops and through:
Green Hill Arts, Fore Street, Mortonhampstead
Newton Abbot, Devon TQ13 8LL
Tel.: 01647 440775
Email: contact@greenhillarts.co.uk
Website: greenhillarts.co.uk

Printed by Short Run Press Ltd, Exeter, Devon

For Juliane

Acknowledgements

Acknowledgements are due to the editors of the following magazines and publications in which a number of these poems first appeared:

Agenda, The British Journal of Psychiatry, The British Journal of Psychotherapy, The Colebrook Bell, Company of Poets Four, Company of Poets Journeys, Company of Poets Taboo, The Countryman, Envoi, The Green Book, The Honest Ulsterman, Lines Review, Odyssey, Otter, Outposts, Oxford Poetry, Poetry Durham, Poetry Ireland Review, Poetry Wales, Quartz, Raceme, Resurgence, The Rialto, Scratch, Social Work Education, Staple, The Stumbling Dance, Westwards, Weyfarers, Writing Ulster

"Mr Golinski (Tailor) And Me" won a runner's-up prize in the 1990 National Poetry Competition.

"Leslie" won second prize in the 1990 Bridport International Creative Writing Competion.

"You" won joint first prize in the 1991 Aberystwyth Open Poetry Competition.

My thanks to: Chris Haslam, Titus Forbes Adam, Paul Hyland, Nick Naydler, Jeremy Holmes, Lawrence Sail, Dana Littlepage Smith and Jeremy Hooker, for their support and encouragement going back many years. Also in gratitude for the friendships woven in The Company of Poets – long disbanded, and in memory of Steve Sims.

Title page print design thanks to Bea Forshall (www.beaforshall.com)

Cover painting: Catherine Hyde *The Dark Orchard* by kind permission of the artist (www.catherinehyde.co.uk)

Contents

"Everything changes but nothing is lost."

Ovid, Metamorphoses XV

Mr Golinski (Tailor) And Me

It was like an unheated waiting-room
In some provincial Polish station
Where the last train departed
Years ago,
Leaving the absence of its travellers
Lingering with the damp.
He descended the wooden stairs
A minute after the bell
Had settled back into its silence
With the dust
And fingered the cloth, frowning
Without a word.
Then I stood measured in the empty gloom
His foreign hands remembering my space,
Outlining the lost generations
With our hundred faceless bodies folded
Back between two mirrors.
There our shapes were stacked
As if down a tunnel,
A whole family mimicking our movements
To a point where his old arms
Around my chest
Were holding me
And not the measure,
And my head small and unfamiliar
Was resting on his shoulder.

Mount Abu

The man employed to keep
Monkeys out of the garden
Ambles the green shade all day.
The monkeys come and go in droves,
Whole families at a distance
Duck his stones.
Nothing much else happens.
The sun swivels through noon,
Casts long shadows towards tea
And beyond.
A cool edged breeze begins.
The families rearrange themselves
Now sitting high in their trees.
The man dances his stones
On the last of the light
Far into the sinking blue
And turning homeward hums
At his day's work.

Fox

Riding to work, midsummer,
Undulating empty fields –
Suddenly a fox,
Burnished copper brazened
Sat gazing from a pool of light.
Such an instant of fox
Forced my stop,
Jet eyes on mine unmoving
Fixed me like a memory.
And so we eyed each other
In a curious balance
Neither thought to spoil,
As the moment passed
Wide as a river:
Fox on a throne of gold leaves,
Poise of a Buddha's gaze,
No shot of scarlet stealing the night,
No owl's screech undoing sleep.
And what was seen
Or what was asked I could not tell
Yet recognized as something lost
Numinous on the air like scent,
As though all the encounters
Of our lives are really one
Chance crossing – you and me.
Tracks long covered converge
Deep in the breathing forest
And then part
Into the outstretched arms of day.

Post Mortem At Lunchtime

I remember the shock of red
Swilling in stainless steel,
The thin drumming of life,
And how it would spatter into its colour
Like burst buds on the polished surface
And rainbow like oil.
It brought a sudden smell,
The blunt metallic gloom
Of sickening finality
As it trickled down the plug.
And we would peer into the rubbery
White carcass of the patient
We'd greeted yesterday,
Her copper darkness gaping,
Ignoring the clown's slit smile
Of her silvery sawn open head,
Pretending to concentrate on the glistening
Rubies that puckered her liver,
Her delicate jade green bile and
How she came to die.
And we would breathe beer and crisps
And soon forget it all,
Would crowd out into a bustling street
Beneath a narrow burning sky,
The sudden traffic roaring,
A river of people pulsing by.

The Edge

They emerge outside the hospital
Dazed by our day,
In dressing-gown and slippers,
The pale ones,
Searching the sunlight
For something familiar:
The bright cars and brisk
Comings and goings
Of life.
Behind them doors slide
And shadows shelve steeply
To the sound of phones;
Shoes squeal on tiles,
As the mundane
And the routine criss-crosses
With something more fragile.
And no one knows
Where the edge begins,
This strange overlap,
But all through the day
They gather
At the building's entrance,
Anonymous filed numbers,
To lean against warm walls
And breathe town air,

To stand blinking away
The minutes
Of wide blue spaces,
While the dust passes,
Unnoticed,
In and out of light.

Channels

In Zamora a boy threw a stone
And it flew like a bird
Around the walls of the church
Out of sight.
Vanished:
Loosened into the blue
Tracing curves in the air
As if caught in the contours
Of the town's finger-print.

Round and round over our heads
Unseen, whole families gathered,
Swirled into the sky.

The boy whistled his way
Through the open square,
Hands itching,
Veered on the edge of twilight
Like a smudge and was gone.

Leonard

His marble eyes –
Cloudy sclera steep and scarred
Like a white cliff face
Staring down the drop of age,
His dizzy ninety years –
Mouthing words to mother and father
Still waiting for him at home.
He sat in silence
Above polished shoes
Filling his suit like a coat-hanger,
Huge hands blotched and bristling
Clumped together cupping air
Impervious to the century's change.
With only fragments of the child left
He was re-learning its loneliness
Through the vacant rooms of home.
Imagine the glistening road
Leading out of this city
Empty as a runway,
And then the woods and the wet fields
Sloping in silence to the sea,
And all the houses with their mothers
And fathers cradling and cradled.
Who is waiting for whom and in what place
When our time so repeats itself in others,
Becoming unowned as the sand
Patterned beyond words,
Rippling into distances like a new land?

Inside

An old house full of rooms
Moves through me,
Grinds gravel on stone floors,
Spirals a flight of stairs.
A slow opening of doors
Leaves lingering a presence
As rooms turn into rooms:
The long backward pull of childhood,
Soft as a moth against glass
Beating insistent wings.

This house knows me,
Draws curtains, lights candles,
Throbs with the glow of fires,
Defines the unfolding of life
Into a shape centuries old.
Against big windows a purple
Intestinal darkness presses,
Gurgles with the sliding of stars.

I imagine the touch of snow;
Flakes falling surprised
Will discover the earth
In all this stillness
Like the hands of a baby
Learning its mother's face.
It is warm inside.
The rooms hum to me
Right up to the pale throat of dawn.

Seminar Storm

Then the hail happened,
humming the air,
bouncing the sudden moment
knee high on grass.
The roof roared stillness
into our voices so we paused
in the deepening shadow that was cast
as from a planet passing close
that unrolled its darkness,
packed ice-sparkles
trailing like stars.

Then everything slowed.

Years condensed in seconds
and we were left as strangers
awkward at some loss,
an absence we could not prevent
as if charged particles had torn open a hole
into which memory had drained
and hope.

The moment passed.

Heads turned slowly from the
grey skies that slid
beyond those rooms,
the interiors from which we gazed

as we tried again with words
that boomeranged back,
clattered in corners
connected with nothing,
and everyone wanted to leave
and no one knew what had happened.

Leslie

Close up he is stubbled granite
As if chiselled beneath stained pyjamas
Out of a huge grey slab,
Swaying on the edge of his bed
Through the fading light of autumn
Like a weather-worn dolmen,
A strange and uncanny sign of something
Whose significance constrains our love
As might an endless winter sky.

Month after month we wait
For him to carry his mute suffering
Back into history,
But month after month he staggers the ward
As he has for half a century,
Mouthing like a goldfish
Imprecations or love-songs
His breath against the wall
Unreadable as the wind.
At night he lays his landscape down
A mound beneath sheets of snow,
His eyes shut tight as fossils,
Hands resting on his chest
Like two spades on a grave.

Biscay

Far out at sea
Diamonds shimmer on waves
Pulled undulant by gravity
To pencil line horizons.
Our ship's steel bulks the water flat
Three miles above the seabed
Barely touching a blackness
We dare not imagine
Of pebbled silence and cold
Constant night.
Behind we leave a motorway
Of hissing surf churned white
Feathering into distance.
On we labour all day,
The ship's nonchalant weight shuddering
Beneath leaden clouds
Warm with no trace of sun,
Drawing our tidy but transient homes
Imperceptibly nearer.
We shift from railing to railing
As the hours lengthen
And the view tilts unchanged,
Until purple darkness deepens like a bruise
Spreading stars over an obsidian sea
And the wind blows cold with absence
And it seems as if we are passing over
The flat back of a vast sleeping being,
Our separate lives briefly joined
Sinking as one in her ancient memory
Like a grain of sand.

13 February 1945

Minus ten in Dresden, and the sky
On fire with evening.
Children skate circles
Around the Zwinger,
Press raw faces north,
East, south, west, north
Round and round.
Between the palace and anything,
The flat spaces we seem
To fall headlong into,
The over-large squares,
Empty streets runway wide,
A great rising of white
That blankets the years.

Imagine how the darkened city
Had lit up, hour
After hour after hour,
How the sky glowed;
How the horizon rocked
Until later, all that could be seen
In the fire
Was the bow of the Elbe
Running black,
Curved as a question mark.

The lights
Drift across to meet us
Piercing the purple air:
Candles in the ruins of the Frauenkapelle
As if be-jewelled
Placed by ten thousand hands.
All those small flames
Amongst the rubble,
Pointing out of a darkness
To a flat 360 degrees,
As if they had a voice,
As if we could hear,
Night
After night after night

East Germany

And the land is bald and hedgeless.
Two women rake soil against a winter sky,
Bleak as scarecrows,
Their bicycles rusting by the road.
We hum over miles of cobbles
Smoothed by hooves,
Clattering wooden carts,
The stamp of singing armies,
Tyes vibrating history
Into the loose tin of our Skoda.

We pass villages folded in hollows
Frost glinting great
Receding shapes
Across their silent roofs.
A few bullet-ridden buildings
Stand witness around a square
Empty at midday,
Our road rising the other side
Straight as string tied
To a blank horizon.

It is close here and the scars so raw
That the gesture is to look away,
As if all war were rolled into one,
Like the tread of a tank
Repeating itself,
Blindly hammering into the years
Its iron,
Denting a pattern we seem
Unable not to follow.

The city's sudden approach
Brings us into the dusk
Behind a lorry snarling gears.
We slow, catching in our headlights
White faces pointing resolutely home:
The old, the young, indistinguishable,
Wrapped with flakes of snow
Trudge the shovelled pavement,
Dispersing the darkness.

Hysterectomy

I am wide awake
On the slim steel table
Boned by a moon white light
Clear and alien
As the slow stroked incision
That streaks its sudden red.
Then tight rubber gloves
Come up crushed
With my warm and easy blood,
And my dumb skin is tugged,
Split and clamped until
The squeak of metal twisted
Holds me open like a trap.

I wait gaping under hooded heads
Paralysed like all the dead
Suspended in a silent sky,
With blunt teeth nosing me
To the warm black of my depths.
Then the numb ripping,
The long seasons giving way
Until it is dragged out
Into the silvery air
Like a fist clenched with earth.

The hiss and pump of gas
Lifts loose my chest,
Breathes me the smell of sweet hay
As my heart dances across a green screen
Like a flight tracked on radar.

I circle mutely, descend
Through darkness
Back towards voices and light.
Tugged by the searing
Of a long thin thread,
I pirouette on the pin-head
That is stitched across
An emptiness
I will cradle forever.

Krakow Am See

(after Jaan Kaplinski)

Night on the lake
And not a breath of wind.
A leaf is held by water
And passes around the moon:
So many hands have gone before
Holding the dark places tight
That dreaming during the day
We may sleep through the night,
And geese are gathering in the grey
Restless once more.

My love, should we never awake,
Should there be no shore?

The Beach, Berneray

The beach is a bleached drum
Bone white,
Hollowed with crystals of air,
And you are crouched
Your ear printing the sand
Like a shell,
Listening for the echo of my hand
Slamming the ground fifty metres away.

Beneath wind and wave
There is a faint pounding
Like a heart beat buried deep,
Distant beyond light,
Dull as the soft tramping of hooves.

Straightening you smile
Sheer against the sky
And you are tiny suddenly
On the horseshoe bay
And our time terribly frail,
With the waves rolling white
And the mountain's purple clamour
Huge at your back.

Storm

Storm a minute before rain.
You lie
In the middle of a still afternoon,
And head-on the day has turned purple.
Jackdaws call through an open window.
The room has settled like a museum piece
And you have been here
For ever
Waking in the amber air.
Outside, woods float upward as if
The moments lifting were a piece of history
Dislodged from the bottom of a well.
You surface
Somewhere in an open field,
Barefoot through mid-summer
And the valley's veils of drifting grey
Become rain,
The first drops big as cherries.
Finally the wind and
The chestnut tree on fire,
Remembering.

The Man At The Stall

The man at the stall
Selling olives was
Measuring them out like jewels.
Black as jet they bobbed in brine,
Were stroked into spoonfuls,
Then lifted glistening into the light
To bulge their seasons
In small plastic bags.
The market was chaos
And he its calm centre,
As if alone beneath
A blue Greek sky
With the wind and the sea.
He was intent on the steady
Ripening of purpose,
The moment's worth not in question,
With nothing seemingly weighed against
The familiar blur of faces and handbags
Pressing in with a dull Welsh rain.
Our exchange was brief:
The crossing of hands,
The glint of my coin
Sinking back into the dark.

A Back Ward At Glenside Hospital

The years are a tide on this shore
Ebbed into distance
Leaving row after row of bedsteads
Washed-up like driftwood
Where I am called one winter's twilight.
I lock the door behind me
And sink into a fabulous noise
That rises like the keening of gulls
Scattered on a seaweed wind.
Here all our grandparents stand screeching,
Dribbling, half naked on the smooth vinyl.
They stare with the tired eyes of fish
Forgetting what was forgotten
And part as I am led to a bed
In the corner.
For some reason the smell of pine forests
Thick with evening drifts from blankets
Clutched by cold, white fingers
But she is pale and pulseless now
With the smashed crab of nothing-to-be-done
From where she fell
Matted in her hair.
I fill out a form she does not need
And notice in her notes a photograph:
Faded and brown, a young woman
Beautiful, with smooth skin and a squint
Smiling at something
Beyond the camera.

Pigtails, lace collar, dated 1920, insane.
Back behind the curtains
I lift the sheet clear of her face
And meet the same smile and cloudy eyes
Staring beyond my shoulder
To what was always out of sight,
Hidden behind this moment,
Her seventy lost years eddying into night.

Clouds Lie Down

"Unless devotion is given to a thing that must prove false in the end,
the thing that is true in the end cannot enter."

Charles Williams

Clouds lie down on the open field.
Rooks punctuate the sky
As the year's end turns,
A new chapter.

How to know the weight
Of all the words
That have ever been spoken?
And what returns?

Our shared season pushes on,
Tilts towards the next.

There are words of wisdom.
There are words of woe.
There is music for those that can hear.
There is thanks to be given.

Nothing returns.

The wind rises
On the closed door,
Neither holding
Nor letting go.
The woods fill with night.
The fields
Grow dark with care.

Girl

I am
Plain faced
Puffy as flour;
The summer is
A lifetime inside
My bones.

I bend in the wind
Bony knees,
Flail long arms
Like windmills
Turning the seasons
That turn in me
Their ripening dark,
My blood;

The mystery of blood
I sometimes taste,
Iron at the back
Of my throat,
My body.

I am awkward in the broken
Light of my body,
My too short skirt,
My white ankle socks,
My skin's smell of
Cut grass and stones.
I stretch into holidays
And back still flat,
Ache for the swell of
My chest,

Climb high stairs
Night after night
And look out at the moon
Looking in,
Snuffle into sheets like snow
Lulled by the hooves
Of my heart in
My ears,
I gallop away
Swallowing tears

Anorexia

I am as frightened as a rainbow
About to fade,
Fearful of all this sun and rain
Failing me,
This chance glancing
That spreads me so wide,
Lifts me in silence
Transparent as the wind.
My thin curves arch the land,
Hum from the inside
With colours you could touch me by;
My clear crystals chasing light
Hungry in their millions,
Hover before your eyes.
And I could dazzle you all day,
No one need know of the emptiness,
The impenetrable white of my desire
Suffused in its void like chance,
How I span my childhood, suspended
With no beginning and no end,
Made up of this storm's fury
Sealed in a pristine light,
Forever
Just out of reach.

Trying To Take A History From Ada

Eventually, in the corner
I found her,
A drooping flower faded
Wandering miles of childhood
With giddy button eyes always
"Our Dad, our Dad" and she'd begin.
"Beneath a full moon I was
Digging the earth till one in the morning."
Fingers fumble a smooth spade,
"Unable to sleep you see,
The summer and the air . . ."
Bats drop
Unfurling sail-like wings
To purse their whispering
Flight against the stars.
"Digging the earth like a man."
A pause and she pants a little,
Walnut skin blending with
The grain of her chair,
Crumpled clothes, unloved hair,
Pants with the joy of digging.
"Our Dad, our Dad looking for me
Through the empty house,
Woke the cat."
The rows of silver gardens,
Silent
Her shadow on the soil.
"What are you doing girl?"

He calls from out the window.
My pen is poised above clumsy notes,
Impatient for information
But the door has opened onto the last century
And she is ever alive
Crumbling soil
Beautiful in a wind tugging her nightdress
Which billows white like a cloud.
"And what year were you born in?" I ask.
Barefoot tender on grass.
"Our Dad, our Dad, It's me, I'm your girl,
I'm not a wolf."
And she sways with silent laughter
Like a tree shedding leaves
To soften its fall.
"I'll always be your girl."

Our Sam

I remember him, our Sam
Face down on the steel,
His great table of a back
Spread wide with skin unrolled
The way you'd bone a fish,
Easing the knife down
To expose the spine.
But he was tough as old boots
With slabs of skin and
Yellow fat inches thick,
So our delicate dissection
Soon gave way to wrenching
Fistfuls of flesh
Burrowing deeper and deeper
Eager for the wet clay feel
Of his insides.

It was a whole week's work that back
And in between, at lunch, his fat
Nestling behind the nails
Of our fingers gripping rolls
Became an emblem of our club,
His fat
With its formalin perfume,
And then we'd be back
Big with beer
To unstrip his purple muscles
And wrench off his limbs
Until he lay like a box,
Face squashed to a snarl.

The weeks passed
And he was taken apart,
His life broken down to bits,
(As if it would make more sense that way)
All came out and was heaped on the bench
Leaving his grey chest
Suddenly empty
With neck sprouting strings and tubes.
And then the day
We broke into his head:

It was easiest to get the saw going
When set between his teeth
But the boulder-round
Weight of it rocked,
So his stubbled cheeks were held
And pressed into pouting
A long drawn-out
Kiss.

The gritty movement of the saw
Squealed like the wind
Before his skull creaked
And yawned open.

We paused for a moment
In the small shock of it:
Two bowls
Of stretched-pearl membrane,
Shaped like a sea-horse,
Exposed to the light
And all the secret coils
Glistening.
We lifted the two halves
Back together, awkwardly
Re-created a face, but
There was no undoing
What we had done.
There was no going back
That afternoon, ever,
With the sound of pigeons and traffic
Through the open window,
And the sudden pattering
On Whitechapel pavements
Of a summer's rain lifting
The suddenly unfamiliar smell of dust.

C.E.P. (1908–1991)

Whilst driving to visit you –
Chasing great bundles of light
Over the road's open camber
You sat in rooms no longer yours
Listening to the minutes
Of another year's Christmas,
Breathing the sunlight's soft yellow.

How the winter had changed you,
Its pallor sunk into your days
As if already part of the land
And your life's span had settled
Into those collective
Seasons of memory
That return to us all,
Year after year:
The grandsons becoming the grandfathers
Becoming the fields
Becoming the forests
That turn on the earth's axis,
Innumerable small stories
Drawn like gravity,
Life's imperative for change.

I entered your oratory of stillness
Whilst you were asleep,
Saw you as if a cadaver:
The small rictus of an open mouth
Clogged still,
Smooth forehead cabochon cold.
I listened to the room breathing,
Imagined a world without you
Until you woke with a wide-eyed stare,
Fingers dancing on your chest
Frantic for buttons
Or something which was not there.

Barnstaple Market, 1910

In the market hall
A thousand faces
Held in angles
By the camera
Gleam in the spring light
That slants through 1910.
The old and the young,
Inquisitive and resigned;
Pale and familiar faces under
A thousand different hats,
Buying and selling all those
Things handed down
And now lost.
They are busy and resolute
In the detail of their lives,
Teeming around the darkness
Of history,
The penumbra of this moment
That holds me half-way
Up the stairs.
They are the long gone,
And they are the present,
Crowding into each
Permutation of gesture
Something that endures:
The unmoving eyes,
The half smile,
The small open hands.
The camera hovers over them
Like an angel
As I look up.

Summers Unborn

Out there on that thin
Flaked beach,
With the waves' white racing
From Ireland
And the wind's weight nuzzling our backs
With the huge miles of its history,
My grand grandfather pulls a potato clear
Of Antrim soil,
Crumbling the dark and the centuries,
To pearl clean a fragment of flesh.

Our shadows slant fifty yards across sand
Stepping giant strides as if on stilts.
This is how distance magnifies –
I know the details are all there
Lived once and still living:
The cottage and the cow
And the carts of hay leaving
For Belfast before dawn,
The stormy-eyed woman
Bearing twigs on her back
In the stirring of summers unborn.

Edith

She was head back in an armchair
Smiling at the ceiling
With a choir intoning carols
From a wooden record player.
Four walls of old people sitting
Motionless as statues.
I, unnoticed in the noise
Crouched at her side
By tight elephant legs heaped on a stool,
Watching worn and blind hands
Folded in her lap
Moving like a nest of new born mice.
"They're all remembering you see."
And she smiled at the thought
Of some Twenties Christmas
Fading into a photograph
At the bottom of her drawer.
The room was soft with balls of shadow
And crackling carols and nobody moved
But the canary in a cage which tilted its head.
A red winter sun flickered inky with crows.
"They're all trying to remember, you see,
What they cannot remember."
Her words settled like the snow outside
Lacing a pattern of crystals
Over footprints that have faded
For ever now into white.

Listening To Light

All day a winter's sun
Barely clearing the hills
Moved golden shapes across walls.
Each latticed square was magnified
Jewelled as a fly's eye,
Slanting on stone like a net
With the curious symmetry of light
Splayed through glass
Trailing miles of space,
Flung up here high as kites
Sinking in slow motion.
The movement was hardly movement at all
But more like music,
As if in everything there is a tone
Longing to be made whole
Which this meeting of sunlight and stone,
Tilting in us notes unknown,
Had sounded far beyond this afternoon.
The shapes with time paled into plaster,
Thinned from the room like ghosts
And were gone
And we were alone with the sound
Of air rushing through a pigeon's wing,
The woods outside smoking dusk,
The early stars beginning to sing.

Travelling To North Wales

At low tide amongst marsh
A dead heron, a dead sheep
Slip under the glassy
Wing of night.
All the way up the coast
White cottages, small curtains,
A long curve of breakers
Stretching north.
We travel on to where
Slate roofs glisten, smoothed
By the grey of clouds,
To where a whole land
Lies down in rain,
Coughs a language from granite cwms
Tenacious as the wind
That whistles across Tremadoc Bay
Shaking Molweyn Bach and
All the scattered farms.
Down dark and dreary bars
It is drunk like a song,
It's what set faces
Alight across a frontier,
Recalls marching armies
Raised on recalcitrant hills,
Processions of kings, priests,
Leading their people
Through a shibboleth of words
Beyond marsh and mist
And crumbling stone walls.

We arrive behind sparks
As brakes taking hold
Tilt us into a silence
That settles and spreads
The length of the platform
And down into the town,
And out across the midnight bay,
A strange muffled silence
Contracted by darkness
As if pressed between the pages
Of a history long snapped shut.

Esme

Esme like the ward cat
Has good and bad days;
Her hair is a cobwebbed mat
On mottled skin that stays

Tight on the bones of a haunted face
That hisses around the ward:
"I've got no mouth. I've got no taste."
Her eyes are owl eyes scored

Dark as the ocean
Sinking through hours of black,
Frantic in slow motion,
With slippers shuffling steps that lack

Any purpose heard for an hour
Before she totters into view:
"I've got no brains. I've got no power."
And then she has her bad days too.

E.C.T.

All through the slow morning
The gardeners with their rakes
Amble the lengths of lawn
That lap the hospital lying grey
And silent like a beached whale.
And all through the morning
I am the finger pushing the button
That shocks sleep into spasm,
Twists dreams through strange circuits
Of who knows where
As lips smack shut
Grimacing a sudden smile
That tightens and tightens.
Then butterfly eyes flicker out of control
And muscles ripple a useless movement
That spreads with the gentle rage-like shaking
Of rocked dignity
Through the silence of bones.
It is a strange ecstasy
That lapses into stillness
With the final shiver of a storm passing.
Outside patients cross and re-cross
The stained square of window,
Their clothes flapping in the spring wind.
Beyond the daffodils their faces merge
Expressionless into sky:
A vast expanse of domed grey,
Stubbled, blank and tender
Sharing the unwashed day.

Mother's Empty Room

I should never have married him
But he came
Tripping through my cream-coloured days
To disturb the dust of my
Long settled summer,
My wise middle age
Laid straight as a dress
Draped over a chair
In mother's empty room.
And all the purple dawns
With me in the warm air
Clanking my bucket towards the cow,
And then back to my sister stood
In the open door of the farm,
Her smile suggestible as the moon.
My beautiful sister,
Her warm and chafed hands
Busy and strong as any man's,
Polished with the oil of fleeces
And the smooth balustrade we'd glide down on,
The warm wax of seasons
All the way from childhood,
Past the church and the village shop,
And the soil father broke his years on,
The acres patterned with primroses,
All the way until I left with him
As never I should have done,
One morning in a thin rain

With her parting the curtains
To raise a small hand,
Unmoving,
From mother's empty room.

Therapy

She sits dowdy as a dream
Caught in the undercurrent of day,
All darkness and demons
Frowning behind long hair
Which she lowers in plaits
With raw fingers
That twist and twist;
Leaning as from a high window
She moans her song a chair away
Mouthing moon-round words
Into sentences that
Spill like milk.

I imagine a tower and stars turning,
Their pale light pulling
Out of nothing the fabric
Of purple air,
Of mountains,
Of a winding road
White with dust,
As if one trusting leap and she could
Billow down through
Night's soft cloth,
Land on the back of words
That could lead through loss.

Instead she paces the room
Wearing her body like an old coat,
Stares long at the mirror,
Pounds the swollen face that
Stares smiling back with
Such small and
Unheld fists.

Black And White Photograph, 1914, The Kitchens, Arlington Court

She stands peeling a potato
In frock and cap,
Face frozen with purpose;
Her bare arms gleam
And it is summer.

A man has entered the kitchen,
Stares at the camera.

The window is mullioned,
Opens onto white space,
Casts shadows on the
Table before her.
Their black shapes are familiar;
They conjure presence,
Speak of twilight and candles
And the gathering grey we share
A century away:
The outline of bowls and eggs,
Some flour, a tea-cup,
Smooth apples
Her hands have held,

And a pheasant whose head
Hangs from the table.

Golden feathers crimson flecked
Burnished like copper,
Flicker in her eyes,
And then the fiery sunset,
And through the open window
The sound of sheep.
Someone is calling.
The moment is all clamour,
And she turns to face the man
Who has gone.

Reg

It won't be long now
Surrounds you like sunlight
Lifting great waves of dust
In the hazy dawn's stillness
Of the spring you'll never see.
We continue at a distance
With all those small things
Magnified by the minutes
Of your gravel breath dying
Into slow motion masterpieces
Of something set in motion
That shall outlive us all.
You sit crumpled as a scarecrow
Who has left his field
And now bends as at prayer
Still rattling with the wind,
Black hair combed
Straight as a ploughed field
Swept to one side by another's hand;
Buttons and braces hold together
The rest:
The years and the miles and the doors
All closing beneath high blue skies.
From this distance there are craters
Furrowed under your eyes
And your breath sounds like stones
That have been dragged miles.
We watch you slow,
And imagine you're watching us
Treading these small circles of light,
Folding your forgotten body
Into the shape of our days and nights.

The Old Rose Bed

"Only the mystery keeps us alive, only the mystery."

Federico Garcia Lorca.

I

This morning of spring – how
To set it down, these
Passing years,
These moments?
But a brief while
Mouths and hands
Given to praise and hold,
We must learn to sing and let go.
But a brief while
The silence of stone and tree.

The empty bowl of the sky,
Breathes in, breathes out.

II

Summer then arrives with
Its suddenness of sunlight flapping
At the window's edge,
Its skies of spilt blue stitched with swallows
That snap and thrum tight orbits.
A single bird swivelling dips

To clip the pond;
Its beak spoons the water.
Such a small drop
But the pond is aflame
With the dancing sun and sky.

The hills lean back
As the day gives way.

III

Autumn returns the golden woods.
We lay our hearts against the earth.
The swell of an ocean surges
Like the hum of bees,
Rocks in the hollows of our chests.
Beyond the sound of drowning
An answering beat faintly
Rises and falls.
And so the question: for those of us here now
Do we have life
The way the night sky has stars?
Or does life have us?

Who is holding who?
Who is letting go?

IV

Winter I'd climb the high bones of trees
Sway on the wind's pulse
Passing around the world,
Pray nothing would ever change, not knowing
Change is all there is –
The dance in our marrow of a million atoms
We cannot step out of,
Like our own shadow,
Like opening the fridge to find
Time-expired pouches of blood,
Heavy and cold from someone's heart,
Brought home by father to squeeze
On the old rose-bed.

"To help them grow. Good for their roots,"
I remember he always said.

India

We feast on shadows
At the lake
Blurred by jade plumes
And the day's end
Becomes all blue.
They will lift forever
Stump hands
From all the roadsides
Leading here,
Caked in dirt,
Mouthing air.
We have not touched them.
Purple clouds lift
A storm over the plains.
Buzzards circle the mountains.
Toads hold up the night.

What Did The Man Dressing The Girl With A Suicide Jacket Say?

They step out into the light.
He bestows the heavy vest
Lifted high,
Lowers it with gentle hands
Over her head to rest
On ungrown shoulders
Blouse covered so as not to catch
Or chafe her skin.
The clasp he connects and the wires.
He hands her a coat with shiny buttons
Which she fastens at the front with fingers
That dance and quiver and can't keep still.
He looks intently at her and smiles,
His eyes in her eyes,
And for a long while so.
He leads her down the dusty street
So that she is not alone
Until they separate
And she keeps on walking and walking
Until ever-so-close,
Almost too late
Steps out of the light.

Regression During A Lecture

Sitting in a room full
Of people thinking
It was never going to be
Like this, my life,
And then your arm, your bare arm
Is all there is,
Draped over the back of a chair
Caught by the last glow
From a red sun sinking
Beyond the window.
Your hands, your bare hands
Open and close,
Hold nothing, listen to nothing;
Your fingers move in small circles
That almost inscribe words,
Coil soft ovals around each other
That reach higher and higher.
And I am telescoped back
To half remembered
Patterns of curtained light
Shimmering on a bedroom wall,
And outside, wood pigeons calling,
A lullaby, the sound of skin
Moving on skin.

Then there is sudden clapping,
A blur of hunched jackets litters
The crumpled lecture hall
And we all empty into our
Separate ways where
Night is draining purple away
With a big moon
And all the roads are silver
Spreading away from the sea,
And everywhere will soon be still.

Consummation

Outside, blue shadows hum
Over moonlight's skin,

Hum and swell beneath the apple tree,
Shapes that come and go.

I slip between day and night
And tilt into white

All the way,
Stretched like the four

Blank corners of a page,
To return written on

By all the small
Hands of the unborn.

Afterwards
I go down to the stones

That ribbon the dry bed,
(Their cool weight)

For a while know the language
Of the world,

For a while speak
Like a river.

I know I leave a crease
On your mouth

Like a bird that cannot fly,
Or a place unchanged by the years,

The corner above the sink
Where you leave your ring,

How it sometimes catches
The light and will sing

For us all.

Why My Grandfather Waves

I am in the middle of a field
And the waist-high wheat
Whispers.
At the edge of the woods
My house burns with
Sigh and crackle
As flames unroll
Far into the blue.
Over to the right my grandfather
Is waving with one arm
Raised high.
It moves back and forwards
Slowly
Like the wheat.
I stand still
As a summer's day,
Beneath a sky
The most brilliant blue
With my house burning
And my grandfather waving.

You

You in the shower and I'm amazed
At how the light glows around you,
Fills your silhouette with solid morning
Framed against the window,
With the early woods rolling
Soft pigeon notes and you
Intent on the tipping drops
Slipping from your curves like silk.

Our small story is centuries old,
Endlessly shared,
Its dark immeasurable elsewheres
Veiled by this bright pause of dawn,
This innocent fragment of day
That lifts dust into a dance
All around you
The way light inside a flower
Loosens its song.

I think of the inevitable stillness
Of our hearts becoming stone,
The world's wind palming
The shore smooth,
How, in washing, you
Betray a child's honesty
Unaware of the years' strife,
Frail as this summer's morning,
Forever falling
Through and through my life.

Call

Outside, swallows
Are on the telephone line
In their hundreds.
It will sag the smooth
Curve of your call
From halfway
Around the world.
They are restless to be off.
I wait on the edge
Of autumn
Surprised by the soil's red,
The sudden glow of evening
That flares and fades
Ringing west.
Later you speak from the palm
Of my hand;
Your voice is movement
Across a continent,
A fine vibration
Like instinct
That flutes my bone.
I answer with words
That wheel and rise,
Circle oceans of darkness,
Somehow return home.

Finally

Autumn returns:
We have all grown old
With the year
And remember ourselves rounding
This same falling
Perfectly.
The earth is heavier
With the fruit of our numbers
And the blue air
Is still calling.
What is there to do
Beyond this being,
And who can say what has begun,
Or what it is
That is constantly ending?

Postscript

Falling Asleep

(for Alice Oswald)

Waiting on the shore of sleep
To be taken
Is like nothing else;
Settling into a shape that lifts
Backwards in deep space
And never lands anywhere.
The precise moment is lost
Always unready, mid-sentence.
It's like grief in reverse:
Everything in its right place shimmers
Utterly changed, as if startled.
The first pang of impossibility
Dropped from a height
Into a void of no gravity
Falls upwards in greeting.
There is the sound of eyelids closing
Membrane to membrane like a kiss.
The day has passed and is spent;
Birds have settled between stars in their roosts.
Will the measure of my life have been enough?
Will my ordinary love laid out like an old coat
Ever be worn again?
Enfolded we are carried off and never return,
Or never return the same.

WORLD CULTURES

by Phillip W Simpson

a Capstone company — publishers for children

Engage Literacy is published in the UK by Raintree.
Raintree is an imprint of Capstone Global Library Limited, a company incorporated in England and Wales having its registered office at 264 Banbury Road, Oxford, OX2 7DY – Registered company number: 6695582

www.raintree.co.uk

Editorial credits
Marissa Kirkman and Jennifer Huston, editors; Peggie Carley and Charmaine Whitman, designers; Morgan Walters and Wanda Winch, media researchers; Steve Walker, production specialist

Image credits
Alamy: Chronicle, 47, Dan Santillo NZ, 9, REUTERS, bottom 61; Capstone Press: Eric Gohl, 44; Library of Congress Prints and Photographs Division Washington, D.C., 28; Newscom: akg-images, 51, Art Media Heritage Images, 39; North Wind Picture Archives, top 61; Shutterstock: Anastasios71, bottom 60, top right 62, Artur Balytskyi, 8, Asmus Koefoed, Cover, top right 1, barbajones, 19, bkp, bottom right 53, blackboard1965, 59, Catmando, bottom left 62, ChameleonsEye, 6, top 15, chrisdorney, middle right 53, Chris Howey, 11, Cloudia Spinner, Cover, bottom right 1, Constantinos Iliopoulos, top right 53, Dm_Cherry, spread 32–33, 42, Dmitry Pichugin, 12, drosostalitsa, middle 60, Elena Veselova, 55, EpicStockMedia, 22, Evannovostro, 49, Everett Historical, 27, Foodio, bottom right 54, GRSI, bottom right 62, Hein Nouwens, 50, Ildi Papp, 24, Jamen Percy, 43, JASPERIMAGE, 20, Jktu_21, 37, kurbanov, design element, lazyllama, Cover, top left 1, Lukassek, Cover, bottom left 1, Lukasz Siekierski, 36, marcin jucha, bottom left 54, mart, (illustrated columns) 53, mountainpix, 45, mushan, design element, Nagib, (earth texture) Cover, design element throughout, Natalia Kostitcina, 5, Nejron Photo, 31, 35, 41, Norman Pogson, 25, Panos Karas, 56, Paolo Bona, bottom 15, patrimonio designs ltd, 10, Peter Hermes Furian, 16, Rainer Lesniewski, 7, Rawpixel.com, 26, Ruth Black, back cover, Sgvn, design element, Slavik Krassovsky, 58, STILLFX, top left 62, Tom Roche, 40, travellight, 17, ufosnow, design element, Zapp2Photo, 23; Wikimedia: Sergei Kazantsev, 21

21 20 19 18 17
10 9 8 7 6 5 4 3 2 1
Printed and bound in China.

World Cultures

ISBN: 978 1 4747 4587 1

CONTENTS

INTRODUCTION

Why do people from different countries do things in different ways? Where do *traditions* and customs come from? Often, traditions or ways of doing things, have been passed down from one person to the next, or from *generation* to generation. These ways of doing things have meaning that is often linked to the area in which these people lived. These ways of doing things can be defined as *culture* or the ideas, customs and social behaviour of a group of people or society.

The traditions of some past cultures continue to influence people living in their regions today. These traditions and customs include food, language and clothing – among others. Some cultures from the past have influenced people from all over the world.

People from around the world celebrate their culture with special clothing, food and dance. This girl is wearing traditional clothing from Russia.

THE MAORI

History

The Maori are the *indigenous* or native people of New Zealand. Nearly a thousand years ago, the Maori people came from the islands of Eastern Polynesia. These skilled sailors journeyed to New Zealand in canoes called "waka". These Polynesian origins have greatly influenced the Maori culture's food, language, song and dance.

The first Maori leader to make the voyage to New Zealand was Chief Kupe. He arrived there around AD 950 – more than a thousand years ago – in a great waka.

Maori tribe members in a waka

Polynesia and the surrounding area

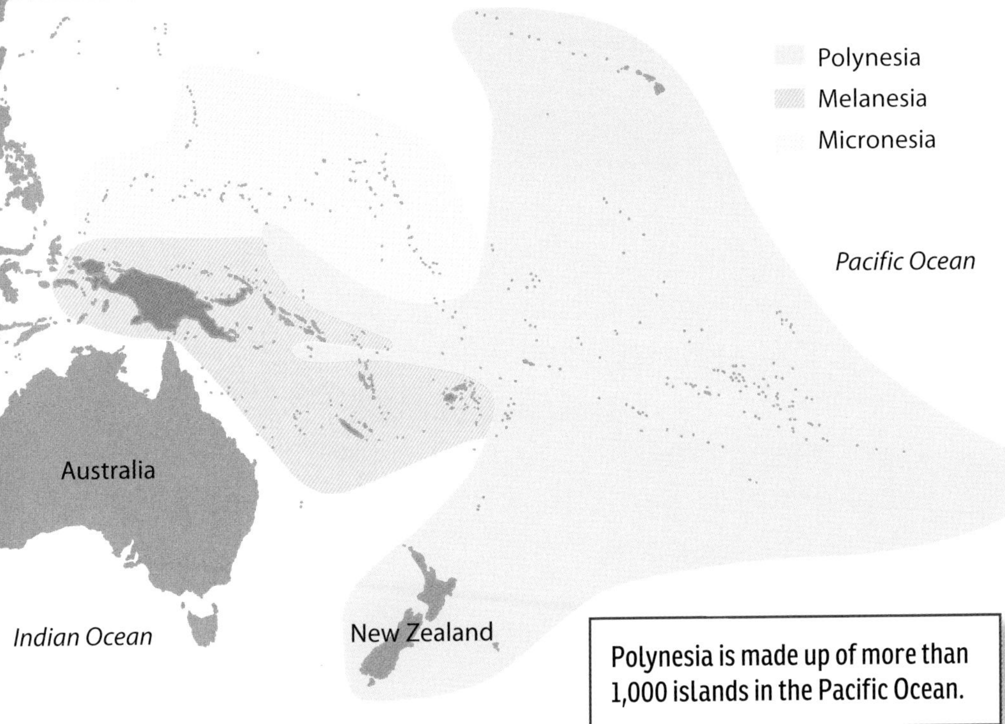

Polynesia is made up of more than 1,000 islands in the Pacific Ocean.

Kupe was so impressed with the new land that he returned home to tell the rest of his people. They followed him back to New Zealand and began settling the untouched land.

In the early 19th century, settlers and whalers from Europe arrived on the shores of New Zealand. Wars broke out between the Maori and the Europeans. In 1840, a treaty known as the Treaty of Waitangi was signed between Maori chiefs and the British. Since that time, the two cultures have gradually merged together. Today the Maori culture, which is rich in tradition and legend, plays an important role in New Zealand society.

Food and food preparation

When the Maori first arrived in New Zealand, there were few mammals native to the area. The Maori brought with them some animals including dogs and rats. But they soon found that there were few animals to hunt in New Zealand, so they relied on fish and birds for food. For hundreds of years, they hunted the many types of birds and fish they found, including a giant flightless bird known as the moa.

Fishing was hugely important to the Maori, and seafood is still one of the biggest parts of their culture. The Maori love the sea, and seafood has influenced the culture of New Zealand as a whole.

The largest moas were 3.7 metres tall and weighed 227 kilograms. They died out or became extinct in the 1300s.

The Maori also brought plants with them from Polynesia. These plants, which most people in New Zealand still eat today, included *taro* and "kumara", also known as sweet potato.

The Maori culture and its origins are often celebrated. In some places, visitors can try Maori food, which is cooked under the ground in an earthen oven filled with hot rocks. This traditional way of cooking, known as "hangi", is still used sometimes throughout New Zealand. Hangis are very similar to cooking methods used in the Pacific islands where the Maori have their origins.

hangi

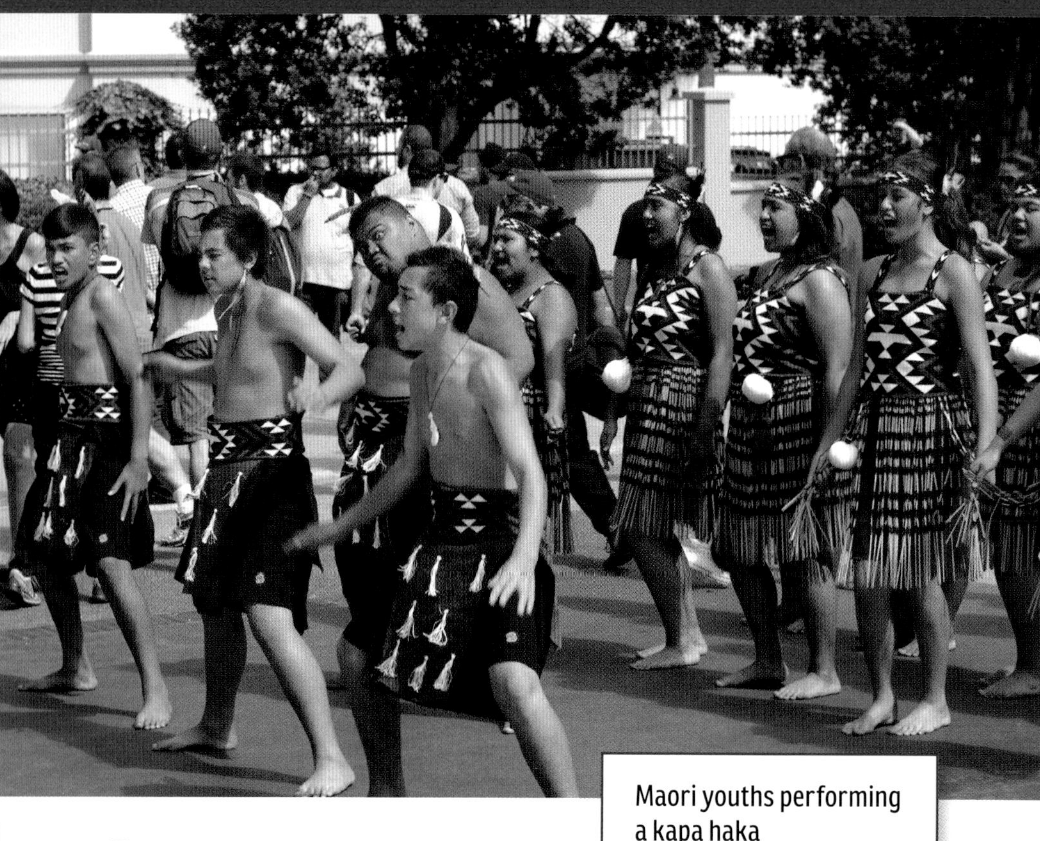

Maori youths performing a kapa haka

Dance

Traditional dances have been kept alive in Maori culture, and most New Zealand schools have a "kapa haka" group. Kapa haka is a type of Maori show that includes singing, dancing and facial expressions.

FACT

New Zealand's armed forces have their own haka dances that they perform on special occasions such as funerals for soldiers killed in the line of duty.

Meeting places

Local meeting places called "marae" are found throughout New Zealand. Marae host social, cultural and religious events within the Maori community. Meeting places similar to these are also found on the islands of Polynesia.

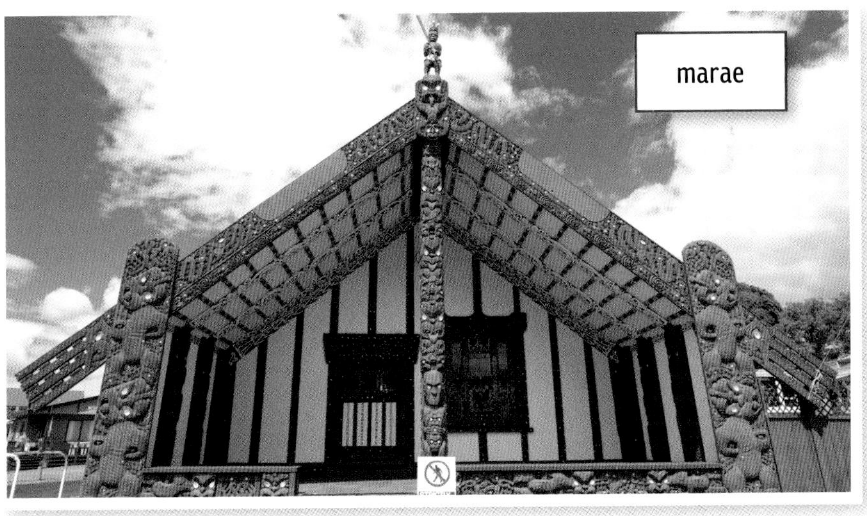

Family

Family ties have always been important to the Maori and are central to their culture. All Maori people belong to a tribe, subtribe and family. These ties are important and have a strong influence on Maori culture as well as New Zealand's culture as a whole. In rural places especially, distant relatives are often referred to as "cousin" or "auntie".

Maori language

The Maori language has its roots in the Polynesian language. It is related to languages spoken on the Cook Islands and Tahiti in the South Pacific. Because the Maori language is the official second language of New Zealand, it is taught weekly in most of the nation's schools.

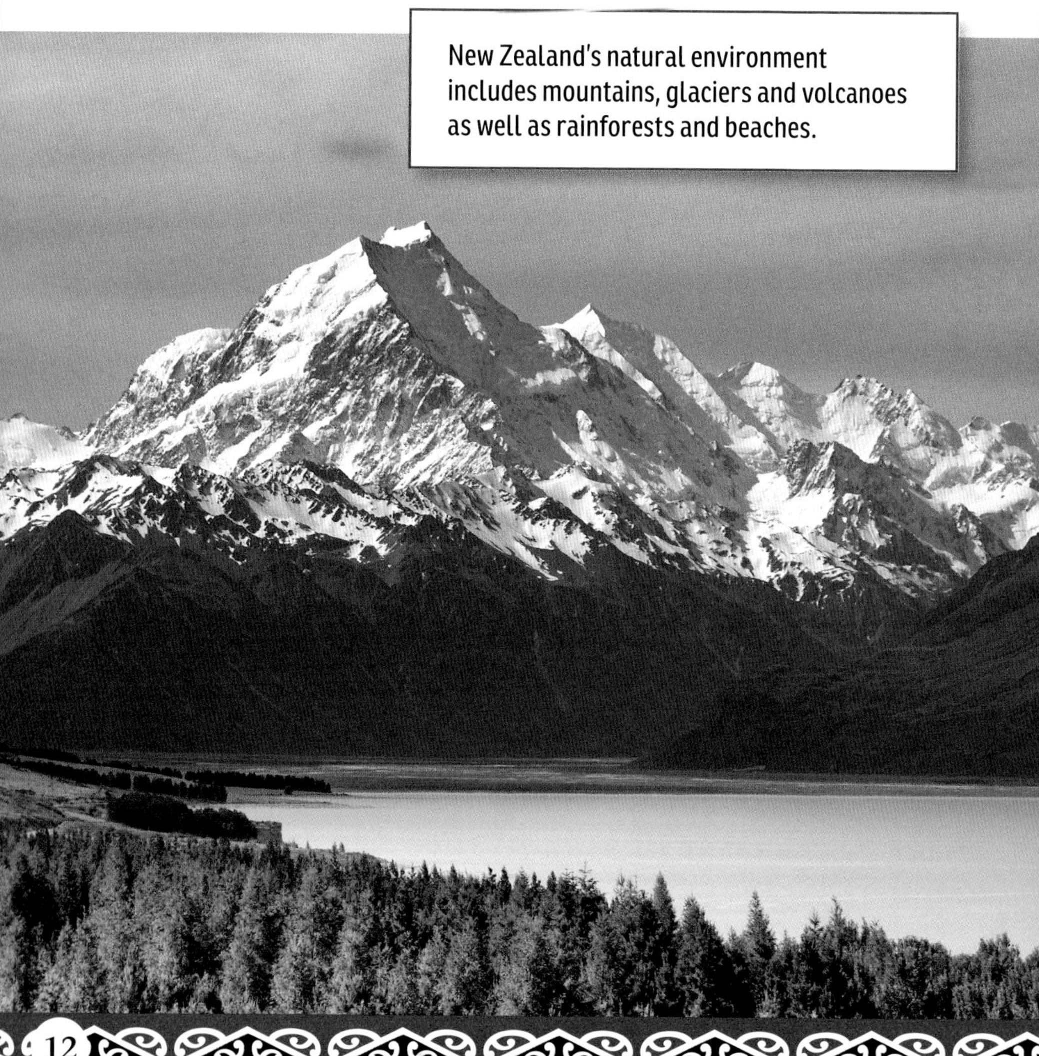

New Zealand's natural environment includes mountains, glaciers and volcanoes as well as rainforests and beaches.

Place names

The Maori culture and language have had a lasting impact on many aspects of life in New Zealand. Many cities, towns, mountains and rivers in New Zealand have Maori names. Some places have two names – an English one and a Maori one. This is because some Maori names are hard to pronounce. But this is becoming less of an issue as more people from New Zealand are learning the Maori language.

Maori beliefs

One of the key beliefs in the Maori culture is the concept of "kaitiakitanga" (kai-tea-key-tanga). This concept has to do with respecting and caring for nature. The Maori have always had a strong connection to nature because the sea and forest were so important to their survival. Kaitiakitanga is a concept that most people from New Zealand value and uphold. It is part of the reason why New Zealand is known for having a clean, natural environment.

Another belief is that of "manaakitanga" (mana-key-tanga). This belief is about being kind to and taking care of guests. It is a concept that most people of New Zealand – including the government – have adopted.

Ancestry

One of the reasons why Maori culture has such a strong influence on New Zealand is because of the number of people claiming direct *ancestry*. In 2013 reports showed that there were 600,000 Maori in New Zealand out of a total population of more than 4 million. Many more have distant Maori ancestors.

Other effects on daily life

Maori culture has influenced everyday life for many people in New Zealand. Today the Maori culture, language and traditions are celebrated throughout the nation. The Treaty of Waitangi is remembered every year with a public holiday on 6 February. New Zealand's national anthem is sung at large sporting events in both English and Maori. Even New Zealand's national rugby team performs a traditional Maori haka before each match.

Maori women sing and dance at a Waitangi Day celebration.

New Zealand's rugby team, the All Blacks, perform a Maori haka before a match.

THE SCOTS

When you think of traditional Scottish culture, you may think of bagpipes and kilts. But there is a great deal more to these people. For more than a thousand years, the Scots have been handing down their traditions and influencing other cultures. Scottish influence can be seen in other cultures across Europe and North America today.

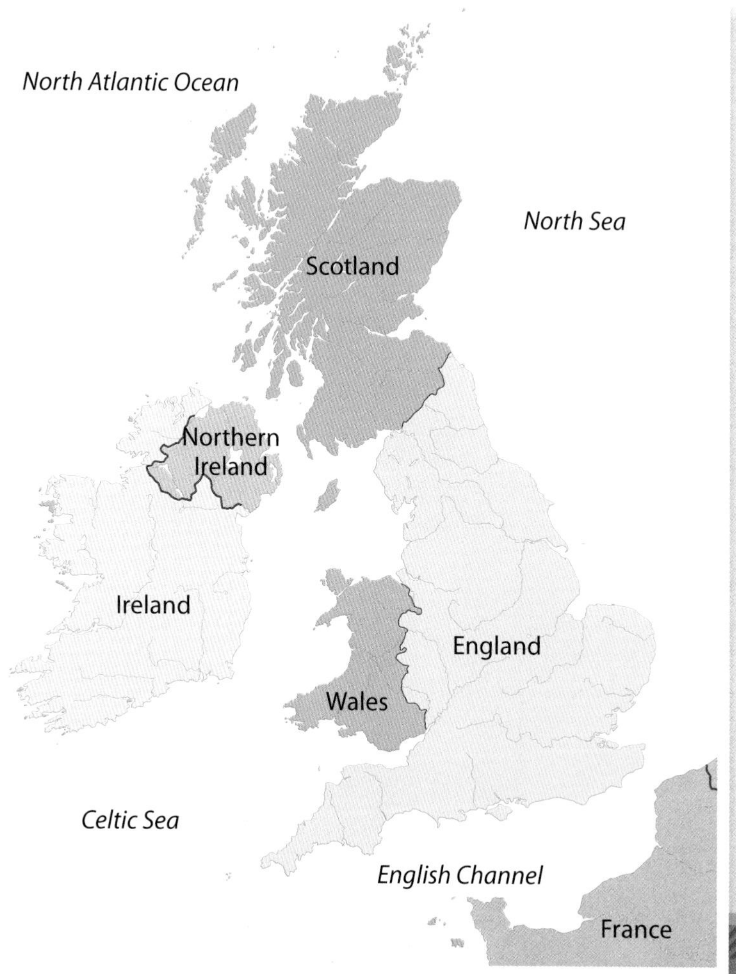

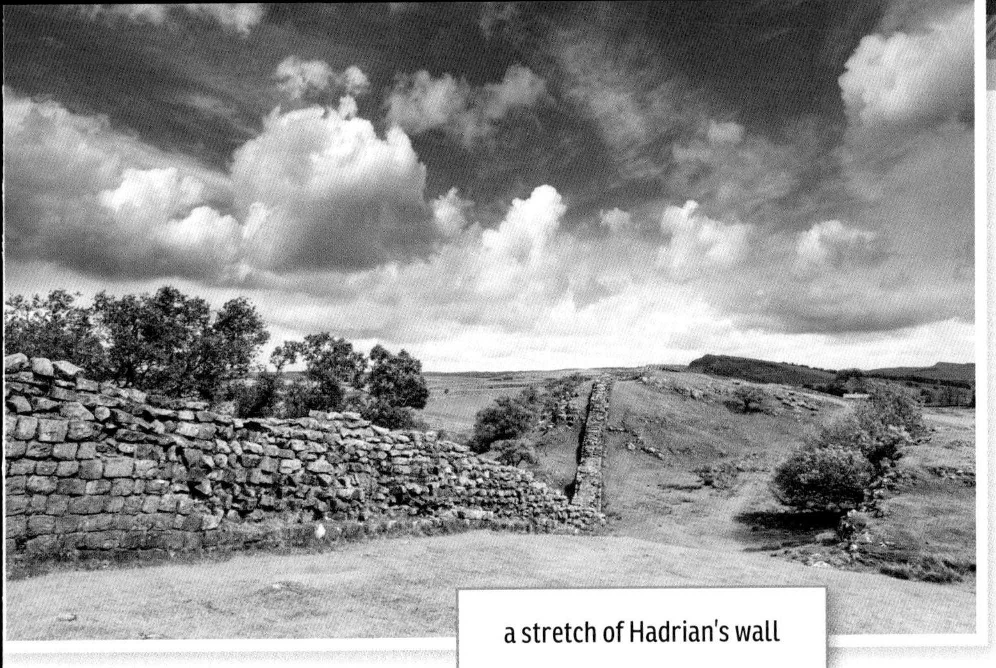

a stretch of Hadrian's wall

History

Scotland has a long and colourful history. Hunter-gatherers roamed the highlands more than 10,000 years ago. The Romans tried and failed to conquer the people in AD 84. In AD 122 – nearly 40 years later – the Roman Emperor Hadrian built a wall to keep the Scots out of the rest of the Roman Empire. Vikings settled in the region around AD 800 and the first *clans* started to appear around the 12th century.

The Scots have never truly been conquered. Over time, they have developed a rich culture, due largely to the clan system. Each clan has its own special *plaid* design called a tartan. The Scots wear their tartan kilts with pride.

Traditional clothing

The Scottish kilt is one of the most recognizable items of clothing in the world. It is a knee-length skirt with a tartan pattern worn mostly by men. Some ancient versions were made of a single piece of long woollen cloth. It was gathered at the waist and held in place with a belt. The extra folds were then wrapped around the upper body, often over one shoulder.

On special occasions, such as weddings, Scottish men also wear a sporran, which is a leather purse on a belt. A tartan cloth is draped over the shoulder. Traditional dress for women consists of a white cotton blouse with colourful patterns and a silk tartan skirt. A tartan silk is often hung over the shoulder. Today tartan is worn in many countries and can often be seen on ties, hats and skirts.

Dance, sport, music and other traditions

Square dancing is a Scottish tradition. In the past, it was a dance performed by the upper class, and it is still alive today in the form of line dancing. The dancers perform the steps to fiddle music.

FACT

Country line dances in the United States, such as the "Texas Two-step" and the "Boot Scootin' Boogie", all have their origins in Scottish square dancing.

The Highland Games are a traditional Scottish contest that feature feats of strength. The Highland Games are held every year to honour Scottish culture. One of the events is the *caber* toss. Many people think the sport is about how far one can throw the caber, but it's not. It's all about how straight the toss is. The winner is the person whose caber lands in a straight line directly in front of him or her, which is called the 12 o'clock position. The Highland Games also include shot-put, the Scottish hammer throw and other music and dance contests.

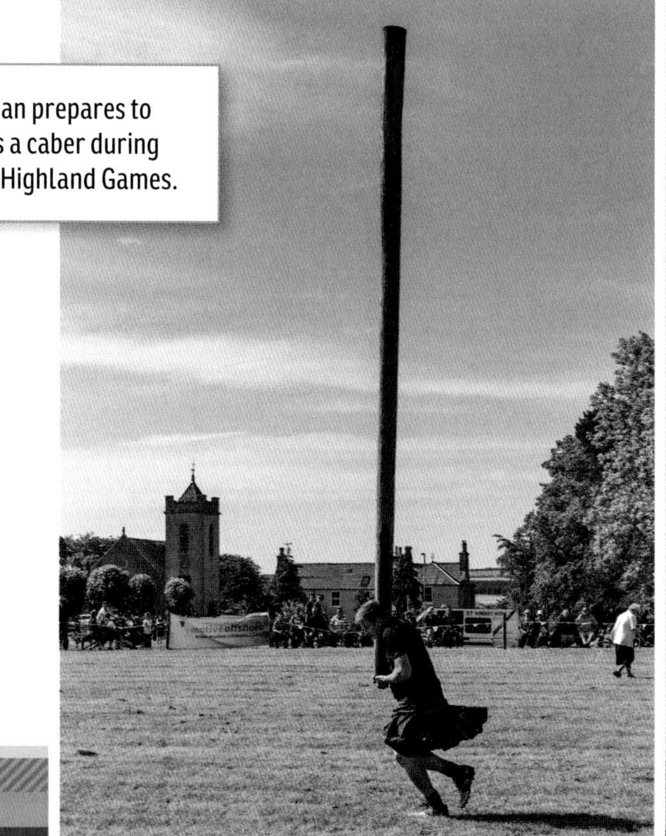

A man prepares to toss a caber during the Highland Games.

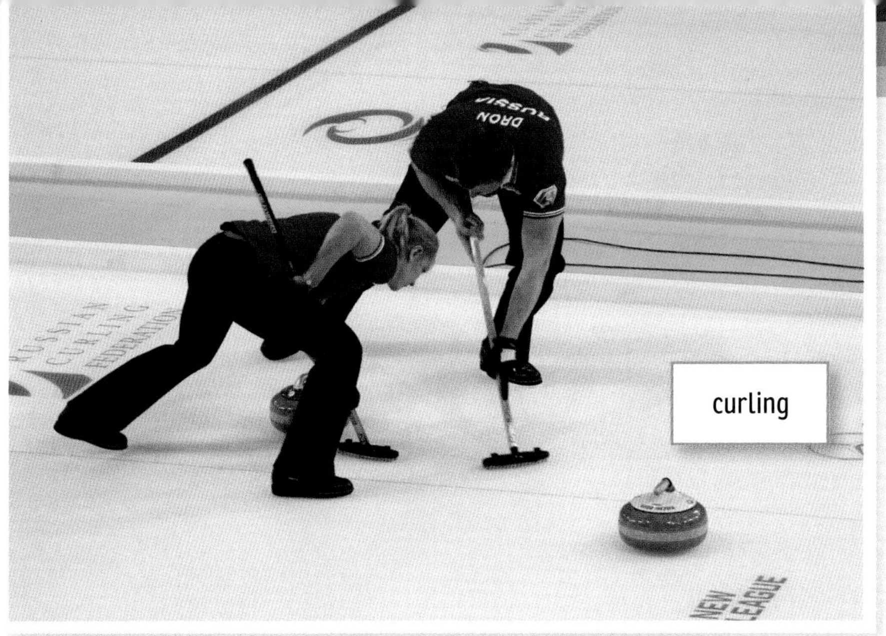

curling

Curling is a sport that got its start in Scotland. It is now popular in the United States and Canada and is a winter Olympic event. In this sport, players slide stones along ice towards a target area called the house. The heavy granite stones are polished so that they slide easily. Players score points by getting their stones closest to the centre of the circle. Two players, called sweepers, follow their stone as it moves along the ice. They use brooms to sweep the ice in front of the stone. This changes the stone's path and moves it closer to the target.

FACT

Throughout the world, countries with large Scottish populations, such as the United States and Australia, host Highland Games each year.

Golf has its origins in Scotland. It started there during the 15th century. Back then, players would hit a pebble around a course of sand dunes, tracks and rabbit holes using a stick. Today golf is one of the most popular sports and is played and watched by people all over the world.

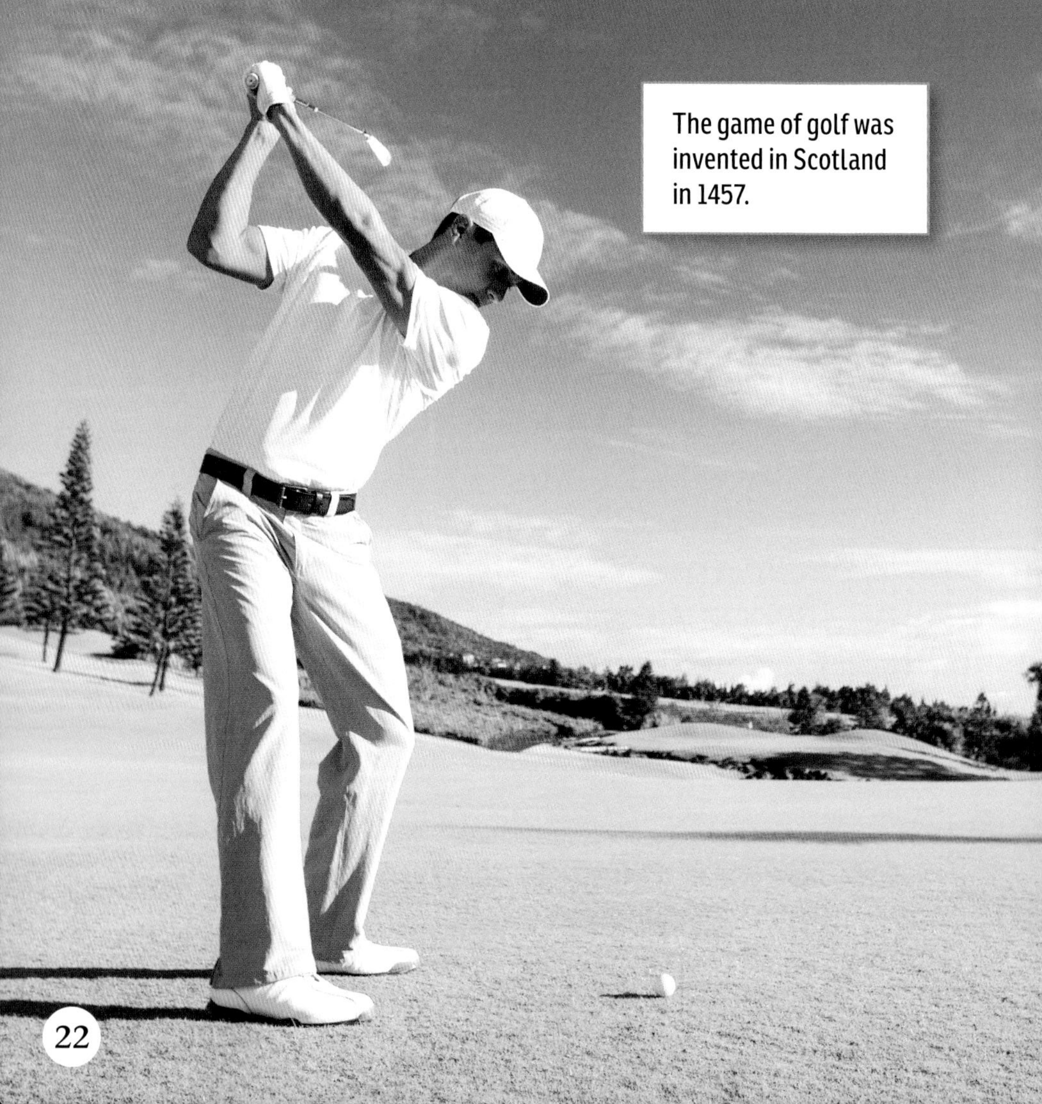

The game of golf was invented in Scotland in 1457.

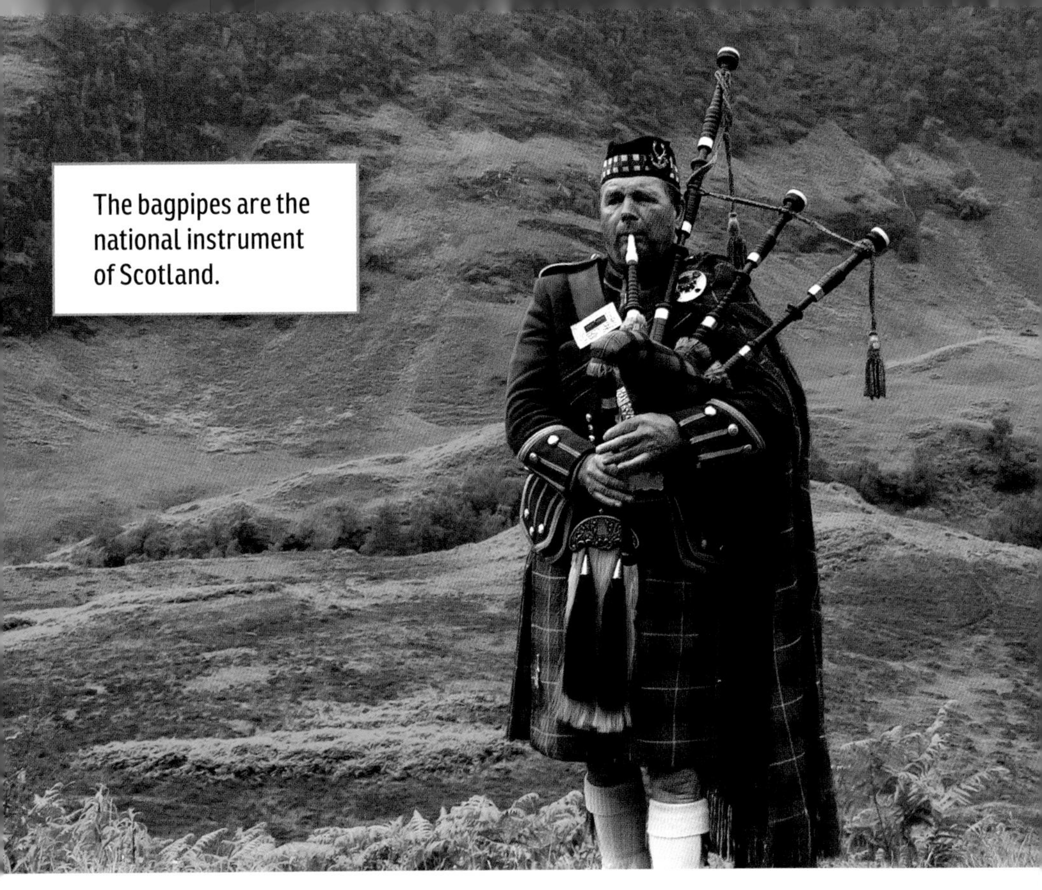

The bagpipes are the national instrument of Scotland.

The Scottish are known all around the world for their music, especially their Highland bagpipes. Although there are more than 30 different types of bagpipes, the Highland bagpipes are the most famous. The bag itself is made from sheep or elk skin. Sticking up from the top of the bag are three pipes called drones, which is where the recognizable sound comes from. People in many countries play the bagpipes for special occasions such as weddings and funerals.

Traditional Scottish food

Traditional Scottish foods include porridge, shortbread and haggis. Porridge is a traditional Scottish breakfast food made from rolled oats and milk or water. It is popular in a number of countries where there is a Scottish influence.

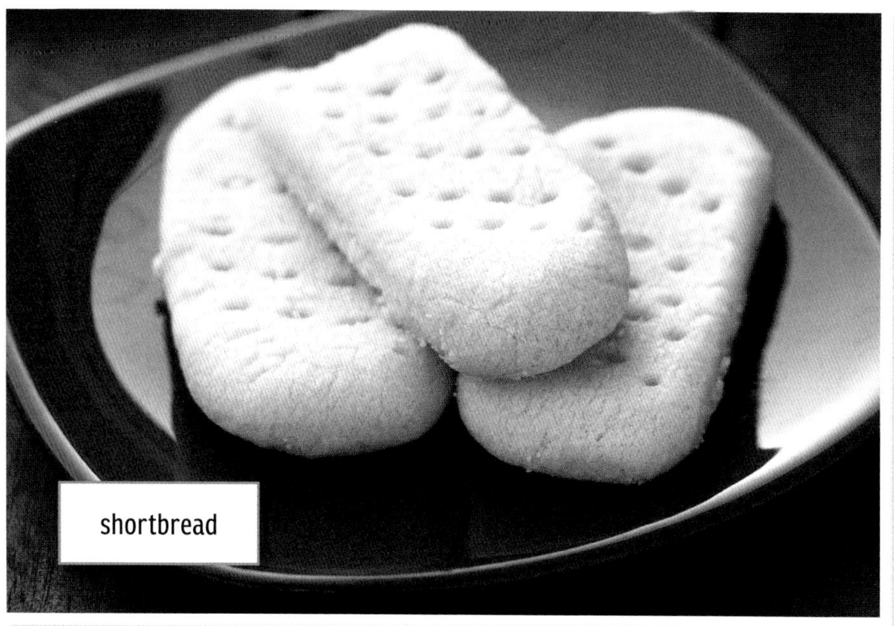

shortbread

FACT

In the Shetland region of Scotland, it is a tradition to break a shortbread biscuit on the head of a bride when she first enters her new home.

Shortbread is a sweet, buttery biscuit that was first made in Scotland. It is a popular treat at special occasions such as birthdays, holidays and weddings.

Haggis is another traditional Scottish food. Haggis is a dish made from the heart, liver and other organs of a sheep, with chopped onions and oatmeal stuffed into a sheep's stomach and boiled. The origin of this meal is unclear. One theory is that women made this meal for the men who were leaving home for days at a time to take their cattle to market. Another theory is that hunters made this meal with the parts of the animal that could not be preserved and would spoil.

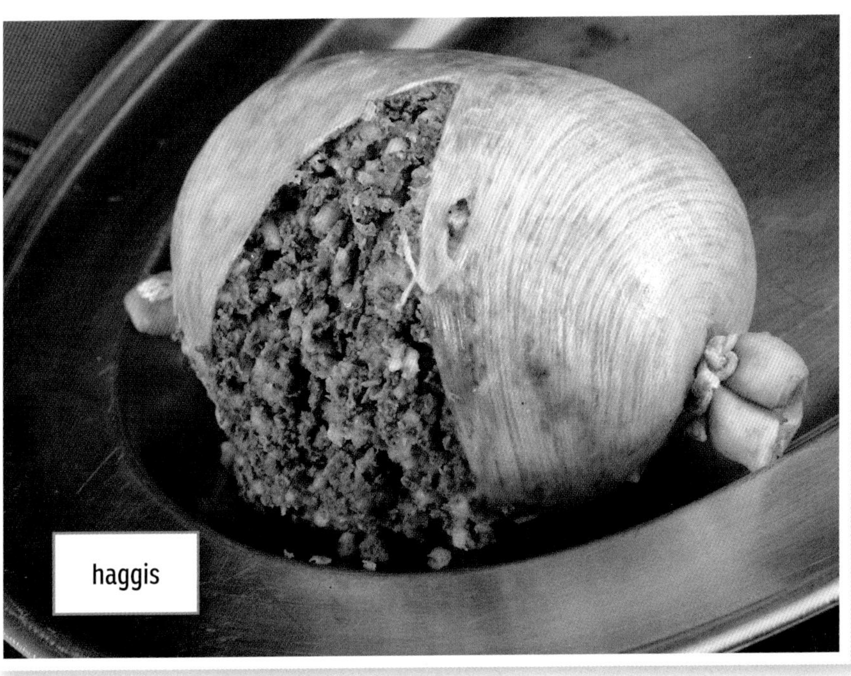

haggis

Holidays

Like many countries, Scotland celebrates Christmas, Easter and other holidays. Scots also celebrate Burns Night and St Andrew's Day. On 25 January, people remember Scottish poet Robert Burns (1759–1796) with a special feast and readings of his works. Burns is best known for his New Year's anthem, "Auld Lang Syne".

Saint Andrew, the patron saint of Scotland, is honoured each year on 30 November. St Andrew's Day is celebrated with traditional Scottish food, music and dancing.

People waving the Scottish flag with pride.

Robert Burns is the national poet of Scotland.

Born in Scotland, Andrew Carnegie founded Carnegie Steel, the largest steel company in the world in the late 1800s.

The Scottish influence

The Scots have a long history of travelling and exploring. As the British Empire spread, the Scots worked as businessmen, teachers, missionaries and soldiers. About 50 million people worldwide claim Scottish ancestry, including those living in Australia, New Zealand and North America. By comparison, the entire country of Scotland is home to only a tenth of that number.

Between 1763 and 1777, 50,000 Scots settled in North America. The influence of the Scots on US society and culture can be seen in many areas, from government to education to business. Many Scots played a role in the founding of the United States. For example, 19 Scots signed the Declaration of Independence.

Many important Scottish figures also made major contributions to the US *economy*. Andrew Carnegie's influence on the US steel industry and David Dunbar Buick's founding of the Buick Motor Company are among the contributions Scots have made to the US economy.

THE VIKINGS

History

Though often thought of as pirates and thieves, the Vikings created a culture that has had a lasting influence throughout the world. The Vikings were people from Scandinavia – Denmark, Sweden and Norway. From the 8th century to around the 11th century, these fearless warriors sailed from northern Europe to take over other lands by force. The lands they took over included Greenland, Iceland and northern Germany. The Vikings were explorers and adventurers who travelled great distances to trade, raid and colonize other places. They brought their culture, language and beliefs with them to each new land they conquered.

The culture of the Vikings is often overlooked because of their reputation as fierce warriors. In truth, their culture was a product of the land around them. *Archaeologists* have found *artefacts,* such as farm tools and iron-working tools, which show that the Vikings were farmers first, then traders and finally raiders.

This man is dressed as a Viking warrior.

As traders, the Vikings travelled all the way to the Middle East and northern Canada. As a result, the Viking influence can be seen in the language and government of people all across Europe, as well as the United States, Canada and other countries. Like many countries today, the Vikings' system of government was a *democracy,* which means "government by the people". They also established what is now the world's oldest surviving *parliament.* It was created in Iceland in AD 930.

The Vikings were also known as poets, artists and excellent metalworkers. They made helmets, axes, swords, spears and other weapons, as well as beautiful jewellery from iron, bronze, copper and gold. But most of all, they were great explorers, arriving in North America nearly 500 years before Christopher Columbus landed in 1492.

The Vikings were masters at making tools, weapons and jewellery from various metals.

Viking ships

Viking ships played a major role in making the Vikings great explorers. The most well known are the longship, which was a warship, and the *knarr,* a cargo ship. Both were built as a result of the harsh travelling conditions in Viking–era Scandinavia, where thick forests covered much of the land. Long, narrow bodies of deep water, called *fjords,* added further challenges for basic travel. Because the seas and rivers were essential for transportation, most Viking settlements were near water.

Despite being somewhat small, longships and knarrs were very stable and were able to cross bodies of water where similar sized vessels struggled. With both sails and oars, they were quick and swift. Both types of ships had small *keels.* A keel is a beam or blade along the centre of the bottom of the ship that keeps it stable and upright. These small keels also allowed the Vikings to better steer their ships and travel up shallow rivers. This enabled them to reach villages and towns that other traders or raiders could not.

The longship was the main type of boat used in Viking raids.

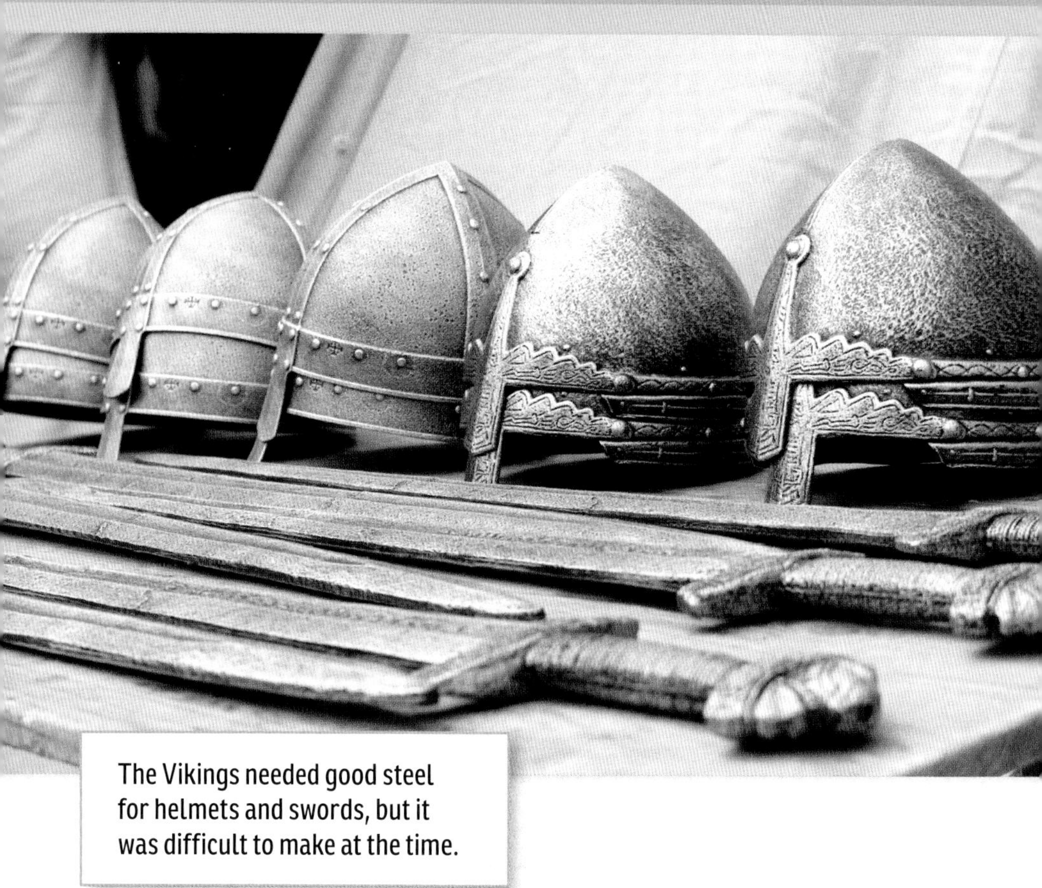

The Vikings needed good steel for helmets and swords, but it was difficult to make at the time.

Exploring, trading and settlements

Their ships enabled the Vikings to travel to faraway places to trade for items they didn't have at home, such as silk and glass. They also sought high-quality steel for swords and silver that could be melted and made into other items. In exchange, they traded furs, walrus hides, amber and iron.

The Vikings traded with countries in Europe, Asia and the Middle East. Their ships allowed them to reach Rome, Baghdad and the Caspian Sea in western Asia. Some archaeologists believe they may have reached Africa, too. Viking writing is carved into the floor of a famous church in Turkey. Artefacts from India and the Middle East have been found in the graves of Swedish Vikings.

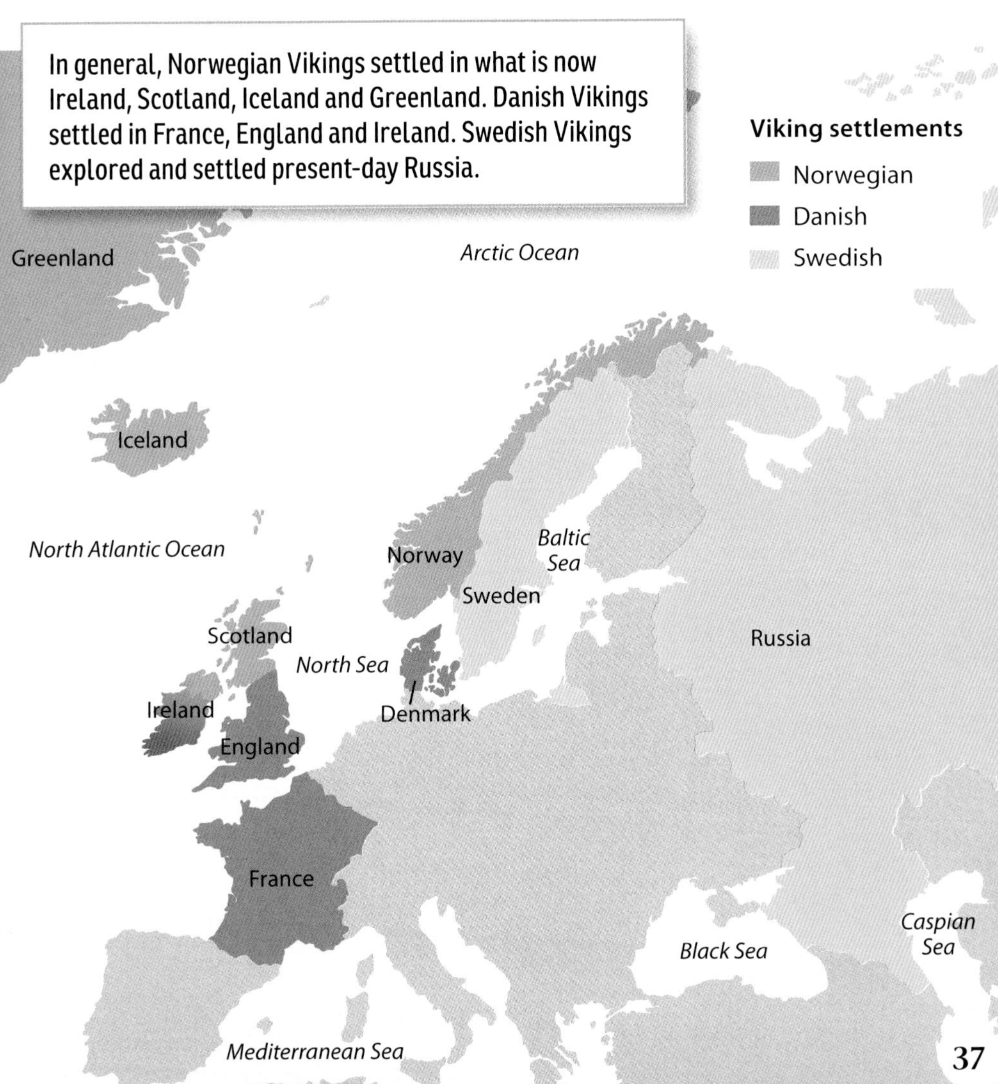

In general, Norwegian Vikings settled in what is now Ireland, Scotland, Iceland and Greenland. Danish Vikings settled in France, England and Ireland. Swedish Vikings explored and settled present-day Russia.

Language

As the Vikings explored, traded and settled places across Europe, they brought their language with them. The Vikings raided England many times and, at one point, they controlled the entire region. Because of this, many words, such as family names and English place names, can be traced to the Vikings. It is believed that nearly 1,000 English words – including "give", "anger" and "husband" – all come from the Vikings.

In France, some Vikings were granted land in the region of Normandy in exchange for becoming Christians and guarding the shores from other Vikings. As a result, a number of place names and family names in France also come from the Vikings.

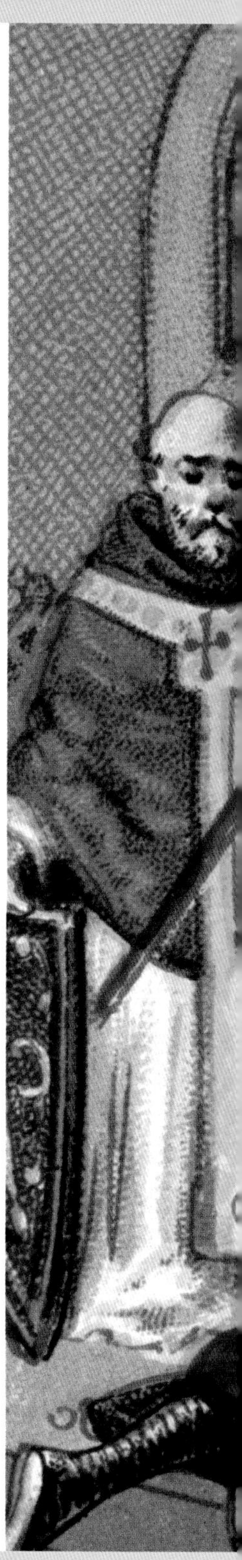

This painting shows Viking leader Rollo becoming a Christian. In exchange, he was granted land in Normandy, a region in France. His followers, called Normans, adopted the French language and customs.

Legal system

Many countries and cultures today can trace their concepts of law and democracy back to the Vikings. Iceland's "Althing" was a group of free Viking men and is thought to be the first such group in Europe. It is perhaps the first true democratic meeting of people. The Althing had the powers of a parliament, such as making laws.

The Althing also acted as a court of law. Laws and lawsuits were brought before the Althing. It was up to the Althing to decide who should be found guilty and punished. Educated men quoted the law, much like lawyers and judges do today. In simple cases, hundreds of people had a say in the judgement. In more important cases, 12 men were chosen to judge. This is the basis of the modern jury system.

All free men were part of the Althing. It paved the way for a democratic future not only for the Vikings but also for many other countries.

The Althing in Reykjavik, Iceland, was established in AD 930. The current building, shown here, was built in 1881.

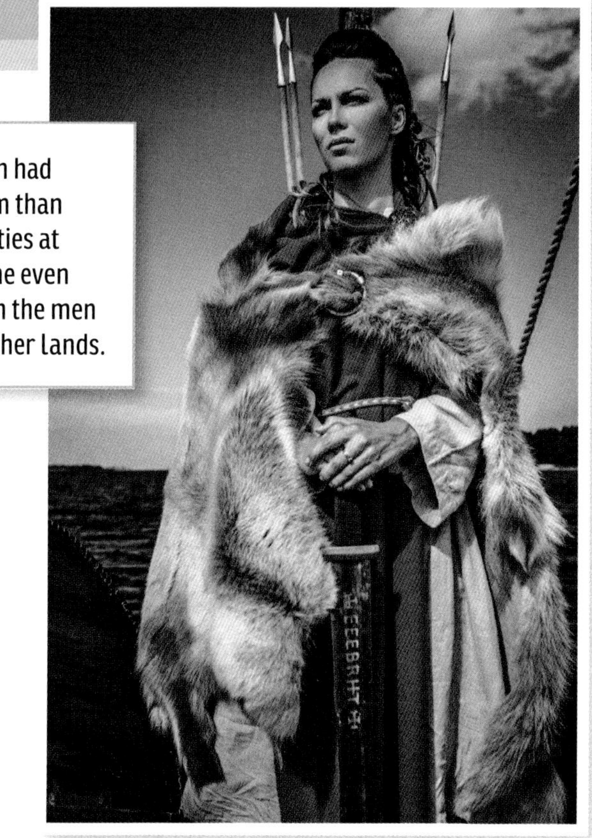

Viking women had more freedom than in most societies at the time. Some even travelled with the men to colonize other lands.

Women's rights

Viking women had more rights than women from many other societies at the time. Viking women were in charge of households and farms, and they could own land. Unlike other cultures, if Viking women lost their husbands through death or divorce, they could keep their property. Viking women also had a say in who they married. Other cultures at this time arranged marriages for women. The women of those cultures had no say in who they married. Over time, the Viking model of women's rights has influenced many modern nations.

Arts and crafts

The Vikings are remembered for their arts and crafts just as much as they are for exploring, trading and raiding. As in modern societies, Viking metalworkers, artists and poets were just as admired as their more athletic friends. Many craftsmen travelled all over northern Europe selling their goods such as timber and iron. Their work was viewed as fine art all over Europe. Craftsmen were often buried with their tools, just as a warrior would have been laid to rest with his weapons.

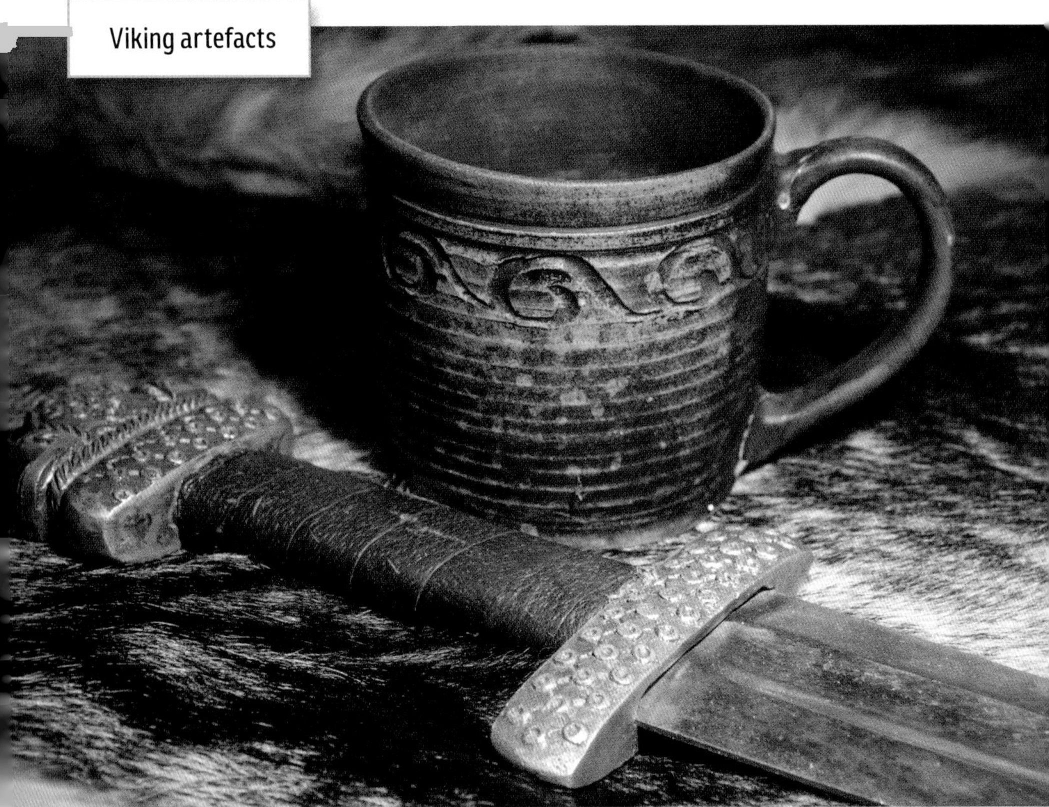

Viking artefacts

Descendants

an ancient Viking rock carving

In Scandinavia, the Vikings' *descendants* formed kingdoms and then nations such as Norway, Sweden and Denmark. The people living in settlements in Britain and Europe married the people from those countries. By the mid-11th century, what we now call the Viking Age had come to an end. But the language and distant relatives of the Vikings spread throughout the Western world and still remain today.

A recent study found that nearly a million British people can claim Viking ancestry. Almost 30 per cent of the population of the northern islands of Scotland have Viking ancestors. And although the Vikings didn't create a permanent settlement in North America, there are still millions of Americans with Viking ancestors.

THE GREEKS

History

The Greek culture has had the longest lasting impact of any other culture in the world. The ancient Greeks have influenced education, government and many other aspects of modern life in countries around the world. Their influence stretches even farther than that of the Vikings.

The term "ancient Greece" refers to the time between 800 BC and 500 BC – more than 2,500 years ago. During this period, the ancient Greeks made advances in technology, art and poetry. This was also the beginning of regions dividing into *city-states* and the true origins of democracy. Their influence affects almost every part of modern culture around the world.

FACT

Each Greek city-state had its own government and army, but they all spoke the same language. Well-known city-states were Athens, Sparta and Corinth.

Many objects from ancient Greece have survived for more than 2,500 years, including this bowl, which was probably used to hold water or wine.

Olympics and international sport

The Olympic Games have their origins in ancient Greece. Every four years, cities would send their best athletes to the games. Although some of the cities often went to war with each other, they agreed to stop fighting during the Games. Back then, there were only a handful of events, and only men were allowed to compete. Events included foot races, horse races and boxing. Roman emperor Theodosius banned the Games in AD 393, but the tradition was brought back to life 1,503 years later in 1896. It has continued ever since.

Democracy

The word "democracy" comes from the ancient-Greek word meaning "people power". This style of government is viewed as the greatest contribution that the ancient Greeks made to modern society and culture. City-states, such as Athens, were governed by the people. They supported equal rights and personal freedom. Many modern governments are modelled on such ideas.

A discus thrower competes in the ancient Olympic Games.

Mythology

Religion was a very important part of life in ancient Greece. The ancient Greeks believed their many gods controlled natural events such as volcano eruptions and earthquakes. To please the gods, the Greeks built temples to honour them. Zeus was the king of the gods and was believed to control the weather. Although the Greek gods are no longer worshipped, myths about them survive in modern culture. One story tells of a woman named Pandora who was given a box and told not to open it. However, the gods had also made Pandora curious, so she opened the box. Once open, all of the world's troubles, such as greed, hate and illness, were released. Today the phrase "opening Pandora's box" means to create problems.

Another myth tells of Zeus' son Hercules, who was said to have super-human strength. Today when something is referred to as "Herculean", it means it takes a great effort or strength.

Many unusual creatures also played roles in Greek *mythology*. One of the most famous was Pegasus, a winged white horse who could fly. Zeus honoured Pegasus by naming a *constellation* of stars after him.

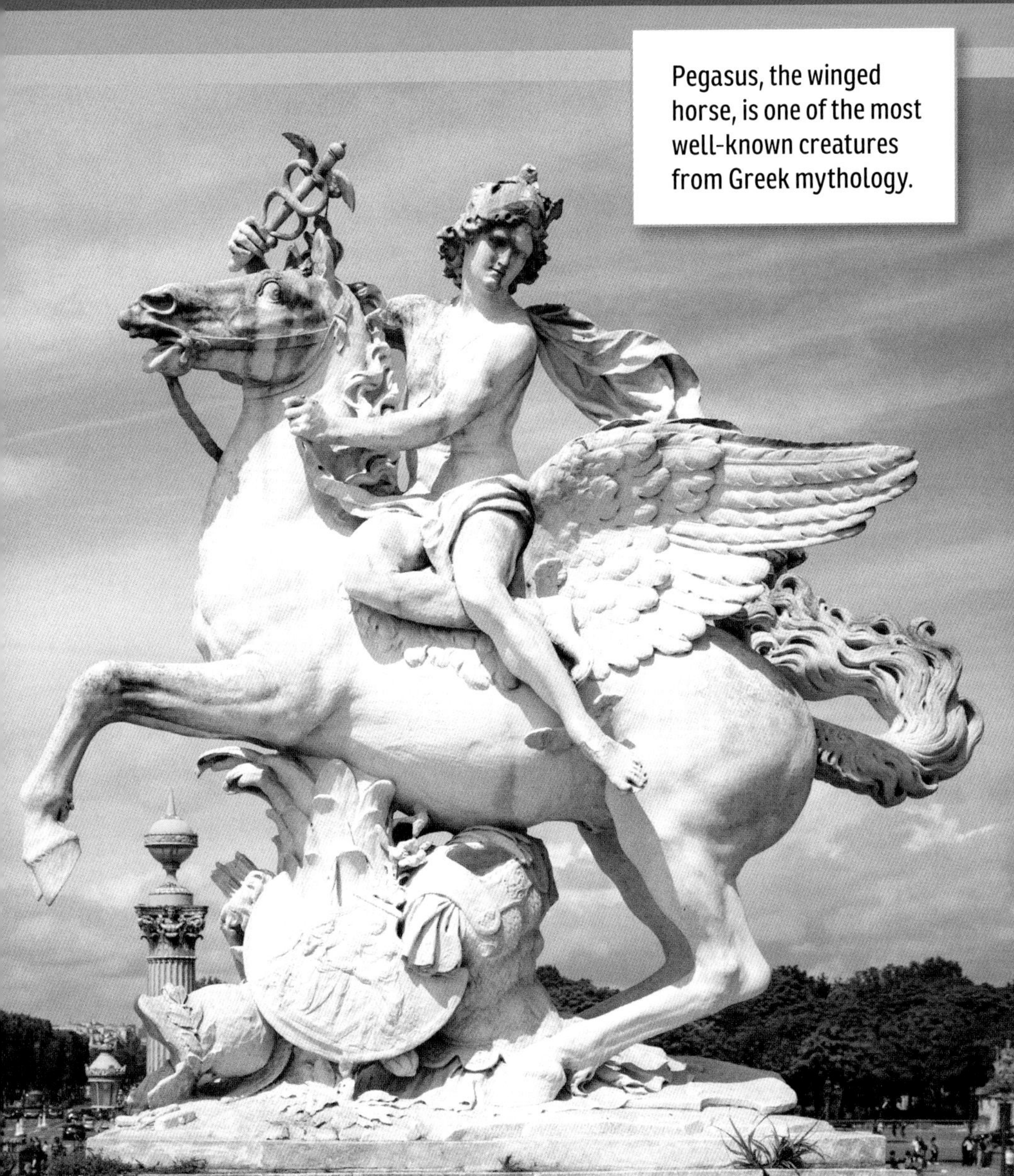

Pegasus, the winged horse, is one of the most well-known creatures from Greek mythology.

FACT

Greek gods have also influenced comic book superheroes. Much like Greek gods and goddesses, today's comic book heroes are larger-than-life creatures with human qualities.

Fashion

Flowing robes were common in ancient Greek fashion, and this style has influenced modern clothing makers. Some clothing makers have even given their designs Greek names. One of the most popular styles of dresses is called the "goddess gown".

Ancient Greek clothing was often made out of wool. Sheep were farmed all over Greece, so wool was easy to obtain. Wool also kept people warm during the cold winters. The ancient Greeks wore simple garments that hung over their bodies and were often belted at the waist. One such item was the "peplos", a sleeveless one-piece garment with holes cut out for the head and arms. Another was the "chiton", which was also a one-piece garment but with sleeves for the arms. Today traditional costumes are often worn during events celebrating Greek culture.

a woman wearing a Greek robe

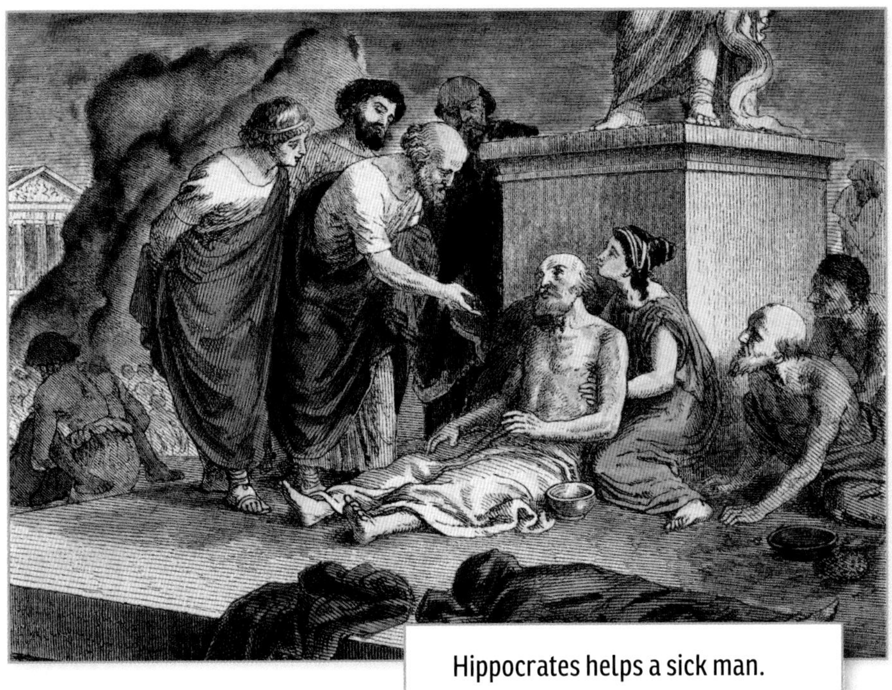

Hippocrates helps a sick man.

Medicine

By the 5th century BC, the ancient Greeks' knowledge of the human body and illness changed the way sick people were treated. Rather than praying to the gods, the Greeks began observing the sick and injured and using common sense to help them. Sickness had human causes and human solutions. This was the start of the field of medicine.

Hippocrates was one of the first doctors and is known as "the father of modern medicine". Even today, doctors finishing medical school still swear an oath or promise in his honour.

Architecture

Ancient Greek architecture has inspired buildings and monuments all over the world. Many of the materials they used, such as wood, unbaked bricks, limestone, marble and metal, are still used today.

But it is the columns that are the true symbol of Greek architecture. All important buildings in ancient Greece had columns in a certain style, based on the time period in which they were built. Doric style columns are the most plain. They can be seen on famous buildings such as the Parthenon. The Ionic style has a bit more detail. The columns on the British Museum in London are in the Ionic style. The Corinthian style is similar to the Ionic, but it has even more flair with leaves carved into the top. The National Archives building in Washington, DC, USA, has Corinthian style columns.

Greek architecture

Doric

Parthenon
in Athens, Greece

Ionic

British Museum in
London

Corinthian

National Archives in
Washington, DC, USA

Food

Greek food was influenced by the climate in ancient times, and that is still true today. Foods that grow well in a hot, dry climate are consumed on a daily basis, including a great deal of fruit and vegetables. Grapes and olives, the most popular fruits in Greece, grow well in the Greek climate. The Greeks do not eat as much meat as many other cultures. But when they do eat meat, it's mostly lamb, pork or chicken. One of the most popular meat dishes in Greece is souvlaki. In this dish, pita bread is filled with meat, cucumbers, tomatoes, garlic and yogurt. These items are easy to find in Greece.

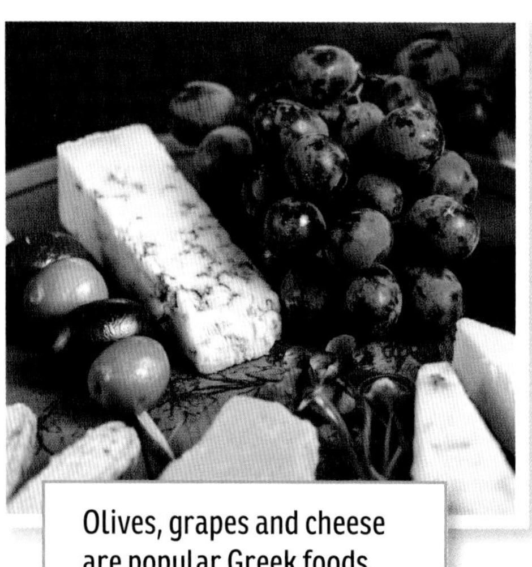

Olives, grapes and cheese are popular Greek foods.

souvlaki

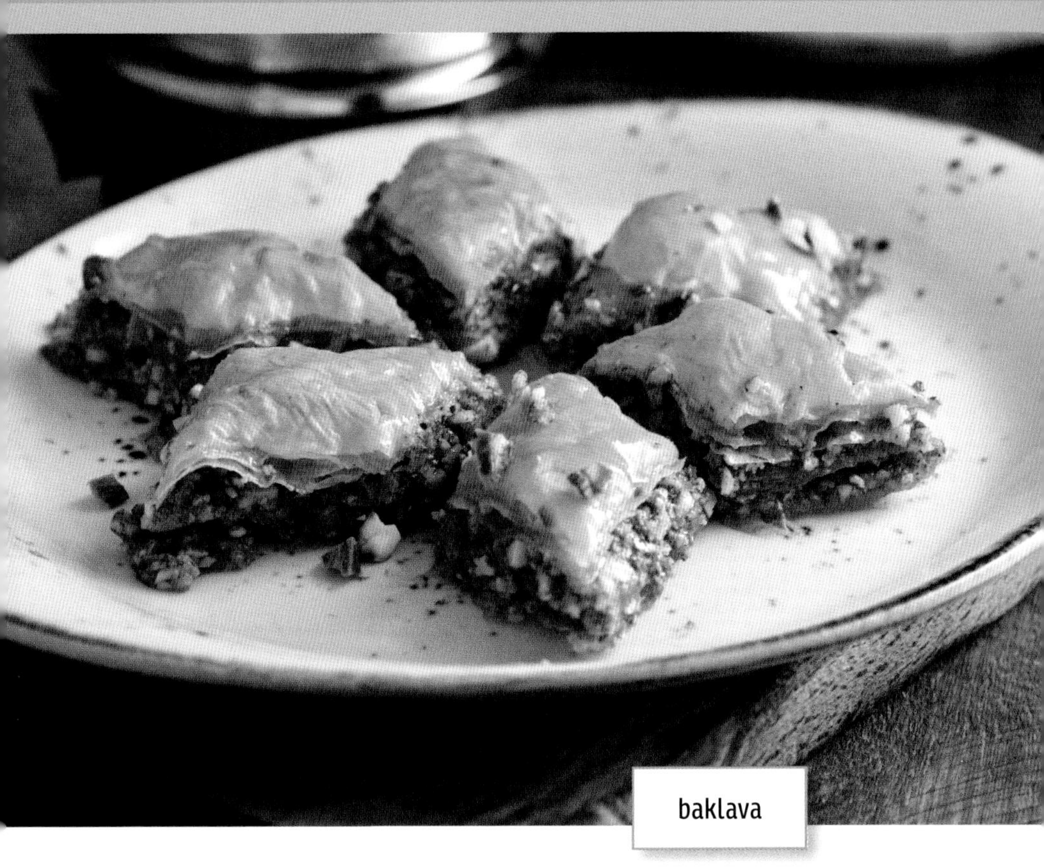

baklava

Baklava is a favourite Greek dessert enjoyed in countries around the world. This sweet pastry is made from thin layers of filo dough stuffed with nuts and honey.

FACT

Ancient Greeks believed that the goddess Athena gifted the first olive tree to the people of Athens.

Story writing

Story writing has its roots in ancient Greek culture. In the 4th century BC, the *philosopher* Aristotle noted that plays seemed to include a problem and a solution as well as a beginning, a middle and an end. Teachers and students of writing still follow this pattern today.

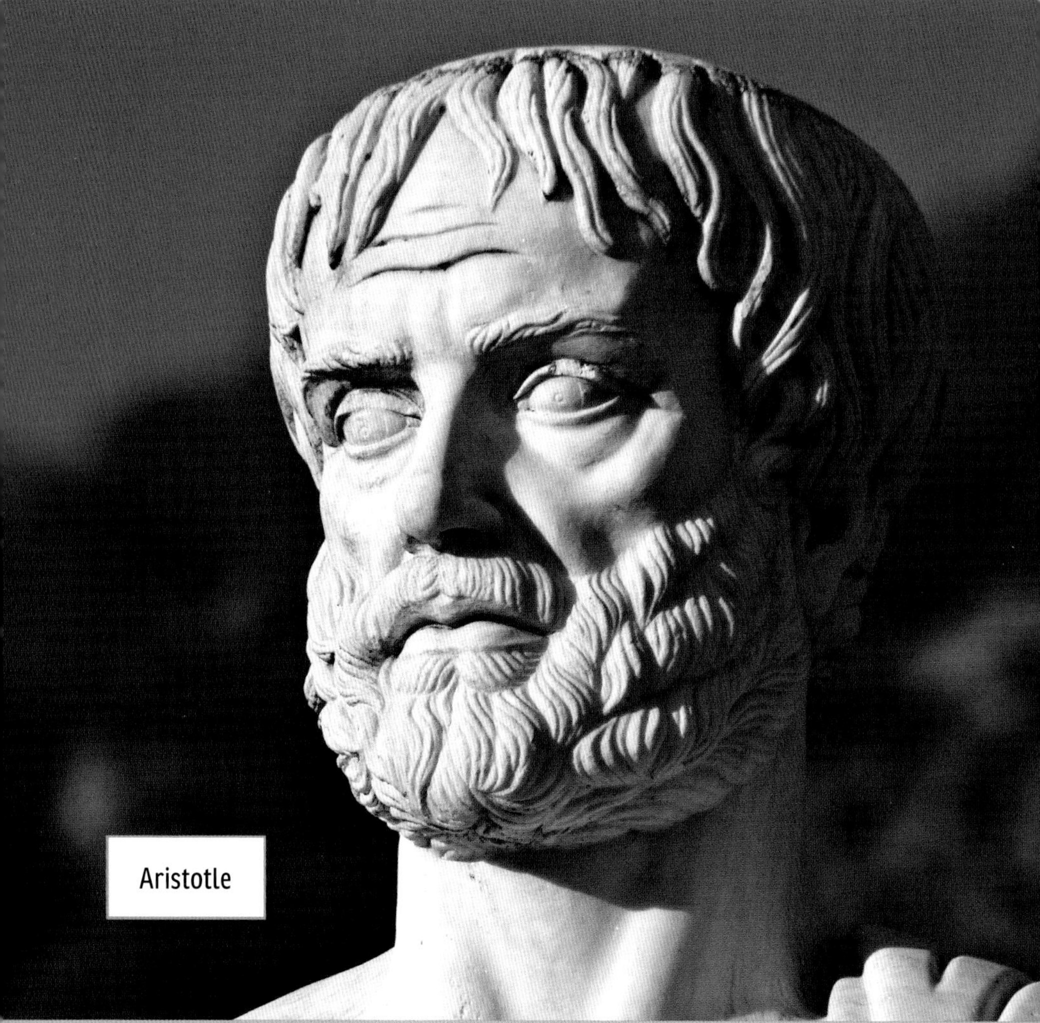

Aristotle

Language

The ancient Greek language influenced many modern languages – especially English. Words such as "idol", "democracy" and "television" all have Greek origins. Many words that begin with "ph" are often of Greek origin. Some examples include "philosopher", "photograph" and "physician".

Music

The ancient Greeks believed that music was a gift from the gods. Certain instruments were believed to be under the influence of different gods. The god Apollo gave a *lyre* to his son. The goddess Athena is linked with the flute, and the panpipes or pan flute are connected to the god Pan. Often these instruments were brought from other cultures, which shows that the Greeks were influenced by other cultures.

Music is still an important part of Greek culture and is often heard at weddings, festivals and religious events. Other popular instruments include the bagpipes, drums and violin, which are all used in traditional Greek folk songs.

Religion

Few people in Greece still believe in the ancient Greek gods and goddesses. Today most Greeks are Christians.

But in ancient times, the Greeks spent a great deal of time praising the gods and goddesses. They built temples to honour certain ones. They said prayers and left gifts in the temples to give thanks to those gods and goddesses.

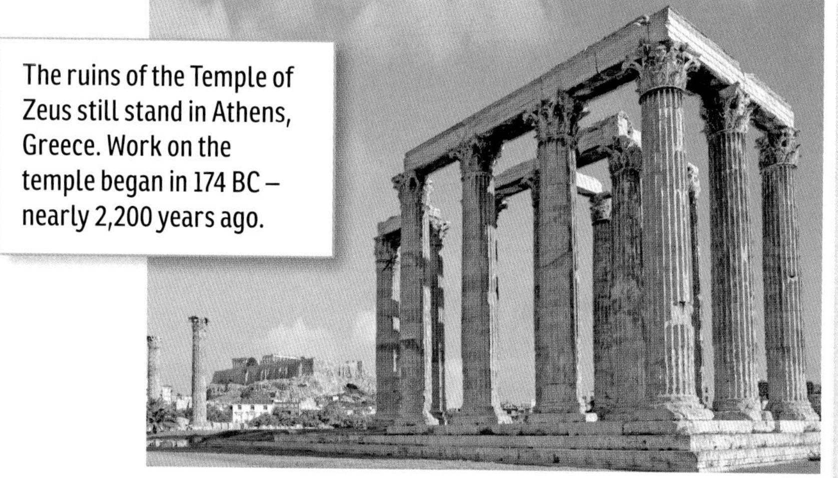

The ruins of the Temple of Zeus still stand in Athens, Greece. Work on the temple began in 174 BC – nearly 2,200 years ago.

Modern festivals and celebrations

Greek gods were also celebrated during festivals and contests such as the Olympic Games. Today many Greek holidays, such as Easter, are centred around the Christian faith.

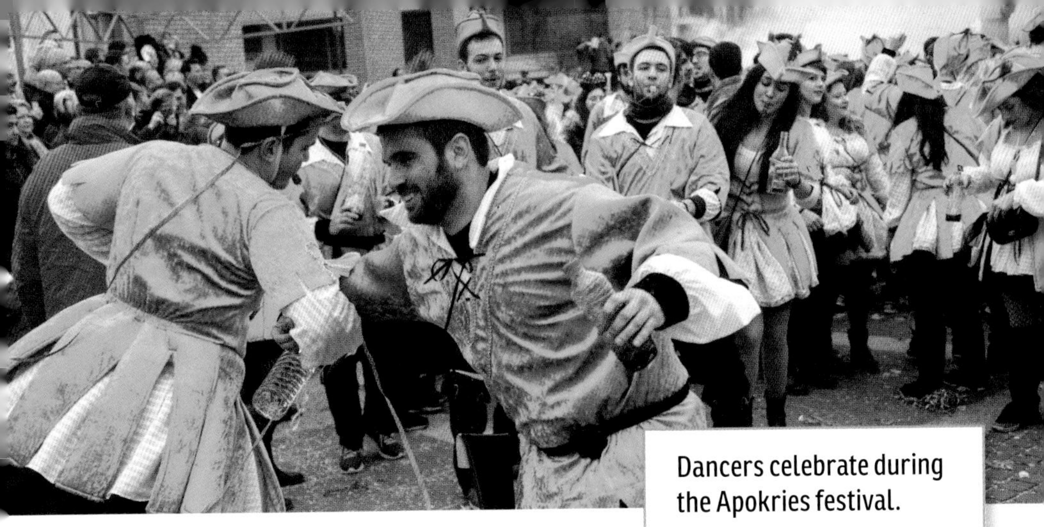

Dancers celebrate during the Apokries festival.

Many Greeks are named after religious saints. Name day celebrations honour a particular religious saint. In Greece a person's name day is more important than his or her birthday.

"Apokries" is a two-week festival held in the weeks leading up to Easter. People dress in costumes and celebrate day and night with music, dancing and traditional Greek food.

The Athens & Epidaurus Festival is held each summer. During this festival, actors perform plays from ancient Greece at a well-preserved theatre. Although the theatre was built in the 4th century BC – nearly 2,400 years ago – it is still known for its wonderful sound quality. It is said that the sound of a pin dropping on the stage can be heard from every seat in the theatre.

Lasting influence

The culture of ancient Greece has had an important impact on modern Greece. Traditions have been handed down for generations. Many of these traditions and ways of doing things have meaning. The influence of ancient Greek culture can be seen in countries all over the world. Many aspects of modern life have been influenced by ancient Greek culture, including education, architecture, language and medicine.

Α Β Γ Δ Ε Ζ
Η Θ Ι Κ Λ Μ
Ν Ξ Ο Π Ρ Σ
Τ Υ Φ Χ Ψ Ω

A B C D E F
G H I J K L M
N O P Q R S
T U V W X Y Z

The Greek (left) and English (right) alphabets are very similar.

The teachings of Plato (left) and Socrates (right) continue to influence modern society.

The modern Olympics (below) were greatly influenced by the ancient Olympic Games, which began in 776 BC.

CULTURE AROUND THE WORLD

Culture explains how and why people do things. It gives meaning to their actions. Culture and traditions are the products of hundreds or thousands of years of progress. They include food, clothing, education and systems of government.

The cultures of the Maori, Scots, Vikings and Greeks have influenced later cultures and continue to impact people today. These cultures have influenced people both in their local regions and those hundreds or thousands of kilometres away. They will continue to do so for many years to come.

GLOSSARY

ancestry line of a person's family or ancestors who lived a long time ago

archaeologist scientist who studies how people lived in the past

artefact object made by human beings, especially a tool or weapon used in the past

caber young tree trunk tossed in a Scottish sport

city-state self-governing community including a town and its surrounding territory

clan large group of families and related people

constellation group of stars in the sky that seem to trace the outline of a person, animal or object

culture group of people's beliefs, customs and way of life

democracy form of government in which the citizens can choose their leaders

descendant person's child and the family members born after that child

economy ways in which a country handles its money and resources

fjord long, narrow inlet of ocean between high cliffs

generation group of people born around the same time

indigenous native to a particular place

keel structure along the bottom of a boat or ship that keeps it stable and upright

knarr type of Viking ship

lyre small, stringed, harp-like instrument played in ancient Greece

mythology collection of myths

parliament group of people who make laws and run the government in some countries

philosopher person who studies ideas, the way people think and the search for knowledge

plaid pattern of squares in cloth formed by weaving stripes of different widths and colours that cross each other

taro plant with roots that people eat

tradition custom, idea or belief passed down through time

INDEX

CW01021091

AQA

AS AND A LEVEL MUSIC

Study Guide

First published 2017 in Great Britain by
Rhinegold Education
14-15 Berners Street
London W1T 3LJ, UK
www.rhinegoldeducation.co.uk

You should always check the current requirements of your examination, since these may change.

Editor: Sarah Patey and Katharine Allenby
Music Editor: Sarah Lofthouse
Cover and book design: Fresh Lemon Australia

AQA AS and A Level Music Study Guide
Order no. RHG140
ISBN 978-1-78558-155-7

Exclusive Distributors:
Music Sales Ltd
Distribution Centre, Newmarket Road
Bury St Edmunds, Suffolk IP33 3YB, UK

Printed in the EU

AQA

AS AND A LEVEL MUSIC

Study Guide

RICHARD KNIGHT &
RICHARD BRISTOW

Contents

The authors

Richard Knight

read Music at St John's College, Oxford, and has been Director of Music at two leading independent schools. He also has nearly 20 years' experience as a senior examiner at A level and is also an examiner for the ABRSM in the UK and overseas. Richard is a prolific composer with a large catalogue to his name including opera, orchestral, chamber and instrumental works (see www.rokmusic.org.uk). His works have been performed at the Tête à Tête Opera Festival in London and in various recitals in the UK and elsewhere. Some of his Christmas church music has been performed by the Ex Cathedra and Tenebrae choirs, and his *Preludes for Piano* are being recorded by the pianist Naomi Kayayan in 2017. Richard also conducts the Malvern Festival Chorus. He has a particular interest in all things South American.

Richard Bristow

read Music at Jesus College, Oxford, before completing his PGCE at the University of Southampton. Richard is currently Director of Music in a highly-successful independent school in London where he oversees the music curriculum and the extensive co-curricular programme. He also works as a senior examiner at A Level, specialising in composition, as well as working for Keynote Education to deliver student conferences and teacher courses across the UK. Richard is active as both a performer and a composer; the BBC Singers have recently performed his setting of the 'Agnus Dei' and he can regularly be found singing with various choirs in London and the South.

Introducing the course

A Level and AS Music with AQA

Fabulous! You have made your subject choices, and you are taking Music on beyond GCSE.

Maybe it was an obvious choice: music is your passion, an obsession, and you have ambitions to be a professional musician. Or perhaps your career aspirations lie elsewhere, but you have always enjoyed making and listening to music and you chose Music as your third or fourth subject to give your schedule some variety and breadth. Or perhaps it was simply that Music was the only subject left on the list after you had eliminated all the subjects you simply can't or won't do.

Whatever the reason, what have you let yourself in for?

Components: Overview

At both A Level and AS there are three components to the course:

	Component 1 **APPRAISING MUSIC**	**Component 2** **PERFORMANCE**	**Component 3** **COMPOSITION**
AS	A written paper of 2 hours comprising: ■ Listening (49 marks) ■ Analysis (17 marks) ■ Essay (30 marks) Two Areas of Study are required for this component (one compulsory, and one chosen from five options)	Minimum of 6 minutes of recorded performance, which can be: ■ Solo and/or ■ Ensemble ■ Instrumental, or ■ Vocal, or ■ IT production To be completed by 15 May	Two compositions: ■ Composition to a brief (25 marks) ■ Free composition (25 marks) Total playing time required: Minimum of 4½ minutes To be completed by 15 May
	96 marks in total = 40% of AS	**50 marks in total = 30% of AS**	**50 marks in total = 30% of AS**

A Level	A written paper of 2½ hours comprising: ■ Listening (56 marks) ■ Analysis and Context (34 marks) ■ Essay (30 marks) Three Areas of Study are required for this component (one compulsory, and two chosen from six options)	Minimum of 10 minutes of recorded performance which can be: ■ Solo and/or ■ Ensemble ■ Instrumental, or ■ Vocal, or ■ IT production To be completed by 15 May	Two compositions: ■ Composition to a brief (25 marks) ■ Free composition (25 marks) Total playing time required: Minimum of 4½ minutes To be completed by 15 May
	120 marks in total = 40% of A Level	**50 marks in total= 35% of A Level**	**50 marks in total = 25% of A Level**

Components in detail

Component 1: Appraising music

This unit is built around a number of Areas of Study (AoS) which enables you to choose repertoire that is most relevant to you, alongside a compulsory Area of Study which provides a shared musical experience with all other A Level musicians across the country.

For each Area of Study, AQA has stipulated some representative composers and artists and some recommended repertoire from these creative musicians that will be the basis of your studies (see the start of each AoS chapter for a complete list of recommended repertoire). The full scheme is as follows:

	AS	A Level
Compulsory Area of Study	**AoS1: Western Classical tradition 1650–1910** Two strands: ■ Baroque solo concerto ■ The operas of Mozart	**AoS1: Western Classical tradition 1650–1910** Three strands: ■ Baroque solo concerto ■ The operas of Mozart ■ The piano music of Chopin, Brahms and Grieg

	AS	A Level
Optional Areas of Study **AS Music** Choose ONE option from AoS 2–6 **A Level Music** Choose TWO options from AoS 2–7	**AoS2: Pop music** ■ Stevie Wonder ■ Joni Mitchell ■ Muse ■ Beyoncé ■ Daft Punk ■ Labrinth	**AoS2: Pop music** ■ Stevie Wonder ■ Joni Mitchell ■ Muse ■ Beyoncé ■ Daft Punk ■ Labrinth
	AoS3: Music for media ■ Bernard Herrmann ■ Hans Zimmer ■ Michael Giacchino ■ Thomas Newman ■ Nobuo Uematsu	**AoS3: Music for media** ■ Bernard Herrmann ■ Hans Zimmer ■ Michael Giacchino ■ Thomas Newman ■ Nobuo Uematsu
	AoS4: Music for theatre ■ Kurt Weill ■ Richard Rodgers ■ Stephen Sondheim ■ Claude-Michel Schönberg ■ Jason Robert Brown	**AoS4: Music for theatre** ■ Kurt Weill ■ Richard Rodgers ■ Stephen Sondheim ■ Claude-Michel Schönberg ■ Jason Robert Brown
	AoS5: Jazz ■ Louis Armstrong ■ Duke Ellington ■ Charlie Parker ■ Miles Davis ■ Pat Metheny ■ Gwilym Simcock	**AoS5: Jazz** ■ Louis Armstrong ■ Duke Ellington ■ Charlie Parker ■ Miles Davis ■ Pat Metheny ■ Gwilym Simcock
	AoS6: Contemporary traditional music ■ Astor Piazzolla ■ Toumani Diabaté ■ Anoushka Shankar ■ Mariza ■ Bellowhead	**AoS6: Contemporary traditional music** ■ Astor Piazzolla ■ Toumani Diabaté ■ Anoushka Shankar ■ Mariza ■ Bellowhead
		AoS7: Art music since 1910 ■ Dmitri Shostakovich ■ Olivier Messiaen ■ Steve Reich ■ James MacMillan

The whole of the Component 1 (Appraising music) paper is based around your choices of Area of Study:

In Section A there will be listening questions based on all the Areas of Study: you answer the questions on the Areas of Study that you have been exploring. As you will be in charge of your own listening via computer, you will be able to ignore the tracks which are not relevant to you.

There is a range of different questions in Section A which will follow the same pattern each year.

AS written paper

The pattern for the AS paper is as follows:

AS Music Component 1					
Section	**Q.**	**Area of Study**	**Type of question**	**Marks**	
SECTION A LISTENING AoS1 is compulsory	**1**	**AoS1 Western Classical tradition 1650-1910**	Extract of Baroque music with short answer Qs	5	
	2		Extract of Classical music with short answer Qs	5	
	3		Aural dictation Q with Baroque or Classical music	4	
	4		Long answer, choosing extract from either Q1 or Q2 and commenting on Baroque or Classical features	10	AoS1 total: 24 marks
Answer ONE set of four questions for the AoS you have studied	**5**	**AoS2 Pop music**	Extract of representative repertoire, short answer Qs	5	
	6		Extract of representative repertoire, short answer Qs	5	
	7		Extract of representative repertoire, short answer Qs	5	
	8		Extract of representative repertoire, long answer Q	10	
	9	**AoS3 Music for media**	Extract of representative repertoire, short answer Qs	5	

	Q	AoS	Description	Marks	Total
	10		Extract of representative repertoire, short answer Qs	5	
	11		Extract of representative repertoire, short answer Qs	5	
	12		Extract of representative repertoire, long answer Q	10	
	13	**AoS4 Music for theatre**	Extract of representative repertoire, short answer Qs	5	
	14		Extract of representative repertoire, short answer Qs	5	
	15		Extract of representative repertoire, short answer Qs	5	
	16		Extract of representative repertoire, long answer Q	10	
	17	**AoS5 Jazz**	Extract of representative repertoire, short answer Qs	5	
	18		Extract of representative repertoire, short answer Qs	5	
	19		Extract of representative repertoire, short answer Qs	5	
	20		Extract of representative repertoire, long answer Q	10	
	21	**AoS6 Contem-porary traditional music**	Extract of representative repertoire, short answer Qs	5	
	22		Extract of representative repertoire, short answer Qs	5	
	23		Extract of representative repertoire, short answer Qs	5	AoS 2 to 6 total: 25 marks
Suggested time: 50 minutes	**24**		Extract of representative repertoire, long answer Q	10	**Section A total: 49 marks**

AS Music Component 1					
Section	**Q.**	**Area of Study**	**Type of question**	**Marks**	
SECTION B ANALYSIS Choose either question	**25**	AoS1	Based on an extract taken from the set works for Baroque solo concerto, both short answer Qs (7 marks) and one long answer Q (10 marks)	17	
Suggested time: 25 minutes	**26**		Based on an extract taken from the set works for Mozart opera, both short answer Qs (7 marks) and one long answer Q (10 marks)	17	**Section B total: 17 marks**
SECTION C ESSAY Answer the essay question for your chosen AoS	**27**	AoS2	Essay question	30	
	28	AoS3	Essay question	30	
	29	AoS4	Essay question	30	
	30	AoS5	Essay question	30	
Suggested time: 45 minutes	**31**	AoS6	Essay question	30	**Section C total: 30 marks**
Total time: 2 hours					**Total: 96 marks**

A Level written paper

The pattern for the A Level paper is as follows:

A Level Music Component 1					
Section	**Q.**	**Area of Study**	**Type of question**	**Marks**	
SECTION A LISTENING AoS1 is compulsory	**1**	**AoS1 Western Classical tradition 1650-1910**	Extract from one of the strands with short answer Qs	4	
	2		Aural dictation Q based on another of the strands	6	
	3		Extract from remaining strand with long answer Q	10	AoS1 total: 20 marks
Answer TWO sets of three questions for the AoS you have studied	**4**	**AoS2 Pop music**	Extract of representative repertoire, short answer Qs	4	
	5		Extract of representative repertoire, short answer Qs	4	
	6		Extract of representative repertoire, long answer Q	10	
	7	**AoS3 Music for media**	Extract of representative repertoire, short answer Qs	4	
	8		Extract of representative repertoire, short answer Qs	4	
	9		Extract of representative repertoire, long answer Q	10	
	10	**AoS4 Music for theatre**	Extract of representative repertoire, short answer Qs	4	
	11		Extract of representative repertoire, short answer Qs	4	
	12		Extract of representative repertoire, long answer Q	10	

	Q	AoS	Description	Marks	
	13	AoS5 Jazz	Extract of representative repertoire, short answer Qs	4	
	14		Extract of representative repertoire, short answer Qs	4	
	15		Extract of representative repertoire, long answer Q	10	
	16	AoS6 Contem-porary traditional music	Extract of representative repertoire, short answer Qs	4	
	17		Extract of representative repertoire, short answer Qs	4	
	18		Extract of representative repertoire, long answer Q	10	
	19	AoS7 Art music since 1910	Extract of representative repertoire, short answer Qs	4	AoS 2 to 6 total: 36 marks
	20		Extract of representative repertoire, short answer Qs	4	
Suggested time: 65 minutes	21		Extract of representative repertoire, long answer Q	10	**Section A total: 56 marks**
SECTION B ANALYSIS & CONTEXT Choose TWO of these three questions to answer	22	AoS1	Based on an extract taken from the set works for Baroque solo concerto, combining short answer Qs (2 marks), medium length Qs (5 marks) and one long answer Q (10 marks)	17	
	23		Based on an extract taken from the set works for Mozart opera, combining short answer Qs (2 marks), medium length Qs (5 marks) and one long answer Q (10 marks)	17	
Suggested time: 40 minutes	24		Based on an extract taken from the set works for 19th century piano music, combining short answer Qs (2 marks), medium length Qs (5 marks) and one long answer Q (10 marks)	17	**Section B total: 34 marks**

SECTION C ESSAY Answer ONE essay question, choosing between the two AoS you have studied	**25**	AoS2	Essay question	30	
	26	AoS3	Essay question	30	
	27	AoS4	Essay question	30	
	28	AoS5	Essay question	30	
	29	AoS6	Essay question	30	
Suggested time: 45 minutes	**30**	AoS7	Essay question	30	**Section C total: 30 marks**
Total time: 2½ hours					**Total: 120 marks**

Course content

This exam structure requires your AS or A Level course to do the following things:

- Study the set works for the compulsory AoS1
- Make a choice of one (AS) or two (A Level) of the optional Areas of Study
- Study a selection of music relevant to the repertoire you have chosen from the optional Area(s) of Study
- Develop your listening skills using related repertoire to your chosen Areas of Study (see chapter on How to listen to music, pages 16-31)
- Cover the technical vocabulary relevant to the Areas of Study you are doing - including the compulsory AoS1 (see chapters 6–12)
- Develop your ability to write essays about music that cover analytical and contextual aspects (see chapter on How to write about music, pages 32-40)

Component 2: Performance

The chances are that you will already have plenty of experience as an instrumentalist, singer or in music production via IT. With this unit being worth 30% of marks at AS, and 35% at A Level, it is important that you commit to good, regular practice.

Often a student's instrumental or vocal studies happen away from the classroom and will involve a specialist teacher who may not know the AS and A Level requirements. Good communication between instrumental teachers and subject teachers in school is therefore very important, and the person best placed to ensure this happens is you.

There is plenty of advice on how to prepare your performance or production submission in chapter 5, How to perform music. The most important message is that your submission should be the end result of several terms of focus on what you need for AS and A Level, not just a last-minute decision to use something you are working on for another reason (such as a grade exam, or a gig with your band).

Your instrumental/vocal/music production activities should not be left to develop in isolation. Look for opportunities to connect practical music-making with the analytical work you will be doing in class. Playing the phrase, cadence or rhythm that you have just learned about is a great way to reinforce the new technical information you have been given; similarly, you could try sequencing a passage from one of the scores you look at. Combining in ensemble with your fellow students is a fine way to build a sense a team spirit among yourselves. Try arranging one of the set numbers from *Le Nozze di Figaro* for a group of you to play or sing; then go and see a live performance and your pleasure will be much increased. Music-making should always be creative, imaginative and fun!

Component 3: Composition

If you took GCSE Music, you will already have experience of composing as part of an examination specification.

- At AS and A Level you will be learning much more about the technicalities of how musical language is used by specific composers and artists in your lessons on the Areas of Study. Alongside these studies, you should try to integrate aspects that appeal to you, and about which you have new understanding, to develop a more sophisticated, imaginative and controlled approach to composing

Like performing, composing is something that should be practised frequently. Try keeping a collection of 'sketches' stored either on a computer, in score or audio form, or on manuscript paper. This should build up your confidence.

For the examination, at both AS and A Level, you need to compose two pieces:

- Composition 1: Composition to a brief
- Composition 2: Free composition

The two compositions are weighted equally - both are marked out of 25 - and their combined playing time should be a minimum of 4½ minutes. If the combined playing time is less, no marks can be awarded.

AQA's specification challenges candidates to make creative use of:

- Musical elements: melody, harmony, tonality, sonority and texture, and tempo, metre and rhythm
- Resources and techniques: instruments, voices and IT, and various ways in which they can be used
- Musical devices: such as ostinato, fugue, EQ and compression
- Conventions: including types of structure and instrumentation

Music for acoustic instruments and voice should be submitted as a fully notated score and/or lead sheet, or by using music software as appropriate, to include an audio facility.

Music intended as a production style composition (i.e. generated entirely digitally) should be submitted via music software, to include an audio facility, and with an accompanying annotation.

Composing briefs

Each year AQA will release the briefs for Composition 1. Note that there are different ones for AS and A Level, so check that you are using the ones you need.

The briefs will correspond to the Areas of Study. At both AS and A Level, the brief for Area of Study 1 will take the form of some technical exercises using the traditional harmony context of a Bach Chorale. For other Areas of Study, the briefs will be less tightly prescriptive, allowing a wide variety of approaches.

It is not necessary to tackle a brief that corresponds to an Area of Study you are using in Component 1. In many cases, however, it may be a very good idea to do so: it will give you a suitable context in which to use all the technical understanding you have gained about that repertoire in a creative way in your own composition. Nevertheless, if you like the look of one of the other briefs, you are free to choose it.

Among the types of brief you might find on AQA's Briefs Paper are:

- Bach Chorale harmonisation (the regular AoS1 brief)
- Some lyrics to set to music
- A story to portray in music, perhaps in the form of a timeline or picture-board for a film
- A pictorial title for a piece
- A melodic idea, perhaps a note row, scale or motif
- A chord sequence
- A bass line or riff
- A given opening to a piece
- A defined ensemble of musicians
- An occasion or performing context
- A picture, drawing or photograph

There is a lot of guidance about developing your composing skills, ideas and habits in chapter 4, How to compose music. It can be a very exciting part of your course, and – with commitment, patience and imagination – you should find your composition work becoming far more rewarding now that you are taking fewer subjects and have more time to devote to Music.

VOCABULARY

As you work through this book you will notice some technical words are in bold: definitions for these terms are in the glossary at the back of the book. You will need to learn what they mean and be able to use them correctly when writing about music.

Check the AQA specification at aqa.org.uk/7271 (AS) or aqa.org.uk/7272 (A Level) for the full list of technical words you are expected to know for each AoS you are studying.

How to listen to music

Jan Brueghel the Younger: Allegory of Hearing

Listening not hearing

You will, of course, feel that you know how to listen to music. Put your headphones on, kick off your shoes, lie back and let the music flow while you check up on your social media.

It can be that simple; however, there is a lot more to it.

Have you ever stopped to think about the fact that we have two verbs for what our ears do: listen and hear? Why is this?

It's the same with eyes: we can see, we can also look. We see the moment our eyelids open in the morning; seeing is an involuntary thing that we do all the time, it is what happens when light hits the retina at the back of the eye. This is not looking. Looking is what happens when we consciously engage with the information received through sight. We look at our phones, we look at a score, we look at a view; we look through a telescope, down a microscope, up a periscope; we look into a problem, we look up an old friend, and look out for danger. Looking is a conscious and focused activity.

When our sight is reporting something familiar, our brain may see but not really look. When you get to your bedroom to crash out, a momentary glance will tell you that everything is familiar and your consciousness will not be focused on visual information but on the feeling of relaxation as you flop onto your bed. Bliss. Lying there, however, you may need to look to see whether your phone charger is in the socket next to you; you probably would have seen whether this was the case as you entered your bedroom, but you weren't looking out for it, so lying there you can't be sure.

Similarly, when you get to your music lesson at school, your sight will tell you that everything is as you would expect, and you are unlikely to focus on what colour shoes your teacher is wearing today, even though your eyes will – in all likelihood – see your teacher's shoes at some point. If, later in the day, you were asked 'what colour shoes was your music teacher wearing this morning?' you might well reply 'I don't know: I didn't look at his/her shoes'.

So it is with our ears: we hear all the time. We do not have earlids, so we have our ears 'open' all the time; whenever soundwaves are travelling through the space we are in, they will reach our ears. This does not mean, however, that we are listening to everything. As with eyesight, we choose what we focus our hearing on: at a party, for instance, among the buzz of many conversations we focus on the one that we are having with a friend.

Music makes all sorts of challenges on our ears. We can just hear it, or we can choose to listen to it.

Of course there are many scenarios where we use music as a background part of our experience:

- In a film we concentrate on the images on screen and not the music in the soundtrack (which is usually subsidiary to the sound of the dialogue), though, as anyone who has seen *Jaws* will testify, the music can very strongly influence our mood
- In an Indian restaurant we focus on the flavours of the food, and the conversation with our friends, but the atmosphere will be enhanced by the sitar music in the background
- Out running, we are mindful of the physical feeling – the tiring muscles, rapidly beating heart, the heavy breathing – though the strong beat of the music coming through the headphones will motivate us to push on harder

Even when we are listening to music, we can easily listen to only part of it, and only hear the rest. For instance, we can focus on the words that are being sung and miss the shapes in the melodic line to which the lyrics are being sung; similarly, we can listen to the driving beat from the drummer and miss the moment the chord pattern or tonality changes. In orchestral music, we may listen intently to the main tune in (say) the woodwinds, but miss the intricacies of the accompaniment in the strings and horns.

By choosing to *study* music to AS or A Level, you are volunteering to become far more expert in the use of your listening faculties. Remember, this is not just an activity for your ears; it requires the full concentration of your brain too.

Developing expertise

Behind listening is curiosity; curiosity as to what is actually happening in a piece of music – not just enjoyment of how it sounds.

Curiosity is the beginning of becoming an expert in any field:

- The chef at some point ate food and thought 'I wonder how you make this', or possibly 'I wonder how you could make this better'
- The professional snooker player at some point thought 'I wonder how you play that shot', or maybe 'I wonder why that shot went wrong'

- The astronomer at some point looked at the night sky and thought 'I wonder what's out there', or possibly 'I wonder why it's there'

In each case the wondering led to a focused pursuit of knowledge and skills: hours spent in the kitchen, or at the snooker table, or looking through the telescope.

Gradually, as knowledge and skill was gained, the initial pleasure turned into expertise and a much deeper identity with the subject:

- The chef began to find much greater understanding of fine food, and a more heartfelt delight in creating and savouring excellent cuisine
- The snooker player began to have a far better sense of the tactics required to play at a high standard, and a deeper appreciation of the skill of the best opponents
- The astronomer began to look at the night sky with much deeper engagement, thrilled to be able to follow and understand the movements and cycles of the cosmos

At the start of your AS or A Level course, when you have chosen Music as one of your specialisms, there is great cause for excitement in the way the study of the subject will deepen your understanding and delight in experiencing music.

Of course, there is a range of skills that come with music. You will be keen to develop your instrumental and/or vocal skills, and there is a great opportunity to take your musical creativity further in the composition; however, at the heart of music is listening to it. The purpose of music is for it to be listened to, and good listening is at the heart of performing and composing well: in both disciplines, you need to listen carefully to the sounds you are producing.

Once you become a skilled listener, you get inside music and music gets inside you.

What is good listening?

Just as the chef benefits from a good kitchen, the snooker player from a good table, and the astronomer from a good observatory, so listening is best under the right circumstances.

These are:

- In an environment where the only sound to be heard is the music you wish to listen to
- Somewhere where there is no visual distraction – for example, a phone, movement of other people, etc
- At a time when your brain is ready to concentrate

There are other important aspects:

- You should listen regularly to unfamiliar music: try different artists, different composers, different instruments, different genres, different musical traditions
- You should listen to a piece more than once: the best music repays listening to several times because you notice more each time
- You should try to follow a score: the combination of your eyes and ears giving your brain the same information in two different formats means you take in more of the musical detail
- Alternatively, you can watch the piece being played, perhaps on YouTube
- Best of all, try to attend live performances: large parts of the repertoire are intended to be experienced 'live' and not through headphones

A very good idea is to keep a listening diary: somewhere you can record the music you encounter and your impressions of it. This will enable you to look back and see how your own personal repertoire of music that you know is developing in quantity and scope. It might look something like this:

Listening diary

1st Oct

'Chan Chan' from Buena Vista Social Club – Spotify

Really liked this: a mellow Cuban song with some cool guitar playing. The main chord pattern has a syncopated feel. Great use of two male voices, and a trumpet instrumental section. Latin percussion effects.

3rd Oct

'Our Love Is Easy' by Melody Gardot – YouTube

A moody song with female vocalist in a minor key. Quite lush strings accompaniment that has a falling bass line. There are some other elements in the accompaniment inc. brushes on the drumkit and some sax. There's a strange solo instrumental break – not sure what it is. Not quite my thing, but suspect Dad would love it!

4th Oct

'You Know I'm No Good' Amy Winehouse – iTunes

I've always liked this song, but really listened to it this evening. There are some great sax moments. The instrumental sections have the band in an octaves texture over the drums which is really effective. I'd not noticed the chromatic bit in the bass riff before, and I think there is a chromatic chord at the end of the verse... it might be V of V which we learned about in class yesterday!

6th Oct

Symphony No.3 'Eroica' Beethoven – Live concert

This was part of our school concert trip to hear the Hallé Orchestra. They were awesome! My favourite section was the third movement that started quite delicately but had some big dynamic changes and lots of energy. I really enjoyed watching the conductor. <u>Must listen to this again!</u>

7th Oct

The Archers theme tune – Radio 4

This tune has always irritated me whenever Mum listens to it, so I decided to actually listen to it and work out why. I think it's the combination of skippy $\frac{6}{8}$ rhythms and loads of major chords. Also, I realise the tune never goes outside an octave: the top note is the tonic and so is the bottom note. This is kind of boring!

What am I listening out for?

In a word: everything. It is so easy for our brain to respond to first impressions, positive or negative. Yet the first impression is inevitably going to be just that: an impression.

It can easily be the audio equivalent of a glance: a sense of the mood of the music, how energetic and loud it is, perhaps which instruments are playing. Yet there are many more details which our ears will hear, but our brains might fail to listen to.

Our eyes do the same thing. Take a long, careful look at this picture by the distinctive Dutch artist Maurits Escher.

Maurits Escher, Day and Night, 1938; woodcut in black and grey, printed from two blocks

Now cover the picture, and – being honest with yourself and without looking back at the picture – have you noticed the following things in this drawing?

- A white, twisting river on the left
- White birds flying to the right
- A patchwork of fields
- That the dark fields and light fields have stripes in opposite directions
- Four boats on the river
- A bridge across the river that leads to a tree-lined road
- Part of the bridge across the river that is narrower (presumably it is a lift bridge)
- A town on the edge of the river (front left)
- A church in the town that has a spire
- The town is surrounded by a canal
- Two ships that are moored up in front of the town on the canal

- Two bridges across the canal into the town
- A windmill on the opposite side of the canal to the town
- A dark, twisting river on the right
- Black birds flying to the left
- A bridge across the dark river leading to a tree-lined road
- Part of the bridge across the dark river that is narrower
- A town on the edge of the dark river (front right)
- The dark town also has a church with a spire and light coming out of its windows
- The dark town is also surrounded by a canal that has moored boats and two bridges
- The dark town also has a windmill on the opposite side of its canal
- In fact, the right hand side of the image is the negative (i.e. black and white reversed) of the left hand side
- That it is not an exactly symmetrical image

In this one two-dimensional image there is an enormous amount of detail. It is small enough on the page that our eyes will 'see' it all in one go; in order for our brain to take it all in we need to spend a significant amount of time 'looking' at it, concentrating our focus on different areas of the image. If we are going to appreciate fully the artist's intentions and skill we also have to make comparisons between one segment of the image and the others: both with the direct symmetrical opposite (left to right) and with shapes that evolve across the picture - consider, for instance, the second line down of flying birds allowing your gaze to travel from right to left to understand how the lead bird on the right morphs into a vaguely bird-shaped view of fields way below a flock of black birds.

All this invites us to engage with our sight and our mental processing; yet the image never changes. The changing aspect is the focus of our eyes.

Now that you have spent time finding all the detail in this Escher picture and understand the clever relationships within it of symmetry and evolution from 'white' to 'black' (or, possibly, daytime to night-time), take another, fresh look at it.

Ask yourself:

- Is my reaction to this picture the same now as when I first saw it?
- If it has changed, do I like it better or less than was initially the case?

Music is different from visual art. Music only exists in the dimension of time; its sounds pass by our ears controlled by the composer and performers. Although we 'hear' all the notes of a piece in an initial experience, in order to be able to understand all the detail and comprehend all the connections between the notes we may have to 'listen' to the music several times. What do we need to be ready to listen to? Potentially, there are many aspects, as shown in this table. (If some of these terms are unfamiliar, you will find them in the glossary, and many are explained further on in the book.)

Tempo:	Is there a regular pulse to the music?
	How fast or slow is it?
	Does the speed of the pulse change?

Metre: Is there a regular stress to the pulse (creating a predictable first beat of the bar)?

Is the beat divided into halves (**simple time**) or thirds (**compound time**)?

Rhythm: What is the rhythmic detail of the music?

Is it consistent throughout, or are there passages of contrast?

Does the rhythmic detail create energy or tranquillity?

Melody: Is there a prominent melodic content?

In what register is it heard?

Does it cover a wide range of notes, or a narrow range?

Is its predominant character rising or falling?

Does it usually move by gentle steps or bold leaps?

Is it **legato** (smooth) or **staccato** (detached)?

Tonality: Is there a clear sense of key?

Is it major, minor or modal, or so chromatic as to be uncertain?

Does it change between major and minor?

Does the tonic change at any point (i.e. **modulation** occurs)?

Harmony: Is the main effect one of **consonant** or **dissonant** harmony?

How varied is the palette of chords used?

How frequently does the harmony change, and does it do so regularly?

Are both major and minor chords used?

Does the harmony use accidentals to create chromatic (colourful) moments?

Are there important **cadences** along the way?

Texture: How many notes are heard at any one time?

Are the multiple notes created by **doubling** the melody, providing an obvious accompaniment to the melody, or by providing two or more melodic lines simultaneously?

Are there any **drones** or **pedal notes**?

What registers are being used? How far apart are the notes being heard?

Instruments: Which instruments / voices are heard?

What is the role of each one? Do these roles change?

Are any particular instrumental techniques used (e.g. **pizzicato**, **mutes**, **flutter-tonguing**, **pedalling**, **overdrive**, humming, etc.)?

Are there any especially interesting blends of instruments being used?

Structure: How uniform is the musical substance and character of the piece?

How is contrast achieved?

Does the opening music return later on, and - if so - in identical or altered guise?

Style: Does the music represent a clear historical, geographical or cultural style?

Is a combination of stylistic influences discernible?

Character: What is the emotional or aesthetic character(s) of the music?

Armed with this long list of questions when you approach an unknown piece of music, you should feel like the musical equivalent of an explorer setting foot on a newly discovered island. How large is it? What are the landmarks? What is the terrain like? What creatures will you meet? Is it inhabited? Does it have hidden treasure? Imagine you need to draw a map of it to guide the next visitor to the island (or listener of the piece).

Here are three listening exercises to try out your explorer's instincts.

LISTENING EXERCISE 1

Find a recording of the 'Air' from the Orchestral Suite No. 3 in D major by Bach – it is the second movement of the piece.

There are five angles of approach; for each you angle you should listen to the music once or twice. You may like to use the questions as the basis for a discussion with a fellow student.

There is a good performance at: **http://bit.ly/BachAir**

First angle of approach – general impression

a. What was the tempo of the music?

Very slow Quite slow Quite fast Very fast

b. Did the tempo change?

Frequently Occasionally Only at the end Never

c. What was the mood of the music?

Tragic Angry Peaceful Excited

d. What instruments were playing?

Just bowed strings Bowed strings and harpsichord

Bowed strings and organ Bowed strings and piano

e. What is the structure of the piece?

AABB (binary) ABA (ternary)

AABA (32-bar song form) ABACA (rondo)

Second angle of approach – melody

Answer TRUE or FALSE for each of the following statements about the melody of the 'Air':

a. The melody is always played at the top of the texture by the first violins

b. The second note of the melody is just a step higher than the first note

c. The second phrase is a falling sequence

d. The A section ends on a lower note than it begins

e. The B section starts with the same phrase as the A section but at a lower pitch

f. There is a rising sequence in the B section

g. The melody ends on the same note on which it begins

Third angle of approach – bass line

Underline any of the following features that you hear in the bass line

Rising octave leaps Falling octave leaps

Descending scale Rising scale

Passing note Auxiliary note Suspension

Even rhythm Dotted rhythm Syncopation

Chromatic notes Rests Pedal note

Pizzicato Arco Crescendo Diminuendo

Fourth angle of approach – inner parts

On this listening, follow the 2nd violin and viola lines on the score below. Ring any places where you can hear either part being especially important in the texture.

Final angle of approach – a more in-depth experience

You have now considered much of the detail of Bach's piece: the structure and instrumentation, features of the melody and bass lines, and places where the inner parts provide significant extra features. This time listen with eyes shut and discover whether your different focused 'listenings' allow you to have a richer experience when you 'hear' the complete piece one more time.

Answers at the back of the book

LISTENING EXERCISE 2

For this exercise you need to have access to the original version of the 1967 song 'A Whiter Shade Of Pale' by Procul Harum.

It can be found online here: **http://bit.ly/ProculHarum, or search for alternatives.**

The structure of the song is as follows:

Instrumental	Verse 1	Chorus	Instrumental	Verse 2	Chorus	Instrumental	Chorus
Melody played by Hammond organ	A1 A2	B1 B2	as before	A1 A2	B1 B2	as before	B2 fades out

The 'B' phrases of the chorus are easy to spot: they begin with the highest note used in the vocal line throughout the song.

Here is a set of questions on each of the three main sections that comprise the song: answers can be found at the back of the book.

The instrumental sections

a. The solo melody on the organ begins with a long note. How many beats does this note last for?

3½ beats **4 beats** **4½ beats** **5 beats**

b. On which beat is the organ's second long note heard?

bar 2^4 **bar 3^1** **bar 3^2** **bar 3^3**

c. This second long note is heard after a rising leap. What is the **interval** used for this leap?

major 6th **minor 7th** **major 7th** **octave**

d. How much higher is the second long note compared to the opening long note?

minor 3rd **major 3rd** **perfect 4th** **perfect 5th**

e. The bass line descends in **conjunct** motion at the start of the instrumental section. Which of the following represents the pattern of the bass line?

i. 

ii. 

iii. 

iv. 

f. How far down the scale does the pattern move before changing direction?

Six steps down to the mediant **Seven steps down to the supertonic**

Eight steps down to the lower tonic **Ten steps down to the submediant**

g. At the end of which bars does the drummer give additional percussive detail rather than just playing the repeating pattern?

Bars 2 and 8 **Bars 2, 4 and 8**

Bars 2, 6 and 8 **Bars 2, 4, 6 and 8**

h. In the following table tick boxes to match bars where the listed features occur:

	bar 1	bar 2	bar 3	bar 4	bar 5	bar 6	bar 7	bar 8
A major chord on the **downbeat**								
A minor chord on the downbeat								
The melody note is a compound 3rd above the bass note on the downbeat								
The second beat of the bar is a first **inversion**								
The bar uses three different chords leading to a faster **harmonic rhythm**								

The vocal sections

a. How many bars long is the A1 section?

b. How many bars long is the A2 section?

c. How many bars long is the B1 section?

d. How many bars long is the B2 section?

e. The word setting is almost entirely syllabic, but at the ends of some phrases the final syllable sometimes receives a 2- or 3-note embellishment. Fill in the following chart to show where this occurs in both verses. Either put a cross for 'no embellishment' or '2' or '3' for the number of notes used for the final syllable:

verse or chorus?	section	phrase	verse 1	verse 2
verse	A1 section	first phrase		
		second phrase		
		third phrase		
	A2 section	first phrase		
		second phrase		
		third phrase		
chorus	B1 section	first phrase		
		second phrase		
	B2 section	first phrase		
		second phrase		
		third phrase		
		fourth phrase		

f. What feature occurs in the organ part to link into the B2 section and becomes very prominent going into the final B2 phrase (the fading outro)?

g. What cadence is heard at the end of the B2 phrase?

Plagal **Perfect** **Imperfect** **Interrupted**

Overall impression

a. In what ways are there similarities between 'A Whiter Shade Of Pale' and the 'Air' from Bach's third Orchestral Suite?

b. What are the significant ways in which Bach's 'Air' is different from 'A Whiter Shade Of Pale'?

LISTENING EXERCISE 3

For this you will need a recording of the first movement from Beethoven's 5th Symphony in C minor.

First approach – motif spotting

Before you listen to the music, read the following information about the music:

Beethoven grew up with the music of Viennese Classicism – composers such as Mozart and Haydn; indeed, he had some lessons with Haydn. His early music, including his 1st and 2nd Symphonies, reflects this strongly; however, from his 3rd Symphony of 1803/04, his music belongs more to the new Romantic style of the 19th century.

The famous 5th Symphony follows in this new style. One aspect is the way Beethoven derives much of his musical material from a single 4-note motif: the famous 'pa-pa-pa-PA' with which the first movement begins. This is never far away in the first movement and is used with a variety of registers, dynamics, instrumentation, alterations of the falling interval, and other techniques.

It is remarkable just how much of the movement is built from this simple 4-note shape. As you listen to the music, listen out for the following versions of the motif: some are obvious (for instance, loud and at the top of the texture) others are more subtle (maybe p and in the bass). See how many you can spot over the course of the movement! There are many others too.

Now listen to the whole of the first movement, concentrating hard on finding all the **motivic** patterns.

Second approach – feeling the emotional temperature

Now read this alternative introduction to the same music:

> *Beethoven was born in Bonn, then a small town, and as a young man arrived in Vienna, the musical capital of Europe, intent on pursuing a career as a pianist. In his early 30s he became aware that he was losing his hearing; it drove him to despair. His ambition to be a renowned performer was over. In the Heiligenstadt Testament of 1802 – a letter to his brothers – Beethoven wrote of considering suicide, but that he had chosen to continue as a composer.*

The 5th Symphony is sometimes given the nickname 'Fate'. There is an immediate sense of doom with the dark minor key and dramatic falling shape. Much of the opening movement has a tempestuous and stormy character, with some warmer, sunlit passages in passing that seem like a memory of less troubled times as a carefree youth. The intensity of Beethoven's frustration becomes overpowering in the final part of the movement. As the whole orchestra hammers out the repeating quavers, one can imagine Beethoven at his fortepiano, thrashing the keys belligerently, desperately trying to hear the notes he was playing.

Now listen to the first movement again.

Comparing the two approaches

When you have completed the listening exercises, reflect on the two listenings; you may like to share your thoughts with a fellow student:

- How influential was the information you read before each listening?
- How different was the experience of listening to the music?
- Which listening experience was the most interesting?
- Which listening experience was the most emotionally charged?

Final thoughts

Good music repays repeated listening. The more we listen to the detail of a piece, the more we become familiar with it, and the more we can savour and enjoy it on subsequent encounters.

We can approach listening to music from a variety of angles, some technical, others emotional. As we become familiar with the music, we can gain intellectual understanding of it, informed admiration for the skill with which it was composed and is being performed, and emotional enrichment. If we listen well, we can soon find an unfamiliar piece becoming a new favourite in our listening repertoire. We can also gain greater understanding of how musical language works, which can enhance our performing and composing skills.

Traditionally, teachers tell AS and A Level students that they need to be 'reading around the subject'. This is also true for music, but more important is to be *listening* around the subject.

Among your targets should be:

- Different performances/versions of the music you are studying
- Other pieces by the artists/composers whose music you are studying and/or performing
- Music by other artists/composers working in the same style/context as the ones you are studying and/or performing

In short, aim to make your *listening to* (not *hearing of*) music a habit. Make it frequent, focused and fun - ***fff*** in fact - and it will have a big impact on your progress.

How to write about music

Why write about music?

Composing, performing and listening are all aspects of the essence of music.

Without composing, the performer would have nothing to perform; without performing, the listener would have nothing to listen to; and without listening, there would be no appreciation of either the composer or the performer. All three are assessed at A Level; however, considerable weighting is also given to being able to write about music. Why is this?

Words can sometimes seem to get in the way of the purpose of music. Your favourite band, your song of the moment, or the piece you most enjoy playing on your instrument, will make a direct appeal to you. This will be due to emotion and feeling; trying to describe and explain this process may seem unnecessary or even intrusive. It can seem similar to explaining what makes a joke funny.

Throughout the history of music, words have played a very important role in its development and evolution. In the medieval era, theorists played a more influential role than composers.

Think how words on their own have influenced your own musical journey, from explanations by your instrumental teacher about technical or expressive aspects of your playing, to recommendations from friends (or arguments with them) about new songs.

After a while, the music takes over again, but your instinct has been enhanced through assimilation of the words used. You forget your teacher's explanation of the correct technical method or expressive idea, and you forget your friend's endorsement of a song; but meanwhile, you enjoy the fact that your technical fluency has improved, the emotional feel of your interpretation has been intensified, or the new addition to your listening repertoire.

Writing about music, therefore, is a vital way to develop your understanding of music, an understanding which you have chosen to take to Advanced Level. Through writing about a great piece of music you can:

- Learn to identify all the features of the music, those on the surface and those in the background (where they can, nonetheless, have a very significant impact)
- Intensify your listening experience, through improved understanding of what is happening in the music in all its layers and dimensions
- Gain a deeper appreciation of a composer or artist by appreciating his/her individual musical identity and stylistic development
- Enhance your performance of a piece due to an improved understanding of its significant structural and expressive features
- Develop your compositional skills through a more confident approach to using techniques to gain control of expressive intent

And, of course, it is through writing about music that you can communicate your musical intelligence to an examiner. Writing about music can be found in programme notes, reviews of concerts and recordings, websites and books, and it is the backbone of the academic area called musicology.

Content

Writing about music is akin to putting it under a musical microscope.

We have three lenses. In order of ascending power these are:

- Musical context
- Musical **affect**
- Musical detail

These levels connect in both directions. Consider the following scenario:

- A new James Bond film provides a context for a title song
- The context is commercial: the song will be written to affirm the Bond brand, tailored for an iconic celebrity singer, and released prior to the film premiere to enhance the profile of the new film
- In order to maximise the potential of the context, the music needs to make a strong and specific affect that is recognisably Bondian. There needs to be suspense, there needs to be romance, there needs to be yearning, and there needs to be a whiff of opulence
- To create the affect, the composer needs to choose musical detail carefully. For example: minor key and prolonged **appoggiaturas** will bring darkness and tension; long lyrical melodies will sound lush when played on big string sections in more than one octave; horn countermelodies with some wide upward leaps will suggest longing and eroticism

Discuss with a friend the following list of moods, and suggest a piece that creates each one. Then try to explain what it is about the music that creates this atmosphere in the music. Think of a wide range of music: songs you know, pieces you have played on your instrument, music you hear on TV, and so on.

Exuberance	Dreaminess	Sadness
Happiness	Fear	Anguish

Some pieces of music concentrate on capturing and sustaining a single emotion; others use contrast as a way of creating drama or structure in a piece. Sometimes there is a subtle blend of emotion, or a kaleidoscopic mix. Some take the listener's emotions on a journey (from darkness into light, for instance).

Let's consider again the music for 'Happy Birthday'. Which of the following adjectives might be used to describe the music of the song?

Happy	Scary	Boisterous
Excited	Cheesy	Warm
Cold	Sad	Complex
Simple	Tranquil	

For the adjectives you have chosen as being appropriate descriptions of the song, now consider what aspects of the music are responsible for creating this characteristic. Some of these might be a feature that is true of the whole song (e.g. the key), others might be one particular moment (e.g. an accidental).

Musical context

Musical detail and musical affect are aspects of a piece which can be studied through listening to the music and (probably) following the score. Musical context requires a more wide-angled lens. There are various possible aspects to consider:

- Reasons for the piece to be composed: commission, patron, occasion, muse, etc
- Aspects of the intended first performance: venue, performer(s), audience, etc
- The cultural climate at the time and place of composition: the typical style, aspects of tradition, influential new ideas and technologies, etc
- Personal aspects of the composer's life and background: age, romantic issues, religious factors, state of health, etc

Of course, not much of this is very relevant to something as traditional and brief as 'Happy Birthday'. A 2015 court case in America established that we do not know who composed the melody. Nonetheless, it would not be the song it is if it did not have its everyday context: a song that all can sing from memory to wish their family and friends a happy birthday whenever and wherever this might be. A longer song or a more elaborate song would be less easy to remember and harder for untrained musicians to sing.

Getting the balance right

For a good A Level music essay, you will need to know something of the musical context of pieces you are writing about, be comfortable describing the musical detail using appropriate technical vocabulary, and be able to describe the musical affect.

It is important to get these in an appropriate balance. This is a qualification in *music*; long descriptions of context that dwell on biographical details of a composer or artist, or the story of why the music was created, don't really belong in a good essay on music. Such aspects are best mentioned in a brief contextual sentence that shows you have an awareness of the background to the piece(s) you are writing about.

You must aim to show that you understand music in detail; it is far more important to focus your efforts on identifying repertoire relevant to the question and pinpointing the key aspects of the musical detail. Depending on the music and the question you are answering, this might be the shape and structure of the melodic ideas, the choices of tonality and harmony, the rhythmic identity of the music in terms of metre, note values and accentuation, the approach to texture or the ways in which the instruments are used and combined.

You must also show that you are familiar with the sound of the music: the musical affect. It is therefore hugely important that you do not just learn technical facts about pieces you study with the intention of reciting them in your essay in the exam room. You need to be able to marry the technical analysis of the music with the resulting sound, and link the two in what you write. In fact, this should make learning your exam facts much easier: when you are able to recall the sound of the music in your inner ear in the silence of the exam room, this should trigger your knowledge of the technical detail you have studied.

Writing in short paragraphs is a good habit to adopt, and leaving a line between each paragraph helps the examiner to understand how you are approaching the music.

For each paragraph you should:

- Have a single, relevant main point to make
- Have one or two musical passages in mind that will provide evidence for your point
- Give a clear location for the music you are going to write about
- Explain accurately the relevant musical detail using technical vocabulary
- Describe the sound of the music produced from the musical detail you have explained

Putting it into practice

In this chapter you have considered both the musical detail and musical affect of the song 'Happy Birthday'. Imagine you were asked to write an answer to the following question: 'What makes "Happy Birthday" the world's best known song?'

Below is a possible answer to this question. Read through this carefully, and use three different coloured highlighter pens to highlight words, phrases and sentences that fit the three categories of (in this order):

- Musical context - background information and comment
- Musical affect - descriptions of what the music sounds like (adjectives)
- Musical detail - technical examination of the notes

SAMPLE ANSWER

A song that is intended to be sung by everyone and anyone whenever someone celebrates their birthday was always going to have a good chance of becoming the world's best known song; however, the right song had to be composed for the purpose.

The happy mood is guaranteed by the choice of major key and a moderate tempo. Though it is only eight bars long, there are many other features that also contribute to its cheerful character.

The tune is perfectly balanced, like a simple poem, in four 2-bar phrases. Each of these begins with an anacrusis in the form of an energising dotted rhythm giving a defining feature to an otherwise simple melodic rhythm of crotchets with minims at the end of some phrases. The triple time metre lends an attractive sense of lilt to the rhythm (particularly underlined by the harmonisation).

The contour (shape) of the melody is particularly effective. The first three phrases each have a sense of upward character, enhancing the positive feel of the music. Much of the tune is conjunct, which aids amateur singing, but each phrase has one rising leap. These intervals become wider: a 4th in the first phrase, a 5th in the second phrase, and an octave in the third phrase, helping the tune to sound increasingly bright. The final phrase begins a 7th above the end of the previous phrase, and - with a different role in the tune - brings the song to its close by descending to the tonic. There is a perfect match between the start of the tune - up a step and back to the first note (D–E–D) - and the way it ends (G–A–G).

This simple tune is so well shaped and affirming that it is, on many occasions, sung in unison. The homophonic harmonisation provided above enhances the musical affect further. The purely diatonic first half confidently establishes the key, balancing the I–V^7 progression of the opening phrase, with V^7–I in the second phrase. The move to Ib on the third beat of bar 1 is mirrored by a move to V^7b in bar 3; together these subtle chord changes add a little sophistication and underline the typical long-short subdivision of the bar available in triple time. These chords also give the melodic notes at bar 1^1 and bar 3^1 the function of being accented auxiliary notes (i.e. non-harmony notes) which increases the charm of the music.

The harmonisation becomes more complex in the second half of the song. Having based the opening two phrases on tonic and dominant harmony, the third phrase is essentially a counterbalance of I–IV, but this is enhanced by some colourful chromaticism with the use of D♯ in the alto line. This third phrase does not have the same accented passing note as its predecessors at bar 5^1, but instead it treats the downbeat of bar 6 as a non-harmony note. The resulting augmented 4th in the tune (F♯) over the C in the bass is complemented by similar movement in alto and tenor parts in order to create a triple appoggiatura on the downbeat before the chord resolves at bar 6^2 onto the C major chord the bass sets up the beat before. This creates the perfect musical opportunity to emphasise the name of the person to whom the song is being sung; moreover, this emphasis is further underlined by the customary ritenuto and pause at this point.

Chromaticism remains the characteristic of the final phrase, especially in the alto line which has five successive notes of a falling chromatic scale, resulting in a suitably sentimental ending reminiscent of the close harmony singing of the barbershop style. The final perfect cadence ensures an emphatic conclusion.

All these details ensure that 'Happy Birthday', while simple enough to be remembered by even the least habitual singer, has in its eight bars an unmistakable feel-good positivity and this explains why it has an assured place as the world's best known song.

When you have finished highlighting this answer, you should find that a large majority is highlighted in the colour you chose for musical detail, with frequent individual words or phrases in the colour you chose for musical affect. The third colour - for musical context - should only be seen in the introductory and concluding paragraphs, plus a short phrase near the start of the fifth paragraph.

All your essays will have unique factors depending on the music you are writing about, but the proportion between detail, affect and context should be similar to this example.

The sample essay answer includes the following technical vocabulary, all of it relevant at A Level. You should check any terms of which you are unsure in the glossary at the back of this book.

Melody:	contour, conjunct, intervals, non-harmony notes, auxiliary note, passing note, appoggiatura
Tonality and Harmony:	major key, diatonic, chromatic, Roman numeral shorthand for chords, perfect cadence
Rhythm:	tempo, ritenuto, dotted rhythm, anacrusis
Texture:	unison, homophonic

Who would have thought just how many details can be found in just eight bars of music? There are only 68 notes in the version of 'Happy Birthday' we have been using, yet once we put it under our musical microscope, we find an enormous amount of musical logic in the melodic, rhythm and harmonic shapes that these 68 notes form; we can explain why this simple piece of music has been such a success, and we can take a better understanding of melodic contour and structure, harmonic colour and rhythmic handling of triple time forward with us to our next musical experience, be it performing, composing or listening.

Should you find yourself singing 'Happy Birthday' to someone in the few days after working through this chapter, you may well find yourself thinking as you sing 'Gosh, this is a really skilfully constructed melody.' If you do, you are benefiting from musicology: the study of music. It is a fascinating and absorbing activity and one which makes us better musicians; like a new pair of shoes, it can seem a rather uncomfortable fit for one's brain at first, but once you make it your own it can soon become a favourite part of your identity.

YOUR FIRST WRITING TASK

So much for 'Happy Birthday'; now choose your own piece of music to write about. Choose something short (less than a minute of music), selecting a passage from something larger if necessary.

TV theme tunes might be a good place to start as these are usually short and intended to create a strong sense of character to match the style of programme.

If you choose something for which you don't have a score, you will still need to be able to give locations for the detail you want to mention. This can be done be referencing a clearly audible moment ('where the opening tune returns', or 'when the drums enter') or you could use a timeline ('at 0'12"...'). Remember to focus on musical detail, but explain the affect that this detail creates.

When you have finished writing about the music, try reading your work to a friend and see if they can work out which piece of music you have been writing about. If they can, the chances are that you have made a good start at writing about music.

Writing essays about music

In the Analysis and Contextual Understanding Essay part of each AoS, you are required to have studied three of the artists listed in the following ways:

- How each artist's/composer's use of musical elements for **at least two** published works reflects the style of the genre and their purpose and intentions for the work
- How the style of each artist's/composer's music has varied over time through comparison of published works
- Use musical vocabulary and terminology relevant to the work and the specific AoS

The AoS 2 to 7 chapters in this book include sample essay questions. They will give you the opportunity to practise this kind of writing. When writing an essay, you may find it useful to bear the following advice in mind:

- **Answer the question**: what is it asking? What is it not asking?
- **Use examples**: be sure to support your argument with examples from the music you have studied
- **Give context**: address the question fully by giving relevant musical detail from the pieces you have studied
- **Focus on the music**: if your music supports words, or a plot, remember that you are writing about the *music*, so only describe as much of the poetry/plot as you need to explain the effectiveness of the music. You can assume your reader knows the story, so don't get side-tracked into detailed narrative!
- **Plan your essay**: before you start writing, make notes on how your argument will develop, and which examples you are going to use
- **Look after the introduction**: this is often the hardest part to write, so consider writing it after you have written the main body of your essay, allowing your confidence to develop

How to compose music

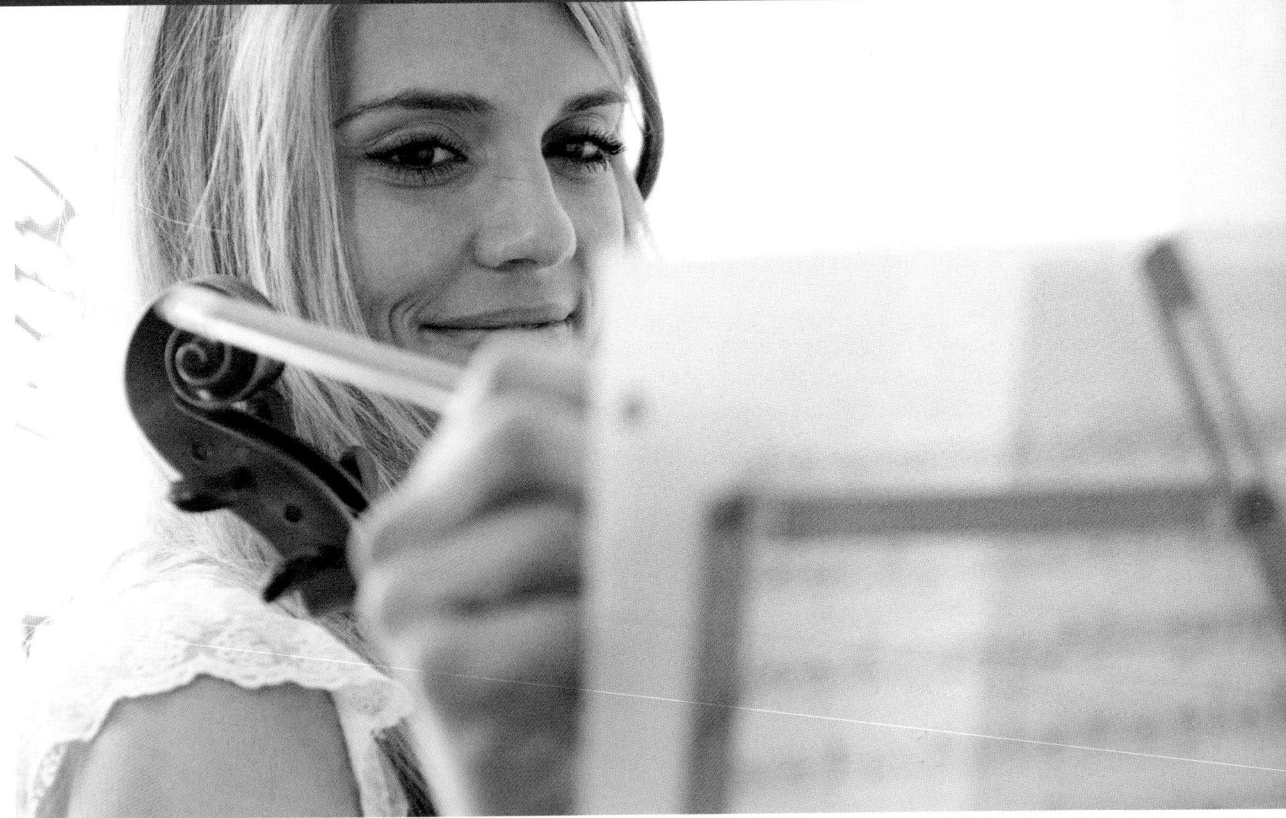

First thoughts

Composing music is an amazing thing to do. The possible combinations of notes are close to infinite; meanwhile, the language of music enables us to express ourselves in extraordinary and extraordinarily diverse ways.

Take, for instance, the following examples:

- Mozart taking delight in human relationships and insecurities in his opera *Le Nozze di Figaro*
- Beyoncé expressing the cares and issues of her generation in her song 'Jealous'
- Bernard Herrmann terrifying cinema audiences with his music to the shower scene in *Pyscho*
- Claude-Michel Schönberg bringing the drama of the French Revolution to life in his music for *Les Misérables*
- Miles Davis blending the sounds of acoustic and electronic instruments in 'Shhh'
- Anoushka Shankar combining Indian classical sitar music with electronica beats and **synthesised** sonic backdrops in *Oceanic*
- Shostakovich speaking for the Russian people oppressed by Stalin in his Fifth Symphony

Some of these pieces you will be studying; what a remarkable diversity of music is represented here! Consider the following aspects for each of the pieces listed:

- The nationalities of the composers and artists
- The years in which the pieces were written
- The singers and instrumentalists required by each piece
- The intended venue for hearing the music
- The emotions expressed by the music
- The style of the music

For AS and A Level music, you are required to compose two pieces of music, one of them in response to one of the briefs set by AQA. Together your two pieces have to last between 4½ and 6 minutes, and you need to upload appropriate materials so that the examiner can listen to your pieces and follow the compositions via a score, lead sheet or annotation.

And that's just about it. If there were a formal exam paper, the question would read 'Compose a piece of music'. Twice. Just think - if there were an equivalent exam in words rather than music and the question was 'Write a passage of words', what would you do?

Among the things you could write would be:

- A fictional story
- A news report
- A poem
- A set of instructions for driving a car
- A letter
- A recipe
- A legal contract
- Something in Norwegian

This immense freedom for composing music of your choice is - in a way - wonderful: you can use your musical experience, talent, skills and personality to compose something that connects strongly with you. It is also a pressure: sometimes when we are faced with a wide choice, it can seem impossible to make up our mind. In a sense you are setting your own exam question, and there are various ways in which you might set yourself a badly chosen question:

- Something too ambitious for your level of experience as a composer
- Something too simple for AS or A Level standard
- Something musically illogical through unlikely choice of instrumentation

Make sure you take advice on the suitability of your concept for an AS or A Level piece before getting too far into the project.

With all this potential variety in the music you can choose to compose, it might seem that each individual project will have a unique starting point and process to match its unique finished result. While this is true to some extent, there are various aspects that all good composing has in common. Now that you are studying fewer subjects, and you are having more lessons of Music per week than before, your AS or A Level course is a very good time to consider these things and develop your approach to composition beyond your GCSE experience.

Before you start

An analogy

If you were about to get creative in a visual way by painting a picture, you would at this point be looking at a blank canvas: a two-dimensional empty space.

It is highly likely that you would spend some time contemplating the empty space: its dimensions, its orientation and its emptiness. Onto this canvas you would begin to imagine the picture you are going to paint: whether it is to be figurative or abstract, whether it is going to have strong or blurred outlines, which colours you are going to employ. You would also start thinking about the process you were going to follow: which parts of the project would be best put in place first, which colour paints you are going to need to have ready, which brushes and other apparatus will be required.

We have a turn of phrase for this, we say things like 'I can see in my mind's eye...'

In your mind's eye you advance your picture far beyond a simple sketch or outline; you have a clear perception of what you are aiming for with your new painting.

This image, which is known only to you until the painting is completed, can be inspired by a wide range of different things:

- A desire to capture in art something you can see: a view, object or person
- A fascination with some specific shape: stripes, geometric designs or flowing patterns
- An interest in a particular colour or contrast of colours
- An experiment with some aspect of painting technique or technical aspect of the artist's materials
- A wish to make an artistic statement with an image, maybe something political or the expression of a particular mood you are feeling
- An intention to deliberately mimic a particular work or the style of another artist in order to improve your own artistic understanding and facility
- A commission from a patron that you have accepted in order to earn money

As you start to bring your painting into being, the image in your mind's eye will guide your progress; simultaneously, your progress – which you actually see with your real eyes – will cause the image in your mind's eye to be modified as the project develops. This evolving of both the imagined painting and the real painting will continue, with your mind's eye leading the way, until you decide that the painting is finished.

How does composing music relate to this?

In many ways the process is similar. The music we create fills a space: the space that music fills is silence.

It is relatively simple to appreciate the space of the artist's 'blank canvas': you can gain a very accurate impression of it in a very brief glance. Whatever other things around about catch our eye – other paintings, pots of paint, the paraphernalia of the artist's studio – the empty space of the blank canvas will stand out.

This is not the case with the composer's pre-composing blank space. In order to get an accurate estimation of, say, a 3 minute silence, you have to hear silence for 3 minutes. You will not feel how long a 3 minute silence is in a ten-second quick listen (the aural equivalent of a glance), neither will three minutes of silence be apparent to you in a room where lots of noises are to be heard.

So the best starting point for the composer is to have silence and to listen to it – just like the artist will look at the empty space of the canvas. And in that silence to imagine the way music might be created and shaped to fill that empty space. The silence is your blank canvas.

In short, you need to imagine with your mind's ears...

And because you need to be imagining how you are going to fill your blank canvas – the silence – you need to do your imagining in silence. This could be in a silent classroom or your bedroom at home; it can sometimes work to take yourself outside into a quiet space (the countryside, for instance: this worked for Beethoven).

How do I get started?

In order to trigger your imagination, you may like to try one of the following approaches:

- Imagine a piece you might play on your instrument
- Imagine how you might express a mood you have been experiencing recently
- Imagine how you might capture a non-musical thing in music; animals, places, weather conditions, times of day, etc. are all good potential topics for music
- Imagine how you might explore a musical journey of opposites: quiet to loud, low to high, slow to fast
- Imagine how you might put a poem or set of lyrics to music
- Imagine a pattern of notes that could be used repeatedly and also imagine how the pattern might gradually change as it is repeated

What am I trying to imagine?

Imagination is a deeply personal thing – you can't show someone else what you are imagining, or how you started imagining it. There are lots of things you could imagine about your piece before you start putting notes into a computer or onto manuscript paper. These include:

- The energy level of the music
- The tempo of the music

- The dynamic of the music
- The instrumental and vocal sounds required for the piece
- The register of the music (which octaves are used)
- The rhythmic feel of the music
- A sense of the texture of the music
- A sense of the tonality required
- The rise or fall of a melodic line

Once you have some answers to these questions, you may want to spend some time finding some specific notes that utilise these imagined ideas. Few of us imagine complete musical ideas with note-by-note precision, but with the help of the instrument we play, or a computer, we can find a close representation of the musical sounds we have been imagining.

One aspect of our imaginations is that they tend to rely on a short-term memory capability: what you imagine tomorrow is unlikely to be the same as today's results. When you have found the notes that capture your imagined idea, it is valuable therefore to make a sketch of them.

These sketches could take many forms, including:

- A melodic shape

- A bass riff

- A chord progression

Or...

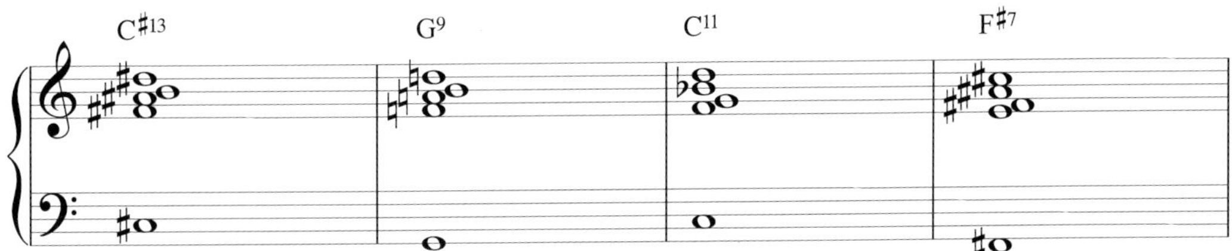

- A rhythmic groove

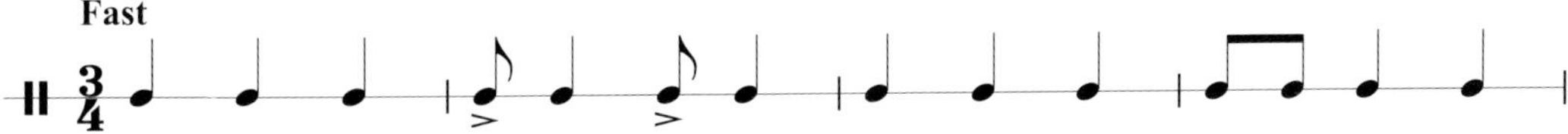

■ A distinctive texture

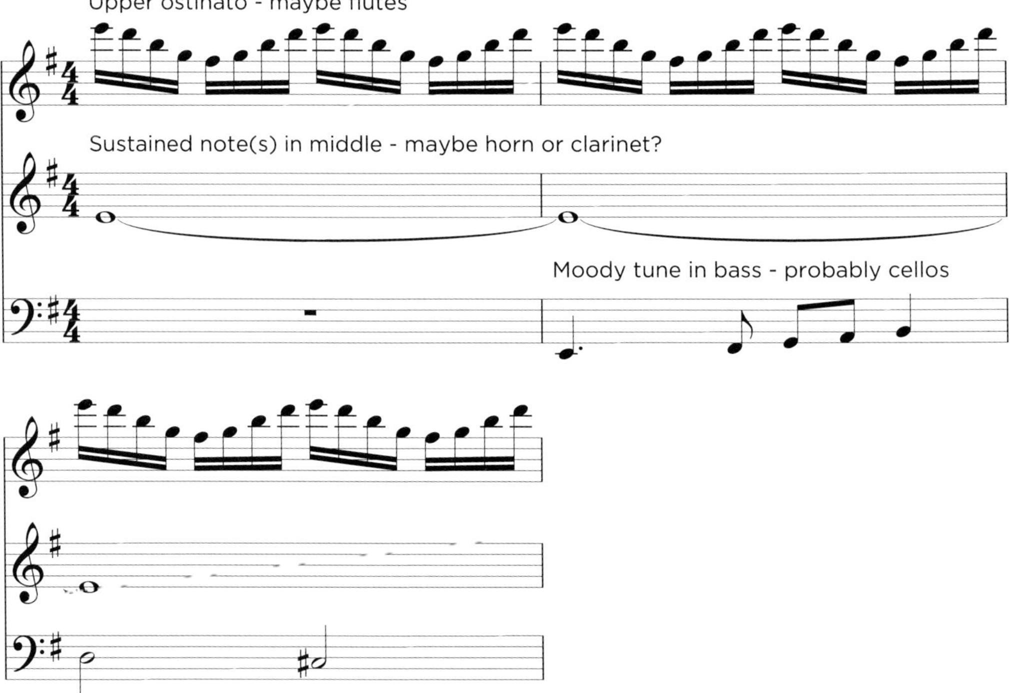

The artist we thought about earlier will probably have made a lot of sketches before starting work on the canvas itself; you will benefit from doing likewise. In the same way that daily practice on your instrument will help you make progress towards the performance component, daily work at your composition will increase your creative fluency. Regularly imagining how your music might fill the blank canvas of silence, and keeping a 'sketchbook' of resulting thoughts, will provide you with a collection of musical ideas, some of which may become part of your composition submission.

What makes for good musical ideas?

In short, CHARACTER – something that makes the melody, rhythm, harmony or texture clearly recognisable: a strong sense of musical identity. It is not easy to say what musical character is, but you know it when you hear it. As with people, some character traits are attractive, positively charged and sunny, others are unattractive, negatively charged and dark. In music – because we are dealing with something artistic – both types can generate excellent results; sometimes one can involve both types in a piece.

Each element of music can provide or contribute to musical character. There are many ways this can happen, each with a wide range of nuance, and it would be a never-ending quest to try to define every musical gesture as in a bilingual dictionary; however, the examples in the chart might provide some insights and encourage you to find musical character in your sketches:

Element	Feature	possible character
Melody	Stepwise / **conjunct diatonic** motion	easy-flowing feel
	Rising leaps	bold, energetic, yearning
	Falling leaps	submissive, nostalgic, noble
	Reliance on semitones	playful, sinister, stressed
Harmony	Major chords	confident, bright, calm
	Minor chords	dark, cold, depressed
	Dissonance	anger, pain, intimidation
	Slow harmonic rhythm	permanence
	Fast harmonic rhythm	energetic, skittish
Metre	$\frac{4}{4}$	formal, striding, assertive
	$\frac{3}{4}$	graceful, lilting, swaying
	$\frac{6}{8}$	skipping, jolly (when fast); lullaby-like (slow)
	$\frac{5}{8}$	energetic, lop-sided, quirky
Rhythm	Fast tempo	high energy
	Slow tempo	low energy
	Triplets	skipping or lilting feel
	Dotted rhythms	formality, confidence, military feel
	Dance rhythms	strong forward momentum
	Syncopation	high spirits, panache

Texture	High register	bright, serene (*p*), piercing (*ff*)
	Low register	dark, depressed (*p*), menacing (with *cresc*)
	Widespread texture	expansive
	Melody in the tenor	rich, warm
	Short rests on beats	energising
	Pedal note	developing tension
Timbre	**Pizzicato**	playful, brittle
	con sordino (strings)	mournful, distant
	Sul ponticello with **tremolando**	ghostly
	Lowest 5th of the flute range	luxurious, exotic
	Solo **legato** oboe	lonely
	lowest octave of clarinet (**chalumeau register**)	dark, oily

By contrast, there are a number of ways in which music can become low on character. The chart below lists various ways in which music can have weak character; each by itself is not a fault, but the composite effect of several of these can mean that little clear musical character comes across to the listener:

Description of potential character-low feature	Possible remedy
Melodies that are entirely conjunct	Include one or more well-placed leaps in the melodic line.
Melodic rhythm and contour fail to suggest any phrase structure	Melodic phrases tend to end on longer notes, and these are likely to come on notes that fit either the dominant or the tonic chord; rests before the new phrase begins are also effective, especially using a quaver rest on a third or fourth beat to create **anacrusis** into the new phrase.

Purely diatonic writing in melody and harmony	Remember, '**chromatic**' means 'coloured'. **Melody**: lower auxiliary notes can be chromatically adjusted to become semitones to the harmony note. **Harmony**: any chord can be prefaced by its own dominant 7th which usually requires accidentals; other chromatic chords can be used such as the minor version of chord IV in a major key, or the **Neapolitan** in a minor key. Modulation should be explored.
All chords are in **root position**.	Other **inversions** of chords are available and have their own personality - listen carefully to them. Try using a pedal note.
The **harmonic rhythm** never changes throughout the piece (usually one chord per bar changing on the downbeat)	Be more adventurous with harmonic rhythm - the results are often very stylish. You might use a faster harmonic rhythm for the B section of a **ternary form**, or the pre-chorus in a ballad. Baroque composers often had faster harmonic rhythm leading into a cadence. A section of very slow harmonic rhythm can create a serene character. Try having an asymmetric harmonic rhythm (chords changing on downbeats of odd numbered bars and beat 3 of even numbered bars, or at a syncopated moment in jazz, such as the 'and' of beat 2).
Rhythms that have long stretches of a single note value (e.g. bars of crotchets or quavers)	Mix note values rather more: imagine combinations of crotchets and quavers, using triplets on some beats, dotted rhythms, etc. Don't let notation software trap you into a limited variety of note values.
Textures that are constructed from notes that are only mid-register	Explore the full range of the instruments you are writing for; where appropriate change clef, or use 8va- - - - - - -┐ signs. If improvising at the piano, do not always play in the central octaves in front of the piano stool.
An absence of rests	Use rests! It is not good (or necessary) to have all instruments playing all the time; in fact, there can be some moments of complete silence in a piece. Some instruments are tiring to play all the time - e.g. the oboe.

The melodic line is always at the top of the texture as a single line in the treble	Vary the texture through: ■ Monophonic melodic writing (perhaps with intermittent chords) ■ Doubling the melody in octaves (or two octaves apart) ■ Having the melody in the tenor or bass register ■ An **inverted pedal**
A lack of differentiation between different lines making it difficult to understand which part is the most important and which are of secondary importance	Combine lines of different character into one texture and make the melodic line have a distinctive contour and/or rhythm compared to other lines. The bass line might also be given its own profile.
No consideration of **articulation**	As soon as you imagine an idea, consider whether it is **legato** or **staccato** (or a mix); are any accents appropriate? Do not think that dynamics and articulation are something to add into the music at the very end.

Making a plan

If you were writing a play, you would need to devise your characters at the outset.

You would probably make sure that there were some contrasts between them since this would allow for dramatic tension. You would also need to create a plan for your play: a plot in which the interaction of your characters would be interesting, perhaps comical or tragic.

Similarly, now that you have some characterful musical ideas for your piece, you will need a plan for exploring them, a structure that will allow you to develop your ideas and create contrast at appropriate moments.

Along with musical character, STRUCTURE is the other vital element in a composition. Once you have some sense of the character of your piece, and how that is to be created through the fundamental choices of instrumentation, tempo and tonality, your imagination should turn to consider structure.

Standard forms

Depending on the kind of piece you are going to be composing, its style and mood, there are a number of common structures you might consider. These include:

- **Binary form**: two repeating sections, the first modulating to the dominant or **relative major**, the second returning home
- **Rounded binary form**: similar to binary form, but with the opening idea reappearing towards the end of the second section
- **Ternary form**: A musical sandwich of matching outer sections with a contrasting middle section (ABA)

- **Sonata form**: A version of ABA, where two themes are presented in the A section with the second in the dominant; themes are developed in the B section, and then both themes are restated in the final section, with the second themes now in the tonic
- **32-bar song form**: common in music theatre, this uses an AABA structure of phrases for the main section (with variants of the A phrase) and then maybe an intro and **coda**
- A pop song form such as: Intro - verse 1 - pre-chorus - chorus - verse 2 - **instrumental bridge** - chorus
- A single musical journey presenting a progression from one idea (slow/quiet/low/minor/ **monophony**) to its opposite (fast/loud/high/major/dense **polyphony**), or maybe a return journey to create an arch-shape structure
- A contrapuntal approach such as **canon** or **fugue** for those interested in **contrapuntal** music

There is more to structure than just choosing one of these labels, however. The essence of composing is to create structure through the music you invent, not to create music to fit the definition of the form (as though you were fitting a carpet).

Another analogy

Composing your piece is not unlike writing a story. There can be a structure of chapters; within each chapter, there can be a structure of paragraphs, and within each paragraph there can be a structure of sentences.

The level of change between sentences is less significant than the level of change between paragraphs; then the level of change between chapters will be something greater still.

You might illustrate this with the following chart:

First chapter	First paragraph	Description of a place	First sentence	Introducing the view	*'From the top of Quaver Hill that summer morning, the villages below looked quite...'*
			Second sentence	A detail...	*'To the south, the village of Cellohampton was asleep, curtains in its cottage windows still closed...'*
			Third sentence	Another detail	*'The River Melody twisted its way through the fields and under the distant suspension bridge...'*
			...and so on...		
			Final sentence	Summary of the view	*'All in all it was a perfect 5 July.'*

	Second para-graph	Entry of a character	First sentence	Arrival on the scene	*'Peace was broken by song from an approaching farmer – a walking bass climbing up the hill…'*
			Second sentence	Descrip-tion of person	*'Each morning Farmer Fraser scaled the hill: it was the same sequence every day – breakfast, walk…'*
			…and so on…	More info about him	
			Final sentence	End of descrip-tion	*'From his viewpoint high above his fields, leaning on his five-bar gate, Farmer Fraser felt all was well.'*
	Third para-graph	Some-thing happens	First sentence		*'Suddenly, a gunshot rang out from behind him, causing Farmer Fraser to leap from his resting place'*
			Second sentence		*'Farmer Fraser's dog ran to the edge of the hill and began to bark and scratch with its paws…'*
			…and so on…		
			Final sentence		*'The farmer wondered whether the gunshot might have been accidental, but it didn't seem natural.'*
	…and so on…	Other aspects to first chapter scenario	Various sentences in several para-graphs		
Second chapter	First para-graph	A change of place	First sentence	Intro-ducing a different scene	*'When the staccato gunshot sounded from the top of Quaver Hill, Mrs Fraser – back in the farmhouse kitchen – had just finished plucking a chicken…'*

The musical equivalent

When we are composing, we need to build similar structures: musical phrases that combine to make sentences; musical sentences that combine to make paragraphs; and musical paragraphs that combine to make chapters.

So starting with one of our sketched ideas (the result of our imagining while contemplating the blank canvas of the silence) we need to find a way to:

- Continue the idea with enough continuity to make a sentence
- Sustain the essence of the idea further but with some changes to create a further sentence (or several)
- Retain some aspects of the idea while introducing a more significant change to create a further paragraph (or two)
- Create the start of a new chapter with a contrasting idea, while keeping enough consistency of style and substance to prevent the contrasting section from sounding as though it should be in a totally separate piece

A creative composer can find many ways to achieve this gradation of change in a piece to build a convincing structure. This table might provide some useful guidelines:

Structural extension	Possible type of change (choose one or more from...)
Extending the initial idea to make a musical sentence	A repetition of the melody with some small tweak; possibly a melodic sequence; A change of cadence to create an answering phrase.
Extending the sentence to make a musical paragraph	A change of dynamic; a contrast of register; some enhancement of texture (e.g. melody doubled in octaves or 3rds); a wider harmonic palette - perhaps using chord IV if the start only used I and V, or maybe secondary triads; a subtle enhancement of timbre and sonority.
Extending the paragraph to make a musical chapter	Greater exploration of the melodic idea - perhaps using **fragmentation**, widening one of the intervals, or looking at the inversion; a richer harmonic vocabulary using chromaticism such as secondary dominant 7ths or modulation; a faster harmonic rhythm; greater textural complexity; some new material too, possibly.
Creating a contrasting new musical chapter	A change of tonality; a new rhythmic profile; a new melodic idea; possibly a change of metre and/or tempo; a different timbre for the main melodic line.

Extending an initial idea

There are many ways an initial idea might be extended at the start of your piece; of course, it depends on the shape, style and mood of your idea.

Here are some examples:

Melodic ideas

Do you remember the melodic sketch from earlier in the chapter?

Its two constituent phrases allow for many different options, including:

1. Treating each phrase to sequence

2. Using inverted versions of the phrases

3. Chromatic alterations

4. Repetition with decoration

Similarly, the bass can be manipulated in various logical ways. The original sketch was:

Among the ways it might be extended are:

i. Sequential treatment

ii. Extension through addition and repetition

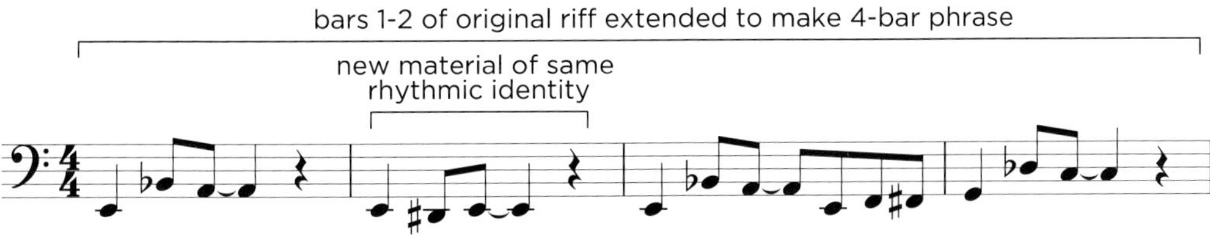

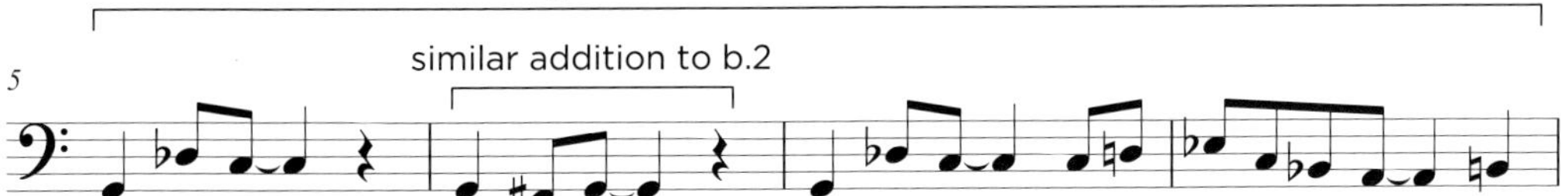

iii. Rhythmic augmentation, fragmentation and repetition

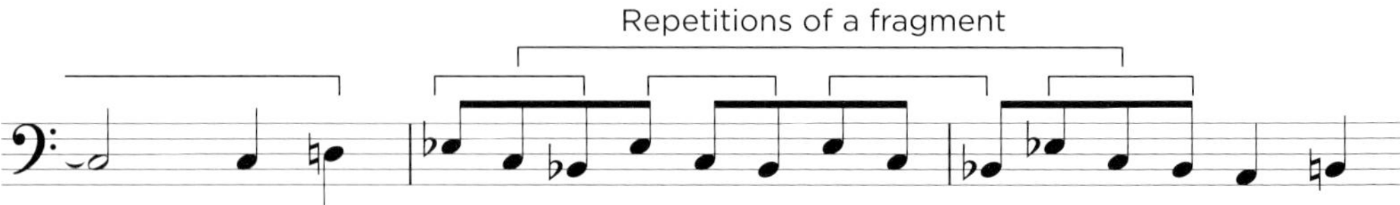

Harmonic ideas

This is the chord progression from earlier:

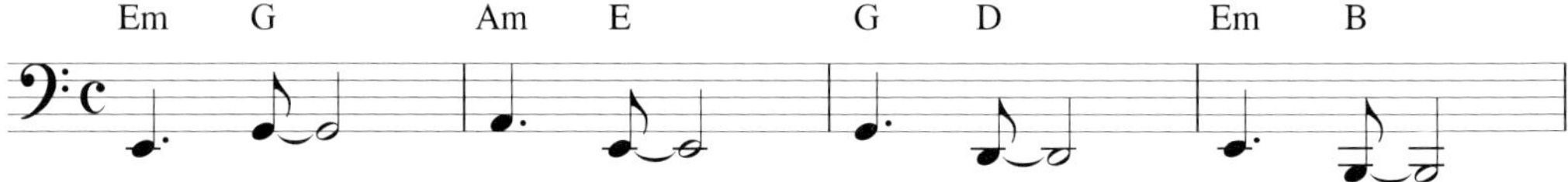

It is easy to build music for a while based on a repeating chord pattern such as this, but it can soon become too predictable to the listener (and the examiner!). The knack is, having repeated it two or three times to build up the expectation of further repetitions, to make small unexpected changes.

1. Swap the occasional major chord for a minor one, or vice versa

2. Alter the harmonic rhythm

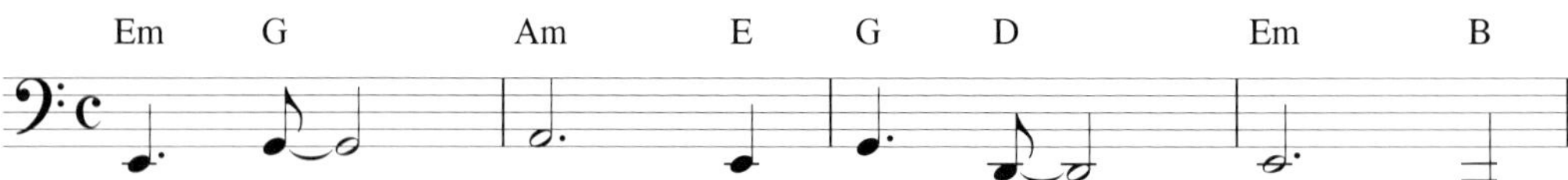

3. Substitute a couple of alternative chords into the progression

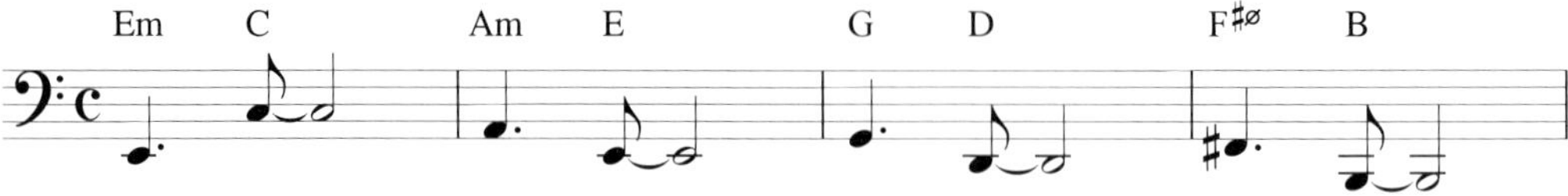

4. Further well-chosen chord substitutions can build a sense of climax for the end of the paragraph or chapter

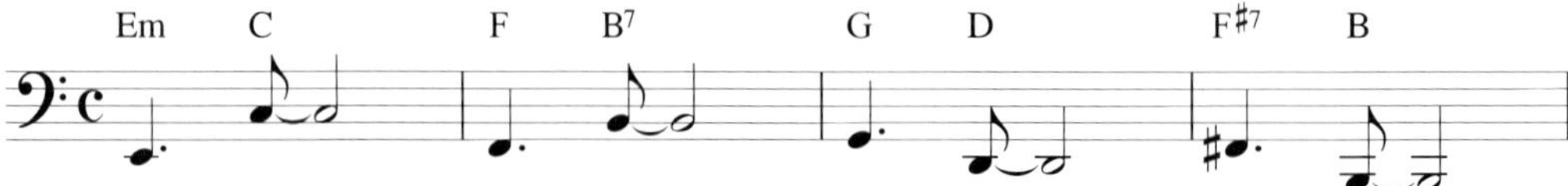

It is important to maintain a similar sense of style in your choice of chords through a sentence or paragraph. The other chord progression sketched earlier in the chapter uses colourful jazzy chords and needs to continue in much the same way.

C♯13 G9 C11 F♯7 B13 Fø B♭13 E♭m13

ø symbol indicates a half diminished chord

Rhythmic ideas

Sometimes ideas can be extended by leaving out some detail, rather than adding in more. Remember that whenever you are composing you can always use a rest instead of a note. The rhythmic idea sketched earlier lends itself to this treatment – silence is all the more effective because the listener is expecting the syncopation heard first time around:

Alternatively, repetition of the bars of interest (2 and 4) can make an attractive effect that breaks the expected 4-bar pattern, creating instead a 6-bar version.

Building to a complete piece

Two compositions follow, both based on ideas discussed earlier in this chapter.

Both pieces were composed following closely the method outlined above:

- Listen to silence
- Sketch some ideas
- Think how ideas can be extended, developed and explored
- Compose the piece thinking of the structure of phrases, sentences, paragraphs and chapters

In addition, some thought was given to using limited space for the score in this book, so the number of instruments was kept small, and the ternary forms depend on a **da capo** of the A sections; in practice it can be a good idea to re-work the A section a second time around to provide greater interest and surprise for your listeners, and – of course – impress your examiner further!

Recordings of both pieces can be found at **http://www.rokmusic.org.uk/project/flute-flurry** and **http://www.rokmusic.org.uk/project/combo-combat**, and there is also a version of *Combo Combat* with guitar parts in tab and alto saxophone in E♭ (i.e. ready to play from).

Flute Flurry

20
mf
mp
26
mf
32
tr
mp
f
37
f
p
molto cresc.

42
To Coda
f
mp espress.
47
half speed 𝅗𝅥. = 36
p
51
mp dolce
56
p
mp

61
cresc.
7
f
mf
65
mf
mp
70
tempo primo
mp
75
mf
D.S. al Coda
p
Coda
ff

Composer's insights on *Flute Flurry*

- The piece is only 2 minutes long; this candidate would need to write a composition to a brief lasting at least 2½ minutes in order to fulfil the specification requirement that two submitted pieces should have a combined playing time of a minimum of 4½ minutes
- The Introduction was the last part of the piece to be composed. How else would it be able to refer to the first bar of the main A section tune at the start, or to the syncopated rhythm of the A section in the piano part at bar 5?
- The melody of the A section is based on the sketch of a rhythmic idea made earlier in this chapter:
  - It occurs unaltered four times at the start of the section (bar 10–25) in the flute
  - The 6-bar version (invented above in 'Extending an initial idea') then occurs in the flute bar 26–31 and is answered by the piano in bar 32–37
  - The original version of the rhythm returns in the flute in bar 38–41
  - Only the final phrase of the section departs from the rhythmic idea
- The harmony of the A section is initially based on a rising scale in the bass. Note the chromatic steps along the way which introduce diminished 7th chords in bar 13 and 15
- The augmented 6th chord in bar 37 leads (as is often the case) to Ic and four bars of a dominant pedal, which brings a contrasting character to the original rising scale in the bass
- Use of the Neapolitan 6th chord in bar 43 prior to the closing perfect cadence completes all the standard chromatic harmony of the A Level specification
- The main characteristics of the A section are triple time, fast tempo, minor key, a jaunty melody due to the combination of angular leaps and syncopated rhythm, and a transparent accompaniment texture using many rests and strong use of staccato articulation
- By contrast, the main characteristics of the B section are slower tempo (half speed), major key, a more lyrical melody (fewer leaps, no syncopation), and a more sustained accompaniment texture
- The B section is based on the sketch of a melodic idea made earlier in this chapter:
  - It is presented in its original form in the piano at bar 47–50 and immediately treated in sequence in bar 51–54
  - The flute has the 8-bar version extended by sequence (invented above in 'Extending an initial idea')
  - The flute then has the 8-bar version that incorporates inversions of the two constituent phrases (also invented above)
- There is a twist of tonality in the B section; it starts in the relative major (C major), but goes to E♭ major at bar 64. This then drifts towards its relative minor (C minor) and ends with an imperfect cadence which allows for a B♮ in the melody; as this is sustained, the harmony slips from a G^7 chord to an E^7 chord - a different dominant 7th that points the way back to A minor
- Much of the harmony of the B section makes use of tonic pedal notes, adding to the sustained, lyrical feel; these occur at bar 47–49, bar 56–60 and bar 64–66

Combo Combat

10
mf
13
16

19
p
mf
mp
22
26
f

29
To Coda
mf
mp
mp
mp
ff
f
f
f
32
f
mf
mf
mf
35
5
mf
f
f

38
mp
mp
mp
5
p
41
mf
mf
mf
mp
44
f
mf
f
mf

47
50
53
mp
mp
mf
p
p

56
cresc.
cresc.
cresc.
mp
mf
59
p
mf
mp
63
D.S. al Coda
mf
mp

Coda
67
ff
f
f
f
69
71
p
p
p
f
p

Composer's insights on *Combo Combat*

- The piece is approximately 2'40" in duration, and therefore over half the minimum aggregate time for the Composition component
- The A section is based on the chord progression sketched as an 'initial idea' early in this chapter; some of the variants explored earlier are also used:
  - bar 3–6: bass line only
  - bar 7–10: with the original chords in the guitar
  - bar 11–18: two further repetitions of the original progression under the sax melody
  - bar 19–22: a slight change as the third chord in the pattern (A minor) is changed to A major
  - bar 23–26: this time there is the change of harmonic rhythm in the second and fourth bars suggested above in 'Extending the initial idea'
  - bar 27–30: as suggested earlier, a change of chord is made this time: instead of G major as the second chord in the progression, C major is used
  - bar 31–34: the same change is kept, and - in addition - the penultimate chord is changed from E minor to a half diminished 7th on F♯
- The overall character of the A section is largely dominated by the syncopated chord progression with the 3+3+2 rhythmic groove never far away
- There is a subdivision within the A section:
  - bars 11–18: two matching phrases that share the same opening two bars, the first then climbs higher, whereas the second falls lower
  - bar 19–26: alternating melodic 2-bar melodic phrases in **antiphony** between guitar and sax (the change of harmonic rhythm in bar 23–26 sustains slightly longer phrases that continue to the next downbeat, these are also more angular and energetic); the drums are more prominent in the guitar phrases
  - bar 27–34: although the underlying feel of the chord progression remains the same, the melodic material is distinctly different: a focus on repeated, syncopated notes in the sax (note the articulation) and a **cross-rhythm** semiquaver figuration in the guitar; the drums are much livelier
- The B section is built on the riff sketched as an 'initial idea' earlier in the chapter; some of the variants explored earlier are also used:
  - bar 35–37: monophonic first appearance in the bass guitar (and drums)
  - bar 38–40: restated, **doubled** in octaves by guitar (and additional countermelody in sax)
  - bar 41–44: treated in canon (a bar behind) in the sax
  - bar 45–52: the extended 8-bar version as developed earlier in the chapter is used here
  - bar 53–58: the version using rhythmic **augmentation** appears here with some imitative **counterpoint** in the guitar and sax
- The overall character of the B section is dominated by the angular riff which is a different length (three bars) to the chord progression of the A section (four bars); there is less sense of tonal stability here and the driving rhythm of the bass and offbeat snare drum at the start of the section create a strong rhythmic contrast
- Like the A section, the B section also has a tripartite internal structure with contrapuntal influences enclosing a strong melody and accompaniment passage in bar 45–52

Presenting your compositions

The AQA mark scheme for composition requires the examiners to take account of the quality of the way you communicate your composition on paper to them.

Of course, one good way to communicate your composition is to provide a classic full score in music notation with all notes and performance directions included. It would help the examiner if you printed this as a 'concert pitch' score; there is no need to provide parts as well. Think carefully about the size of the staves you use; there is a happy medium between large, which leads to a very small number of bars per page and therefore frequent page turns, and so economically small that it is not so easy to read.

Some styles of music, especially jazz, by custom do not require every note to be shown; guitar parts may just require chord symbols, drum parts can just give an indication of patterns and identify places that require a 'fill', and sections requiring melodic improvisation can be marked as such. It would be advisable to give some detailed description of the musical content you (as composer) require of the player - maybe a mode, rhythm, register or mood. Guitar tab is acceptable, though examiners would be pleased if you used the software capability to 'translate' it into music notation.

It is perfectly acceptable to submit an annotation instead of a music score; however, bear in mind that the examiner will reflect the quality of your annotation in your mark. You therefore need to think carefully about how to design your annotation and make sure that it conveys all the important information about structure and musical character.

A good way to do this is often as a timeline of your piece. *Combo Combat* might be represented as an annotation as follows:

Combo Combat

This piece is for an instrumental quartet of alto sax, semi-acoustic guitar, bass guitar and drums. It is a fast (140bpm) ternary piece which has E as its tonic. An outline of the piece is as follows:

INTRODUCTION

0'00" The piece starts with two bars on the ride cymbal.

0'03" The main riff is heard in the bass guitar for the first time, the guitar joins in on the second playing of the riff with the main chord syncopated chord sequence:

Em-G-Am-E-G-D-Em-B (The drums continue on the ride)

A SECTION

0'17" The alto sax enters with a melody of four phrases that is mainly in conjunct quavers and includes chromatic and syncopated characteristics. The first and third phrases are identical; the second climbs higher, the fourth falls lower. The drums continue with quavers on the ride, bass and snare underline the harmonic rhythm.

0'31" The guitar starts a passage of alternating phrases with the sax; the drums become more energised under the guitar phrases. Some alterations are made to the chord progression, including using A major instead of A minor, and some adjustments to harmonic rhythm.

0'44" The final passage of the A section is rhythmically more assertive with semiquaver triadic figuration high in the guitar, syncopated repeated notes in the sax, and a busy drum part including crash cymbal and various fills on the toms.

The chord sequence has more adjustments here, C major instead G major as the second chord, and a half diminished 7th on F♯ instead of E minor in the final cadence.

B SECTION

0'58" A new 3-bar riff is heard in the bass guitar which has more syncopation and various **blue notes**:

Second time, it is doubled an octave higher in the guitar, and there is a fragmentary countermelody on the sax. There is a heavy drum part with bass drum on every beat and snare on the offbeats.

1'08" The new riff is heard in canon between the guitars and the sax a bar later.

1'15" The riff is developed into an 8-bar phrase and the sax plays a very energetic new melody largely in semiquavers. The drum groove changes into a Latin 3+3+2 feel, and the guitar reverts to playing strummed chords.

1'29" The original version of the section B riff is now treated to rhythmic augmentation as part of a contrapuntal texture that has imitation between guitar and sax. The drums here start on ride, but end the B section with a prominent drum fill on the toms.

1'39" The Introduction returns, but there is a new sax melody over the first reappearance of the A section riff.

A SECTION

1'53" The A section is largely played as a *da capo* of its first appearance.

There is a slightly altered ending, starting with the use of an F♯^{7} chord at 2'32".

2'34" A semiquaver flourish on the drums colours the final cadence.

2'36" The final chord is surprisingly soft after the energetic final passage and hangs in the air with added 9th, 11th and 13th. There is a delicate roll on the ride.

Composing to a brief

As mentioned in the Introduction (pages 14-15), one of your two compositions has to be in response to one of the briefs released by AQA each year.

There are various types of brief possible:

AoS 1:

Bach Chorale harmonisation

This is a traditional style of compositional technique exercise. For more information see below (pages 76-87).

AoS 2-7:

Briefs that give you a musical idea

- A melodic idea, perhaps a note row, scale or motif
- A chord sequence
- A bass line or riff
- A given opening to a piece

Composing a piece on one of these briefs is essentially the same as the method recommended for your other composition, except that AQA have sketched one of the main ideas for your piece ready for you. You will need to explore ways of extending the idea they have given, and also imagine other ideas that might complement it. The examiners will be looking for imaginative and interesting creative use of the musical idea they provided. You will still have to plan a structure, of course.

Briefs that appeal to your imagination

- A story in the form of a timeline or picture-board for a film
- A pictorial title for a piece
- A defined ensemble of musicians
- An occasion or performing context
- A picture, drawing or photograph

Composing a piece to one of these briefs is essentially the same as the method recommended for your other composition, except that AQA provide stimuli for your imagination. The examiners will be looking for an appropriate musical response from you. You should therefore consider how each of the musical elements - melody, harmony and tonality, rhythm, metre and tempo, texture and sonority - can be used to relate to the stimulus. Once you have imagined and sketched your ideas, the compositional process is essentially still the same: you need to experiment with ways to extend and develop your initial musical ideas, and make sure you design a suitable plan for the piece. Sometimes this will also be governed by the brief, for instance where the examiners have provided a story, otherwise you can choose your own structure that best suits your musical ideas.

Briefs that provide you with lyrics

Writing music for lyrics is a rather different challenge. It shares quite a lot with briefs that appeal to your imagination: the brief does not give you any musical substance, and you have to imagine appropriate musical ideas for the words.

Throughout the composing process, however, you know something about what has to happen next, and that is the next word or syllable. This is bound to have some profound impact on the structure of your piece.

You should consider:

- Is there a section of the lyrics that reoccurs and can be used for a refrain section?
- Does an opening line return later on, suggesting a return of the first tune?
- Do the words suggest long or short phrases?

In addition, the lyrics are likely to suggest specific musical requirements:

- The meaning and mood of the words may influence your choices of tonality, tempo, dynamic, register and melodic contour
- The natural sounds and stresses of the words are likely to influence metre and rhythm

Compare these two settings of the same words:

Version 1

Version 2

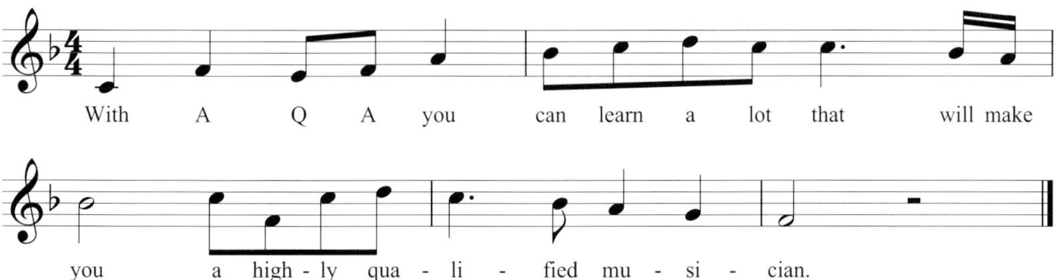

Have you noticed that, with only one note different, these two tunes have almost the identical pitch contour? And have you tried singing the tunes? If so, how did you get on?

Despite the close similarity of pitch, only one of these tunes suits the words. In version 1, the words and syllables on the stressed first and third beats of the bar are the ones you would naturally emphasise if you were to say the words:

With AQA you can learn a lot that will make you a highly qualified musician

... but in version 2 this emphasis is very clumsy:

With AQA you can learn a lot that will make you a highly qualified musician

Also, there is the change of note between the two versions on the word 'highly'; not only is the 'high' syllable in version 1 on a high F (instead of the low F in version 2), but the resulting falling 4th onto the '-ly' syllable is far more akin to the natural spoken intonation on the word 'highly' than the rising 5th in version 2.

If you are setting lyrics, therefore, think carefully about the natural rhythms and intonation of the words when spoken.

The chorale harmonisation brief

What you have to do

Chorale harmonisation exercises are the brief associated with AoS1 in both AS and A Level specifications. In each case you have to carry out two tasks:

AS

Question 1: A chorale in which the cadences (including preparation chords) are missing alto, tenor and bass parts, which you have to complete.

Question 2: A chorale in which the melody and bass lines are given; you have to write the alto and tenor parts.

A Level

Question 1: A chorale in which the melody and bass lines are given; you have to write the alto and tenor parts.

Question 2: A chorale in which only the melody is given; you have to write parts for alto, tenor and bass.

The important basics of the style

Bach chorale harmonisation has long been held in high regard as an academic skill in music. It requires from you:

- A good awareness of tonality and modulation to related keys
- An ability to invent strong harmonic progressions and cadences
- The imagination to write interesting lines for the altos, tenors and basses to sing
- Technical control so that you avoid a variety of errors in the patterns created by the horizontal (vocal lines) and vertical (chords) patterns that you write

To succeed at the highest level in this area, you need both artistic imagination to make an effective chord progression, and an almost mathematical mind to create an error-free solution (the thought processes are not dissimilar from doing a Sudoku puzzle, as you have to consider horizonatal and vertical dimensions simultaneously).

The best way to learn the skill is to play, sing and listen to examples of Bach's own chorale harmonisations on a daily basis. There are several hundred and they can be found in a famous volume edited by Riemenschneider. Bach nearly always finished each of his cantatas with a chorale, and we have around 200 of his cantatas (although it is believed he wrote many more), so this is a good place to start if you want to listen to them in performance, perhaps on YouTube or Spotify.

Vocal ranges

Chorales are best written in closed score on two staves, like the arrangement of 'Happy Birthday' on pages 34-35:

- Soprano - top stave (treble clef) with all stems pointing upwards
- Alto - top stave (treble clef) with all stems pointing downwards
- Tenor - bottom stave (bass clef) with all stems pointing upward
- Bass - bottom stave (bass clef) with all stems pointing downwards

There is no universally accepted rule as to the limits of range for each voice part - context can make exceptions acceptable - but, as a general rule, it is advisable to keep to the following guide:

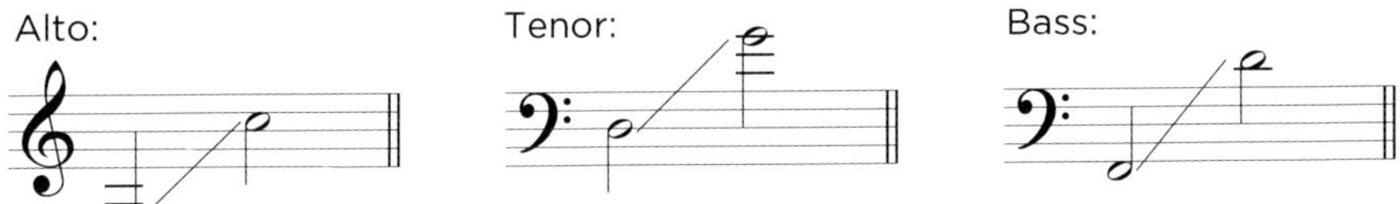

Note that it is very common for the tenor to be above the bass clef stave and using leger lines.

Writing good vocal lines

When you are writing your vocal lines, you should remember exactly that: they have to be suitable for singers. The best way of checking this is to try singing the lines you have written yourself; if this proves difficult at any point, it is probable that you have written something unidiomatic in your harmonisation.

In particular:

- Avoid leaps of a major 6th or wider
- Avoid augmented intervals (be alert especially for augmented 2nds and 4ths)
- Where you do use a wide leap, have the following note proceed in the opposite direction and by a smaller interval (ideally stepwise)
- Be aware of any note that is the 7th of the chord (most probably the dominant 7th); to make a convincing vocal line this needs to fall by step
- Bass lines tend to have a somewhat different profile; although stepwise motion is common, leaps of 4ths and 5ths are also a frequent feature (especially at cadences, of course). Also falls of a diminished 5th (and sometimes a diminished 4th) are a stylistic feature which Bach used regularly

Choosing good chord progressions

For any note in the melody, three chords are available as consonant options for harmonising the note: the melodic note can be the root, 3rd or 5th of the chord. For instance, in C major the available diatonic chords are:

The consonant chords for each degree of the scale in the melody are therefore as follows:

Melodic note	C (1)	D (2)	E (3)	F (4)	G (5)	A (6)	B (7)
Chord if melody note is 5th	F major (IV)	G major (V)	A minor (vi)	B dim. (*vii*)	C major (I)	D minor (ii)	E minor (iii)
Chord if melody note is 3rd	A minor (vi)	B dim. (*vii*)	C major (I)	D minor (ii)	E minor (iii)	F major (IV)	G major (V)
Chord if melody note is root	C major (I)	D minor (ii)	E minor (iii)	F major (IV)	G major (V)	A minor (vi)	B dim. (*vii*)

There are, therefore, lots of possible permutations to the chords you might choose to harmonise a complete chorale tune. This means there are lots of possible good answers (as well as, of course, many less good ones!).

The following guidelines should be borne in mind when choosing chords:

- Chords I and V are the most common and give an immediate sense of key
- The dominant chord will often use the 7th, most likely as a passing note (see cadence patterns below), but sometimes on the beat, especially when in first inversion (chord V^7b)
- Chord IV is also common, but often chord II is used where chord IV might appear – especially in front of chord V
- Chord VI is less common
- Chord III is rare and usually best avoided
- Chord VII is a diminished chord; in root position the tritone (B to F in C major) is an ugly sound, so it is only ever used in first inversion; it is sometimes used as a more subtle option where the dominant might otherwise be used since its three notes belong to the dominant 7th chord
- The progression V to IV and I to II are best avoided

In a minor key, the available chords (following the *harmonic* minor version of the scale) are:

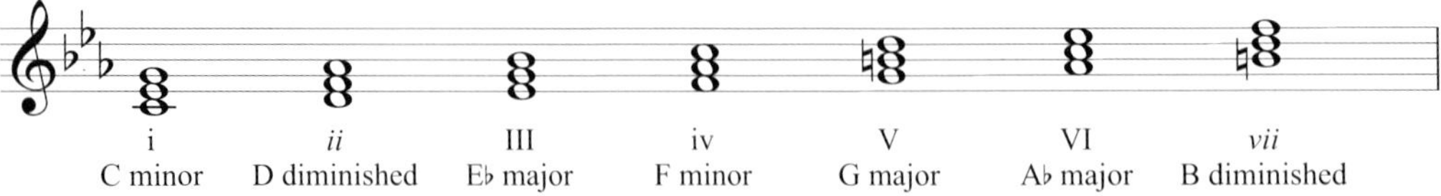

Note that chord II is now diminished (as well as chord VII) and must therefore be used in first inversion.

Handling choral texture

Chorale harmonisation is for a 4-part texture; most chords have three different notes (root, 3rd, 5th). It is therefore necessary to double one of the notes.

The following guidelines should be followed:

- Usually the root of the chord should be doubled
- Sometimes the 5th of the chord can be doubled (for instance in chord Ic – see example below)
- The 3rd can occasionally be doubled in a minor chord if it helps to avoid consecutive 5ths or octaves
- The major 3rd should not normally be doubled; it can be done with care, but the two 3rds should be in lines that move in contrary motion:

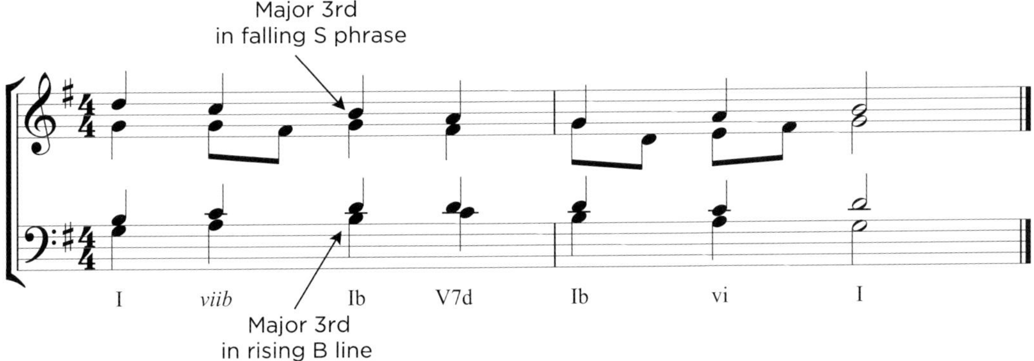

The spacing of chords is important. Alto and tenor parts should be kept high wherever possible; this will probably mean using many leger lines in the tenor. If there is a large gap between any pair of parts, it should be between tenor and bass.

Consecutives

An essential part of good harmony is to have each vocal line moving in complementary relationships with each other. This involves avoiding any instance of two parts moving in parallel octaves or parallel 5ths, or 5ths in contrary motion. Usually you only have to avoid parallel motion in perfect 5ths, but if one of the parts involved is the bass, it is also best to avoid motion from a diminished 5th to a perfect 5th (or vice versa).

All the following are incorrect:

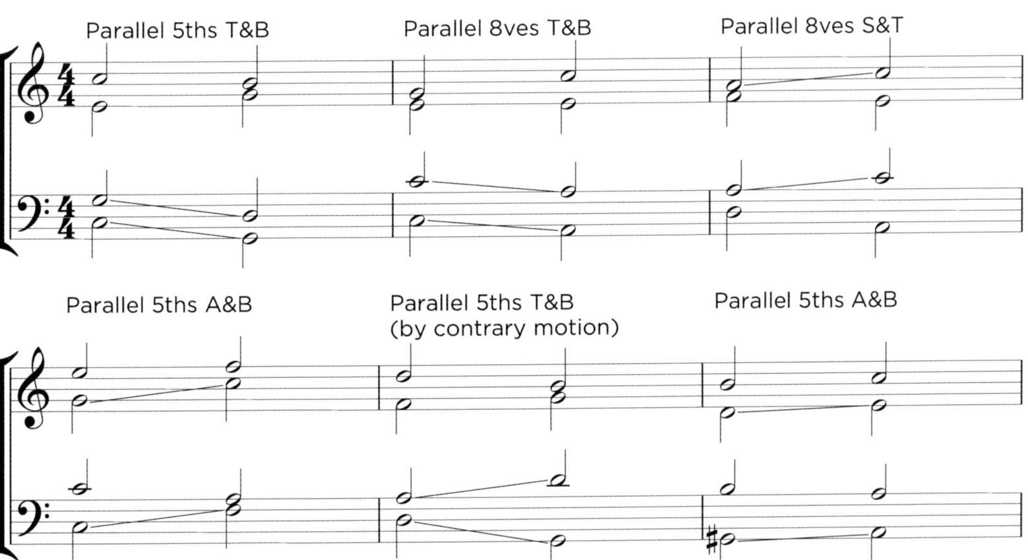

Cadences

Chorale tunes were commonly used by the Lutheran church in Germany for hymns to be sung. As hymns are a form of religious poetry, they comprise short lines of words, which dictate short musical phrases. At the end of each phrase is a cadence, and these often follow one of a limited number of patterns.

It well worth learning these patterns and practising them in a variety of keys (up to four sharps and flats, major and minor). Not only is this the focus of question 1 in the AS Brief, but cadences also form a significant proportion of the chorale set in question 2 of the A Level Brief.

The patterns shown here are common in the chorale idiom.

Perfect cadences

Where the tune descends 3–2–1:

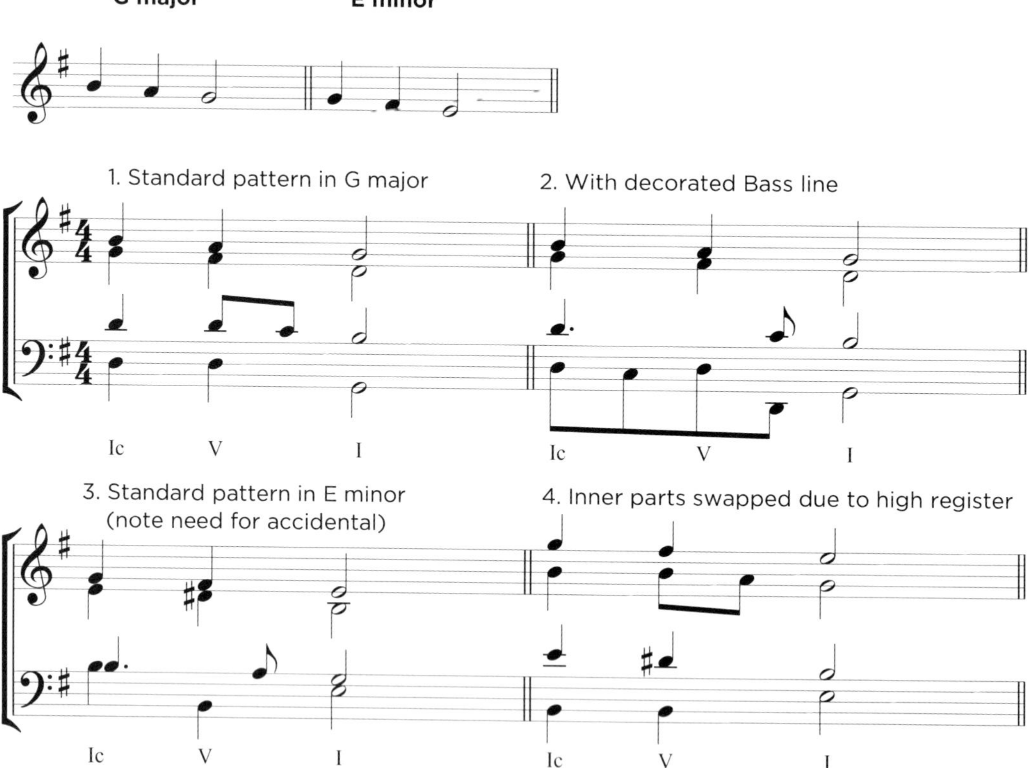

Where the tune descends 2–2–1:

1. Standard pattern in G major
2. With decorated Bass line

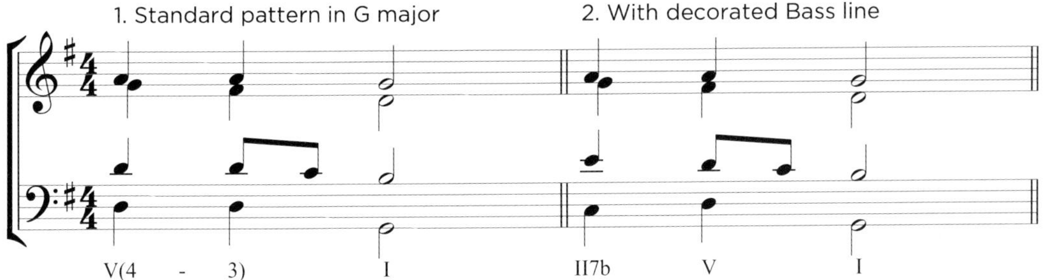

3. Standard pattern in E minor (note need for accidental)
4. Inner parts swapped due to high register

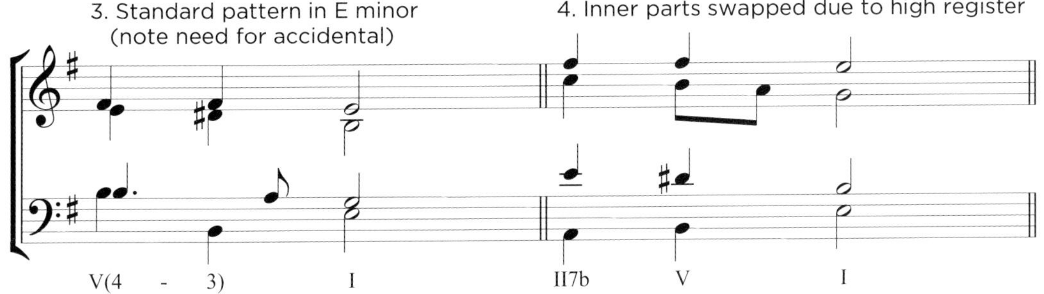

Where the tune finishes 8–7–8:

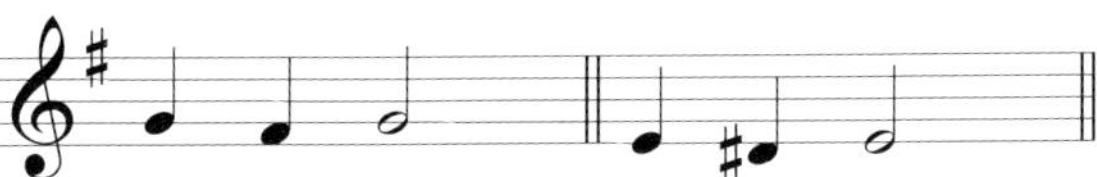

1. Standard pattern in G major
2. Chromatically altered using secondary dominant 7th

3. Standard pattern in E minor
4. Chromatically altered (note: 2 accidentals required)

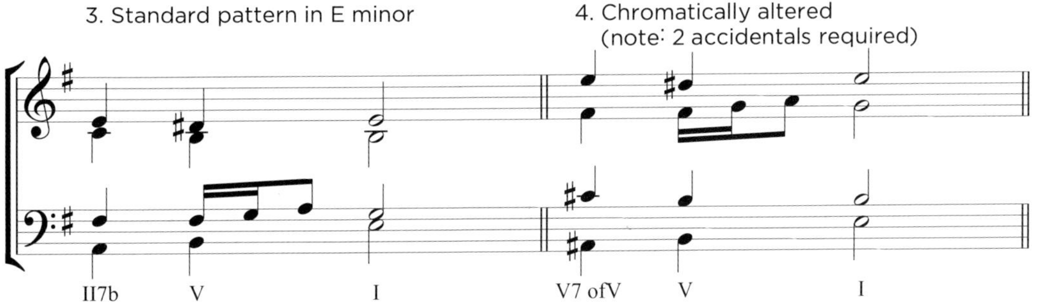

Plagal cadences

Plagal cadences are not common in chorales, but the following are useful patterns to be able to use where an appropriate opportunity arises:

Where the tune finishes 8–8:

Where tune ends 6–5:

Imperfect cadences

Perfect cadences – V to I – of which there are many in chorales, and plagal cadences – IV to I – of which there are very few, are tightly defined as particular chord progressions at the end of phrases. Imperfect cadences – and there are quite a number of them in chorales – come in many different progressions: I to V, Ib to V, V^7b of V to V, ii to V, iib to V, IV to V, IVb to V, vi to V. The thing they all have in common is that they end on chord V.

Consequently, it is not so possible to recommend just a couple of patterns to learn. The following are all found in Riemenschneider, and it is recommended that, if possible, you play them at the piano, and in various keys.

Imperfect cadences in G major

Imperfect cadences in E minor

It is worth paying particular attention to the last of these: ivb to V in a minor key. This is called the Phrygian cadence, because – like the Phrygian mode – there is a semitone at the bottom as the bass moves from C to B, and a tone at the top as the soprano moves from A to B. It is quite common in chorales, even in those that are in a major but which visit minor keys in the middle.

Interrupted cadences

Interrupted are the same as perfect cadences, except that there is a surprise on the final chord: instead of the tonic chord, some other choice is made. Traditionally we often think of an interrupted cadence being V to VI, but other surprises are possible including chord I, but with a flattened 7th (try the 7th in the bass for extra tension), and a diminished 7th.

One of the important aspects of using an interrupted cadence is to use it in the correct place. There has to be a sense that the music is about to finish for it to be fully surprising; therefore, the music needs to be in the tonic key, and it is not going to be early on.

The penultimate phrase is a favoured place for an interrupted cadence, when the chorale has returned to the tonic key by this point.

Modulation

Nearly all chorale tunes will have one unavoidable modulation, probably to the dominant if it is a major key, or the relative major if it is in a minor key. In this exercise, however, we are attempting to emulate the great master, J. S. Bach, and he was very adept at finding potential for other modulations.

Bach's tonal world comprised a network of six closely related keys:

For a major key		
Subdominant (e.g. F major)	TONIC (e.g. C major)	Dominant (e.g. G major)
Relative minor of the subdominant (e.g. D minor)	Relative minor (e.g. A minor)	Relative minor of the dominant (e.g. E minor)

For a minor key		
Subdominant (e.g. C minor)	TONIC (e.g. G minor)	Dominant (e.g. D minor)
Relative major of the subdominant (e.g. E♭ major)	Relative major (e.g. B♭ major)	Relative major of the dominant (e.g. F major)

It is a good idea to draw out this chart and work out the appropriate keys before starting to choose cadences and chords, as it enables you to see more options. If you do not find some variety of keys to use in your harmonisation, your mark will be restricted even if there are few actual errors. It is a matter of style.

In choosing when to modulate, you should have an overview of the whole chorale as a complete piece of music. It could be destabilising to modulate to, say, the relative minor of the subdominant in the first phrase or two. Usually, the best option will be to establish the tonic at the start, move to the dominant (or relative minor) as a first change of key, and then find one, two or even three of the other keys later on before returning to the tonic for the end.

It is always a good idea to suggest the new key early in a phrase (by using the significant new accidental) rather than wrenching the music into a new key just for the cadence at the end of the phrase.

Two examples

Consider the following chorale melody:

What key is this chorale in? How can you tell? What are the possible related keys you might visit? Which of these options can be used, even though there are no accidentals in this melody?

Here are two possible solutions to harmonising this chorale melody:

Version 1:

Version 2:

Try playing and singing the two versions and consider what the strengths and weaknesses are.

Here is a comparison of how an examiner might be thinking of each version:

	Version 1	Version 2
Phrase 1	Successful consonant harmony but no quaver motion.	Quaver motion occurs on four beats spread across A, T and B. Bass agile with 4ths and 5ths.
bar 1	Some first inversions used; opportunities for passing notes in the bass line not taken.	First inversions on beats 2 and 3 give graceful flow, enhanced by rising quaver passing notes.
bar 2	Imperfect cadence works; however, rather solid feel with all chords in root position.	Chord *viib* on the downbeat has a 7–6 suspension in the A. Imperfect cadence. Doubled major 3rd but in parts that are in contrary motion (S and B). Bright, high T part.
Phrase 2	More confident harmony, but still no quaver motion.	Continued quaver motion. Strong B line: conjunct motion and leaps of 4th and 5th.
bar 3	Static inner parts. Consecutive 5ths between S and A across the barline into bar 4.	S and B move together in 3rds; More good quaver motion.
bar 4	Straightforward perfect cadence in the tonic using 4–3 suspension in T for some interest.	Stylish II7b–V–I perfect cadence. High bright 3rd in the T on final chord.
Phrase 3	Stays in the tonic key; missed opportunity to modulate.	Modulates immediately to C minor (relative of the subdominant).
bar 5	All root position chords; consecutive 5th between T and B beats 3–4 (passing note does not rescue the situation).	Stylish move to C minor via *viib* on beat 2. Excellent quaver motion which includes strong accented passing note.
bar 6	Pleasing quaver motion in B for the imperfect cadence, but upper parts are very static.	Another strong II7b–V–I perfect cadence, this time in C minor which gives two chromatic notes (A♭ and B♮).

Phrase 4	This phrase is treated in the subdominant (E♭), but manages to avoid featuring A♭ - the chromatic implication is therefore not made explicit. No quaver motion.	A strong move to E♭ major with four occurrences of A♭ in the phrase. The high register of the S line is complemented with busy lower parts.
bar 7	All root position chords and consecutive 5th between A and B beats 1 to 3.	Very strong conjunct descending B line starting an octave higher than previous phrase ended. Good A movement too.
bar 8	Strong octave leap in the B for the cadence, and 4–3 suspension in the T. Opportunity for dominant 7th (A♭) not taken.	Another strong II^7b–V–I cadence in E♭ major.
Phrase 5	More consonant harmony, but no quaver motion or colour.	A successful culmination.
bar 9	More crotchet chords; chords I to ii is not stylish. Consecutive 5ths in S and A across barline.	Pleasing use of descending conjunct quavers in all parts.
bar 10	An efficient perfect cadence using 4–3 suspension, but slightly bland.	A strong final cadence with chromatic inflection to give V^7b of V–V^7–I. The bright timbre of the high T is well used.
Overall	Tidy cadences and some successful consonant chord choice; however, no clear modulations and no chromaticism. Very limited quaver motion. This results in a diluted sense of idiom.	Strong modulations to two other keys and additional chromaticism in the final cadence point to a clear understanding of tonality. Consistently convincing quaver motion. The idiom is confidently and imaginatively embraced.

How to perform music

Why do we perform?

Many students cite the performance component as their principal reason for wanting to study music at A Level.

Performance encompasses everything, from a formal concert or gig at a prestigious venue with a sizeable audience, to a more informal session with no audience; it can be as public or as private as we decide.

Performance strongly influences our sense of individual musical ownership and many of us will have our favourite recordings of pieces that somehow appeal to us. The art of achieving an excellent performance is to understand how to communicate the notated composition into an aural experience that will effectively speak to the audience. Performance is more than simply playing the notes of a composition usually written by someone else; it is about understanding what the composer of the music is trying to tell the audience and enhancing this to make the music come alive. Simply put, we must perform with subconscious passion and fully conscious intelligence.

Within this component there are two principal choices you can make – either solo/ensemble performance on an instrument/voice, or a production via music technology. You can choose to do one of these options, or a combination of both. The full requirements can be found on pages 5-6 of this book. Make sure your recital meets the specification in terms of duration: a minimum of six minutes for AS, or a minimum of ten minutes for A Level. Look at the specifications to understand how your performances will be assessed: **www.aqa.org.uk/7271** for AS, and **/7272** for A Level.

- A **lead sheet**, which should contain pertinent information to explain how your performance meets the composer's or arranger's intentions
- A **guide recording**, which should only be used if a score and/or lead sheet are unavailable, with your performance being based on a recording of another performance of the same piece

EXPRESSIVE CONTROL

If your score does not contain expressive markings (a Baroque piece may not), consider adding a few markings to show you have thought about the expressive control of the piece.

Improvisation

Improvisation is permitted as a part of this component. However, you must ensure that you provide information about what the improvisation is based on - for example a chord sequence, melodic fragment, a riff, a scale or a mode - so that your recording can be assessed.

It's not advisable to submit a piece that is entirely improvised, because the nature of the assessment demands that you provide documentation on how your performance was derived.

Recording

There are many ways to ensure that your recording is of an appropriate quality for this component. It is important to consider the venue in which you are performing, its acoustic, and the time of day that you are performing.

Make sample recordings, listen critically and identify ways to improve your work. Check the balance of the final mix to ensure the performance is being captured in a way that truly reflects the performance you give.

RECORDING QUALITY

Nurture it! Remember that the recording is the *only* way your performance will be assessed.

Performing

When you step up to perform, ensure you give eye contact, smile, breathe deeply and connect with the audience.

There is much power in taking a few seconds before you start to perform: allow a moment's silence for the audience to settle and to encourage them to focus on what is about to happen. Similarly, after your piece has finished, consider waiting for a second or two before moving, allowing what you have just performed to ring around the room and end without a sense of haste.

Even though your performance will be assessed only through the recording, this communication with the audience will come across and will greatly aid the musical energy of your work.

Summary for live performance

When planning your recital it is useful to remember the following points:

- Build variety into your recital pieces through changes in style, period, approach or technique, or a combination of these
- Aim for pieces that are ambitious in standard but not beyond your technical control as a musician
- Time your pieces to ensure they meet the specification requirements
- Research your pieces to establish where the emotional peaks and troughs of the piece are, keeping a 'performing log' to track your work
- Highlight areas that are more technically complex in your pieces and devote regular practice to meeting these challenges, remembering that slow practice is best to secure the music to muscle memory
- Establish clear practice routines from the very start of the course, including tuning your instrument and communicating with your accompanist
- Perform your pieces often, establishing which audience base works best for you
- Record your performances, so that you can listen back to them and gain an understanding of which areas are successful and which require more work
- Be active within the recording process: where the microphone is placed, the acoustic of the room, the balance of the recording are all important factors

TASKS FOR LIVE PERFORMANCE

1. Looking at the AS Level electric guitar recital above, listen to the tracks in order and consider if the recital works as a musical whole. Would you change any of the pieces? Would you change the order? Why?
2. Doing the same for the A Level vocal recital, list areas where this recital might enable you to score highly on the assessment scheme. Which parts are more complex and might cause marks to be lost?
3. Now consider your own AS or A Level recital. Make a list of potential pieces for your recital, listing the positives and negatives of each piece, as well as the level of difficulty and the timings.
4. Discuss your ideas with your fellow students, other musicians and friends. This will not only enable you to improve your recital, but also help your fellow A Level musicians in their work.

Production via music technology performances

Production performances refer to music produced using music technology software, including sequencers (such as Cubase or Logic) and multi-track recording using a range of microphones to capture live sound.

While the initial skills demanded by this option might seem very contrasted to the live performance option, the overall effect is similar - the desire to produce a musical performance that is satisfying to the audience's ear.

Assessment

The mark scheme for performances using production via music technology uses similar titles to live performing, but with different descriptors for each.

Technical control

This assesses the accuracy of pitch, rhythm, articulation, phrasing and the clarity of capture of your chosen pieces. Take care to ensure that the sounds you hear are accurately sequenced to sound the same, and that microphones are sensitively placed, avoiding distortion.

Expressive control

This assesses your choice of timbres, dynamics and use of dynamic processes, including control of **compression** and **EQ**. Thought should be given to the overall shape of the music - does your use of dynamic processing aid the overall musical effect, allowing for the overall mix to be rounded and well-balanced?

Performance quality

This assesses your performance style, balance, blend, **panning** and use of effects, including the appropriateness of these devices for the style of the piece. Consider your use of the stereo field as well as how to use the multitude of effects available to enhance your performance, enabling you to show an affinity with the stylistic requirements of the piece in question.

Ambition of project

Also similar is the availability of 5 marks for the ambition of project for your chosen repertoire. Clearly the comparison to accredited music grades is not appropriate here, but notice the requirements in the descriptor boxes in the specification (see **www.aqa.org.uk /7271** or **/7272**), where the expressive variety and complexity of the piece is assessed alongside the number of total tracks used. A similar sense of caution should also be exercised here, as for live performances: it is better to perform at a standard where you are confident, perhaps losing a few marks in ambition of project, than to perform a set of pieces that are beyond your capabilities as a musician and risk significantly compromising the overall effect.

Essential equipment

This performing option is reliant on having good quality music technology equipment available to enable you to show the full range of skills required in the assessment scheme.

At a basic level, you should have access to and a full working knowledge of:

- Sequencing software (e.g. Cubase or LogicPro) and VST instrument/MIDI keyboard
- Notation software (e.g. Sibelius)
- Mixing desk
- Condenser microphones
- Dynamic microphones
- High quality speakers and headphones

DON'T ATTEMPT THE IMPOSSIBLE

If your school or centre does not have the right equipment, or you do not have access to it, it's probably wiser to opt for a live performance.

Preparation

Many of the points discussed for live performance are true for this unit also. It is vital that you fully research your chosen pieces and listen to them carefully to understand their individual characteristics, recording your thoughts as you progress by using a performance log.

TAMING THE TECHNOLOGY

Establish which programs you use most effectively: are there any aspects that you need to work on to develop your skills? Consider short exercises to develop your understanding.

The challenges in this unit come from your technical ability to use the technology available to you. Remember that performers who are completing a live performance may well have been having lessons on their instrument for many years, allowing for them to progress to a high standard. You need to be proficient on the software you are using to complete your performance, and this may include doing many small projects to familiarise yourself with the technology prior to starting work on your final recital.

Some points to help you plan your recital effectively:

- If your production requires the use of other musicians to perform pieces for you to capture, remember to be organised. Give them plenty of notice of when you would like to record the music. Be active within the process, ensuring they are performing the music with technical and expressive control
- Experiment with your recordings and use of sequencer, producing different versions which use the software to its full potential. Remember that the mark scheme awards successful use of software and variety of timbre
- Ensure you have a thorough knowledge of the instruments you are using in your performance. How can you make an acoustic guitar sound strummed on a sequencer? How is the original effect being achieved, and how can you produce something similar?
- Give thought to pieces as you practise and develop your technological understanding. How many tracks are involved in each piece? Does the programme offer variety, high complexity of musical character and considerable expressive variety?

- Experiment with microphone placement, noticing how the recorded sound quality alters when the position of the microphone or the type of microphone changes

Performance documentation

You need to provide evidence to enable your performance to be assessed against the mark scheme.

Unlike the live performance option, this can be an **annotation** that contains all the details of the processes, devices and techniques used, as well as any other information that you feel is pertinent. You should provide as much information as possible to explain how your final recital has been produced.

Summary for production

When planning your recital it is useful to remember the points mentioned under the live performance area (earlier in this chapter) as well as the following:

- Ensure you have a full working knowledge of the music technology available to you
- Experiment with different pieces to ensure you have this working knowledge - for example, by spending time experimenting with panning in one section of a piece and microphone placement in another
- Build variety into your programme to give expressive and technical variety to your work and demonstrate your abilities as a musician

TASKS FOR PRODUCTION

1. Research, define and create short musical examples to demonstrate the following processes:
   a. Panning
   b. Quantise
   c. Reverb
   d. EQ
2. Consider how you might use the production software to imitate closely the following features of live musical performance, producing short examples to demonstrate your points:
   a. Acoustic guitar - strumming
   b. Piano - pedalling
   c. Strings - changes in bowing
   d. Woodwind/brass - breathing
3. Consider which microphones you might use and how you might place them for the following acoustic instruments:
   a. Electric guitar
   b. Singer
   c. Drum kit

Being accurate and expressive

No matter which option or combination of options you elect to take for this component, there will come a point where you might be able to perform your piece accurately but yet it does not yet quite have the emotional control to enable it to be fully effective.

Your teacher may well comment that the performance is accurate but lacks interest. How can we achieve both?

AIM FOR BALANCE

The best performances balance accuracy with good expressive control, so keep focusing on both.

When we are learning a piece of music we often focus on learning the notes in front of us, perhaps by interpreting a score or lead sheet, and there can be no doubt that this is a vital first stage in the learning process. However, this is only half of the story; while we might be playing the notes in the right order, we need to understand how to communicate the expressive demands of the piece beyond what the score is telling us.

When you research your pieces by listening to different recordings you will hopefully find many contrasting performances - some by professional musicians who have a career as a performer, others from amateur musicians who are performing for the love of making music. Listen to as many varied performances as you can, commenting on how each performer interprets the specific features of the music. To what extent does each performance communicate a sensitive and mature understanding of style and period? How does your favourite recording achieve such an accolade?

Example performance activity

This activity can be done with any piece, providing you have two or more contrasting recordings. Completing this exercise for some or all of your chosen pieces would be a useful way to engage with the assessment criteria.

Using YouTube, Spotify or a recording, listen to two contrasting performances of the same piece. This piece could be in any style and in any situation - a professional soloist in a concert hall, or an amateur musician playing in a classroom. Assess to what extent they meet the requirements of the top band of the mark scheme, especially on the need for subtlety and expressive control.

As a class, listen to the performances, marking these short extracts to the assessment scheme in the specification and adding a comment to justify the mark awarded. Consider specific moments where you are awarding or taking away marks, noting down why you feel this is appropriate. Discuss your ideas with fellow musicians and friends. You may wish to use a table like this to order your thoughts:

Assessing performance

		Performance 1	Performance 2
Ambition of project	5		
Technical control	15		
Expressive control	15		
Performance quality	15		
Other points for discussion			

During your discussion, consider:

- Did you award similar marks? Were there differences? Why might these have happened?
- Where in the piece did you award marks for expressive control? Where did you feel this control was not being met?
- How could the performer improve communication via the recording?
- What advice would you give the performer for each performance?

PERFORMANCE TASKS

1. Complete the assessment activity above for your chosen repertoire using performances available online or via a recording. Consider how each performance would score when measured against the assessment criteria.
2. Build these features into your own performances, taking care to ensure an overall sense of stylistic appreciation of each piece.
3. Finally, assess your own recordings in the same way against the assessment criteria, setting yourself suitable practice targets to gain credit for your work.

Western Classical tradition 1650–1910

OVERVIEW

There are three strands to this AoS:

- Baroque: the solo concerto
- Classical: the operas of Mozart
- Romantic: the piano music of Chopin, Brahms and Grieg

For AS you study only the Baroque and Classical strands. For A Level you study all three strands.

THIS AREA OF STUDY IS COMPULSORY

What do you have to study?

For each strand you will study set works. These are as follows:

AS	A Level	Set work
Strand A: Baroque solo concerto		
		Purcell: Sonata for trumpet and strings in D major Z.850
✔	✔	first movement
✔	✔	second movement
✔	✔	third movement
		Vivaldi: Flute Concerto in D major Op. 10 No. 3 'Il Gardellino' RV428
✔	✔	first movement
	✔	second movement
	✔	third movement
		Bach: Violin Concerto in A minor BWV1041
✔	✔	first movement
	✔	second movement
	✔	third movement

Opposite: J. S. Bach

Strand B: Classical - The operas of Mozart		
		Mozart: The Marriage of Figaro (*Le Nozze di Figaro*) K. 492, Act 1
	✔	Overture
✔	✔	No. 1 Duettino (Figaro and Susanna, including following recitative)
✔	✔	No. 3 Cavatina (Figaro, including the previous recitative)
✔	✔	No. 4 Aria (Bartolo)
✔	✔	No. 5 Duettino (Susanna and Marcellina)
✔	✔	No. 6 Aria (Cherubino)
	✔	No. 7 Terzetto (Susanna, Basilio, Count)
	✔	No. 9 Aria (Figaro)
Strand C: Romantic - The piano music of Chopin, Brahms and Grieg		
	✔	Chopin: Ballade No. 2 in F major op.38
	✔	Chopin: Nocturne in E minor Op. 72 No. 1
	✔	Brahms: Intermezzo in A major Op. 118 No. 2
	✔	Brahms: Ballade in G minor Op. 118 No. 3
	✔	Grieg: Norwegian March Op. 54 No. 2
	✔	Grieg: *Notturno* Op. 54 No. 4

How does it fit into the exam?

Music from this AoS will appear in Sections A and B of the 'Appraising Music' paper (component 1) in both AS and A Level.

AS paper

Section A – Listening: There will be four questions on AoS1 in Section A, which account for 24/49 marks in this section.

- Question 1: Extract with short answer question on Baroque Music (5 marks)
- Question 2: Extract with short answer question on Classical Music (5 marks)

- Question 3: Aural dictation question on either Baroque or Classical Music (4 marks)
- Question 4: Long answer question which you can choose to answer on the music of either question 1 or question 2 (10 marks)

Section B - Analysis: You answer one of two questions; each is worth 17 marks.

- Question 25: Based on an extract from one of your Baroque set works
- Question 26: Based on an extract from one of your Classical set work movements

In total, therefore, at AS, AoS1 work accounts for 41/96 marks available on the paper overall.

A Level paper

Section A - Listening: There will be three questions on AoS1 in Section A which account for 20/56 marks in this section.

- Question 1: Extract with short answer questions based on one of the three strands (4 marks)
- Question 2: Extract with aural dictation question on another of the strands (6 marks)
- Question 3: Extract from remaining strand with long answer questions (10 marks)

Section B - Analysis: There will be three questions, from which you answer two; each is worth 17 marks, and this Section is therefore worth 34 marks.

- Question 22: Based on an extract from one of your Baroque set works
- Question 23: Based on an extract from one of your Classical set work movements
- Question 24: Based on an extract from one of your Romantic set works

In total, therefore, at A Level, AoS1 work accounts for 54/120 marks available on the paper overall.

Musical language for this AoS

In order to understand music and communicate your understanding to others - especially an examiner - you need the vocabulary for describing and defining features in a piece.

Each of the optional AoS has some specialist vocabulary that is applied to specific styles; AoS1 requires both knowledge and understanding of general musical vocabulary.

It is important not only to learn these words, but to make them part of your regular vocabulary when playing, listening to and thinking about music. Some will already be familiar to you - perhaps your instrumental teacher uses them. If others seem foreign to you, then make yourself use them and you will soon be speaking them fluently, and better still, using them to think about music wherever you meet it: in orchestra rehearsals, going to a concert or listening to music online.

Melody words

The specification requires you to know the following melody words for AoS1. How many do you already know? Check the glossary at the back of the book for definitions of words you are not sure of.

- Contour - ascending, descending, stepwise, conjunct, disjunct, scalic, triadic and arpeggio
- Intervals, including compound intervals

- Phrase lengths - equal, unequal, balanced
- Ornaments - trill, mordent, turn, acciaccatura, appoggiatura
- Passing notes - accented, unaccented and chromatic
- Auxiliary notes - upper, lower and chromatic
- Note of anticipation
- Echappée note
- Portamento
- Melodic devices - sequence, motif, fragmentation, repetition, intervallic augmentation and diminution

Many of these melodic features are found in the following piece.

Melodic Featurefest 1

Melodic features to note here are:

Bars 1-4

- The opening of the piece comprises two **balanced phrases** of equal length
- Both phrases start with a bar of **triadic** contour (based on a C major chord in bar 1 and a G^7 chord in bar 3)
- The first note has a **mordent** on it - an ornament that emphasises the note by briefly visiting the upper note:

- The first note of bar 3 also has a **mordent** on it - a similar ornament that uses the lower note for emphasis:

- Bars 2 and 4 are decorated with **turns** - an elegant ornament typical of the Classical period which uses both upper and lower notes:

- Both of the first two phrases reach their final consonant note a beat after their final chord and from the note a step above which is dissonant to the chord. Each of these penultimate notes is therefore an **appoggiatura**

Bars 5-6

- These bars start with a **descending scalic** contour in semiquavers; in the second half of each bar there is an **ascending arpeggio** contour
- The last note of bar 5 has a momentary sounding of its lower neighbour immediately before it, known as an **acciaccatura**
- Bar 6 is the same as bar 5, but with every note lower by a step, making it a **descending sequence**

Bars 7-8

- Bar 7 has three notes (B, D and F) each of which is decorated by **lower auxiliary notes** - notes that are briefly dissonant to the bass. Two of these notes (the A♯ and C♯) are notes that are not in the home key of G major, making them **chromatic lower auxiliaries**
- In bar 8, the resolution from the supertonic (D) to the tonic (C) goes via a step in the opposite direction, making the E an **echappée note**

Bars 9-12

- These bars make use of **fragmentation** - using only the first three notes of the opening melodic idea to create **motif**. This is treated to **repetition** in bar 10, **rising sequence** in bar 11 and **intervallic augmentation** in bar 12, where the rising 6th is stretched into an octave

Bars 13–17

- This 5-bar phrase makes for an **unequal phrase length** to finish the piece
- The phrase starts with two bars of **conjunct** motion. In order to create this, many **passing notes** are used. In bar 13 the D and B on the second and third beats fit the harmony of these beats (D major first inversion and G major root position), so the intervening C on the half beat is an **unaccented passing note**; however, the B on the fourth beat is dissonant with the bass, and so this is an **accented passing note**
- The melodic line in bar 15 leaps by more than an octave, creating an interval of a **compound 5th**
- In bar 16 the first C is consonant in a second inversion C major chord (a cadential 6/4), and so is the D on the third beat; this makes the C♯ a **chromatic passing note**
- The D in bar 16 is decorated with a **trill** – a fast oscillation with the note above. The C at the end of the bar (which is dissonant with the G^7 harmony in this perfect cadence) announces the final note of the piece, and is a **note of anticipation**

PLAY IT!

If you are a pianist, you should try playing this piece. The melody is also well suited to being played on the violin (perhaps with a cello on the bass line) or a clarinet (maybe with a bassoon).

Intervals

The melody of this short piece is also good for checking your understanding of intervals. The method for measuring intervals is as follows:

1. Count through the alphabet from the lower note to the upper note. Including the notes themselves, the number of letters you count gives you the number (remember after G to go back to A). For example, low D to higher B would be... D, E, F, G, A, B – so this must be a 6th of some sort; F♯ to B♭ would be... F, G, A, B – a 4th of some sort.
2. Now ask yourself whether the upper note appears in the major scale that begins on the lower note.

3. Use the diagram below to find the adjective required for your interval:

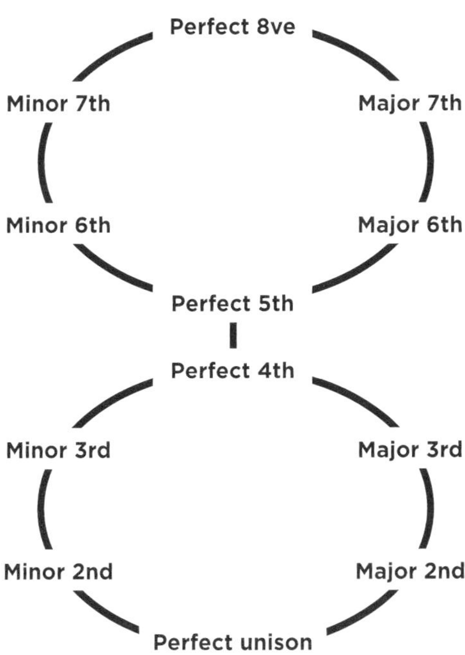

4. If your answer to step 2 is 'yes' the interval is either 'perfect' (for 4th and 5th) or 'major' (for 2nd, 3rd, 6th and 7th).
5. If the upper note is too high to make your answer to step 2 'yes', then the interval is 'augmented'.
6. If the upper note is too low *by a semitone* then the interval is either 'minor' (for 2nd, 3rd, 6th and 7th) or 'diminished' (for 4th and 5th).
7. If the upper note is too low by two semitones to be a major 2nd, 3rd, 6th or 7th, the interval is 'diminished'.

So in our two examples, the 6th of D to B has to be a major 6th as D major has a key signature of F♯ and C♯, making its sixth degree a B♮; meanwhile, the interval of F♯ to B♭ has to be diminished 4th, as F♯ major uses a B♮ and B♭ is smaller (but being a 4th, there is no 'minor 4th' available in the chart above).

INTERVAL QUESTIONS ON 'MELODIC FEATUREFEST 1'

1. In the opening 2-bar phrase of 'Melodic Featurefest 1', between which two notes can each of the following melodic intervals be found?

Minor 2nd	**Major 2nd**	**Minor 3rd**	**Major 3rd**
Perfect 4th	**Perfect 5th**	**Minor 6th**	**Major 6th**

2. What is the interval in bar 3 between B and F?
3. Where in the piece is there a melodic interval of a 7th, and what kind of 7th is it?

Answers at the back of the book

'Melodic Featurefest 2' has been composed to focus on melodic features. Study the score and/or play or listen to it, and then answer the questions below:

Melodic Featurefest 2

QUESTIONS ON 'MELODIC FEATUREFEST 2'

1. What word best describes the melodic shape in bar 1?

   Motif **Phrase** **Theme** **Tune**

2. How does the melody in bars 2–3 relate to bar 1?

   Falling sequence **Intervallic diminution**

   Intervallic augmentation **Rising sequence**

Bars 20–23

- This phrase begins in B♭ minor but continues to have quite a chromatic complexion
- The downbeat of bar 21 has another **bass suspension**
- In bar 22 the chord is a dominant 7th with B♭ as its root, but with A♭ (the 7th) in the bass, making it the **third inversion** or V^7d
- V^7d always resolves to Ib which happens here on the downbeat of bar 23, but there is a **7-6 suspension** in the tenor (F-E♭)

Bars 24–29

- Bar 24 is another **secondary dominant 7th** - this time in **second inversion** (C^7 with G in the bass) forming V^7c of F minor which is reached in the next bar
- In bar 25 there is a **7-6 suspension** in the alto
- Bar 26 is the **dominant 7th** of B♭ minor in **first inversion** (V^7b); as it resolves on the next downbeat, there is a **double suspension** (9-8 in the tune, 4-3 in the alto)
- Bar 28 is an **augmented 6th chord**; here the chord is built on D♭ and the B♮ is the augmented 6th, meanwhile there is a major 3rd (F) and an augmented 4th (G) making this a **French 6th**
- Bar 29 is a C major chord (reached from A♭ major as an imperfect cadence in the relative minor of F minor); halfway through the bar an A♯ is added to the chord, making another **augmented 6th chord**. This time the chord only has the augmented 6th interval (C-A♯) and a major 3rd (E) making this an **Italian 6th**

Bars 30–33

- This is the return of the opening phrase of the piece, but the music is now in the **tonic minor** of E minor; for three bars there is a **dominant pedal** in the bass
- The phrase ends with an **interrupted cadence**: we expect V^7-I in E minor, but the final chord is an E^7 chord in first inversion which is demanding resolution onto A minor on the downbeat of bar 34

Bars 34–38

- Bar 36 presents an F major chord in root position - the chord of the flattened 2nd or **Neapolitan** (but not Neapolitan 6th as it is not in first inversion); it is preceded in bar 35 by its dominant 7th-C^7
- There is a **9-8 suspension** on the Neapolitan chord
- Although this final section is in E minor, the last chord is the tonic major, thereby providing a closing **tierce de Picardie**

'Harmonic Featurefest 2' has been composed to focus on tonal and harmonic features. Study the score and/or play or listen to it, and then answer the questions on it.

Harmonic Featurefest 2

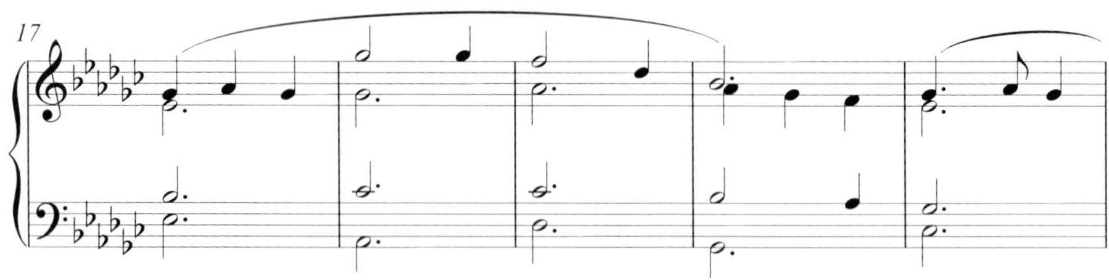

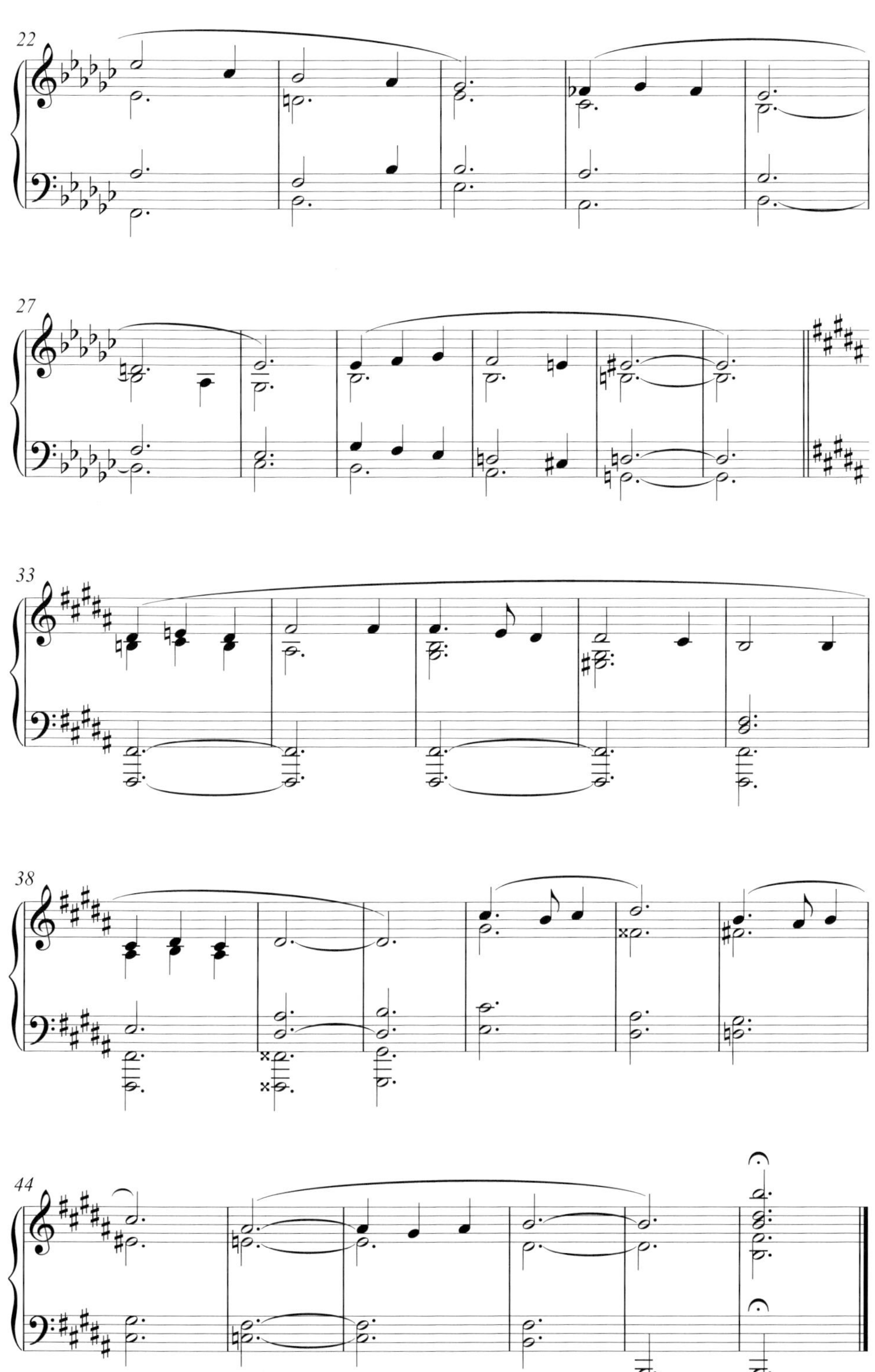
22
27
33
38
44

QUESTIONS ON 'HARMONIC FEATUREFEST 2'

1. The piece begins and ends in the same key. What key is this?

   B major E major F♯ major G♯ minor

2. What term best describes the harmony of the opening phrases (bars 1–8)?

   Chromatic Circle of 5ths Diatonic Tonic pedal

3. Which of the following represents the chords on the downbeats of the first three bars?

   I-II-III I-Vc-Ib I-Vc-VIc I-VIIb-Ib

4. There is a suspension in bar 4. What type is it?

   4–3 7–6 9–8 bass

5. What type of cadence occurs in bars 6–7[1]?

   Imperfect Interrupted Perfect Plagal

6. What type of cadence occurs in bars 7[3]–8[1]?

   Imperfect Interrupted Perfect Plagal

7. What type of chord occurs in bar 12?

   Augmented 6th Diminished 7th Neapolitan 6th Secondary dominant 7th

8. At the change of key signature in bar 17 the music enters a minor key. Which of the following is this the enharmonic equivalent to?

   Tonic minor Relative minor of the subdominant

   Relative minor Relative minor of the dominant

9. The passage from bar 17 is based on a circle of 5ths progression. For how many bars does the circle of 5ths govern the chord progression?

   7 bars 8 bars 9 bars 10 bars

10. There is a suspension in bar 20. What type is it?

    4–3 7–6 9–8 Bass

11. What type of chord occurs in bar 25?

    Augmented 6th Diminished 7th Neapolitan 6th Secondary dominant 7th

12. What type of cadence occurs in bars 27–28?

    Imperfect Interrupted Perfect Plagal

13. The chord in bar 30 is a dominant 7th. In what position does it occur?

    Root position First inversion Second inversion Third inversion

14. The chord in bars 31–32 is an augmented 6th chord. What type is it?

    French German Italian

15. What harmonic device is used in bars 33-38?

Circle of 5ths progression **Dominant pedal** **Modulation** **Tonic pedal**

16. What kind of cadence occurs in bars 38-39?

Imperfect **Interrupted** **Perfect** **Plagal**

17. How is the bass line in bars 41-47 best described?

Descending major scale **Descending minor scale**

Descending chromatic scale **Descending whole tone scale**

18. In bars 41-47 at what interval does the alto line follow above the bass line?

Major 6th **Minor 6th** **Major 10th** **Minor 10th**

19. What is the best way to describe the cadence in bars 41-42?

Half-close **Imperfect** **Interrupted** **Phrygian**

20. The chord in bars 45-46 is an augmented 6th chord. What type is it?

French **German** **Italian**

Answers at the back of the book

Texture words

ADDING TEXTURE

Texture is a very characterful aspect to music. The more you think about the texture of music you play, sing or listen to, the more imaginative and varied your own composition is likely to be.

For AoS1 you may need to know the following terms associated with texture:

- Solo, monophonic, unison, octaves, parallel thirds
- Melody and accompaniment, homophonic, chordal
- Polyphonic, contrapuntal, imitative, fugal, canon
- Antiphonal
- Trio sonata texture
- Polarised
- Countermelody, descant

'Texture Melange' (on the following pages) uses many of these textures.

Texture Melange

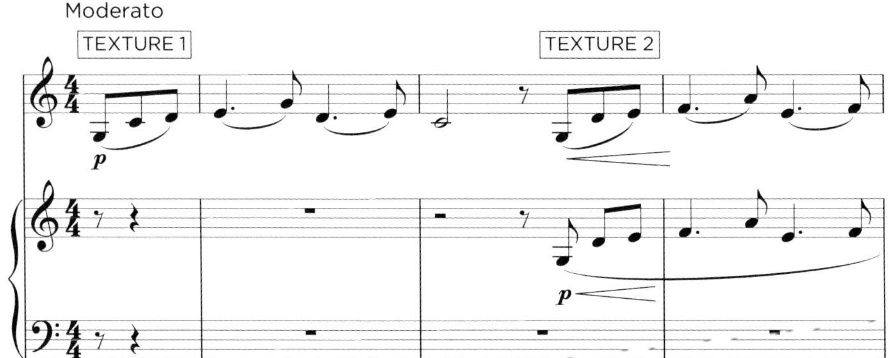

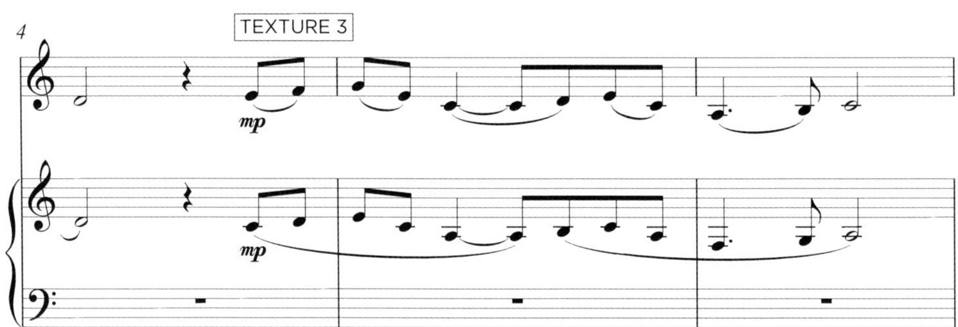

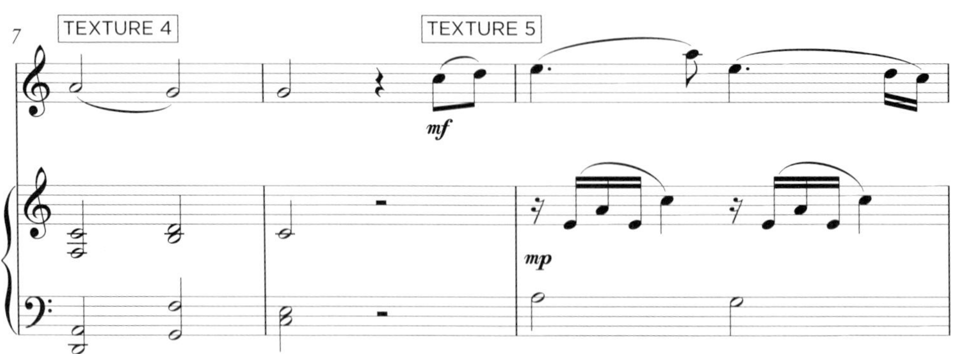

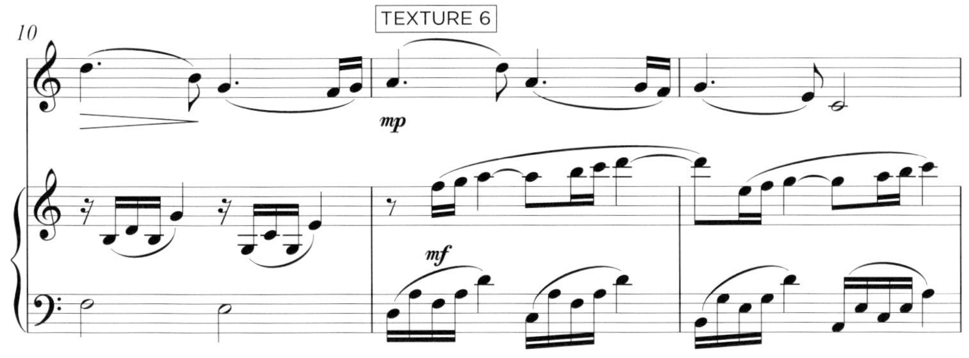
TEXTURE 6
10
mp
mf

TEXTURE 7
Swing
TEXTURE 8
13
p
cresc.
p
cresc.
mf

16
mf

20
mp
mf

23
Straight
TEXTURE 9
mf
f
26
TEXTURE 10
TEXTURE 11
28
ff
f
ff
f
32
rit.

- Direction and profile of melodic contour
- Length of melodic motif
- Homophonic or antiphonal texture

Bar by bar: the second movement – Andante

It is difficult to imagine a concerto movement in which the solo instrument does not play; however, in this pre-concerto sonata, the trumpet is *tacet* (silent) throughout this second movement.

In this short work, this helps to make a clear contrast between the three sections. Not only do the tempo and timbre provide contrast, the tonality too is different. Purcell chooses to have the Andante in the relative minor. This is another reason for the trumpet's silence: remember those notes that the valveless trumpet can play – the harmonic series of D major? There are not many Bs available.

The strings and continuo music is very chordal. It is unclear whether the harpsichordist was intended to improvise elaborately on the chord progression. In the absence of strong Purcellian melodic material, now is an excellent time to practise your harmonic analysis. Here are the opening four bars analysed for you:

Simple as this may seem, there is a moment of harmonic daring typical of Purcell where the 7th in the fairly standard dominant 7th chord at bar 3^3 resolves directly onto another 7th chord in the rather unusual subdominant 7th chord at bar 3^4. The open 5th at the end of the phrase is also a favourite Purcell trick – a very cold, barren colour at the end of a phrase in a minor key.

The second phrase of the movement (bars 34–37) is almost identical, although it is now transposed to E minor and ends with a tierce de Picardie.

Now it's your turn to consider the second half of the movement. There are some fascinating chromatic moments for you to ponder which perhaps only Purcell would have used in this period. The strange chord on the downbeat of bar 42 is a particular favourite of his. Enjoy the expressive downbeats of bars 44 and 45 – what accounts for the plangent quality here?

Bar by bar: the third movement – Allegro

After the short, but plaintive slow movement, there is a welcome return to jollity with this gigue-like finale, back in D major.

Bars 50–64

There is a striking, skipping melodic idea of four bars following a regular rhythm, immediately announced on the violins:

Three subsequent entries, the last on the trumpet, give a sense of fugal texture, though it is a simplified example, as all parts begin from A, unlike in a true fugue with alternate entries having a tonic-dominant relationship, but then tonal processes in the 17th century were still developing.

Bars 65–81

This passage has two ideas:

- Bars 65–75 – a non-imitative antiphony between repeated semiquaver chords in the strings (energised by entering after the downbeat each time) and falling triadic shapes in the trumpet; this culminates in a strong cadence in D major (which has a sense of hemiola)
- Bars 76–81 – a phrase of flowing semiquavers which has some similarities with the opening tune. The cadence in 80–81 is a strong hemiola which become clearer if we slightly adjust the layout of the notes:

Bars 82–112

This is clearly another quasi-fugal section; indeed, the tune sounds quite similar in fact to the opening of the movement.

This is not just a coincidence: Purcell has turned his original tune upside down and is now using the **inversion**:

This time Purcell does something unexpected and twists the music to a cadence in B minor (complete with another hemiola) at bars 93–95 before the trumpet is heard with the final entry of the inversion at bar 96.

There is then some high-spirited imitation between trumpet and strings using a simple shape of a rising 4th and falling 3rd before a single statement of the original fugal tune and a big D major cadence (a hemiola once more).

Bars 113–129

The final section of the sonata focuses on the repeating note figure first heard at bar 65. The repeating semiquavers are now in the trumpet as well as the strings; the effect is almost drum-like, not least because the harmony is completely static – 11 bars of tonic root

Among the tricks Vivaldi uses for this sonic painting are:

- A high register
- Rapid oscillations between A and D
- Trills

Should you wish, you can compare Vivaldi's fluted impersonation with the real ornithological thing at **http://www.british-birdsongs.uk/goldfinch** (but don't expect a very close match!).

Bars 21–26

This is clearly another ritornello passage – the strings re-enter and we immediately recognise the head motif; however, due to the flute solo being anchored to D and A (tonic and dominant of the home key for the concerto), the music has not yet had a chance to modulate and this second ritornello is therefore also in the tonic, unlike in the generalised description above. This is not particularly unusual for Vivaldi.

The fact that we are still in D major perhaps leads Vivaldi to truncate the ritornello theme and he stitches together the head motif and tailpiece to give us, literally, a 'little return'. Even the three descending scales are now only played twice:

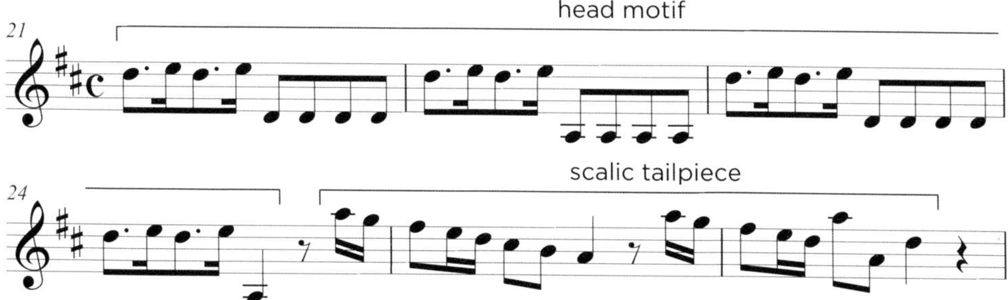

Note that this actually produces a section that is 5½ bars long rather than the initial 12; the asymmetric nature adds an unpredictable quality that is beguilingly charming.

Bars 26–47

This is a more typical solo passage, as it has a light accompaniment and the music modulates.

There are three subsections here:

- Bars 26–31 – reminiscent of the initial unaccompanied solo passage with the flute continuing to flutter about very much tethered to the perch of D and its major scale; however, the violins add a little further tweeting (of a non-21st century kind) with semiquavers and trills in parallel 3rds
- Bars 31–39 – a passage of triadic semiquavers in the flute over a bass line of quavers in the violas (a good example of the nuanced scoring to support the soft flute). This has the feel of a rising sequence: there is a 2-bar phrase of semiquavers based on D major, then two bars based on E minor, and finally two based on F♯ major; however, there are some subtleties here:
  - Each phrase is articulated by half a bar which allows the flautist to breathe, a gap covered by violin trills
  - The harmonic implications are not consistently sequential: in the D and E minor phrases, these triads operate as tonics, alternating with their respective dominants. However, in the F♯ major phrase, F♯ is a dominant which alternates with its tonic of B minor – the relative minor for the concerto

- Nonetheless, the momentum of all these semiquavers and the rising in pitch undeniably has the effect of increasing tension and excitement:

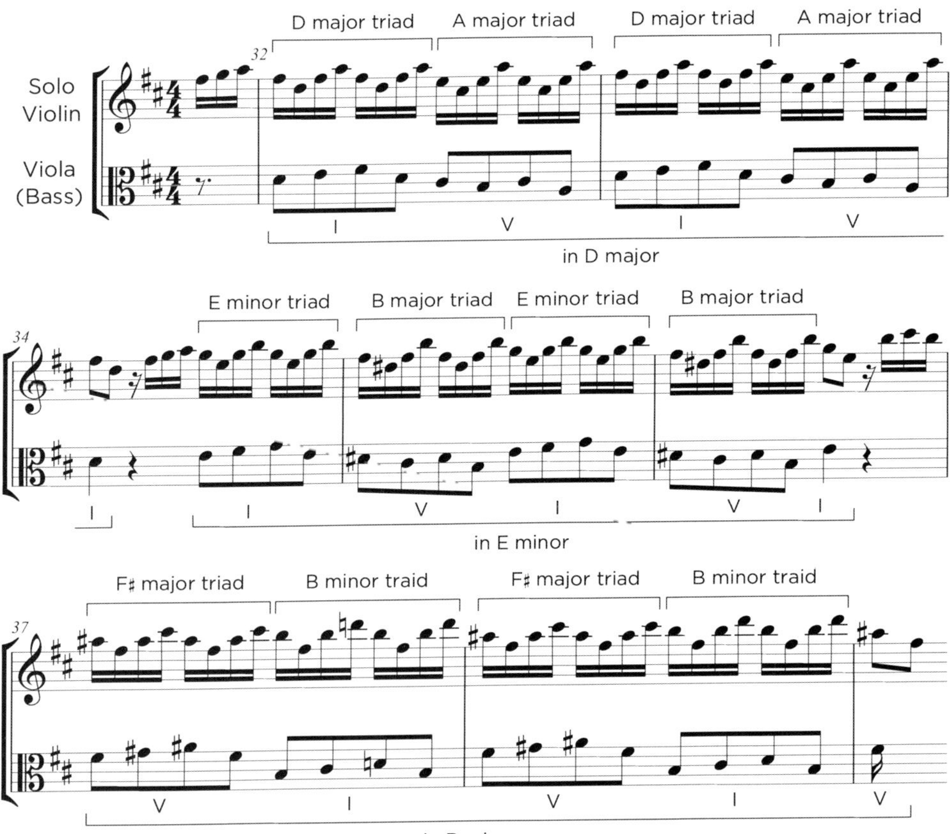

- Bars 39–47 – a passage that provides the perfect counterbalance to the previous one: after the changing tonal centre, this is firmly anchored in B minor, and where the previous one had an effect of rising sequence, here the melodic line of the flute has a straightforward descending sequence:

Bars 47–53

This is another version of the shorter version of the ritornello, but now in the relative minor (B minor). A few small details are changed.

Interestingly, there are no A♯s in the string parts to heighten the sense of B minor, though the figured bass at bar 52[4] indicates that the continuo player (organist, probably) should play an F♯ major chord in the cadence.

Bars 53–95

This final solo passage is remarkably long and discursive, amounting to 43 bars. The whole movement is only 100 bars, so it makes for a rather asymmetric structure to the movement; however, bear in mind that there are two further movements in the concerto that can bring balance.

The main subsections are:

- Bars 53–64 – two similar phrases, both of which begin with a rising chromatic scale (each note played four times) in the flute and end with oscillating semiquavers (that were originally heard in the opening ritornello). There are differences, however:

First phrase, bars 53–58	Second phrase, bars 59[3]–64
Six bars long	Five bars long
Starts on B and in B minor	Starts on F♯ and in F♯ minor
Ends on F♯ and in F♯ minor	Ends on B and in B minor
Lower register	Higher register
Bass line in quavers provided by violins	Bass line in quavers provided by violas

Vivaldi's harmonic palette is quite resourceful here, including a Neapolitan 6th and various secondary dominant 7ths:

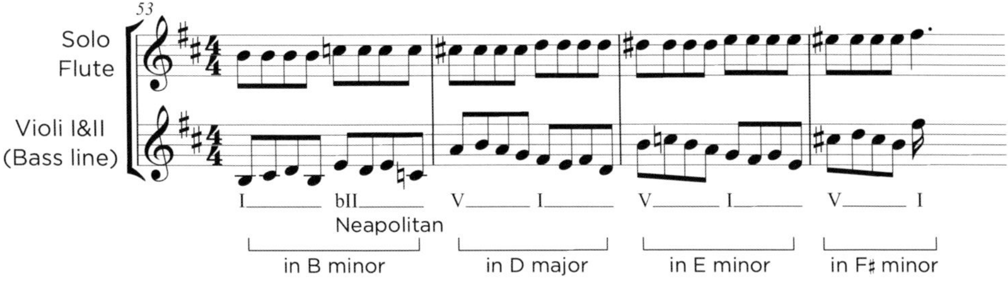

The speed of harmonic rhythm, chromatic spice and rising pitch all add to the sense of forward intensity, yet Vivaldi is careful to have only a very light texture that is essentially just two parts.

- Bars 65–68 – in answer to the two previous intensifying rising phrases, Vivaldi now provides a bright falling phrase. This is largely diatonic, treating the starting B minor chord as though chord VI in the home key of D major, and gives the illusion of descending sequence (due to intervallic alterations, it is not strictly so). G♯s in bar 68 hint at the dominant key (A major); violas provide a simple bass line:

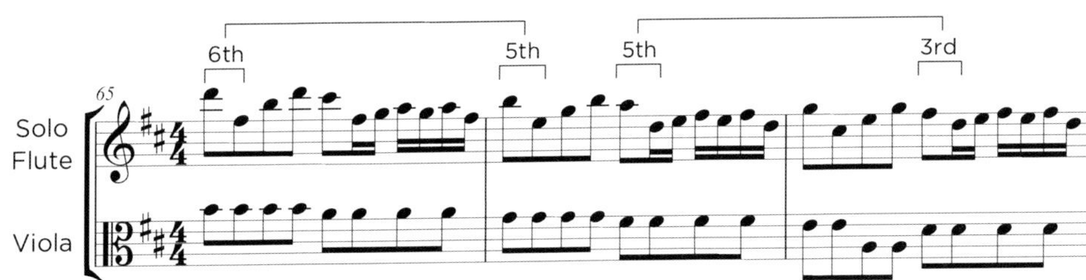

- Bars 69–76 – with D major very much back in the air, Vivaldi delays the return of the tonic chord in root position with this passage built over a long dominant pedal. It is another very chirpy passage with the solo flute and first violins almost engaged in some goldfinch courtship ritual, full of trills and repeating quavers
- From the viewpoint of the continuo player (harpsichord/organ) the bass line is marked ***Tasto solo*** – an indication that the composer does not expect lots of chords to be improvised here, instead just the pedal note itself
- Bars 77–84 – triadic semiquaver figuration, of a type previously met in the movement, dominates the flute part here. After a simple move towards E minor in bars 78–79, a simple diatonic circle of 5ths progression (chord changing every half bar) steers the music back to D major. The violas again provide a bass line in quavers; the full strings only play to bridge breaks in the flute part
- Bars 85–95 – By now the return of the ritornello in the home key is overdue. Vivaldi prolongs its arrival with a kaleidoscope of ideas. Some refer to music we have already heard: the rising arpeggios in the flute in bars 85 and 87 remind us of the opening ritornello and there are oscillating semiquavers in the violins; others are new surprises, such as the sudden turn to the tonic minor (D minor) in bar 88 and the half-close mini-cadences on the downbeats of bars 89 and 90. The long solo passage ends with a final lengthy flute solo accompanied only by viola quavers

Bars 96–100

The long awaited ritornello in the tonic key is remarkably brief, Vivaldi allows us just about enough of the head motif (about half a bar) to recognise it and then finishes with the tailpiece descending scales. It is fair to say we might feel slightly short-changed; but then, there are two more movements to follow.

The overall structure of this movement can be summarised in the following table:

1-12	13-20	21-26	26-47	47-53	53-95	96-100
Ritornello 1	Solo 1	Ritornello 2	Solo 2	Ritornello 3	Solo 3	Ritornello 4
12 bars	8 bars	6 bars	21 bars	6 bars	43 bars	5 bars
D major	D major	D major	D major to B minor	B minor	B minor via F♯ minor to D major (and hint of E minor)	D major

The asymmetry is very evident here, and points strongly to the fact that bar 100 is not the end of the piece.

A LEVEL ONLY

Bar by bar: the second movement: Cantabile

The slow movement of this concerto is in the same key - D major. Aware of the delicacy of the solo instrument for which he is writing, Vivaldi dispenses with his string players and accompanies the flute with just basso continuo.

Basso continuo is the mainstay of all instrumental Baroque music. The term denotes a complementary pair of instruments: one bass register bass instrument - typically cello or bassoon, and one harmony instrument - usually a keyboard instrument such as organ or harpsichord, though lute was another possibility. The bass player would follow the notes on the stave; the harmony player would improvise their part around the implied harmony of the bass line and a numerical code under the stave known as 'figured bass'.

The outcome in 'Il Gardellino' is a slow movement that would fit equally well in an intimate flute sonata or in a larger-scale flute concerto.

Vivaldi chooses a compound metre - $\frac{12}{8}$ - 4 slow beats in the bar which are subdivided into three. The frequent use of the rhythm pattern ♩. ♪ ♪ ♩ ♩ gives the music a gentle lilt usually associated with the Baroque dance style of the siciliano. In keeping with this, the music is in a simple binary form: two matching halves, each repeated; the first modulating to the dominant, the second returning to the tonic. Often the route home is via the supertonic minor. This provides balance as it injects some minor colour into the movement, and also it is the relative minor to the subdominant - i.e. on the flat side of the tonic to counteract the move sharpwards to the dominant in the first half.

Here, Vivaldi follows this plan to the letter, as highlighted by the D♯ in the bass in bar 7. On the way to E minor he uses - quite innocuously - a diminished 7th chord at bar 7^3. When this phrase is treated to descending sequence from bar 9 to return the music to D major, the corresponding diminished 7th creates quite a striking effect with the B♭ in the flute melody; modern ears might even think of it as a 'blue' note.

It is possible for a binary form to be just a little too neat in its balancing of phrases. Here, there is just enough subtlety to Vivaldi's plan of 2- and 3-bar phrases to avoid complete predictability; indeed, there are six bars in the A section and seven in the B section. The layout below illustrates the deft design:

* Some editions (e.g. Dover Scores) have G sharp throughout this bar, others (e.g. Eulenberg) have the first half of the bar as G natural.

The elegance of this melody lends itself to elaboration when being repeated. This offers potential not only to the flautist, but also to the continuo player who can respond to the enhanced melodic shapes that the soloist plays in each repeat. The recording with The English Concert directed by Trevor Pinnock is a very good example of the continuo player reflecting the elaborations of the flute soloist.

A LEVEL ONLY

Bar by bar: the third movement - Allegro

If the slow siciliano of the slow movement has a hint of a solitary goldfinch feeling somewhat lonely, the opening of this fast finale clearly has a sense of the first violins providing company. For much of the first 23 bars the two lines move in parallel 3rds.

As is common in the Vivaldi concertos, this finale is again in ritornello form. The ritornello theme itself is easy to spot: it starts with a scurrying descending scale with the top tonic separate from the rest of the scale (see bar 1):

Its significant structural appearances are as follows:

- **Bar 1** D major
- **Bar 40** A major
- **Bar 89** B minor
- **Bar 112** D major

ANALYSIS OF THE ALLEGRO

There is a plenty here for you to explore and analyse further in Vivaldi's music. Although the triple time metre ($\frac{3}{4}$) creates a different character, many of the features are similar to those found in the opening movement and discussed in detail above. These include:

- Use of trills
- Repeating staccato quavers
- Triadic figuration
- Dominant pedal
- Light string textures
- Dotted rhythm patterns
- Oscillating semiquavers
- Melodic sequences
- Rising leaps of a perfect 4th

Can you find examples of all these?

EXPLORE VIVALDI

There is an amazing range of concertos by Vivaldi to enjoy in your further listening. Most famous, of course, are 'The Four Seasons', but try concertos for different instruments: cello, bassoon or mandolin.

Bach: Violin Concerto in A minor BWV1041

Context: The composer

Johann Sebastian Bach (1685–1750) is one of the great figures in Western culture and widely respected as one of the greatest composers of all time. He was born at Eisenach (Germany) into a musical family in a time and place of enormous potential musically:

- Northern Europe had settled after the disruption of the Thirty Years' War earlier in the 17th century
- The Lutheran religion (a part of the Protestant Christian Church), to which he belonged, had become fully established as a strong force that embraced the power of music in its services
- Composers were increasingly moving away from modal habits to explore the potential of tonality
- Instrumental music was on the rise, aided by improved instrument making
- Princes desired orchestras at their courts and had the wealth to fund them
- Various dancing traditions had given rise to an array of different musical style: the corrente from Italy, the sarabande from Spain, gigues from England, the gavotte from France, etc

Bach had the skills to exploit all this potential: he was a prodigious organist and grew up with the Lutheran tradition of chorales; he also played the violin. He was exceptionally hard working: for much of his career as a church musician he had to compose a cantata (maybe twenty minutes of choral music, with solo arias, all accompanied by orchestra) each and every week, having it ready for performance on Sunday morning. He had a strong sense of personal mission to build a musical tradition for the Lutheran church that was fit for God. Above all, he had a remarkable intellect that combined inventiveness in all aspects of music (melody, harmony, contrapuntal texture, rhythm, etc.) with supreme technical control.

Strangely Bach's music fell into obscurity when he died. The contrasting styles of his sons (three of them were able composers) were considered more fashionable in the second half of the 18th century. Gradually scholars rediscovered the riches of his achievement. Mozart and Haydn were introduced to his music, Mendelssohn revived the St Matthew Passion (one of Bach's greatest works) in 1829, and by the end of the 19th century the Bach-Gesellschaft (Bach Society) had published a comprehensive edition of all his music.

In more recent years, the renewed interest in recreating 'authentic' performances on period instruments has given Bach's reputation even more lustre. Bach's music appears three times (more than any other composer) on the 'Voyager Golden Record' now flying through deep space.

BACH'S RANGE

Bach's contribution to Western culture was immense, and while his concertos are wonderful, his choral works, such as the B minor Mass, and instrumental pieces, such as the Six Suites for unaccompanied cello, are warmly recommended.

As you get to know Bach's music, you will become familiar with its intensity and momentum. It may not be quite as sunny as that of the Italian Vivaldi, but it has a remarkable degree of invention and drive.

Bach's orchestral music

Although Bach's career was dominated by his work for the Lutheran church, for six years (1717–1723) he worked as Director of Music (*Kapellmeister*) for Prince Leopold at Cöthen. Leopold's religion was Calvinist, a more puritanical train of Protestantism that did not allow music in church, so Bach's duties were focused on instrumental music and some secular cantatas.

Many of his greatest instrumental works date from this period, including the Brandenburg Concertos, Book 1 of the *Well-tempered Clavier*, the six suites for unaccompanied cello, and the sonatas and partitas for solo violin. In all likelihood, so too does our set work concerto, but the original score is lost and had to be reconstructed from the instrumental parts.

Violin Concerto in A minor

Bach knew and admired Vivaldi's concertos – well, at least some of them. We know this because he made transcriptions of some of them, converting them into solo organ pieces, among them Vivaldi's Concerto for two violins in A minor RV522:

Vivaldi's violin concerto

Bach's version for organ

It is, therefore, not surprising that when Bach came to write his own solo concerto for violin, he followed Vivaldi's plan: three movements (fast – slow – fast) and embraced ritornello form. However, he also had his own ways of thinking musically, and these included more complex contrapuntal textures, a more significant harmonic dimension with a stronger sense of harmonic progression, and a more highly charged rhythmic energy.

The concerto is available in several different editions from various publishers; the miniature score published by Eulenberg is a sound choice. There are many recordings available. The 2015 recording by Alina Ibragimova has received excellent reviews.

Bar by bar: first movement: Allegro

Bars 1–24: the opening ritornello

This is long and full of characterful melodic shapes and eager rhythms. The solo violinist plays as though just one of the first violins throughout this section.

The overall effect is one of energy and restlessness due to a number of factors:

- The opening leap of a rising 4th from the anacrusis to the first downbeat – it is a striking start to the head motif (bars 1–4)
- Melodic interest being spread across all four lines in the texture; consider, for example, the second violin and viola parts from bar 8, and the cello line from bar 13
- Melodic lines that give both a melodic direction and harmonic implications at the same time; for example in bars 5 and 6 the 'main tune' is a rising scale in crotchets that is heard in the 1st violins, but they also provide some significant harmony notes with the A-G♯-A semiquaver repeating pattern; meanwhile the cello doubles the 'main tune' a 10th lower, but also manages to suggest a dominant pedal at the same time:

- Long passages of continuous semiquavers that are passed from one part to another; for example, from starting with an innocuous pair of semiquavers in the cello in bar 4 there is a constant flow of semiquavers, immediately in the 1st violins, then in the 2nd violins from bar 8, passing to cellos and the line from bar 13 and lastly back in the 1st violin in bar 15
- Frequent use of tied notes over the barline in the violins and viola which keeps a sense of arrival (i.e. on the downbeat) at arm's length and propels the music forwards

- A modulation to the dominant key of E minor which is initially hinted at in bar 13 where the first D♯ appears in the viola, and more strongly pointed to in bar 14 with the first B^7 harmony
- Opportunities are sidestepped to cadence in the new key: perfect cadences in E minor could be completed on the downbeats of bar 18 (in fact it sidesteps to II^7b) and bar 20 (which is IVb with 7–6 suspension), but instead it charges onwards
- Several dramatic plunges in the bass line – a major 7th bars in 19–20 to the open C-string (lowest note) of the cello, a diminished 7th in bars 20–21, and a major 6th in bars 21–22

The density of these and other features is extraordinary; here is an annotated version of the last eight bars of this opening ritornello:

Bars 25–39: First solo

The opening ritornello ends in E minor, but the tierce de Picardie means that its final chord can operate as a dominant and the music immediately heads back into A minor for the first solo passage.

There are three subsections to the solo passage:

- Bars 25–28 – a classic 4-bar phrase that has a sense of two 2-bar sub-phrases, the first based on I-V harmony, the second on V-I (the Classical period was just around music history's corner...); note how the intervals in the second of these stretch further with delightful result:

- Bars 29–32 – tumbling sequential semiquavers over a clear circle of 5ths progression, the chords of which change every crotchet, making for a faster harmonic rhythm:

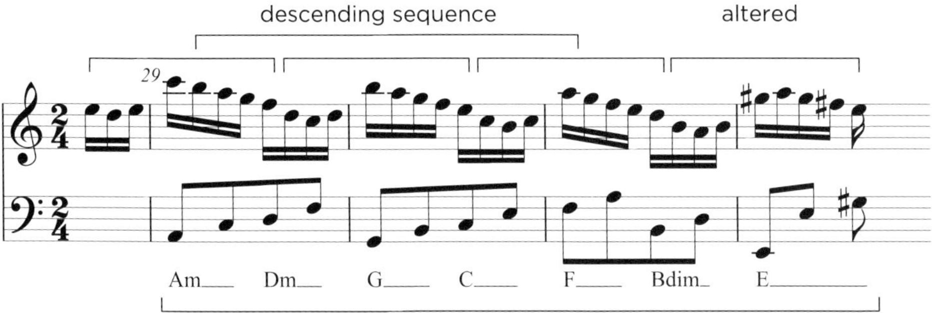

- Bars 33–39 – continued solo semiquavers and another circle of 5th progression, but now the harmonic rhythm is slow – one chord per bar instead of two – and the orchestra plays the head motif of the ritornello (just the first two bars) in the background (*p*) in a descending sequence:

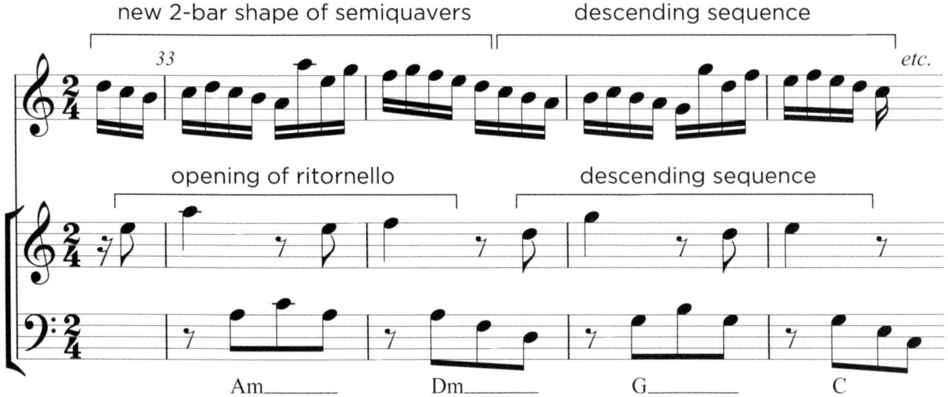

Bars 40–43: Mini-ritornello

The head motif has been in the background for a while; it now briefly comes to the fore – still in the tonic (A minor) – for its opening four bars. (You may recall that in the 'Il Gardellino' Concerto, Vivaldi's second ritornello was also very short and still in the tonic key.)

Although this has a sense of being a moment of structural articulation, the solo violinist barely takes any notice and continues with freely spiralling semiquavers.

Notice also that the bass line from bar 4 is maintained as this short passage ends.

Bars 44–51: second solo

This relatively compact solo passage starts in A minor and takes the music to C major.

There are three strands to the texture:

- A new playful, syncopated figure in the solo violin that has a pair of demisemiquavers on the beats
- The bass shape at the end of the mini-ritornello
- A softly pulsing chordal backdrop in the orchestral violins and viola

The harmonic content here is quite sophisticated in its use of inversions and chromatic inflection:

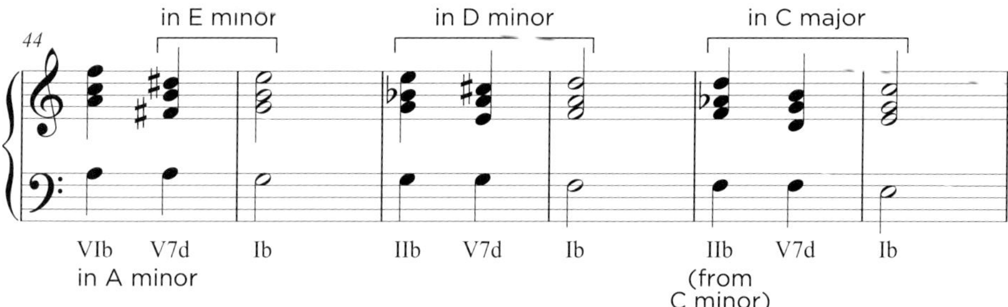

However, this simplifies at bar 49 when the orchestral strings stop playing. After the chromaticism and shifting keys, there is a strong sense that C major is going to be affirmed, a sense that is only reinforced by the passing secondary dominant 7th (V of V) at the end of bar 50.

Bars 52–84: ritornello

As expected, C major is embraced with a substantial ritornello section. This has various elaborations:

- Some flamboyant rising arpeggios in the solo violin in bars 52–53 which give a sense of the solo section overlapping with the ritornello
- Two moments where the orchestra stops and there are short unaccompanied passages for the soloist (bars 61 and 65).
- A perforated orchestral texture in bars 73–76 which sustains a sense of *tutti* passage while allowing the soloist to be in the spotlight again
- A modulation over the course of the ritornello so that it ends in E minor at bar 84

The remainder of the movement

We have reached about the halfway point of the movement here (bar 84 of 171 bars); now it is your turn to look into all the details of the second half of the movement. To help you on your way, here are a few clues:

THERE IT IS AGAIN!

Throughout the whole movement, listen out for just how much use Bach makes of the first two notes: the rising 4th that begins on an offbeat.

- In bars 89-99 there is another passage using the circle of 5ths progression but now with a slowed harmonic rhythm of each harmony essentially lasting for two bars (but harmonically decorated in the meantime)
- At bar 102 the ritornello appears in D minor
- At bar 123 the ritornello appears in A minor
- At bar 135 there is an extraordinary passage of harmony where each of G minor, D minor and A minor (circle of 5ths again) is prefaced with its Neapolitan 6th which changes into the dominant 7th in third inversion (no change of bass note required) before resolving onto the principal chord
- At bar 143 the substantial final ritornello commences - in A minor of course. It is interesting to compare this to the Vivaldi. You will recall that the final ritornello of the first movement of 'Il Gardellino' is quite short; here - after all the complexities encountered in this substantial movement, the final ritornello is long. This substantial, tonally stable section is needed to bring balance to the movement

A LEVEL ONLY

Bar by bar: second movement: Andante

Vivaldi wrote all three movements of 'Il Gardellino' in the same key. Here Bach chooses a related key for the slow movement: the relative major - C major. After all the energy and momentum of the opening Allegro, this movement has a sense of respite to it, like a meditation in the middle of a frantic day. There is, of course a regular pulse, but it feels as though time itself has been slowed.

There are two important strands to this music:

- A motivic idea in the bass of a tonic pedal note repeating in quavers, with every fourth quaver replaced by a rising shape that seems to be lifting the heavy weight of the repeating bass note over a barrier into the next half bar. Although the ear is drawn towards this slow-motion action in the bass, the upper strings - playing detached chords on the beats - give this almost riff-like bass a rich harmonic connotation:

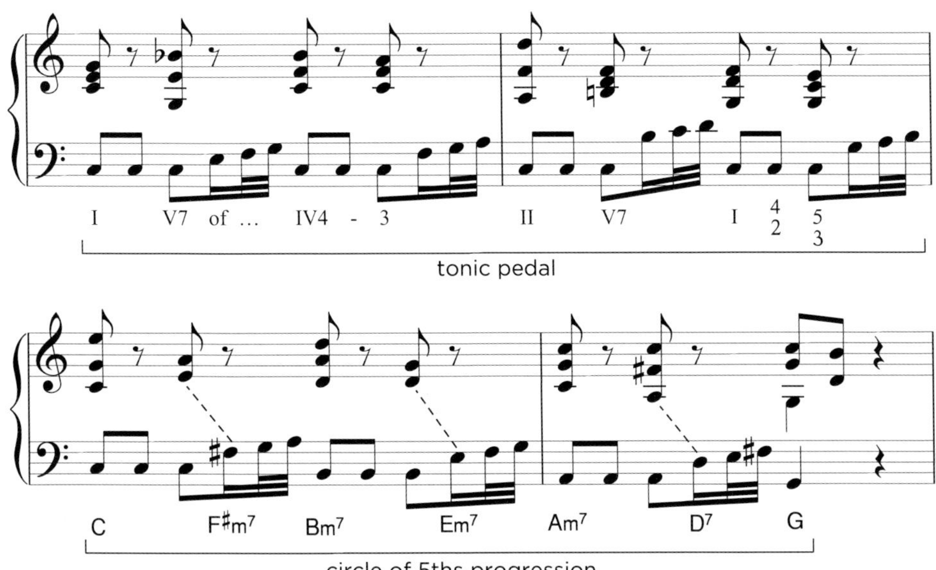

The effect of this backdrop is rather like listening to the ticking of a fine traditional clock, the rising shape on the fourth quaver reminiscent of the escapement mechanism operating on the pendulum.

When the motivic idea is not being played in the bass, the cellos are silent, leaving the more delicate violas to underpin the texture with repeating quavers.

- A beguiling melody in the solo violin that wanders across three octaves (the open G in bar 32, to the G an octave above the stave at bar 15), weaving an entrancing, elegant and intimate thread of exquisite beauty. After an initial bar, the main rhythmic characteristic is triplet semiquavers. There is a wonderful sense of freedom and spontaneity to this melodic lines caused by:
  - The use of ties and trills
  - The changing placement in the bar of longer note values
  - The mix of triadic and conjunct motion
  - The twists and changes of direction of the melodic line

There is almost something here that, two centuries ahead of time, foreshadows the spirit of an improvised jazz solo over a riff or chord pattern.

The structure of the movement comprises a series of 2-bar segments. These can be varied in the following way:

- Whether or not the solo violin is weaving its line over the top
- Whether or not the bass quasi-riff is played
- Changes of tonal centre
- Shapes in the melodic line
- Distinctive harmonic colours such as the descending viola bass line in bars 13–14, or the diminished 7th harmony in bar 17

Particularly wonderful moments to savour are the violin phrases that begin with semibreves.

TEST YOURSELF

Complete the following chart of the movement.

Bars	Bass motif Y/N	Solo violin Y/N	Tonal centre	Notable melodic features	Notable harmonic features
1–2	Yes	No	C major		Tonic pedal
3–4					
5–6					
7–8					
9–10					

11–12					
13–14					
15–16					
17–18	Yes	Yes	Moving to D minor	A single semibreve in bar 17 to start the phrase, then a falling D harmonic minor scale	A single diminished 7th chord for a whole bar, then a perfect cadence in D minor
19–20					
21–22					
23–24					
25–26					
27–28					
29–30					
31–32					
33–34					
35–36					
37–38					
39–40					
41–42					
43–44					
45–46					

A LEVEL ONLY

Bar by bar: third movement: Allegro assai (fast enough)

After the oasis of the C major slow movement, Bach returns both to A minor and a spirit of verve and momentum for the finale of the concerto. The movement is in the compound metre of $\frac{9}{8}$ which is a double layering of a triple division: three beats per bar, and each beat subdivided into three. Despite the minor tonality, this creates something of a feel-good dancing spirit in the music.

There is also use of ritornello here, and - as with the first movement - the solo violinist plays with the 1st violins through the opening *tutti* section.

Bars 1–24 Opening ritornello

The 1st violins start with a gigue-like melody of constant quavers; like the opening movement, this begins with a dominant anacrusis that leaps to the tonic on the downbeat. There is then a falling A melodic minor scale; in bars 2 and 3, notes on the main beats emphasise tonic and dominant chords which the other quavers decorate, as highlighted below:

At bar 5 the 2nd violins enter with the same tune, but transposed a 4th lower (though the anacrusis is a 5th lower - a modification to match the dominant-tonic 1st violin lead to the first entry with a tonic-dominant answer here). In due course, at bar 9 the same tune - now at its original pitch occurs in the bass line. This makes the ritornello have a fugal texture, and Bach hasn't completed his dazzling contrapuntal plan yet: at bar 15 the violas have the tune, though now in the relative major (C major). The music returns to A minor for the cadence at the end of the ritornello into bar 25.

Bars 25–42: first solo

There are four subsections to this solo passage:

- The solo passage starts with two elegant matching phrases, each two bars long, the first over a I–V progression, the second over V–I:

If this description sounds familiar, you should look back at the first solo passage in the opening movement: the metre and melodic contour are different, but the structural idea of two balanced phrases being used to define the tonality though tonic and dominant harmony is identical.

The remarkable feature here is the long dissonant note in the second bar of each phrase - the D♯ in bar 2 and the G♯ in bar 4. These act as long lower appoggiaturas, eventually resolving to harmony notes on the last quaver of the bar. The piquancy of the dissonance is softened by the violins of the orchestra entering into the sparse texture (it is largely just soloist and basso continuo at this point) with a short melodic gesture in sweet parallel 3rds - a shape of motivic significance that comes from bar 3 of the ritornello theme.

- From bar 29 there is a more free-flowing passage that is built over a descending bass line; in bar 31 the first semiquavers of the movement appear: these give a scurrying character that will be exploited in due course
- At bar 33 a sequential passage built on a circle of 5ths progression begins:

Listen carefully for the detail in the articulation of the bow markings here

- From bar 40 there is a burgeoning sense of momentum as the music heads towards its confirmation of E minor (dominant key) for the imminent ritornello; the long dissonant D♯ in the first bar of the solo section is echoed at the end of bars 39 and 40

Bars 43-45

The expected E minor ritornello arrives, but there is little respite for the soloist as Bach trims it to just three bars at this point.

The remainder of the movement

If you have worked through all three concertos of this Strand up to this point, you should now be able to explore the rest of the movement for yourself. In particular, look out for:

- Appearances of the ritornello and the keys in which it returns
- Register, contour and rhythm of the solo material for the violinist
- The balance of silence, simple harmonic support and significant detail in the violins and violas of the orchestra

In particular, listen out for the string-crossing passagework from bar 82, and the special technique of *bariolage* in an extended passage from bar 105.

Bariolage (from the French meaning 'multi-coloured') exploits the juxtaposition of notes that are played on an open string (in this case the E) and those played by 'stopping' the string with a left hand finger. Throughout this passage, notes with upward pointing stems - always an E - are played on the open string, those with downward pointing stems - which includes some other Es - are played 'stopped'. You should be able to hear the distinct difference of timbres this creates.

STRAND B:
The operas of Mozart

Context: Introducing opera

By the time Mozart was writing his operas in the 1770s and 1780s, opera had been part of European culture for the best part of two hundred years. Originating in Italy with a group of composers, the most famous of whom is Monteverdi (1567–1643), opera had already had immense success in France with Lully (1632–1687) and Rameau (1684–1764), and in England with Purcell and Handel (1685–1759).

Opera is an art form in which drama is told primarily through music, while performed on a theatre stage with acting, costume and lighting to enhance the effect. If you think that sounds like musical theatre, the two are clearly similar, and the differences are not easy to define. In musical theatre, the constituent elements of the lyrics, acting, dancing and music are usually in a clear balance, whereas in opera, the music is given predominance over the others. This is why operas are very much credited to their composer rather than their librettist (the person who writes the words).

In the 18th century Vienna was the capital of the powerful Habsburg Monarchy. It was a city where musicians and artists from much of Europe prospered, among them the opera composer Gluck (1714–1787). He reformed many of the traditions of opera, to make it less governed by conventions (such as recitative and arias), and more built on continuous, melody-focused music that conveyed emotion.

Portrait of Mozart painted by his brother-in-law, Joseph Lange in 1782/3. In her old age, Mozart's widow said this was the best likeness of him

Wolfgang Amadeus Mozart (1756–91)

Mozart is one of the most celebrated composers in Western culture. He was a remarkable child prodigy, and his father – a court musician – promoted him and his talented sister around the palaces and high society of Europe during a three-and-a-half-year journey that began when he was seven and his sister ten. This included performing to King Louis XV of France and several concerts in London.

As an adult, Mozart was drawn to the splendour of Vienna. He first travelled there as a musician in the employ of the Archbishop of Salzburg (his birthplace) and he soon wished to make the capital his home. This led to a break in relations with both his employer and his father, but from 1781 until his death ten years later at the age of 35, Vienna was his home. Here he was known as the city's finest keyboard player, and he composed a continuous stream of wonderful music: concertos, symphonies, chamber music and, of course, opera.

Mozart started writing operas when he was 11. In all he worked on over 20 opera projects, most in Italian, some in German; a few were not completed or performed in his own lifetime. The most significant are:

Date	Title	Librettist	Language
1780–81	Idomeneo	Giambattista Varesco	Italian
1782	Die Entführung aus dem Serail	Gottlieb Stephanie	German
1786	Le Nozze di Figaro	Lorenzo da Ponte	Italian
1787	Don Giovanni	Lorenzo da Ponte	Italian
1790	Così fan tutte	Lorenzo da Ponte	Italian
1791	La clemenza di Tito	Metastasio	Italian
1791	Die Zauberflöte	Emanuel Schikaneder	German

Le Nozze di Figaro

Introduction

Le Nozze di Figaro – The Marriage of Figaro or, most commonly, just 'Figaro' – was Mozart's first collaboration with librettist Lorenzo da Ponte. The story is based on a play by French writer Beaumarchais and is something of a domestic comedy centred on the intended marriage of Figaro and Susanna who are respectively servants to the Count Almaviva and his wife Countess Rosina. Inevitably, since this is an opera, there are misunderstandings and contrary motives from some characters along the way, but it is a piece with a happy ending.

There are many opera fans for whom this is their all-time favourite. It is not just that Mozart's music is full of gorgeous tunes that you will soon find yourself humming as you get to know the score; Mozart took delight in human beings and their emotions. In this story of love, confusion and resolution, his delight is never far from the surface.

The opera is in four acts and lasts around three hours. It is one of the most frequently performed of operas; it is highly recommended that you try to get to a live performance of it - this way you will really enjoy the full experience of the live music reinforced by the acting onstage. A night at the opera is a treat! If this is not possible where you live, there are several full performances of 'Figaro' available on YouTube.

The cast of the opera is as follows:

Count Almaviva	Bass
Countess Rosina - wife of the Count	Soprano
Figaro - personal valet to the Count	Baritone
Susanna - the Countess's maid	Soprano
Cherubino - the Count's page	Mezzo-soprano
Dr Bartolo - the Countess's former guardian	Bass
Marcellina - Bartolo's housekeeper	Soprano
Don Basilio - a music master	Tenor
Don Curzio - a notary (lawyer)	Tenor
Antonio - a gardener, Susanna's uncle	Bass
Barbarina - Antonio's daughter	Soprano

There is also a chorus of villagers and servants. Mozart's orchestra comprises two flutes, two oboes, two clarinets, two bassoons, two horns, two trumpets, timpani and strings; a harpsichord or fortepiano (arguably more authentic) is also needed to accompany the recitative sections.

It is a good idea to get to know the whole opera: you will only really have a complete understanding of each of the characters whom you meet in Act 1 by following the opera through to the end. Both the finales at the end of Acts 2 and 4 are especially brilliant.

A LEVEL ONLY

Bar by bar: Overture

Mozart's overture to his opera has no direct connection with the themes of the rest of the opera, but in its fizzing, bustling four minutes of presto scampering, it perfectly sets the mood for what lies ahead.

Structurally, the overture follows most of a sonata form design:

Exposition	First subject	tonic
	Transition	modulating
	Second subject	dominant
	Codetta	dominant
Development	exploring the potential of the musical ideas in a variety of keys (avoiding the tonic) and ending on the dominant to lead back into...	
Recapitulation	First subject	tonic
	Transition	rewritten so as not to modulate
	Second subject	tonic
	Codetta	tonic
Coda		tonic

Mozart, however, appears to be in a hurry to get his opera started and misses out the development section entirely. This is sometimes known as 'abridged sonata form'.

The detail of the Overture is as follows:

Bars 1–138: Exposition

Bars 1–35: First subject

There are two main ideas in the first subject:

1. A line of scampering quavers heard at the start in octaves in the strings and bassoons. Curiously for the Classical period, it is seven bars long, but it highlights the notes that were most important to the Classical composers: the tonic and the dominant:

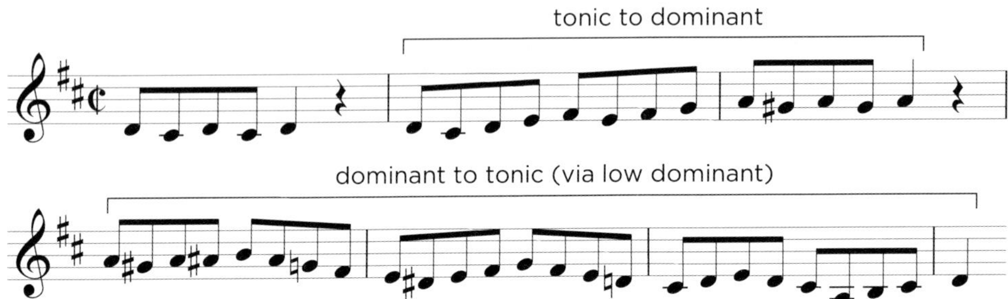

The use of the bassoons in unison with the cellos gives the combined sonority more of an edge and, moreover, the dry timbre of the bassoons hints a little at some humour in the opera ahead.

2. A more homophonic idea, initially for the winds, and then the whole orchestra, all over a tonic pedal. The melodic line at the top of this is built from the descending scale and ascending arpeggio of D major:

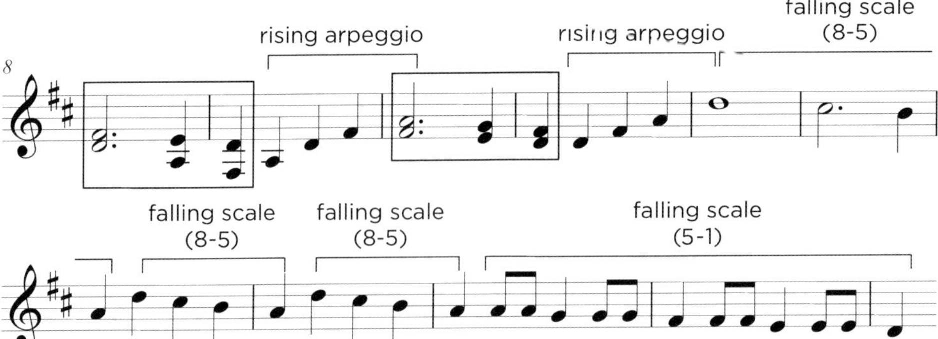

Notes in the boxes are played by horns, which were – of course – 'natural horns' (i.e. without valves) in Mozart's day, which explains the musical idea: only these notes were available to the horn players with 'horns in D'.

The whole of the first 18 bars is then played again, only this time Mozart adds a countermelody in the flute above the strings (and also a harmony line in the first oboe) which adds a dash of charm and sophistication to the music.

Bars 35–88: Transition

The transition increases the sense of anticipation and excitement by its strong dynamic contrasts and continued quaver energy. Over another tonic pedal, the violins play tumbling scales; the scales themselves may be descending, but their starting notes get higher, creating increasing forward momentum. Trumpets and timpani mark the downbeats.

Then in bar 41, the scale is ascending, matched in the next bar by an ascending scale in the bass, and the music remains ***f*** in a *tutti* section of considerable brilliance. The use of crotchet rests on the second beat of the bar (remember we're in $\frac{2}{2}$) in bars 45–47, each preceding a falling triadic shape in the bass, is very energising and propels the music towards a new pedal note on A from bar 51. Over this pedal, the triadic shapes, now rising, appear in the violins.

The pedal note is a little ambiguous; coming soon after the D pedal, it sounds initially rather like a dominant pedal, and there have been no G♯s to suggest otherwise; however, this clearly being music of the Classical style, we are expecting sonata form, and the pedal could easily be the new tonic.

Bars 36–49: Transition

Musically, this passage effects the modulation towards the dominant, the first C♯ occurring at bar 43, and the fleeting appearance of G♯ in bar 45 ensuring that the option of modulating is going to be taken.

Dramatically, Mozart makes use of the Classical convention that transitions often start with a restatement of the first subject to create a humorous passage in which Susanna is trying to get her fiancé's attention. She compromises her melodic line by adopting the repeating crotchets that the violins were playing as part of his theme; Figaro, however, is not paying attention and continues to focus on his measuring.

So, after a while and a number of 'hint-dropping' shorter phrases, Susanna imposes herself more with a 4-bar phrase from bar 46, for which she has the support of the whole orchestra.

Figaro and Susanna in a production of *The Marriage of Figaro*

Bars 49–59: Second subject

The music arrives in D major and Figaro finally stops measuring and pays attention to Susanna. He does so, by adopting her tune, now a 'proper' second subject in the dominant key; however, for Figaro the theme is accompanied by 'his' strings. The woodwind flourish in semiquavers in bar 51 seems to convey Susanna's delight that she has won her man's attention.

The second subject ends with a simple, reiterated cadence figure that allows Mozart to create brief dialogue between the lovers.

Bars 59–67: Linking passage in lieu of development

Mozart realises that now is not the time for elaborate development; instead Figaro and Susanna share a tender moment, singing in parallel 3rds and the pedal note underpinning this passage conveys a sense of stability and security.

The pedal note starts as being the tonic of the second subject key, but soon C♮ turns it into a dominant pedal; we sense that the music is returning home for what would usually be called the recapitulation.

Bars 67–end: Recapitulation

The music clearly returns to the tonic of G major at bar 67. It would, of course, be dramatically contradictory to return to the same music that was heard at the start of the exposition: we do not want Figaro to stop attending to Susanna and return to his measuring. Instead, the young couple continue to sing Susanna's theme in flowing parallel 3rds. It is, therefore, essentially a recapitulation of the second subject only, and another example of the composer adapting musical convention for dramatic purpose.

With the recapitulation therefore being rather shorter than the exposition, the couple's bliss is prolonged by a charming codetta from bar 81. Recapitulation and exposition are all totally diatonic.

Bar by bar: Recitative after No. 1

Recitative was developed by Baroque composers as an expedient way to get through large amounts of narrative and dialogue and so move the music on to an aria that could reflect on a character's state of mind. It is found mainly in operas by composers such as Handel and Vivaldi, but also in works like cantatas and oratorios by composers such as Bach.

Traditionally, recitative is characterised by:

- A free sense of rhythm (i.e. no strong pulse) so the singer can get through the text using normal speech rhythms
- A syllabic setting of the text – i.e. one note per syllable
- Accompaniment from the basso continuo: a combination of a bass instrument (cello, bassoon) and a harmony instrument (harpsichord, organ, lute)
- The harmonic element is indicated by numbers under the stave ('figured bass') and not notated as full chords by the composer; it therefore includes some improvisatory element from the player
- A tonal freedom – modulations can occur quite frequently as harmony is the main way to give some colour to the musical setting of the text in recitative; this is useful as recitatives can link between movements by beginning in the key of the previous aria and ending in the key of the next one

The first recitative in *Figaro* gives opportunity for Susanna to quiz her fiancé as to why he is measuring the floor; when he explains it is for the bed that the Count is giving them as a wedding present, she raises an objection, suspecting not wholly honourable motives from the Count.

The recitative begins on a G major chord – the key of the previous duettino; it ends on an F major chord which operates as a dominant into the next movement which is in B♭ major. This fluid tonal journey is facilitated by having many of the chords of the recitative in first inversion – a softer, less tonally assertive position of the chord.

TEST YOURSELF

Fill in the chart below to examine the harmonic content:

Bar	Text	Chord	Inversion
1	S: *Cosa stai misurando, caro il mio Figa-*	G major	first inversion
2	*-retto?* F: *Io...*		
3	*...guardo se quel letto, che ci destina il Conte, farà buona fi-*		
5	*-gura in questo...*		
5	*...loco.* S: *In questa...*		
6	*...stanza?* F: *Certo, a noi la...*		
7	*...cede generoso il pa-*		
7	*-drone.* S: *Io per me te la dono.* F: *E la ragione?* S: *La ragione l'ho...*		
9	*...quì.* F: *Perchè non puoi far, che passi un pò...*		
11	*...quì!* S: *Perchè non voglio;*		
12	S: *sei tu mio servo, o nò?* F: *Ma non ca-*		
13	*-pisco perchè tanto ti spiace la più commoda stanza del pa-*		
15	*-lazzo.* S: *Perch'io son la Su-*		
16	*-sanna, e tu sei...*		
17	*...pazzo.* F: *Grazie...*		
17	*...non tanti e-*		
18	*-logi; guarda un poco, se potria meglio stare in altro loco.*		

Bar by bar: Act 1 No. 3 Cavatina (Figaro)

Preceding recitative

In this lengthy recitative, Susanna explains to Figaro that Count Almaviva has intentions towards her and that Figaro should not be so naïve. Apparently Susanna's music master, Don Basilio, is not to be trusted either.

This is a lengthy passage of recitative and illustrates well just how useful this type of music is for injecting pace into the telling of a story. It can seem like a very simple musical style (very few notes), which could become facile.

There are two factors that allow composers as good as Mozart to keep dramatic vitality in the music:

- Melodic contour – for example in bar 23, when Figaro sings *'Chi? Basilio? Oh birbante!'* ('Who? Basilio? The rascal!') the rising contour on '*Basilio?*' suggests a question (and his incredulity) and *'birbante'* is set to Figaro's highest note of the recitative so it can be delivered with disdain
- Harmonic flexibility – the recitative both begins and ends on a C major chord, but in between there are harmonies ranging from A major (bar 3) to E♭ major (bar 23); the changing tonal implications help to convey the spirit of intrigue in the narrative and prevent every aspect of the music from being simple

Cavatina

In this aria Figaro is alone and imagining what he would like to say to his master now that he is aware of the Count's improper intentions towards Susanna.

There is an unusual structure of four different sections to the music, with the outer ones being the same. This gives an ABCA pattern.

Bars 1–20: A section

Using dancing as a metaphor for the Count's scheming, the lyrics here are *'Se vuol ballare, signor Contino, il chitarrino le suonerò'* ('If you want to dance, my dear little Count, I'll play the tune for you on my guitar'). It is not surprising, therefore, that Mozart writes music for this passage that is based on the Menuet – a popular aristocratic dance of the day in triple time.

There is a clarity to the music here that conveys the fact that Figaro's eyes have been opened:

- A simple rhythm – largely crotchets with just enough dotted patterns to suggest the lilt of the dance
- Purely diatonic use of pitch and largely conjunct melodic lines; only the third phrase has a triadic contour which may be an attempt to portray the guitar mentioned in the lyrics here
- A clear phrase structure of four 4-bar phrases, the final two bars then reiterated
- Treatment of the first phrase as a rising sequence beginning a 3rd higher
- A straightforward harmonic palette: the first two phrases and the final one only use tonic and dominant harmony, ending with perfect cadences; the third phrase provides contrast through using chords VI and IIb in bar 11 (and hence a faster harmonic rhythm) to effect an imperfect cadence

In the orchestration to this section the horns, with 18th-century connotations of hunting, are very much to the fore.

Bars 21–63: B section

This section begins with the music still in the tonic F major, but Mozart balances the heavy preponderance of tonic/dominant harmony of the previous section by starting the vocal phrase over chord IV (bar 23). The text here references being at school; this might explain the amount of repeating phrases (or 'copying') that occurs in the melodic line.

The music moves to the dominant from bar 31, with a cadence in C major at bar 42. Immediately C is turned into a dominant pedal under a most exquisite passage with various strands in the texture:

- The pedal note itself in the cellos and basses
- Sustained chords in the rich timbres of oboes, bassoons and horns
- Restless off-the-beat-reiteration of the harmony in the second violins and violas
- A skilfully woven countermelody of rising scales in the first violins
- The vocal line

LISTENING IN DEPTH

Spotting and savouring moments of characterisation such as the harmonic sidestep in bar 51 (of which there are very many) is all about good quality listening - really focusing on the changes of melodic direction, harmonic colour and accompanimental texture, while following the lyrics. Once you begin to unlock this approach to listening, listening to the music becomes a whole lot more rewarding.

Just when we might expect resolution of the dominant pedal to its tonic, Mozart creates a harmonic sidestep of a diminished 7th chord (bar 51) and the rest of the section is pointing to the relative D minor. The text here is *'Meglio ogni arcano dissimulando scoprir potrò'* ('best to hide secrets: by dissembling I can discover it all'): it contrasts Figaro's 'direct approach' against the shady scheming of the Count by having Figaro singing on a monotone (A) in the middle of an elaborate web of chromatic notes such as the lower chromatic auxiliary G♯ in the violins and juxtaposition of C♯ and C♮ (both found in the melodic scale of D minor).

Bars 64-103: C section

Instead of changing key here to the expected D minor, Mozart changes metre and tempo to give more insight into Figaro's eager defence of his fiancée.

Details you should listen out for include:

- Trills
- A passing modulation to G minor
- Bars in which the strings do not play
- Rising and falling sequences
- 7-6 suspensions

Bars 104-123: A section

This is a straightforward reprise of the opening section. A short codetta follows which reverts to the music of the C section.

Bar by bar: Act 1 no. 4 Aria (Bartolo)

This is Bartolo's first appearance in the opera and from the outset he is determined to have vengeance on Figaro: previously in the story Figaro had facilitated the wedding of the Count and Rosina, while Bartolo had intended to marry Rosina himself. Mozart writes his aria in D major, thereby allowing the trumpets and timpani to add to the character of the music.

This is another movement in which principles of sonata form can be seen. A clear sense of sonata **exposition** is found:

- Bars 1–14: First subject (D major)
- Bars 15–29: Transition (modulating – starting in B minor and ending on A)
- Bars 30–50: Second subject (A major)

Throughout this section Bartolo's melody is quite assertive and declamatory, owing to:

- Disjunct contour
- Wide register
- Use of rests to articulate phrase structure

Other details to listen out for include:

- Frequent dynamic contrasts in the orchestra that convey a sense of outbursts of rage
- A long line of impetuous semiquavers in the second violins in bars 5–12
- The staccato wind chords to accompany '*gli oltraggi*' ('the outrages')
- The second subject beginning, surprisingly, on the dominant chord (E major) of the dominant key (A major) and then having its secondary dominant (B^7) – perhaps inspired by the words: '*coll' asuzia, coll' arguzia*' ('with cunning, with wit')
- The Italian 6th chord used in bars 46–48

From bar 51 there is less sense of sonata form. The music returns to D major and then instead of a development section Mozart writes a contrasting **middle section** which tests the singer with a long line of triplet quavers at high speed: the words here refer to the possibility of having to read 'the whole legal code'.

The middle section ends at bar 72 on the dominant chord (approached via the tonic minor – D minor); bar 73 brings a sense of **recapitulation** with the return of the start to the aria. This is not prolonged, and the perfect cadence at bars 86–87 leads to a **coda** in which the semiquavers return to the second violins, supported this time by the violas.

Bar by bar: Act 1 no. 5 Duettino (Susanna and Marcellina)

This duet puts Susanna and Marcellina together in a scene of mistrustful competitiveness hidden under social niceties. These two contradictory levels are captured by the clever accompaniment texture with an elegant melody at the top in the first violins (which sometimes the singers double) and the restless triplet quavers simmering away underneath in the second violins.

Other features to listen out for include:

- The **introduction** of two bars that begin on E which, it emerges as the bass moves down the scale to A, is only the dominant
- The **first section** beginning with dialogue (or antiphony) in the phrases between Marcellina and Susanna
- Subsequently, the two sopranos singing in parallel 3rds (bar 14) in two matching phrases, the first led by Marcellina, the second (bar 17) by Susanna
- An early modulation to the dominant begun in bar 9, leading to a perfect cadence in bar 21 at the end of the first section
- The **second section** beginning in E major (bar 21) with the same melody that began the first section (bar 3)

- A modulation back to A major begun in bar 25 with V^7d, leading to a perfect cadence in bars 37-38
- The **third section** from bar 38 begins with a turn to the subdominant, then quickly returns to the dominant before finding its way home to A major at bar 46

Bar by bar: Act 1 No. 6 Aria (Cherubino)

This aria introduces Cherubino, the adolescent page, who is preoccupied with thoughts of love (or possibly lust). This is captured by a slightly breathless quality to the music generated by the energy of the rests in the violin accompaniment pattern and the motor-rhythm of the vocal part being constantly two quavers and a crotchet.

It is curious that two years after 'Figaro', Mozart used the same rhythm for the first theme in his 40th Symphony:

Le Nozze di Figaro 1786:

Symphony no.40 in G minor 1788:

This is also the first time in the opera that Mozart allows the clarinets to be the main accompanying instruments in the wind section. We can only speculate why this was - was it something to do with their sound for an aria about love, or that the clarinet was the 'new kid on the block' in the 1780s and this seemed appropriate for the youngest character in the opera? Whatever the reason, their sound is something fresh and very beautiful in this aria.

The aria has a composite structure: two halves, each with its own internal structure:

First half: bars 1-52

This half falls into three sections and could be seen as ternary, though it is also possible to see the middle passage as a second subject given it starts and ends in the dominant key, and then the word section acts like a recapitulation (after all, we have already seen examples of Mozart using sonata form without a development section).

The two schemes are shown below:

Bars	Seen as based on abridged sonata form	Seen as ternary form
1-15	First subject E♭ major	A section E♭ major
16-35	Second subject B♭ major after minimal transition in bar 15	B section B♭ major
38-51	Recapitulation E♭ major	A section reprised E♭ major

Points to notice:

In the first subject / A section:

- The similarity in contour of the first two phrases, but also the difference: the second uses intervallic augmentation to intensify the fervour being expressed in the lyrics
- The quickening harmonic rhythm which suggests increasing impetuousness
- The repeating third phrase, but the repeat is one note shorter, allowing for an earlier anacrusis into the next phrase
- Another repeated phrase in bars 9–15 which utilises a top G as the climax of the section; the first version of this phrase ends with an imperfect cadence, its repeat with a perfect cadence
- One solitary chromatic inflection in bar 13 – A♮ in the bass to point the final cadence in the section

In the second subject / B section:

- Considerably more chromaticism here which provides contrast and gives a much more colourful setting of the words
- A more melodic bass line, often in 3rds with the vocal line
- Frequent use of appoggiatura the end of phrases creating a sighing feeling; especially affecting is the D♭ to C on '*desio*' ('need') in bar 27 and 32 because the appoggiatura forms a diminished 7th above the E♮ in the bass

Second half: bars 51–91

This half is in two sections (bars 54–72 and 73–91) which have many similarities with each other – including the same text – but also some differences.

TEST YOURSELF

Compare closely the two passages and fill in the chart below to reveal the similarities and differences:

Italian text	English translation	Musical similarities	Musical differences
Parlo d'amor vegliando	I talk of love when waking		
parlo d'amor sognando	I talk of love when dreaming		
all'acqua, all'ombre, ai monti	to the water, to the shadows, to the mountains		
ai fiori, all'erbe, ai fonti	to the flowers, to the grass, to the fountains		

all'eco, all'aria, ai venti	to the echoes, to the air, to the winds
che il suon de' vani accenti	and the sound of my useless words
portano via con se	is carried away with them
portano via con se	is carried away with them

There is a small **codetta** from bar 92 which has a slower, thoughtful phrase that expresses some loneliness (it is almost like recitative) and which sets up a final phrase that is the perfect culmination to a fabulous aria.

LIBRETTOS AND LANGUAGE

Most of Mozart's operas have Italian librettos – opera was invented in Italy; however, he also wrote some operas in German, most notably *The Magic Flute (Die Zauberflöte)*.

A LEVEL ONLY

Bar by bar: Act 1 No. 7 Terzetto (Susanna, Basilio, Count Almaviva)

In the previous lengthy recitative Don Basilio has been voicing gossip and malicious rumour to Susanna while both Cherubino and the Count are hiding. This leads to a dramatic scene when the count emerges from behind a chair, and later, at bar 139, when the Count discovers Cherubino.

In opera, such shenanigans need dramatic pace that could be slowed by adhering closely to well-known musical structures; on the other hand, a complete absence of structural awareness will soon make a long movement take on a musically rambling, unsatisfactory quality which would be very alien to the Classical style.

Mozart finds a midway path here, which he achieves by capturing each character's mood and motive as the action unfolds (not without a degree of farce), but by carefully controlling his tonal centres and by having a sense of connection at various points in the music – for instance, the return of the Count's opening melodic idea at bars 101 and 147, and the re-use of Basilio's tune from bar 16 at bar 85 (though in a different key).

To understand the composer's great skill in this trio, complete the chart below:

Bars	Character(s) singing	Dramatic mood	Key	Musical means through which the dramatic mood is achieved
1–15	Count Almaviva	Authorative, disapproving	B♭ major	Short, blunt melodic lines with dotted rhythms Diatonic music throughout Energised fragments of rising scale in full string section in 8ves
16–23	Don Basilio	Obsequious, ingratiating	B♭ major	Conjunct falling phrases; homophonic accompaniment with chromatic twists that avoid any strong cadences
23–42	Mostly Susanna, Count & Basilio in backgound	Susanna is flustered and ashamed; Basilio and Count still in previous moods	F minor	Susanna's pain immediately conveyed by the upper chromatic auxiliary note on *ruina*. In the downward scale in bar 26, each step is foreshadowed by an anticipatory note on the previous half beat giving quite a breathless feel. As the emotion intensifies her entry on top A♭ (bar 35), followed by a diminished 7th fall, is quite melodramatic
43–61	Don Basilio & Count			
62–69	Susanna			
70–84	Don Basilio & Count			
84–92	Don Basilio	Obsequious again	E♭ major moving to B♭ major	Similar melody and accompaniment to bar 16
93–100	Susanna			
101–121	Mainly the Count, the others in support			
121–146	Count Almaviva			

The **final passage** of the trio from bar 147 to the end is the most substantial and involves all three characters singing most of the time. Both Count Almaviva and Don Basilio return to their initial melodic ideas at various points.

Keep an ear open for the bass line: there are some very effective dominant pedals which intensify the suspense of the dramatic situation and require resolution (as does the drama). There is also some wonderful chromatic harmony to enjoy, especially this passage at bar 195:

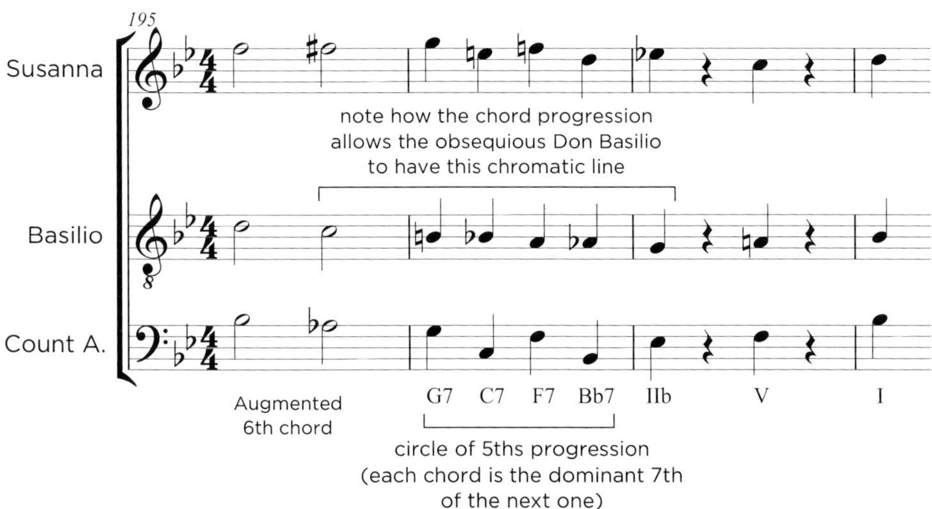

From bar 201 there is a winning passage with flowing quavers in octaves in the strings, sustained chords in the winds and the voices singing on the second and fourth beats of the bar; the combined effect is one of growing excitement and momentum as this long ensemble movement nears its close.

A LEVEL ONLY

Bar by bar: Act 1 No. 9 Aria (Figaro)

Non più andrai – Figaro's aria that brings Act 1 to a finish – is probably the best known tune form the entire opera. Cherubino is being sent away to become a soldier; Figaro teases him that this means an end to his adolescent flirtations with the ladies at court.

The opening section with its jaunty dotted rhythms and simple tonic-dominant harmony is immediately playful – but, in terms of the drama, in an ironic way – and has a once-heard-never-forgotten tune due to its clever design:

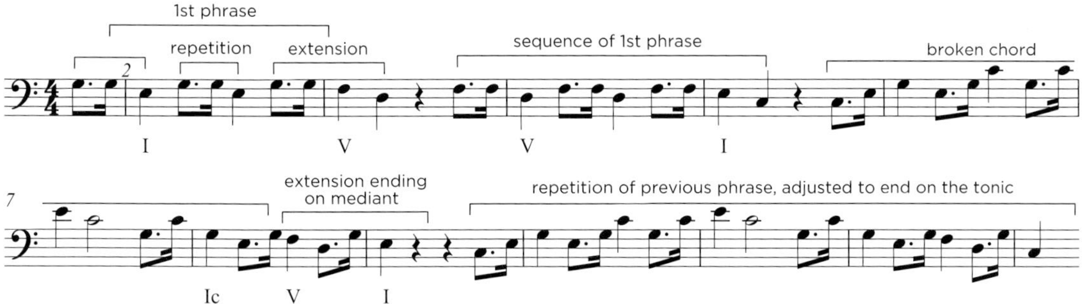

The term 'hit song' probably did not exist in 18th century Vienna, but it seems likely that Mozart knew this tune would be well received because he chose to make this aria a Rondo, and this melody is heard three times in an ABACA structure:

- **1 bar of introduction**
- **Bars 2–13** section A C major
- **Bars 14–31** section B G major
- **Bars 32–43** section A C major
- **Bars 44–77** section C starts in C major, passes through G major (bars 50–51) and E minor (bars 54–58), returns to C major (bar 61) and finishes in G major (from bar 70)
- **Bars 78–89** section A C major
- **Bars 90–101** coda C major
- **Bars 101 to end** Orchestra 'play-out' to end of Act 1 C major

TEST YOURSELF

Search this aria for two contradictory colours: things that are playful and pretty, and things that are militaristic and bombastic. You may wish to continue these lists:

Act 1 no.9 Aria	*Non più andrai*
Playful and pretty aspects	**Militaristic and bombastic aspects**
■ Turn played on downbeat of bar 3 and 5 by violins ■ Mini-flourish by oboes in 3rds at bar 9^2 ■ Sparkling semiquavers in 2nd violins and violas bar 14	■ $\frac{4}{4}$ = 'march' time ■ Dotted rhythms ■ Simple tonic-dominant harmony

A LEVEL ONLY

STRAND C:
The piano music of Chopin, Brahms and Grieg

Context: A brief introduction to Romanticism

The Classical style of Mozart was very much suited to the splendour of the Habsburg court and civic life in Vienna at the end of the 18th century. It encapsulated proportion, order and elegance. The 19th century, perhaps inevitably, brought new ideas to music and the arts in general. These fall under the umbrella of an aesthetic called Romanticism.

Among the ideas and influences on music in the 19th century were:

- Exploration and expression of the emotions
- The influence of the natural world
- The rise of virtuosity and celebrity among instrumentalists epitomised by the violinist Paganini and Liszt the pianist
- Improvements in instrument design and manufacture
- Programmatic music - music that tells a story (e.g. Berlioz's *Symphonie Fantastique*)
- Extremes of size from gargantuan pieces to intimate miniatures
- Nationalism - expressing a country's identity through music, perhaps with folk influences
- Increased complexity of musical language seen in greater chromaticism, more elaborate textures and new ideas on structural principles
- The rise of a wealthy middle class who embraced concert-going and were entranced by musical showmanship and precociousness

Many of these ideas were set in motion by Beethoven, who learned his craft in the Vienna of Mozart and Haydn, but took a new direction with the Eroica Symphony in 1803. He was also a pioneer in writing for piano with works of considerable diversity ranging from the mighty Hammerklavier Sonata to the six Bagatelles Op. 126.

The piano in the 19th century

After the harpsichord of the Baroque era, the Classical era had embraced a new instrument: the fortepiano. This allowed for greater dynamic range, but limited resonance and range of tone colour.

The early years of the 19th century saw some important developments that made the instrument more like the piano we know today (though there was still a long way to go). Its role was changing: it was a concert instrument rather than a domestic one. Composers were encouraged to see new potential for how they could write for it - the piano was a vehicle for pyrotechnics and social impact; yet their imaginations developed faster than instrument-makers could match - Liszt was known to break pianos in performance.

Compared to the fortepiano, the piano of the 19th century was an instrument of far richer tone, with more potential for sustaining sound and varying sonority. The sustaining pedal was more useful in producing rich texture and harmonic colour, and the instrument was more reliable across a wider range of pitch. This encouraged new ideas in how to compose for the instrument, for example the filigree flourishes that frequent Chopin's works, Brahms weaving the melody into a middle register often shared between the hands, or Grieg's open textures with ringing 5ths derived from mimicry of the Norwegian folk fiddle from Hardanger.

Fryderyk Chopin 1810–1849

Context

Chopin was popular with high society from an early age, both in his native Poland and subsequently in Paris for much of his life after 1831. He wrote almost exclusively for the piano and played in salons – venues for the wealthy aristocracy.

Detail from a portrait of Chopin by Eugène Delacroix painted in 1838 and now in the Louvre, Paris.

Although he wrote some large-scale pieces – three sonatas and two concertos – most of his pieces are single-movement pieces of a few minutes' duration. These come in various genres: preludes, waltzes, etudes, polonaises and mazurkas (both Polish dance forms) and nocturnes – a 'night piece' invented by the Irish composer John Field and taken up by Chopin to much acclaim.

These shorter pieces proved fertile ground for his music, which is often characterised by delicacy, elegance and intimacy. Their relative brevity dilutes the focus on structure and provides an appropriate timeframe for a more improvisatory approach to composition; many of his works were written down subsequent to performance in the salon.

LISTENING TO CHOPIN

Chopin's music is central to the piano repertoire. There are, therefore, many recordings, but a good way to hear it would be to ask pianists you know to play some for you and ask them about what makes his music so suited to the instrument and enjoyable to play.

Bar by bar: Nocturne in E minor Op. 72 No. 1

Chopin wrote 21 nocturnes, which are modelled on John Field's Nocturne. The Nocturne in E minor was first published in 1855, after the composer's death, but it was written quite early in his career, perhaps in 1829, and was Chopin's first attempt at a nocturne.

The tranquil mood of this reflective night piece is immediately set by the accompaniment pattern that is heard by itself for the first bar and continues throughout the piece with very little change of character to its flowing triplet quavers. These, in essence, form harmony through broken chords, but in the contour of the broken chord (with a mix of upward and downward leaps) and the frequent feature of the fifth note in the pattern being an upper appoggiatura to the sixth note, there is considerable beauty in the detail:

The structure of this Nocturne is not dissimilar to abridged sonata form (i.e. sonata form without a development):

- **Bars 2–22** A section (= first subject?) E minor (Exposition?)
- **Bars 23–30** B section (= second subject?) B major (dominant major)
- **Bars 31–46** A section E minor (Recapitulation?)
- **Bars 47–54** B section E major (tonic major)
- **Bars 55–57** Coda

However, as we shall explore, it doesn't sound like the sonata-form-dominated style of the Classical period, and this seems unimportant; instead there is a focus on sustaining the mood in a highly emotion-centred, Romantic manner.

Bars 2–22: A section

The A section begins with an 8-bar phrase which clearly comes in two 4-bar sub-phrases, and is – up to a point – immediately played twice:

However, there are various ways in which this is not a standard example of Classical periodic phrasing:

- The second 4-bar sub-phrase is very unlike the first
- The second phrase, instead of balancing the original 8-bar phrase, extends in a rather relaxed way to 13 bars
- Neither phrase cadences in the tonic
- The first half of the second phrase is a rather intricate variation of the first phrase

These traits point clearly to a more 19th-century aesthetic. Other Romantic factors include:

- The prefatory acciaccatura to the melody that leaps upwards by a 6th to the main melodic note
- Duplet quavers in the RH against the continuous triplets in the LH in bars 2 and 4
- Stretching of the beat at bar 3^4 through having the semiquaver that completes the dotted quaver in the right hand after the third triplet in the left hand
- Chromatic harmony used early in the piece: diminished 7th chords at bar 5^2 and 7^{3-4}, and an augmented 6th chord at bar 6^2 which is further spiced by a false relation between E♯ and E♮

The second half of the second phrase, in bars 14–22, is essentially in B minor, but the harmonic progression is very chromatic, including substantial use of the Neapolitan chord (C major) in root position *and* with its dominant 7th (G^7) in bars 14^3–15^4; before the 19th century, the Neapolitan chord was nearly always used in first inversion.

The ending of the A section on a tierce de Picardie in B minor sets up the potential for what happens next:

Bars 23–30: B section

This section offers a different melodic idea, which starts with simple minims in parallel 3rds, the second of which becomes a long, unadorned accented passing note. There is some sense of the tonality being B major, though the whole section is over a B pedal, and it can be seen as eight bars that decorate the dominant, not least due to moments suggesting E minor harmony at bars 25^4 and 29^{3-4}.

Although this section has some of the properties of a second subject (new idea in a dominant-related key), it does not feel like it makes for a sonata exposition:

- It is disproportionately short compared with the 'first subject'
- Its effect with the pedal note is more one of tranquil codetta than contrasting structural counterbalance

Bars 31–46: A section

The prolonged B major harmonies of the B section lead back to E minor and the return of the A section theme. One might conclude that this is a recapitulation, but its character is something else: it is altogether an intensification of the musical mood.

This is achieved through:

- The ***f*** dynamic
- Considerable elaboration of the melodic line using ornaments, fioritura (including sextuplets and demisemiquavers) and extremely high register

The restatement of the second A section phrase is less elaborate, but takes a different direction to stay in E minor, which – as before – it completes with a tierce de Picardie.

Bars 31–32 combine falling conjunct crotchets as found in the cadences of the opening phrases with the quaver upbeats at the start of the piece; the 2-bar pattern is then repeated but in a minor harmony version.

Subsection A'

This is based on the opening four bars of the piece, but with the first two bars with the melody inverted:

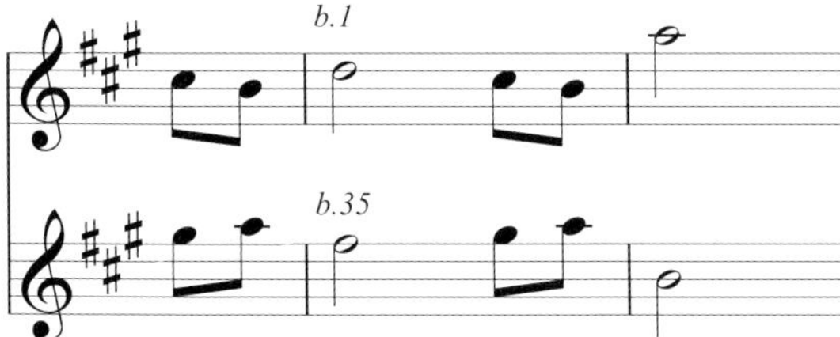

Other changes of melody and harmony are made here.

Subsection B'

This is similar music to the passage starting at bar 17, though the pedal note is now the tonic rather than the dominant. Also, Brahms now takes his cross-rhythms further here, incorporating a hemiola in bars 40–42, which starts unconventionally on the third beat of the bar:

Effect of cross-rhythm:

Section B

Subsection D

The move to F♯ minor brings a wistful quality to the music that is complemented by the duplets in the right hand against the triplets in the left hand. There is a Classical sense of proportion to the melody - two related 4-bar phrases - but there are typical Brahmsian hallmarks:

- The substructure of the melodic phrase, which instead of being four three-beat shapes is 4 beats + 3 beats + 2½ beats + 2½ beats
- The alteration to the segment of the melodic phrase, which is treated sequentially
- The harmonic rhythm, which gives a different asymmetric substructure in the left hand: 5 beats + 3 beats + 1 beat + 1 beat
- The tenor register countermelody split between the top of the left hand and bottom of the right hand, which echoes the melody almost canonically
- The intervallic augmentation used to convert bar 49 into bar 52 in both melody and countermelody

So here are three different rhythmic substructures happening simultaneously: the assumed triple metre, the melodic cross-rhythm and the harmonic cross-rhythm.

All of this, as well as the change of tonality and first use of triplets in the piece, gives a sense of a new section (the middle of the ternary form), but woven into the music are conjunct descending crotchets and these link the music to what has already been heard: bar 49^2 - 50^1 in the melody relate to bar 30^3 - 31^2, for example, and the pairs of crotchets in the countermelody are reminiscent of subsection B (bar 17).

Subsection E

This passage is the 'middle of the middle' and provides an oasis of rich homophonic music at the heart of the piece. Its main differences to the previous passage are:

- Tonality - we are now in the warm key of F♯ major
- Texture - after the three contrasting strands woven together in the previous passage, Brahms now writes with chords of six or more notes
- Rhythm - the flowing triplets and legato duplets of the previous passage are stilled; instead the music moves in hymn-like crotchets

Not all is new, however: the opening melodic shape here (bar 57) is the same as the previous section (bar 49), only converted into the major mode. The first four bars turn towards the relative minor of the dominant; as this is the very remote A♯ minor (key signature - seven sharps), for the ease of the pianist, Brahms writes two of the chords enharmonically, though this makes understanding the harmonic progression more challenging! The chord at bar 59^3 is actually chord II^7b; strictly, this should be a half-diminished 7th on B♯. The next chord at bar 60[1] is chord V, which would properly be written as an E♯ major chord, complete with G𝄪!

Subsection D

The return to F♯ minor brings back the main theme of the middle section. For four bars the texture is inverted so that the countermelody is now at the top of the music, while it is the main melody that is passed between the hands in mid-register. The accompaniment is again triplet quavers in the bass.

A few bars of extension (bars 73–76) lead back to the return of section A.

Section A

This is very largely the same as the first third of the Intermezzo; there are a few details that are altered for you to notice. The most significant is that subsection A is only played the once this time around.

Bar by bar: Ballade in G minor Op. 118 No. 3

Marked 'Allegro energico', this ternary form ballade certainly has energetic, even stormy, outer sections, but at its heart is a beautiful and unhurried middle section.

Bars 1–40: section A

This A section is itself also in ternary form:

- **Bars 1–10** subsection A G minor
- **Bars 11–22** subsection B E♭ major
- **Bars 23–32** subsection A G minor
- **Bars 32–40** codetta / link

Bars 1–10: subsection A

There is a muscular ***f*** opening with a chordal texture and resonant octaves in the bass and some staccato and accent markings. The subsection falls, unusually, into two 5-bar phrases, both essentially descending G melodic minor scales, the first dropping to the dominant at the end (to fit an imperfect cadence), the second finishing on the tonic (and a perfect cadence).

A feature of considerable effect is the harmonic rhythm. In the first two bars, there are two chords, but they are split asymmetrically to give 3 beats + 1 beat; in bar 3 this pattern is treated to rhythmic diminution with four chords in a dotted crotchet + quaver + dotted crotchet + quaver pattern:

Outline of opening:

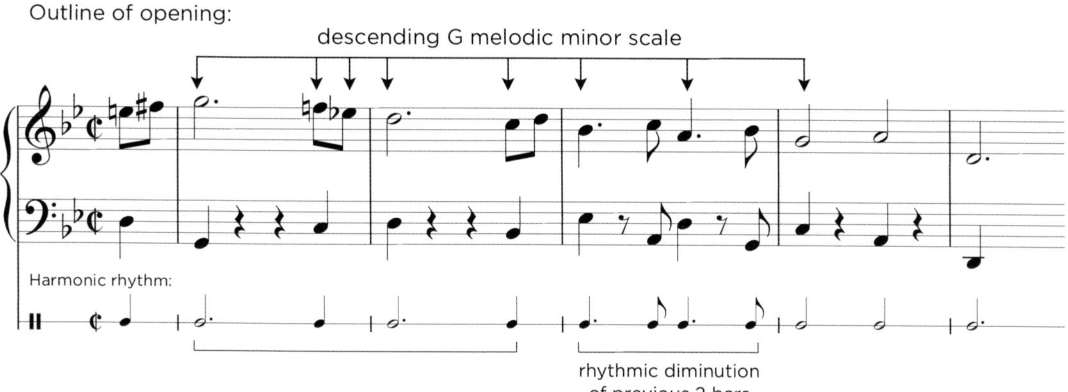

There are some important harmonic features here:

- The initial right-hand notes act as lower appoggiaturas to the subsequent D^7 chord
- The right-hand notes on the fourth crotchet of bar 1 are accented passing notes to a C minor chord (IV)
- The right-hand notes on fourth crotchet of bar 2 are lower auxiliaries; the subsequent chord is a colourful hybrid of a D major chord in the RH (V) but with a B♭ in the left hand that is the dominant of chord VI on the next beat
- The chord in the second half of bar 4 is a secondary dominant of D (V of V)
- The harmonic progression in bar 3 is based on the circle of 5ths

Bars 11–22: subsection B

Based in E♭ major – relative major of the subdominant, and therefore on the flat side – this passage sounds rather more mellow in character. The musical material is similar, however, but stretched over six bars, thereby delaying the momentum of the bar of faster harmonic rhythm.

As in subsection A, there are two matching phrases here; you may like to compare the harmonic progression that starts each one: they complement each other beautifully.

Bars 23–32: subsection A

The first phrase here is the same as the start of the piece. You may like to compare the respective second phrases to uncover some differences.

Consider:

- Anacrusis
- Melodic contour
- Harmonic progression

Bars 32–40: Codetta/link

The tonic major chord (G major) of the tierce de Picardie is sustained, with some decoration, throughout these nine bars, but almost immediately an F is introduced to suggest it has turned into a dominant 7th. Perhaps the middle section is going to be in the subdominant (C)?

Brahms has a better idea in mind. Though – literally – he never spells it out, he treats the F♮ as though it were an E♯ and therefore leaves the chord as though it were an augmented 6th chord on G and not G^7:

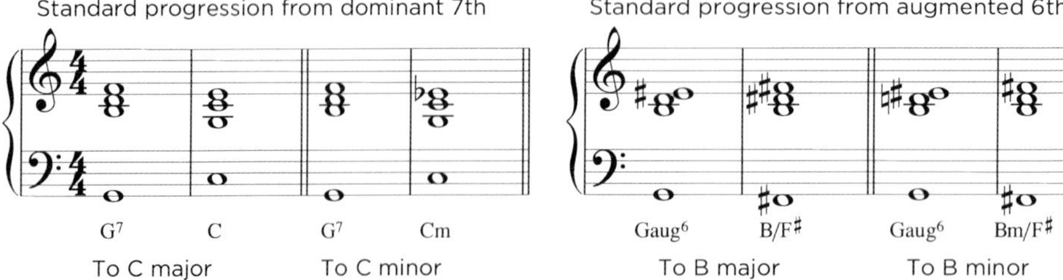

So the middle section of the ternary form will arrive in B major.

Bars 41–72: section B

The middle section is in many ways very contrasting, yet the ratio of ¾ to ¼ - as found in dotted minim + crotchet or dotted crotchet + quaver - remains very important here and ensures that there is no disconnect between the main sections of the ballade.

TEST YOURSELF

Use the chart below to find the important ways in which the A section and B section are contrasting:

	Section A	Section B
Mood		
Key		
Dynamic		
Articulation		
Phrase length		
Harmonic rhythm		
LH figuration		

There is an interesting moment midway through section B at bar 53 where a reminiscence of the section A material is heard for four bars, now in D♯ minor.

Bars 73–117: section A

The main body of this section is the same as the opening third of the piece; where it differs is in the codetta.

Here there is no tierce de Picardie at the main cadence (bar 108) and the G minor harmony dominates the closing bars. Just as an echo of the section A material appeared in section B, now the main section B idea appears in G minor at bar 114 to finish the piece.

OVERVIEW

The ballade has three significant tonal centres. In the following chart, fill in what material occurs in each:

G minor	
E♭ major/D♯ minor	
B major	

Now consider these three tonics – G, B and E♭/D♯. Can you see anything significant about them? What is the pattern they follow if you play them as an arpeggio over several octaves?

Edvard Grieg (1843–1907)

Context

Grieg was born in Bergen, and is – by a distance – the most famous composer to have come from Norway. That may seem like trivia, but it is highly significant: Grieg, on the fringes of Europe, found new ways to make music, embracing sounds that were indigenous to life in the isolated fjord communities of Norway rather than the eminent musical traditions of cultural centres like Paris and Vienna.

Portrait of Edvard Grieg by Eilif Peterssen painted in 1891.

GRIEG THE NORWEGIAN

Grieg wrote several pieces based on the 'Halling', a Norwegian folk dance. His final set of Lyric Pieces (opus 71) includes a fine example. Listen out for the drone-like perfect 5ths in the bass, present from the start, that imitate the sympathetic strings of the traditional Hardanger Fiddle (see http://bit.ly/GriegHalling).

Grieg's education included being sent away from home to study at Leipzig Conservatory from the age of 15. Thus he was able to find his own unique synthesis of mainstream European ideas and traditional Nordic musical instincts. As a result, he is considered one of the nationalist composers of the late 19th century – composers who captured a national identity in their music that was distinct from the dominant Austro-German tradition. Others in this category include Dvořák and Sibelius.

Among the features that Grieg assimilated from the folk traditions around him were:

- Melodies that have the dominant of the scale as their focus instead of the tonic
- Dance rhythms in compound time or triple time, especially emphasising the last beat of the bar, or final triplet of the beat
- Familiarity with, and fondness for, using modal scales
- Frequent changes of tonality during a melody
- Use of mordents to decorate melodic lines
- Use of open 5th as drones and pedal notes, derived from the 'sympathetic' (i.e. freely reverberating) strings of the local Hardanger fiddle

Also, from Norwegian folk music came his fascination with a simple three-note melodic shape that he used so frequently, sometimes known as the 'Grieg motif'. There are two versions: either a falling tone + minor 3rd, or falling semitone + major 3rd:

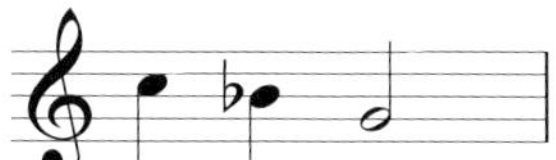

Much of Grieg's music was written for his home audience and therefore tends to be intended for domestic performance: piano miniatures and chamber music. There is a fine portrait by Peder Krøyer of Grieg at the piano accompanying his wife Nina, who was a singer; indeed, you can still visit his home near Bergen and imagine them there making music in their living room. Nonetheless, he wrote possibly the best known piano concerto of all time (it starts with the 'Grieg motif...').

Lyric pieces Op. 54

Many of Grieg's piano miniatures were published in ten collections called *Lyriske småstykker* (Lyric pieces); the first set was published in 1867 and the last in 1901. In total there are 66 pieces; many tell stories, capture a folk dance or simply distil a mood. The overall effect is like an artist's gallery.

The Op. 54 set is the fifth collection and contains six pieces; it was published in 1891. The complete set suggests some facets of Norwegian life:

1. *Gjætergut* (Shepherd's Boy)
2. *Gangar* (Norwegian March)
3. *Troldtog* (March of the dwarfs)

4. *Notturno* (Nocturne)
5. *Scherzo*
6. *Klokkeklang* (Bell-ringing)

The pieces set by AQA are numbers 2 and 4.

Norwegian March Op. 54 No. 2

This piece is a fascinating blend of march - two strong beats per bar, at times strongly articulated in the left hand - and dance, heard in the skipping compound rhythms of the melodic ideas. The form is a simple ABAB with a short coda to finish. Curiously, there is little sense of tonal contrast: the whole piece is essentially in C major, but chords from other keys occur in juxtaposition to add colour to the harmonic palette.

Section A: bars 1–40

There is a four-part texture at the start:

- The melodic line at the time
- Largely conjunct dotted crotchets in the inner parts that move in parallel 6ths
- A tonic pedal note that changes to the dominant at bar 6

The melodic phrase has various Grieg fingerprints - a syncopated rhythm that creates a dance feel with the tie from the third quaver of the first beat onto the second beat, mordents decorating the melody in bars 2, 6 and 7, and various appearances of the Grieg motif:

It is also very typical of Grieg that this tune, starting on the tonic, heads for the dominant as its destination. There is no complementary answering phrase; instead, the whole tune is immediately played a second time from bar 9.

From bar 18 the first phrase of the theme is used as the basis for a sequential passage where the melody is antiphonal between bass (left hand) and treble (right hand). Essentially, this is four bars of decorating an E major chord, first as a dominant chord (bars 18–19) and then as a tonic chord (bars 20–21), before doing exactly the same process to a G major chord:

In bars 26–40 there is little sense of melody; instead, the music fades away, the open 5ths in the left hand are reminiscent of distant church bells, and the filigree figure in the right hand like the echo of a Norwegian folk dance. The impression of bells is enhanced by the harmonic vocabulary here which has a series of unresolved dissonances in the chords:

Bars 27–28	D^7 / G moving to a G^{11} chord on the second beat
Bar 29	G^{11} moving to G^9
Bar 30	C^7 with no 3rd
Bar 31	F^9
Bar 32	a half-diminished 7th on B
Bar 33	E^{-9}
Bar 34	Am^7
Bar 35	Dm^9
Bar 37	G^9

These advanced chords are, of course, built on a circle of 5ths progression.

Section B: bars 41–79

If the final passage of section A is reminiscent of receding bells, the whole of section B would seem to be drawing ever nearer to church bells. The whole passage is built on the opening theme of the piece and makes full use of the wide range of registers available on the piano.

The internal structure of the section is:

Bars 41–44	Topmost register: an initial 4-bar phrase that is based on a C major chord
Bars 45–52	Topmost register: beginning with the same first bar, Grieg constructs an 8-bar phrase which – through various twists and turns – descends an octave. The melody is built from sequences, and – despite its register – is the bass line to some ultra-high chords:

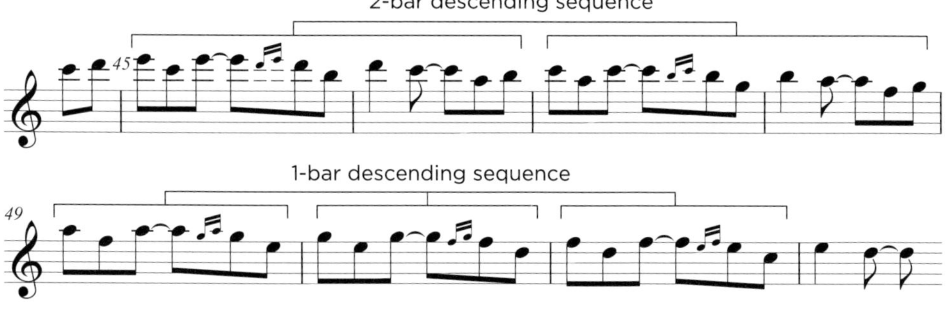

This passage is marked ***ppp*** throughout (but for the accents)

Bars 53–60 Treble register: this is an exact repeat of the previous eight bars, but played an octave lower and taking the music further down the registers.

This passage is marked with *cresc. molto*

Bars 61–68 Bass register: the same eight bars are played again; however, not only is this down an octave, but the left hand melody is now doubled at the lower octave.

This time the dynamic markings are ***f*** and *più* ***f***

Bars 69–72 This 4-bar phrase is, in essence, the same as the 4-bar phrase that began section B (bar 41), but with some significant differences:

Bars 41–44	Bars 69–72
Topmost register	Bass register
ppp	***ff***
Melody in single notes	Melody in octaves
Based on C major chord	Now played in A♭ major, though still with the melody starting on C

The other difference at this point is that the accompanying chords, which for the previous 24 bars were above the melody, are now exchanged for left-hand chords in the deep bass register.

Bars 73–76 The same four bars are played again, but now back in C major – the detour into A♭ major was for its rich colour as the music reached the low register, and not for structural purposes. The return of C major is marked with ***fff***.

Thus section B has explored a complete range of piano registers and a complete range of dynamics.

PIANO DEVELOPMENT

In registers and dynamic range this section is making distinct use of the 19th-century advances in piano technology.

Remainder of the piece

The whole of the first half of the piece is played again, but for a contraction of the opening 18 bars which are replaced with a simple, related 4-bar shape marked ***p*** *tranquillo.*

A similar phrase is used at the start of the short coda (bar 148) and from there it only takes another eight bars for the music to melt away on the tonic chord of C major with reminders of the dancing syncopated rhythm that has dominated much of the piece.

Notturno Op. 54 No. 4

Context

To gain a full understanding of this delicious miniature, it is important first to understand what was happening in the musical circles of Germany at the time. Earlier in this chapter we met Brahms and noted the fact that he was at the centre of the more conservative camp in a rift in German musical life. On the opposite side was the colossal figure of Richard Wagner.

Wagner does not appear on the AQA specification, so a disproportionately small amount needs to be said about him here. Where Brahms wrote Classically proportioned symphonies, Wagner wrote massive operas (or music dramas, as he preferred to think of them) – typically five hours long. Wagner's creativity (or at least his own estimation of it) knew no bounds: he wrote the words, he wrote the music; he required singers to sing like they never had before, and demanded new instruments to be invented; he even designed the theatre in which his pieces were to be performed.

Why is this relevant? Well, in 1876 Wagner's theatre opened with three complete performances of his *Der Ring des Nibelungen* (a four-opera cycle with approximately 17 hours of music), and in the audience was Edvard Grieg.

Midway through composing 'The Ring', Wagner had paused to compose a different opera – *Tristan und Isolde* – and in its opening bars he wrote one of the most (some would say *the* most) famous chords in all music:

There are some important aspects to this:

- The chord itself is, enharmonically, a half-diminished 7th. This would usually be written F, C♭, E♭ and A♭. It is called 'half-diminished' because the 5th is diminished, but not the 7th; a full diminished 7th on F would have A♭, C♭ and E♭♭
- It moves out onto a dominant 7th on E which is left hanging in the air in an unresolved way
- Although the E^7 chord may seem like V^7 (of either A minor or A major), the Tristan chord itself – with its D♯ – fits neither tonal context; the Tristan chord is therefore often thought of as the beginning of the dissolution of tonality which the 20th century was to bring to music
- The G♯ seems to be a long lower chromatic appoggiatura to the A
- The resolution onto E^7 is then given further chromatic elaboration by the accented chromatic passing note of A♯ as the chord changes, and the 5th of the chord is thereby approached from the sharpened 4th

Enough Wagner! What you will find in this *Notturno* is that Grieg uses many of the same features: the piece is full of chromaticism. He was not the only one: *Tristan* was one of the most influential pieces in the history of Western music. If *Gangar* shows Grieg's Norwegian colours, *Notturno* reveals that he was not an isolated Scandinavian figure, but thoroughly connected to the latest music craze in continental Europe.

The *Notturno* is in a ternary form:

- **Bars 1–14** section A
- **Bars 15–20** codetta / link
- **Bars 21–33** section B
- **Bars 34–54** section A
- **Bars 55–63** codetta

Bars 1–14: section A

It does not take Grieg long to embrace chromatic harmony here – the bass line in bars 1–2 descends the top half of the scale in semitones from tonic to dominant (remember – Grieg's music often leads to the dominant). The internal accompaniment pattern is simply a gently pulsating major 3rd, the ties between beats giving a nuanced character.

The melodic content is minimal: A falling to E in bar 2, though the anticipatory acciaccatura adds some flavour. Bars 3–4 are almost identical, but elaboration of the melodic shape adds a dotted rhythm and a G♯ to create a 'Grieg motif' shape.

In bars 5–8 there is the same descending chromatic bass line, but now rhythmically augmented; over this, rather than a static C major harmony, each bar has a rich chromatic chord:

Harmonic outline:

Analysis:

Bar 5 Half-diminished 7th on F♯ in second inversion

Bar 6 Half-diminished 7th on B, changing to diminished 7th on B on third beat

Bar 7 Half-diminished 7th on E in second inversion

Bar 8 Half-diminished 7th on A, changing to an augmented 6th Chord (German) on the third beat

Bar 9 $D^7 = V^7$ of V

Bar 10 The Neapolitan of G major in first inversion (Neapolitan 6th) – a very rich colour given we are heading towards G major, not G minor (where the Neapolitan is traditionally found)

Bar 11 $D^7 = V^7$

Bar 12 E^7, changing to a half-diminished 7th on A

Bar 13 D^7

Bar 14 G

The obvious aspect to this is all the complex chromatic (and therefore 'colourful') chords there are, but a closer examination will reveal the following roots of chords are being used:

Bars 5–10 F♯, B, E, A, D, A♭ (= G♯)

Bars 12–14 E, A, D, G

In other words, the whole passage, for all its chromatic nuance and complexity, is following a circle of 5ths progression.

The fondness for the chord of the half-diminished 7th is not the only Wagnerian aspect. The accented chromatic lower auxiliaries on the second beats of bars 5, 7, 9, 11 and 13 are distinctly *Tristan*-esque, as is the long flattened 6th appoggiatura of the final chord of the cadence in bar 14 (E♭ falling to D).

Bars 15-20: codetta/link

After all the rich harmonic moves of the previous section, there is considerable stillness in these bars. For bars 15-17 the same chord is used - it seems to be a half-diminished 7th on B, over which the right hand plays a delicate phrase that seems rather like a bird call, until the right hand crossing into the bass supplies a 5th in the bass (quite Norwegian) that makes the chord become dominant in character as G^9.

The music could return to the original tonic of C major here, but instead, Grieg transposes the whole previous phrase up a minor 3rd, similar to what he does in *Gangar* in bars 18-25. In bars 18-19 the harmony is thus a half-diminished 7th on D, and this turns into B♭^{9} through the bass notes (played by the right hand) in bar 20.

Bars 21-33: section B

In this magical passage Grieg indulges in some sumptuous harmonies that continue to move chromatically and which, together with the delicately rippling texture, flowing melodic shapes and extreme dynamic range, might lead the listener to imagine (poetically, perhaps) that he is painting a musical picture of the stars emerging in the night sky during this 'night piece'. Note the pianistic pedalling instructions: una corda in bar 21 (requiring application of the left pedal) and tre corda in bar 27 (the left pedal is released).

The harmonic content here is:

Bars 21-22	E^9
Bars 23-24	E^{11}
Bars 25-26	A♭^{9} in second inversion
Bars 27-28	D^9
Bars 29-32	G^{11}

These chords again form something of a circle of 5th progression, but Grieg is really using them for their sense of opulent colour rather than strong harmonic direction. That said, the choice of second inversion for the A♭ chord allows him to have a descending chromatic bass line - very appropriate for the piece given the way the *Notturno* begins.

Note how Grieg leaves an unresolved dominant 11th chord hanging in the air at the end of this passage - not unlike the end of the first phrase of *Tristan*.

Bars 34-54: section A

This follows the same course as the opening section up until bar 42. Here an additional bar before the Neapolitan harmony carries the music towards a destination on the tonic instead of the dominant (where the original section A finished); the Neapolitan chord in bar 44 is therefore D♭ rather than A♭ (as had been the case in bar 10).

From bar 49 there is a phrase of several bars that ends with a quickening harmonic rhythm and a striking chromatic descent of chords in bars 53-54.

Bars 55-63: codetta

The codetta refers back to the end of the original section A. After a bar's silence, the final perfect cadence is softened by using IIIb instead of V; the bass still goes G to C, but the E minor first inversion chord is softer than a G^7 chord would be. One can consider it a 'surrogate dominant' chord.

Pop music

OVERVIEW

This AoS looks at the changes and developments in pop music by looking at various contrasting pieces composed by six named artists:

- Stevie Wonder
- Joni Mitchell
- Muse
- Daft Punk
- Beyoncé
- Labrinth

This AoS is richly rewarding, because of the diverse styles, genres and emotional impact of the pieces available to study. When selecting your pieces by the named artists, aim to achieve contrast and variety that enable you to discuss changes in artistic style and the contrasting use of the musical elements.

Remember that the examiners are looking for you to communicate extensive musical detail in your responses, showing a full aural understanding of the pieces and artists in question. While it is always a bonus to enjoy the music you study, do keep this academic requirement in your mind when approaching the AoS.

The named artists and suggested listening in this AoS are:

Stevie Wonder
'For Once in my Life', from *For Once in my Life* (1968)
'Signed, Sealed, Delivered', from *Signed, Sealed, Delivered* (1970)
'Superstition', from *Talking Book* (1972)
'You Are the Sunshine of My Life', from *Talking Book* (1972)
'Sir Duke', from *Songs in the Key of Life* (1976)
Joni Mitchell
'Big Yellow Taxi', from *Ladies of the Canyon* (1970)
'River', from *Blue* (1971)
'Carey', from *Blue* (1971)
'A Case of You', from *Blue* (1971)
'Help Me', from *Court and Spark* (1974)

Opposite: Beyoncé

Muse
'Stockholm Syndrome', from *Absolution* (2003)
'Supermassive Black Hole', from *Black Holes and Revelations* (2006)
'Uprising', from *The Resistance* (2009)
'Supremacy', from *The 2nd Law* (2012)
Daft Punk
'Around the World', from *Homework* (1997)
'One More Time', from *Discovery* (2001)
'Harder, Better, Faster, Stronger', from *Discovery* (2001)
'Get Lucky', from *Random Access Memories* (2013)
Beyoncé
'Crazy in Love', from *Dangerously in Love* (2003)
'Listen', from *B'day* (2006)
'Singles Ladies', from *I Am... Sasha Fierce* (2008)
'Best Thing I Never Had', from *4* (2011)
Labrinth
'Earthquake', from *Electronic Earth* (2012)
'Express Yourself', from *Electronic Earth* (2012)
'Beneath Your Beautiful', from *Electronic Earth* (2012)
'Let It Be', from *Take Me To The Truth* (2015)
'Jealous', from *Take Me To The Truth* (2015)

STEVIE WONDER QUESTIONS

'Superstition' questions

1. Create 3–5 bullet points discussing how the following elements are used in 'Superstition'. Make sure you include references to the score/lyrics to justify your points:
   a. Melody
   b. Rhythm
   c. Texture
2. How does Wonder balance repetition and change in this piece? Give examples in your answer, discussing the overall structure of the piece.
3. Check your understanding of the following musical elements by writing a definition for each, giving examples of where they are used in the piece:
   a. Riff
   b. Glissando
   c. Breakdown
   d. Pentatonic scale
   e. Drum Fill
   f. Fade out

Answers at the back of the book

'For Once in my Life' (1968)

Using the analysis above as a guide, listen to 'For Once in my Life', trying to create your own analysis of the musical elements. In particular, consider the use of:

1. Melody and rhythm: the bassist James Jamerson creates a bass part where no two bars are the same, using a mixture of tied quavers, dotted rhythms and syncopation. Listen out for chromatic passing notes that allow the sense of rhythmic movement to continue in a quasi-**walking bass** style. Also, notice the use of **melisma** in Wonder's vocals and where they occur. Finally, check the ostinato figures of the accompaniment and the rhythmic drive this gives the entire piece.
2. Harmony: use of primary and secondary triads, the use of diminished 7th chords and how they are used as extended chords, the use of first, second and third inversion chords, the use of augmented triads, and the extensive use of extended chords, including 7th, 9th, 11th and 13th chords.
3. Tonality: the modulation up a semitone for the bridge, and how this modulation is achieved.
4. Structure: the use of three verses and a bridge, flanked by an intro and fade outro, and the subtle omission of a distinctive chorus section.
5. Timbre: the role of the backing vocals and harmonica, especially during the bridge.

'Sir Duke' (1976)

Listen to 'Sir Duke' and consider the analytical questions below:

1. Play through the three repetitions of the 1-bar riff in the introduction; how are each of the three bars related?
2. Compare the harmony used in the first part of the verse ('Music is a world within itself') with the harmonic progression of the end of the verse ('But just because a record has a groove'). How are they similar?
3. How does the bridge in 'Sir Duke' contrast with the bridge in 'Superstition'? Consider the use of texture and structural elements in your response.

Independent analysis

The specification also names two other pieces by Stevie Wonder that could be used as part of your studies for this unit. Remember that this list is a guide and is not prescriptive and that other pieces could be used if you choose:

- Signed', Sealed, Delivered' (1970)
- 'You Are the Sunshine of My Life' (1972)

For both pieces, create an analysis of the different musical elements, considering the use of instruments and voices, structure, melody, rhythm, texture, harmony and tonality. Each element should contain 3-5 important points with examples from the piece.

Give evidence
Wherever possible, support your arguments with examples from the score.

Joni Mitchell

Context

Born in Canada in 1943, Joni Mitchell is one of the most respected female singer-songwriters of the twentieth century. Her compositions often use a range of different guitar tunings as well as the lyrics frequently raising issues with popular social or environmental concerns. Songs that link to this idea of social change are often called **protest songs**. Her initial folk sound became increasing complex as jazz features, including more complex harmonies, were introduced into her work.

A **protest song** is a song which is concerned with social change – for example, environmentalism, human rights or equality. The songs can be in any musical genre.

'Big Yellow Taxi' (1970)

One of Joni Mitchell's most famous songs, 'Big Yellow Taxi' is known for its environmental concern within a quintessentially folk idiom. The line 'They paved paradise to put up a parking lot' was the most memorable line from the song, highlighting the negative impact of urbanisation on the landscape.

The acoustic guitar in the piece is tuned using an alternative tuning to the standard tuning. The guitar could be tuned to open E tuning (tuning the strings up from concert pitch, and putting them under extra stain) or to open D with a capo on the second fret to move the tuning into E without straining the strings. Both options are outlined in the table below (left to right, lowest to highest).

Standard	E	A	D	G	B	E
Open E	E	B	E	G♯	B	E
Open D	D	A	D	F♯	A	D

Bar by bar: Intro

The intro to the song is eight bars long and consists of strummed chords on the guitar. The first chord we hear is the subdominant (A major), which then has an F♯ added to it on beats 3 and 4 of the first bar. This creates an A^6 chord. This pattern is repeated in the second bar while the third bar moves the chord up a tone to the dominant B major before repeating the B–B^6 pattern for the next two bars. The final four bars are based around the tonic, E, which is played prominently in the bass of the chord while E^7 and A major chords alternate over the top of the **tonic pedal**. These three chords are all **primary chords**.

Primary chords are chords I, IV and V of a particular key. They are called primary chords as every note of the scale can be harmonised with these chords. **Secondary chords** (chords ii, iii, vi and sometimes vii) can be used to add greater harmonic venture to the harmonisation.

Bar by bar: Verses

There are four verses in total, each employing the chords outlined in the intro of the song.

Each verse is eight bars long and can be divided into different sections:

- The first line, lasting two bars. This uses A major and A^6 chords.
- Guitar strummed chords, lasting two bars. This uses the tonic pedal with E, E^7 and A chords over the top.
- The second line, lasting four bars. This uses A and A^6, B and B^6, and the tonic pedal with E, E^7 and A chords over the top.

The second verse uses more developed chord strumming patterns, giving the effect of thickening the musical texture, as well as adding a light percussive backing on hand-held percussion. This is also present in the third verse, which slightly changes the ending of the second line by adding a higher vocal line outlining E–C♯–B on the word 'please'. The fourth verse returns to the opening soundworld of verse two.

Bar by bar: Chorus

The chorus contains the lyrics for which the song has become famous:

Don't it always seem to go

That you don't know what you got til it's gone.

They paved paradise and put up a parking lot.

Shoo bop bop bop bop (repeat twice)

There is a slight change of harmony here, though the use of primary triads continues. Notice the use of E^5 or a **bare-5th chord** at the start of the chorus, which is then filled in to include both the 3rd and the dominant 7th of the chord. The final line of the chorus repeats the opening IV–V–I chord pattern heard in both the intro and the verse. Also notice the introduction of the triangle on the first two lines of the chorus, playing an initial dotted rhythm that becomes increasingly syncopated towards the end of the phrase. This varies the instrumental timbre and marks the change of section.

A **bare-5th chord** is a chord where the tonic and dominant are played without the third. This can also form a **power chord** on guitar.

At the very end of the chorus, a three-part chord is sung to nonsense syllables giving a sense of musical climax to the section. This is sung in close harmony, clearly confirming E major with the repeated E in the bass and B at the top of the chord. The middle voice and guitar change their notes subtly, allowing the final section of the intro to be evoked.

The final chorus is slightly different from the preceding three; it is initially played at a quieter dynamic, with the strumming being less prominent. It is repeated with the addition of a pause after 'that you don't know what you got til it's gone'. This effectively serves as a 1-bar breakdown, disrupting the flow of the music and giving the repetition of the final phrase greater prominence. The coda of the piece is provided by repeating the final line of the chorus, complete with a change in vocal **tessitura** and a final strummed E major chord.

JONI MITCHELL QUESTIONS

'Big Yellow Taxi' questions

1. Check your harmonic understanding by completing the following chords using staff notation:
   a. E^7
   b. Chord V^7 in C major
   c. V^+ in A major
2. How is textural variety achieved in this piece? Aim to give 3–5 points with examples from the piece.
3. Create a revision note for this piece, discussing the use of the musical elements and giving examples from the score.

'A Case of You' (1971)

Look for contrasts
Musical contrast in your set works is vital to allow you to have a range of musical devices to analyse in your work.

There is significant contrast between 'A Case of You' and 'Big Yellow Taxi'. 'A Case of You' is a slow, soulful ballad, complete with accompaniment on the Appalachian Dulcimer and Mitchell's haunting vocals. There is a sense of nostalgic regret throughout the song, including a brief link to Mitchell's place of birth via the Canadian National Anthem. In some performances of the song, an acoustic guitar and light percussion are added.

A **ballad** is a term used to depict a song concerned with the topic of love which is often slow in tempo to create the desired musical effect.

The **Appalachian Dulcimer** is a fretted string instrument with up to six strings that is played horizontally. Mitchell used this instrument extensively in her album *Blue* from which 'A Case of You' is taken.

Create your own analysis for 'A Case of You', using the points below to help. You may decide to structure your work by musical element, or by going through the piece chronologically discussing how these elements are used to create the overall musical effect.

- **Structure**: create a table of the main structural parts to the piece, including intro, verse, chorus and outro. How is repetition and change managed to ensure the music sustains musical effectiveness?
- **Harmony and tonality**: note the use of extended chords in the introduction, as well as the changes in harmonic rhythm - sometimes one chord per beat. What is the effect of the descending harmonic pattern in the verse on the overall effect of the song? How would you describe the vocal F♭ on the words 'northern star'? What happens in the outro? Why might this happen?
- **Rhythm**: note the use of a dotted rhythmic pattern in the verse, the change into $\frac{2}{4}$ for a single bar, and the subtle vocal syncopation including triplets and tied notes
- **Melody**: how does the vocal melody change between repeated sections? How would you analyse the tessitura of the melody in relation to the structure?
- **Texture**: how is textural contrast created throughout the piece?
- **Instruments and timbre**: how are the instruments used? Does Mitchell's vocal style change throughout the piece? Why might these changes happen?

'Help Me' (1974)

This song is from a later album than the pieces discussed so far, and the increasingly complex harmonic sound world showing influence from jazz is clearer. This is an excellent piece to use to discuss how Joni Mitchell's style changed over a relatively short period of time. Listen to the piece and consider:

- **Instruments and voices:** this is a larger ensemble of musicians, so there are more opportunities to hear contrasting timbres. Comment on the role of each different instrument you can hear, remembering that different recordings may use different ensembles of instruments
- **Harmony and tonality:** the piece has a far greater sense of harmonic venture than the songs previously discussed, including a wide range of chords that stray far from the tonic A major. Also consider the use of extended chords - 7ths, 9ths, 11ths and 13ths. Particularly effective is the use of **false relation** between melody and bass on the word 'free'

Having made notes on this piece, write an essay comparing and contrasting 'Big Yellow Taxi' with 'Help Me'. You should comment on the use of harmony and tonality, the use of instruments, and any other musical elements you feel are appropriate.

Independent analysis

The specification also names two other pieces by Joni Mitchell that could be used as a part of your studies for this unit:

- 'River' (1971)
- 'Carey' (1971)

For both pieces, create an analysis of the different musical elements, considering the use of instruments and voices, structure, melody, rhythm, texture, harmony and tonality. Each element should contain 3–5 important points with examples from the piece.

Muse

Context

Formed in 1994, Muse is an alternative rock band comprising Matt Bellamy, Dominic Howard and Chris Wolstenholme, which has released several studio and live albums, as well as touring globally. Their sound is often described as being progressive and aggressive in output, with different albums showing changes in musical style.

'Supermassive Black Hole' (2006)

'Supermassive Black Hole' comes from Muse's fourth studio album, *Black Holes and Revelations*, released in 2006 and entering the UK chart at No. 4. The song has also found fame from being used in *Guitar Hero III* and in the *Twilight* film series. The song represented a new sound world for the band, with disco, funk and R&B all being evidenced in the music. The structure of the song can be seen in the following table:

Section	Bar Length
Intro	16
Verse 1	8
Chorus 1	16
Verse 2	8
Chorus 2	16
Bridge	16
Chorus 3	16
Outro	8

Bar by bar: Intro

The piece opens with a 16-bar intro on bass, electric guitar and drum kit, complete with **distortion** and repeated **tonic pedal** outlining E minor, using a syncopated rhythm which accents the first beat of the bar. This opening section is divided evenly into two sections, with the second section containing greater quaver movement and the use of power chords.

At the end of both the first section (bar 8) and the second section (bar 16) the electric guitar has a decorated fill starting on a B♭ – the flattened fifth degree of the scale which acts as a **blue note** to the tonal palette. The use of N.C. at these points allows the melodic material to achieve prominence.

A **tonic pedal** is where the tonic note is sounded against a changing harmony. They can be found in the bass, or inverted to be on the top of the texture.

Bar by bar: Verses

The verses are made up of two 2-bar phrases which are then repeated, forming an 8-bar section. Power chords outlining the tonic, subdominant and dominant are heard in this section, with the majority of these harmonic changes happening at the end of each 2-bar phrase.

The vocal line, sung in **falsetto**, also contains the blues note heard in the introduction, though it is now notated enharmonically as an A♯ as it resolves up to a B, not down to an A as in the introduction.

Falsetto is the term used for men singing in a high treble or unbroken voice, in the same range as a soprano or alto.

Muse

Bar by bar: Chorus

The chorus establishes greater harmonic venture by using a wider harmonic palette with a steady harmonic rhythm of one chord per bar. Four chords are used in total, each being repeated four times:

A^5 G^5 B^5 E^5

What makes this section stand out from the preceding verse is the use of constant quavers in the bass. Rather than just outlining the triad in root or first position, as in the verses, the bass now anchors the tonic note and has an increasingly chromatic line to allow it to snake between the chord changes. This matches the descending chromaticism of the vocals to the lyrics 'Oh you set my soul alight'.

The second section of the chorus develops the first section by adding backing vocals singing in 3rds, outlining the chordal progression. The initial chorus melody is repeated over the top. The section ends with a 1-bar passage for guitars in octaves, descending from a B towards the tonic E via the flattened 5th note of B♭.

Bar by bar: Bridge

This section is again made up of two 8-bar phrases. The first of these links back to the introduction of the piece, with the guitars anchoring the E minor tonality. Over the top of this the title of the song is spoken with 'black hole' being accented and using crotchets rather than quavers. This section is also used as the outro, giving a sense of unity to the structure.

The second part of the bridge contains some new ideas developing the song:

- The electric guitar solo, which seeks to increase the temperature of the song by means of semiquaver patterns between A and B♭ – the 4th and flattened 5th degrees of the scale
- The bass outlining the chordal progression using a mixture of octaves, open strings and bare-5th chords

- The chords used are the same as in the chorus, with the omission of the B^5 chord and a faster and less predictable harmonic rhythm
- The electric guitar octaves in the final few bars contain a new note - C♯ (the major 3rd to A major) - but the sound world has prioritised distortion and **glissando** to such a degree that the harmonic implications of such a move are undermined

MUSE QUESTIONS

'Supermassive Black Hole' questions

1. What is guitar distortion? How is it used in this piece? What is the effect of this?
2. What are blue notes? How are they used in this piece?
3. How are melody, rhythm and texture used to help define the structure in this piece?

Answers at the back of the book

Uprising (2009)

Using the analysis above, listen to 'Uprising' and create your own analysis, considering the points below to help you:

- **Instruments:** what instruments are used and how are they used? What is drop D tuning? What is the role of the backing singers?
- **Harmony and tonality:** consider the triadic shapes of the opening synth, mixed with the use of pedals in the bass
- **Melody and rhythm:** how are chromatic inflections in the vocal part used? How is chromaticism used in the bridge, especially in the electric guitar? How is syncopation used within the compound time signature?
- **Structure:** consider the role of linking sections to the overall structure. How is the bridge linked to the Intro?
- **Dynamics:** how are these varied to help give the piece even greater contrast?

Independent analysis

The specification also names two other pieces by Muse that could be used as a part of your studies for this unit:

- 'Stockholm Syndrome' (2003)
- 'Supremacy' (2012)

Listen to each piece, analysing them fully. Use this analysis to consider how Muse's music has changed since the millennium.

Variety
Remember that other pieces by the named artists can also be used, providing they offer contrast to each other.

Daft Punk

Context

Daft Punk are a duo of French musicians who are central to the French house movement, writing in a predominantly electronic sound world. As well as many successful chart-topping songs, they also tour widely and are famed for their appearance, never being seen without their robot masks.

House music is a genre of music that emerged in the 1980s in America, characterised by the use of electronic drum machines, a $\frac{4}{4}$ time signature with four-on-the-floor bass drum and syncopated hi-hat cymbals and the use of synthesised instrumental lines.

Four-on-the-floor refers to the use of the bass drum of a drum kit on every crotchet beat in $\frac{4}{4}$ time. This was a central feature of 1970s disco with later house and techno styles using a similar pattern.

Daft Punk

'Harder, Better, Faster, Stronger' (2001)

Originally released in October 2001, this song is also available in a live version, released in 2007, which won a Grammy award for Best Dance Recording in 2009. The robotic nature of Daft Punk's physical look is evidenced musically within the song, with robot voice effects and heavy use of synth sounds. The song itself uses a sample of the song 'Cola Bottle Baby' by Edwin Birdsong, from his album *Funtaztik* (1981).

Sample is the term used for taking an extract of a pre-existing song (for example, a riff, ostinato figure or **hook**) and reusing it within a new piece.

Unusually, the piece does not have a conventional verse-chorus form, instead presenting the main 8-bar idea in an increasingly developed way, including the move to constant vocal quavers in the fifth repetition which extends beyond the 8-bar structure to move into an instrumental bridge section.

The melodic range is extensive, showing the influence of robotic vocals rather than acoustic performance. This includes bottom F♯s ('Our work is never over') which then jump up to a top C♯ – a range of over two octaves at the start of the contrasting bridge section. Here the vocal is increasingly instrumental in quality, as well as having greater rhythmic variety including tied notes and semiquavers, some of which are used in triplet shapes.

There are some particularly adventurous harmonic moments throughout the piece, including:

- The false relation between treble and bass on D/D♯ in the second part of the introduction, played in a one-beat riff, contrasting to the opening B minor syncopated section
- Use of extended chords in the verse including F♯m^{9}, E^{6}, D$^{7\sharp4}$ and F$^{\sharp sus4}$ with the last chord being in second inversion

- Use of a pedal on B with F♯^{7sus4} chords played over the top, helping to give a sense of harmonic ambiguity – the piece clearly starts with a B minor chord but the use of G♯ and D♯ helps to make the harmonic palette more complex
- The presence of C♮ in the break of the instrumental bridge, which acts as a blue note and when combined with the A, F♯ and D♯ of the instrumental parts suggests a passing diminished 7th chord

The electronic sound world is aided by use of technological processes, including use of telephone effect after the chorus. This is where **equalisation** (a type of filtering – in this case band-pass filtering) is applied to the music to change the audio effect.

Equalisation is a music technological process used to edit the low, mid or high frequencies of a particular track, changing the timbre.

Notice how the song ends on the last quaver beat of the bar with the lyrics 'Our work is never over' on octave F♯s with a solitary D quaver in the accompaniment; this helps to create **word-painting** by suggesting that the music itself is incomplete.

'Get Lucky' (2013)

One of the biggest songs of the new millennium, 'Get Lucky' has sold over 9 million copies and went into the Top 10 in 32 countries. The track combines the robotic vocoder sound of Daft Punk with the acoustic vocals of Pharrell Williams.

The song is based around B Dorian, using a chord progression of Bm^7, D, F♯m^7 and E. In a similar way to 'Harder, Better, Stronger, Faster', the use of G♯ gives a greater sense of harmonic venture while also conforming to the sixth degree of the scale in the mode.

A **vocoder** is a device used to synthesise a human voice, used extensively by Daft Punk to characterise their melodic vocal lines.

Dorian mode is a modal scale with a minor 3rd and minor 7th. It is exemplified by playing all the white notes of a piano from D to D, but can be transposed to other tonal centres.

The disco feel of the piece is captured by the common time signature, the tempo of 116 bpm and the use of simple four-on-the-floor drum patterns.

Bar by bar: Verses

The verses are characterised by the same chord progression used in the introduction, complete with vocals which start after a quaver rest on the second beat of the bar. This encourages the melodic lines to have a sense of purpose, further aided by the melodic lines crossing over to the next bar to form an accented passing note. Notice how the accompaniment uses syncopation to create rhythmic excitement, taking the focus away from the repetitive chord pattern.

Bar by bar: Chorus

The chorus features eight bars of more conjunct melodic writing in a higher tessitura followed by 12 bars of contrasting rhythmic ideas. The crossing of the barline, found in the verse, is also present here, as is the use of quaver rests. After eight bars, rhythm becomes the main focus of the song, using syncopation over the 1-bar chord sequence. Later in the song, these vocals are taken over by vocoder effects.

DAFT PUNK QUESTIONS

'Harder, Better, Stronger, Faster' questions

1. What are vocoder effects? How are they used within this piece?
2. What is sampling? Why might an artist choose to do this?
3. How is repetition and change balanced in this song?

'Get Lucky' questions

1. What is B Dorian? How is it used within this piece?
2. This song is one of the best-selling tracks of all times. In your opinion, which features of the music contribute to this? Write an essay discussing these points with reference to the elements of music.

Answers at the back of the book

Independent analysis

Having studied both 'Harder, Better, Stronger, Faster' and 'Get Lucky', consider the two other pieces which are listed on the suggested listening list:

- 'Around the World' (1997)
- 'One More Time' (2001)

Make a table discussing how each piece uses the various elements of music, being sure to give specific examples of how and where these elements feature.

Aural analysis
Listen to a wide range of music by the named artists to truly establish what their sound world is like and refine your aural analysis skills.

Beyoncé

Context

Born in 1981, Beyoncé was the lead singer of the **R&B** girls group Destiny's Child before embarking on a solo career from 2003. As a solo artist, Beyoncé has been exceptionally successful, winning a record-breaking six Grammy Awards in 2010 for her third album *I Am... Sasha Fierce*. In 2015 she was named the most powerful female musician of the year by *Forbes* magazine. Her performances are heavily choreographed in both live performance and on official videos accompanying her music.

'Listen' (2006)

Written specially for the 2006 musical film *Dreamgirls*, 'Listen' is a soul-R&B song discussing love, the power of following your dreams and finding your own way. The song uses a large instrumentation including a standard pop line-up of drum kit,

bass guitar, electric guitars and keyboard, but also adds in strings to help add extra drama at the end of the first verse. The drum kit enters for the first time at the first chorus, again thickening the texture and supporting the higher vocal tessitura during the more dramatic part of the song.

R&B is a genre of music combining elements from rhythm and blues (hence R&B), funk, soul, hip hop and pop. The genre is particularly noted for its use of vocal melisma to embellish the vocal line.

Melisma is the term used to indicate that many notes are sung to one syllable of text.

Bar by bar: Verses

The piece is set in the tonic key of B major. The verses utilise the lower tessitura of the voice, complete with a rather static accompaniment on piano (verse 1) with a chord change mostly every minim. Many of these chords are extended or made more complex by use of suspension.

Listen out for:

- The opening sus2 B major chord, creating a feeling of unresolved yearning
- The use of C♯m^7 in bar 3
- The 4–3 suspension (**sus4**) in bar 4

In the second verse, the voice embellishes the original melody and the piano line is joined by the drum kit on light hi-hat.

Bar by bar: Pre-chorus

The pre-chorus is a 4-bar section that is sandwiched between the verse and the chorus, with the purpose of raising the temperature of the music. Often this happens with changes of instrumentation or a gradual development of musical texture; however, in this song, there is a tertiary modulation from B major to D major which acts as the relative major to B minor – the tonic minor key. This, plus the use of triplets, instrumental glissando, 4–3 suspension and vocal embellishment via a melisma helps the arrival of the chorus to feel all the more acclaimed.

Bar by bar: Chorus

At ten bars long, the chorus does not seem to readily conform to the **32-bar song form** employed in many songs of this genre. On closer inspection it is comprised of two 4-bar phrases with a 2-bar linking codetta at the end.

The chorus is the climax of the piece, and this is achieved by a combination of the following:

- A return to the tonic key of B major
- Greater clarity in the vocal line with the word 'listen' being exemplified by following the bass in octaves
- The change in harmonic rhythm – two bars with one chord per bar followed by two bars with two chords per bar
- The use of V^7d which does not resolve to Ib, but instead to a D♯ first inversion chord (chord V in G♯m)
- The passing modulation to G♯m – the relative minor of B major– just before the codetta. This is achieved via a perfect cadence (notice the F𝄪, which is the leading note to the key)

The chorus is followed by a 4-bar bridge, based on the pre-chorus chord progression and featuring a greater amount of vocal embellishment, including a climactic melisma leading to a developed version of the chorus.

'Crazy in Love' (2003)

Whereas 'Listen' demonstrated a soul-R&B genre, 'Crazy in Love' is more pop-R&B with a strong funk influence. The track features rapped verses by Beyoncé's husband from 2008, Jay Z.

As you listen to the song, consider how the following elements are used:

- **Structure:** a standard verse-chorus form complete with four verses divided equally between Beyoncé singing and Jay Z rapping. These are flanked by choruses and a bridge to create musical contrast
- **Harmony and tonality:** the piece alternates between the chords of B♭ major and G minor with added 7th in the intro and chorus. However, the E♭ required for both these keys is not present; an E is present instead, suggesting the **Lydian mode** on B♭. Notice how the entrance of the vocals at the verse, complete with N.C. bar, outlines D and A - tonic and dominant in D minor - with an F in the bass forming a first inversion chord, matching the key signature of one flat
- **Melody and rhythm:** the verses use a 1-bar vocal riff employing subtle syncopation and semiquavers, making the piece feel faster in tempo than it actually is. The chorus employs a similar device using the notes D, F and G, forming a hook; the last two bars of the chorus use backing vocals to give a complete chord of G minor over the B♭ and Gm^7 chord pattern
- **Instrumentation:** the standard pop ensemble is joined by synth brass, which plays a sample from the 1970 song 'Are You My Woman? (Tell me So)' by the Chi-Lites. Also notice the prominent use of cowbell

The **Lydian mode** is a major scale with an augmented 4th, giving an exceptionally bright character. On the piano, it is best represented by playing all the white keys from F to F.

BEYONCÉ QUESTIONS

'Single Ladies'

Listen to 'Single Ladies' and answer the questions below:

1. What is the effect of the first verse and chorus having N.C. bars with a prominent drum beat?

Less can be more
Remember that the absence of something can also create musical interest and therefore warrants discussion; here, the N.C. bars have a profound effect on the music.

2. At the repeat of the first chorus, the bass enters with a new pattern using C♮. How does this line impact on the harmonic rhythm of the song?
3. Which musical element do you think is most significant to the song's success? Give a detailed explanation for your answer.

Answers at the back of the book

Independent analysis

The suggested listening also includes the following track by Beyoncé:

- 'Best Thing I Never Had' (2011)

Listen to this piece and analyse it for the elements of music you can find in it, giving specific examples of how the various elements are being employed.

Listening

Using any of the tracks listed, make your own listening question showing your awareness of how listening is assessed in the final examination. You should show a range of short answers and longer responses.

Labrinth

Context

Timothy McKenzie, better known as Labrinth, is an English singer-songwriter who was born in 1989 and has had several popular songs since his debut in 2010. Labrinth's style shows influences of electronica, rap, pop and ballad styles, with Tinie Tempah and Emeli Sandé featuring on some of his songs.

'Jealous' (2015)

MTV described this song as being a 'heart-breaking ballad' and from the very first bar it is difficult to disagree with this. The combination of piano, synth strings, backing vocals and Labrinth's haunting voice, together with the expressive five flat key signature and the rubato moderato tempo, all combine to help the emotional effectiveness of the song.

Bar by bar: Introduction, verses and choruses

The introduction, scored for solo piano, is eight bars long and uses a simple melody and accompaniment texture, with the right hand playing a melodic line using acciaccaturas and a simple accompaniment using bare-5th chords in consecutive 5ths motion. The ending of the introduction appears to sample 'Fields of Gold', made famous by Eva Cassidy and later Sting, using an interrupted cadence with a note of anticipation to give a chord of B♭ minor.

The verses are equally divided into 2-bar melodic shapes, making evocative use of the interval of a major 6th and an often downwards falling profile. The accompaniment pattern from the introduction continues, with subtle backing vocals and strings being added in later to develop the music.

The chorus is based around a four-chord pattern of D♭ major, B♭ minor, E♭ minor and A♭ major with a 7th. This corresponds to I, vi, ii, V^7 in D♭ major. To add extra emotional emphasis to the song, the lyrics 'thought you'd come back, tell me, all you found' use an upward resolving appoggiatura on C and D♭, initially producing a sharpened 4th over the chord of G♭ major, then a sus2 over B♭ minor. Such melodic features play to the meaning of the song and help to enliven the harmonic palette.

Bar by bar: Bridge

The bridge offers significant contrast in terms of harmonic venture and increased instrumental roles, changing key towards E major/C♯ minor. This contrast is achieved by using the enharmonic of D♭ (C♯) and more advanced chords including a diminished 7th on G that resolves to an F♯$^{7\sharp9}$ chord, creating a greater sense of harmonic ambiguity. The strings have an increased role to play here with a new ascending countermelody that works in between the vocal triplets. This section leads to a repetition of the chorus, complete with a change in chord pattern on 'but I always thought you'd come back', where a B♭$^{7\flat9}$ chord is used, resolving down to an A major chord. B♭ is the flattened 5th in E major; the resolution by a semitone between the B♭ and A gives an almost **Phrygian mode** quality to the music. It is also the original tonal centre of the piece - word-painting to the words 'come back'. The piece ends with the same interrupted cadence as heard in the introduction, ending on a C♯ minor chord.

The **Phrygian mode** is a minor mode complete with flattened second degree of the scale, giving it an intensely dark character. It is best represented by playing the white notes on a piano from E to E.

LABRINTH QUESTIONS

'Earthquake' (2012)

This piece contrasts strongly with the ballad style we saw earlier, with a more electronic sound world featuring elements of rap with a much faster tempo. Listen to the song, considering the following points to help your understanding:

- **Instruments**: what instruments can you hear? How are they produced?
- **Structure**: how is unity and variety balanced with the different sections?
- **Harmony and tonality**: how would you analyse the harmony of the opening (constant quavers) and the main hook (four bars before the vocals start)
- **Rhythm and texture**: how does the piece create rhythmic variety? How is texture linked to this use of rhythm?

When you have formulated your ideas, share them with your peers to see if they have similar or contrasting points and examples.

'Beneath Your Beautiful' (2012)

This song has many similarities to 'Jealous' in terms of being an emotional ballad. As you listen to the piece, consider the following questions to develop your understanding:

1. Create a table outlining the overall structure of the song
2. Using Roman numerals, analyse fully the opening four-chord pattern
3. What musical term best analyses the melodic line of the opening verse?
4. How does the chorus achieve contrast with the verse?

5. Bar 44 of the song (to the lyrics 'I just wanna know') contains an advanced chord which then resolves to the dominant. How could you analyse this chord?

Having established the answers to these questions, consider making a bullet-point list of how this song uses the various elements of music, giving examples of where they occur where possible.

Independent analysis

The suggested listening also contains two other works which you could use to develop your understanding of Labrinth's musical style:

- 'Express Yourself' (2012)
- 'Let It Be' (2015)

For both pieces, create an analysis of the piece in terms of their musical elements.

SAMPLE ESSAY QUESTIONS

Essay advice
Before you start, review the advice on writing essays at the end of Chapter 3.

Each essay is worth 30 marks and should take 45 minutes to complete.

For AS Level

1. Referring to the music of one or more of the named artists, comment on how their musical style has changed. You should reference at least two contrasting pieces, commenting on use of melody, harmony and tonality, structure, rhythm, melody and texture as appropriate.
2. Referring to the music of one or more of the named artists, comment on the view that a successful pop song relies solely upon a four-chord progression and a memorable hook.

For A Level

3. 'Pop music from 1970 to the present day has undergone some significant stylistic changes.' Referring to the music of at least two of the named artists, describe in detail some of these developments.
4. Choose pieces by two named artists that you have studied, explaining their contrasting approaches to harmony and tonality, rhythm and texture.
5. Choose two contrasting genres of pop music, commenting on how each artist manages to reference this style. You should refer to at least two published works by two different artists.

Music for media

OVERVIEW

This AoS includes a range of fantastic music for film or games written by the following named composers:

- Hans Zimmer
- Thomas Newman
- Bernard Herrmann
- Michael Giacchino
- Nobuo Uematsu

Approaches to this AoS

Within this AoS there are five composers to choose from, each with different examples of their work. The suggested listening list includes blockbuster films, animated films and gaming music.

To try to study every piece in the suggested list would only provide an overview to the AoS and would probably lack the detail required at this level: be selective with your choices.

Film music
Hans Zimmer
Pirates of the Caribbean
Inception
Gladiator
12 Years a Slave
The Dark Knight Rises
Rain Man
The Lion King
Thomas Newman
American Beauty
Skyfall
Saving Mr. Banks
The Shawshank Redemption
Finding Nemo

Opposite: *Gladiator*

Bernard Herrmann	
Psycho	
Vertigo	
Citizen Kane	
North by Northwest	
Taxi Driver	
Michael Giacchino	
Call of Duty or Medal of Honor	
Lost	
Up	
The Incredibles	
Mission impossible III	
Star Trek into Darkness	

Gaming Music	
Nobuo Uematsu	
Final Fantasy	'Opening medley'
	'Rebel Army' (II)
	'Terra's Theme' (VI)
	'Aerith's Theme' (VII)
	'One-winged Angel'
	'Fragments of Memories' (VIII)
	'Vamo' alla Flamenco' (IX)
	'At Zanarkand' (X)
	'Ronfaure' (XI)
Lost Odyssey	'Light of Blessing'/'A Letter'
Blue Dragon	'Cave'

When selecting pieces to study, it is important to know something about each of the named composers and about their style and use of musical devices. When picking your music to study, choose extracts which represent contrasting scenes and emotions to explore how the composers achieve this with their music.

It's important that you understand well how the music is constructed and how it links to the action on screen. Avoid just studying films you enjoy and instead celebrate the diversity of the genre in your approach to the AoS.

In the chapter that follows there is a detailed approach to two contrasting scenes from the 2000 film *Gladiator* as well as a character scene from *Pirates of the Caribbean: Dead Man's Chest*. Subsequent to this are shorter approaches to contrasting pieces by the other named composers, giving you room to extend your understanding of this modern and exciting genre of music independently.

FOCUS ON THE MUSIC

When writing about music, always emphasise musical detail rather than cinematic action or description. Identify the elements of music and link them to the score/soundtrack where possible.

Hans Zimmer

One of the most famous names in regard to writing music for film, Zimmer has worked on many popular and award-winning performances, writing music that is integral to the action onstage and is popular in its own right.

Gladiator

Released in 2000, *Gladiator* took over $450 million at the box office globally, winning many awards including Best Picture, Best Actor (Russell Crowe) and other Oscars at the 73rd Academy Awards. The soundtrack, composed by Hans Zimmer and featuring the distinctive vocals of Lisa Gerrard, was nominated for an Oscar and has become one of the most famous pieces of music for film in recent years.

Hans Zimmer

Excellent resources on the making of the *Gladiator* soundtrack are available online, where Hans Zimmer discusses the creative process he used to create the soundtrack, and how he and Lisa Gerrard worked together to create the final soundtrack. See http://bit.ly/MakingGladiator1, http://bit.ly/MakingGladiator2 and http://bit.ly/MakingGladiator3.

The Battle

This is the first full scene of the film, depicting the Roman army preparing and engaging in battle with Germanic tribes. This battle is of significance, since it is the last pocket of resistance in the Roman Empire. The leader of the Roman army, General Maximus Decimus Meridius (played by Russell Crowe) is victorious in the battle, allowing the war to be won in favour of Emperor Marcus Aurelius. The scene is exclusively seen by the audience from the Roman side, and the extract is excellent in showing the preparation, duration and final execution of battle. It is an exciting start to the action. The analysis is based on the battle scene being 10'02" in duration.

EXPECTATIONS

What might we expect the music to an ancient battle to sound like? Discuss as a class and write down your thoughts including types of instruments, use of tonality, rhythm, melody and texture. Order your thoughts in the way you feel is best to discuss as a class.

Opening Scene (0'00"–0'59" soundtrack, 2'35"–4'07" film)

The epic nature of the film is captured in the opening music; a theme presented with percussive accompaniment evoking the anxiety at the start of the battle.

Consider how this opening idea is constructed:

- The use of 4-bar melodic phrases that effectively give a question and answer feel
- The initial melodic span of a minor 6th
- The modulation from the tonic D minor to the relative major F major at the end of the first phrase and then to other related key centres
- The use of **dominant pedal** (on a C) in the second answering phrase
- The use of **ostinato** in the accompaniment

The instrumentation here is central to evoking the desired effect. Notice the use of strings on the melody and accompaniment, and the use of militaristic percussion playing a repetitive ostinato using a crotchet-crotchet-crotchet triplet rhythm.

The theme uses **diatonic functional harmony**, modulating to the subdominant key of G minor via a perfect cadence before reintroducing C♯ to move the music back to D minor by means of another perfect cadence.

Towards the end of the extract, the melodic idea gives way to more chordal writing, complete with **suspensions** including 4–3 and 9–8, as well as use of first inversion chords.

Notice the move to E♭ major - the **Neapolitan key** of D minor - which helps to intensify the harmonic palette. Despite this apparent change in writing, the opening melodic idea does still feature here - developed by means of rhythmic **augmentation** to make the brief move to an E♭ chord all the more effective. Also notice the rising chromatic scale which starts at this point, presented by high violins and helping to raise the excitement of the unfolding action. This music is extended to match the drama on screen in the film version.

STORYBOARD

Watch this opening scene, using the analysis above to link to the unfolding drama. What is happening on screen when these musical devices occur? Create a storyboard outlining your thoughts. Be sure to include a time frame using timings from the film.

Highlight the musical elements
Your storyboard can include brief plot lines, but should focus on the musical elements in detail. Giving timings is useful where possible.

'Horde say No' (0'59"-1'27" soundtrack, 4'07"-5'07" film)

The scene is broken by new action on the screen. A Roman rider, sent out to negotiate with the Barbarian enemy, is returned on a horse to his comrades *without* his head.

This results in a swift change of musical temperature, including:

- Use of silence for dramatic effect
- Low male vocal sounds with vibrato, using the notes F-E-F-G♯, which creates a sense of harmonic unease, singing nonsense syllables in a moaning, pained fashion
- Increase in use of sound effects, including wind and wave sounds and a **tonic pedal** played four times with **delay**
- Use of a low guitar sound using semiquavers
- The less predictable movement of this section, avoiding regular ostinato figures, creating anticipation

It is clear from this part of the scene that the enemy has no desire to surrender and that a battle is therefore a certainty.

GENRE FEATURES

As you work through this chapter, build up a list of musical features especially characteristic of cinematic music.

'Preparation for Battle' (1'27"–4'37" soundtrack, 5'07"–7'40" film)

The pace of the music continues to increase here with strong use of rhythmic devices to drive the music forward. Notice how the opening theme is now heard in the bass registers in the strings, transforming its effect from anticipation to a sense of foreboding of the action to come.

The combination of rhythmic drive and ostinato figures helps to create a strong sense of excitement. The melodic shapes here are altered to become increasingly chromatic and chaotic, creating a second thematic idea – notice the use of the D minor scale with added C♯ at the bottom and G♯ at the top, creating a whirling effect matching Maximus's line of 'unleash hell'.

Maximus then moves to rally his troops and the music becomes appropriately battle-like, with trumpet fanfare calls with imitation in the lower strings. The music even triumphantly moves to a major key briefly, showing the excitement that the troops have for the battle, and the overall prospect of peace in the Empire.

The music surges with string trills and severe crescendos, building tension as the first flamed arrow is delivered, signalling the start of the battle.

BUILDING TENSION

How does Zimmer create tension in the opening of this scene? What is the effect of this on the viewer?

'The Battle' (4'38"–8'40" soundtrack, 7'40"–11'03" film)

The main action of the scene takes place here and the music also enters its climax. There are sounds of swords clashing, arrows flying and fire-ball canons being launched, and this almost certainly heightens the effect of the film.

The exhilaration of battle is represented musically in several different ways:

- The use of pedals, sometimes inverted to the top of the texture, with brass underneath evoking hunting horns
- The use of **cross-rhythms** and accented weak beats to destabilise the time signature
- The use of the opening theme presented several times in the tonic key of D minor, often with the lyrics 'stay with me' as the characters enter the fight
- The use of the second theme when the Horde are entrapped by the Roman soldiers
- The use of $\frac{5}{4}$ time signature with accents on beats 1, 3 and two quavers on beat 5
- The use of surging crescendo, sudden diminuendo and string trills to create anxiety and excitement
- The use of bells and gongs to heighten the effect of the battle

As the battle continues, the music shifts in focus, suggesting that the battle has been won despite the continuation of fighting.

MUSICAL EFFECT

How does the change in the music here heighten the effect of the visuals? Asking yourself questions like this will help you to analyse the musical effect.

COMPARISON

The score for this scene was subject to a lawsuit from the estate of English composer Gustav Holst, who wrote *The Planets*. The argument was that the music of 'The Battle' had been plagiarised from 'Mars - The Bringer of War' from Holst's suite. Listen to both pieces; to what extent do you agree? You should find both similarities and differences to support your answer.

Victory (8'40"–10'02" soundtrack, 11'03"–12'18" film)

A **tonal** shift to C major marks the turning point of the battle, complete with dominant pedal on G. Here the main theme is presented, in this new major key, representing the Roman victory. However, this is far from being a celebration. The Romans have suffered heavy losses and the music here evokes that sadness.

This is achieved by:

- The use of dominant pedal which lacks resolution to the tonic, instead resolving to a chord of A minor to give an **interrupted cadence**
- The string instrumentation coupled with Lisa Gerrard's haunting vocals
- The use of suspensions including 4–3 and sharpened 4–3, evoking the **Lydian mode**
- The expansive use of dotted minims creating a great feeling of space
- The slower harmonic rhythm
- The **modal** ending, using an Em - A progression
- The lack of resolution to C major despite the use of dominant pedal; when C major chords are heard, they are in first or second inversion
- The absence of the driving second theme, heard so extensively in the battle itself

REVISION NOTES

Create a formal revision note for this scene, outlining how the different parts of the story use the musical elements and musical detail to support the action on screen; track this using precise links to the score/timeline. You should include references to instruments, structures, melody, rhythm, texture, harmony, tonality and the effect of the music.

'Now We Are Free'

In contrast to the opening battle scene, 'Now We Are Free' is taken from the very end of the film, after Maximus has had his revenge on the corrupted Emperor, Commodus. Maximus, injured from the fight, falls to his death having ordered the release of the prisoners and set in motion the reforms required to set up a new Roman Republic.

The film imagery here is central to this musical landscape; Maximus is shifting in consciousness, being both in the present and thinking of his wife and son, to whom he will return in the afterlife. The music clearly evokes rural ideas, heard at the very start of the film, as well as formally presenting a theme that is passionate in character. In contrast to the chaos of the battle scene, here we have a far greater feeling of peace and serenity, as well as a sense of conclusion as the film ends and the credits roll on the screen.

THE FINAL SCENE

Watch the final scene of the film, from just before the fight between Maximus and Commodus to the end. How does the music support the action on screen? Do you feel 'Now We Are Free' is an appropriate ending to the film?

Analysis

'Now We Are Free' is structured in an overall **ternary form** (ABA) with some repeats to allow melodic and instrumental embellishment.

A Section

The A sections are characterised by constant quavers played on a guitar sound effect against a string accompaniment, using a dominant pedal (on E) and an ascending bass line using an additive rhythm of 3 + 3 + 2 quavers. The chord sequence here is established with a harmonic rhythm of one chord per bar:

A	E	A	D	A	E	F♯m7	E	A	E	A	D
I	Vc	Ib	IV	Ic	V	vi	Vb	I	Vc^{4-3}	Ib	IV^9

For the most part, this allows the dominant pedal to continue throughout the chord progression, not only as a consonant note, but also as a dissonant note - for example, by being played over a D major chord, becoming an unresolved sus9 chord. Sometimes this appears on the top of the texture, creating an **inverted pedal**.

The A section then repeats, adding in Lisa Gerrard's hauntingly expressive wordless vocals which sound quasi-improvisatory over the chord sequence. Notice how the constant quavers continue, albeit reduced to the background. The melodic ideas here feature triplets and **push rhythms** which anticipate the beat and suspensions.

B Section

The B section starts with an instantly recognisable theme with a new chord sequence and change in harmonic rhythm.

This melodic idea is full of musical expression, achieved by the following devices:

- The broken chord ascent (C♯–F♯–A) using the additive 3 + 3 + 2 rhythm from the A section
- The melodic fall of a minor 7th (from A to B)

- The move towards F♯ minor rather than A major, though notice the lack of qualifying E♯ to confirm the key
- The change in harmonic rhythm - the fastest harmonic rhythm reaching one chord per crotchet beat, though minim movement is still prominent
- The use of a countermelody an octave higher than the vocal melody on another voice, complete with embellishments to thicken the texture
- The increased role of percussion towards the end of the repeat

The second part of the B section is more upbeat, focusing more on A major tonality. However, many of the chords are **open-5th chords**, lacking the important 3rd. Notice the **conjunct** falling pattern of the melody, forming a 2-bar question and a 2-bar answer complete with subtle syncopation. The countermelody, hushed in the background of the texture, combines with a more active percussion part to become the climax of the piece.

A' Section

The rejoicing of the B section is left hanging on a lonely E (the dominant), instantly reducing the texture and using silence for dramatic effect. This leads into a developed reprise of the initial A section, with some important changes to alter the musical effect.

The tempo is freer, prioritising the vocal inflections, and the harmonic rhythm is again slow, with one chord per bar played on the strings. The ascending conjunct bass line from the opening is also present, though now changed to semibreves rather than having the movement of the additive rhythm. The guitar idea from the opening is also present, but is very much in the background of the texture, making it inaudible in places.

The emotional impact of this closing section is aided by:

- The reduction in rhythmic movement in the accompaniment
- The ascent of the bass, linking to the plot
- The improvisatory nature of the vocals, including use of semiquavers
- Use of suspensions in the vocal part, including 4-3 and 9-8 suspensions
- The final **perfect cadence** which, after a lengthy 4-3 suspension, resolves via a note of anticipation to the final A open-5th chord

COMPARE AND CONTRAST

Compare and contrast how 'The Battle' and 'Now We Are Free' create different scenes to match their respective plots. You should refer to instrumentation, harmony, tonality, melody, rhythm and texture, as appropriate.

Compare and contrast: these words are asking you to discuss similarities and differences.

Pirates of the Caribbean

The *Pirates of the Caribbean* franchise has produced four films with a fifth due for release in 2017, all based upon the theme park ride of the same name to be found at Disneyland. Starring Johnny Depp as Captain Jack Sparrow, the film franchise has taken substantial profits from the box office, with *Dead Man's Chest* earning over $1 billion.

It's worth noting that Zimmer only composed the title music in the first film, *Curse of the Black Pearl*, whereas all the music in *Dead Man's Chest* was scored by Zimmer. As Zimmer is the named composer only extracts written by him have been selected here.

Dead Man's Chest: 'Jack Sparrow'

'Jack Sparrow' is the opening piece on the soundtrack and sets the scene for the character. The music opens with an ostinato rhythmic figure on double bass and cello, complete with a solo cello playing staccato dotted rhythms.

CHARACTER IN MUSIC

Being able to discuss character musically is an excellent way of engaging with the music.

Consider how this theme represents the character of Jack Sparrow:

- Use of short, fragmented melodic line, using beats 3 and 1 of the bar and meandering around the key of D minor
- Use of chromaticism in the melodic line
- Use of a lower mordent
- The low bass and muddy chords, giving a lack of clarity

The music is deliberately clumsy, perhaps even intoxicated in nature, reflecting the humorous character of Sparrow and his penchant for rum.

While the music is often diatonic, there are some chromatic shifts which create a sense of harmonic venture, including:

- One bar of G major in the fourth bar of the theme, moving directly to B♭ major the bar after.
- The bar of E♭ major before a tritone resolution to A major - the dominant key of D minor. What is the relationship of E♭ major to the tonic D minor?

On the repeat of the melody, the instrumentation is developed with the solo cello being replaced by the full cello section and violas and violins adding a new triplet idea as a pedal, thickening the texture.

THE CHARACTER OF JACK SPARROW

How does the opening music evoke the character of Jack Sparrow? Organise your thoughts in a way you are confident with to allow you to discuss your ideas with your peers. Collaborate on your findings by comparing your thoughts with those of others.

Main Theme

The music changes character after this initial idea, moving to a lively $\frac{6}{8}$ time signature and containing one of the most memorable melodic ideas from the different films.

The theme is written in the tonic key of D minor, but B♭s, part of the D minor tonality, are significantly avoided. This helps to suggest the **Dorian mode** and gives the music an intrinsically modal character.

The **Dorian mode** is a mode with a minor 3rd, major 6th and minor 7th, best represented by playing D to D using the white notes on a piano.

A **Lombardic rhythm** is a type of syncopation where the short rhythmic value note is accented, reversing the traditional dotted rhythm. In this case, instead of crotchet-quaver, we have quaver-crotchet.

The melodic rhythm is slightly unusual here, using the $\frac{6}{8}$ time signature but also suggesting a **Lombardic rhythm** given the fast tempo. Also notice the prominence of C♮ over the bare-5th D accompaniment - again showing a modal character.

Further rhythmic vitality is added in with a new cross-rhythm, which challenges the $\frac{6}{8}$ time signature by suggesting an accompaniment in $\frac{3}{4}$ time, with accented quavers on every other quaver beat. Despite this, the jaunty melodic line continues in earnest.

Traditional cinematic devices to create tension are in evidence here, with some significant contrast in dynamics and instrumentation helping to raise the emotional impact. This is often achieved with contrary motion scales complete with crescendo, before a *subito piano* (suddenly quiet) and reduction from full orchestra to solo cello. Tension is also created later on in the piece with an ascending sequential figure in quavers which rises with some chromatic movement - again to the dominant A major which resolves to the tonic D.

The piece climaxes with a near constant inverted tonic pedal, including C♯ to create further movement, and a strident bass melody which occasionally uses additive rhythms and some more chromatic chords including diminished 7th chords.

The ending of the piece returns to the opening ideas, complete with solo cello, eventually developing in terms of orchestration to give the piece a triumphant finale.

COMPARE AND CONTRAST

Compare two contrasting pieces of film music by the same composer which accompany contrasting emotions. How do the pieces help to support the unfolding plot?

Independent study

STUDY THE CONTRAST

Make sure you achieve contrast in your choice of pieces to study. Listening to a wide variety of music will help you to establish key stylistic points for the named composer.

There are many other films for which Hans Zimmer wrote the music listed within the suggested listening list. Try to pick music which is contrasting in musical character to both *Gladiator* and *Pirates of the Caribbean: Dead Man's Chest*, such as:

- *The Dark Night Rises* (2008), 'Why so serious' (9'15"): heavy use of electronic sounds mixed with orchestral timbres create the Joker's sound world. This is a particularly good example for investigating character in film music
- *Rain Man* (1988), 'Rain Man Theme' (3'22"): Zimmer's first big film, the sound world here has a distinctly ethno-musicological feel, but is in fact not specific to one geographical location, linking to the ideas of the characters not entirely knowing where they are on their road-trip adventure
- *The Lion King* (1994), 'Sunrise at Pride Rock' (3'03"): using panpipes, a calm yet majestic sound world is created to depict the rising of the sun over the Lion's kingdom. Choir voices add drama towards the middle of the piece in a minor key, depicting the dark side of the film

REVISION NOTES

Create a series of revision sheets to analyse Zimmer's style in writing music for media, allowing space to add notes about the other named composers in this AoS. These could include:

- Detailed notes, structured element by element
- Examples and links to the score
- Analytical statements to help start an essay paragraph discussing a specific element
- Reduced notes/flashcards, using key vocabulary to help you remember the central facts

Thomas Newman

Thomas Newman is a highly respected American film music composer, famed for his use of electric sounds coupled with expansive orchestral timbres.

As well as writing for blockbusters including *American Beauty* and *Skyfall*, Newman has also written extensively for a varied array of different film genres, including action, animation and more reflective film scripts.

American Beauty

Released in 1999, *American Beauty* tells a story of Lester Burnham, an advertising executive, who becomes besotted with his teenage daughter's friend, Angela. The entire film looks at the complex relationships people have with each other, including the mistaken ideas people can establish when discussing love. While the film is violent at the end, beauty remains at its core.

'Any Other Name' (30'36"–34'43" soundtrack)

This section of music, falling towards the end of the soundtrack and film, demonstrates the expansive sound world Newman creates, suggesting Minimalist tendencies to his writing where melodic development is spared for repetitive and slow-moving fragments. The film score makes much use of sound effects and world instruments, and the former are central to the effect of 'Any Other Name'.

This music comes at the climax of the film, just at the point that Burnham has been shot in the head by a mysterious shooter, whose identity initially remains unclear. As Burnham lies dead over a table, eyes open, he is discovered by his daughter Jane and the next door neighbour Ricky. Over the top, Burnham narrates and discusses how life flashes in front of you the second before you die - but that 'that moment stretches on forever and ever... like an ocean of time'.

The scene then switches between past and present, going from Burnham's memories of star gazing to the present moment of the other central characters of the film hearing the gunshot and reacting to it. As the identity of the shooter is slowly suggested, notice how the character of the music does not alter, remaining calm, serene and above all, beautifully still. Even the plastic shopping bag, flying in the wind, has an odd sense of beauty to it.

As you listen to the piece and watch the scene, consider how Newman creates such a feeling of space and conclusion by his use of:

- Free tempo, including use of **fermata**
- **Parallel harmony**, often using open 5ths
- Fragmented melodic shapes, often using conjunct motion and having no repetitive phrase structure, instead giving the impression of a meandering line
- The subtle use of **acciaccaturas**
- The use of acoustic piano and synth sound effects, sometimes electronic in nature, sometimes using a string-based sound effect

While tonal progression is not prioritised in this piece, the harmonic relationship is worth exploring. The key signature of two flats suggests either B♭ major or G minor but the music itself suggests C minor; however, the use of bare-5th chords means that the first full triad we hear is actually that of F major. This harmonic canvas is further blended with use of sound effects, sometimes of no discernible pitch, which cloud the clarity of the piano writing. This creates **diatonic non-functional harmony**, where cadences are actively avoided to enable the sound world to be prioritised.

Extended chords are also used throughout; these are chords which have additional notes added to the basic triad (for example E♭ major^6 in the textural break between the piano lines) which do not resolve and are not written with specific harmonic function in mind; instead, they are appreciated as sounds in their own right, slowly moving and creating the desired effect. This is shown towards the end of the first section, where the F major^9 chord has a 6th added to it, effectively outlining the pentatonic scale of F major.

EMOTIONAL IMPACT

Watch the scene for 'Any Other Name' and consider how the music helps to reflect the emotional impact of the scene. Format your ideas in a way you feel confident, discussing your ideas with your peers to establish if they have similar or contrasting thoughts on the effectiveness of the whole scene.

Skyfall

Released in 2012, *Skyfall* is the third Bond film to be directed by Sam Mendes, featuring Daniel Craig in the iconic role of James Bond. Adele famously performed the opening song of the same title to the film, with Thomas Newman replacing David Arnold as composer.

The James Bond theme tune (originally composed by Monty Norman) appears throughout the film, especially at moments leading up to high-intensity action. However, there are also more expressive sections which show Newman's typical style and preference for expansive chordal textures with Minimalist approaches to thematic development.

INDEPENDENT ANALYSIS

Pick three contrasting titles from the soundtrack, commenting on how they reflect and support the action on screen. Aim to include different emotions - for example, chase, grief and suspense - to allow you to be able to comment on how Newman creates music for different scenes.

The example on the next page shows one approach that could be taken to complete this task; it's based on the scene in *Skyfall* at the death of M.

PLOT AND MUSIC

In the following table notice how the musical features are expansive while the plot points are minimal. This ensures your focus is directed correctly.

Approx. timing	Film action	Musical features
0'00"–0'20"	M '007–what took you so long?'	■ Silence – focus is on dialogue ■ Silva dies without any music, reflecting his character
0'20"–1'00"	M collapses in 007's arms	■ Music starts, exceptionally quietly – you are not aware of it when it does really start ■ Bare-5th A♭ major chord, strings with electronic effects, slowly changing to B♭ major with A♭ in melody and bass ■ Fade out to allow dialogue, fade in to support silence in dialogue – still ***ppp*** ■ Melodic shapes avoided – chords prominent
1'00"–end	M dies in 007's arms Camera pans out to allow scene to change	■ Brass enter, still quietly, evoking a more majestic sound quality ■ A♭ major for four beats, moving to B minor second inversion and E major for two beats – diatonic non-functional harmony ■ The B minor chord is then diminished by replacing the F♯ with an F♮ ■ Alternation between D♭ and E major – tertiary relationship with extended chords (e.g. E♯7) ■ Alternation of this chord sequence as camera pans out

INDEPENDENT STUDY

There are several other films that could be studied to gain further understanding of Newman's style, including:

- *Saving Mr. Banks*
- *The Shawshank Redemption*
- *Finding Nemo*

Choosing two contrasting scenes from different films from this list, analyse the music and emotional impact to allow you to gain a greater understanding of Newman's compositional style.

REVISION NOTES

Add notes on Newman's style in writing music for media to the revision sheets you started for Zimmer.

Bernard Herrmann

Herrmann collaborated extensively with director Alfred Hitchcock on several famous motion picture scores, including *Psycho,* released in 1960.

Herrmann was also a champion of performing music by composers who were not part of the musical canon, which no doubt helped him to shape his deeply personal and iconic compositional sound.

Psycho

Considered the first 'slasher film', this psychological horror film focuses on a motel run by Norman Bates and the encounters he has with the guests who stay there, including Marion Crane, a young secretary who is on the run, having stolen money.

The film has many twists as key characters are murdered, with the final plot twist helping to make the film one of Hitchcock's most successful. While several of the scenes were originally intended to be unaccompanied by music, Herrmann's score was so captivating that Hitchcock included it in the film, realising how it intensified the entire effect. Scored for string orchestra, the music adds significantly to the imagery on screen.

Psycho

Prelude (0'00"–1'58" film and soundtrack)

This music accompanies the opening credits - grey words on a black background which pan in from screen left and right, always with grey bars missing from the words, allowing them to be slowly revealed. The imagery is not especially dramatic or tense, but the music certainly sets the listener on edge.

Consider how the sense of panic is achieved, using the following devices to help your understanding:

- The opening chord, made up of a B♭, D♭, F and A, creating an augmented triad of two major 3rds played over a B♭ for added dissonance, and with an F in the bass. This creates a B♭ minor major 7th chord - a chord which subsequently has been named 'The **Hitchcock chord**'
- The agitated rhythm of two crotchets followed by a quaver rest, two quaver repetitions of the chord, and a final quaver rest
- The dissonance of the third and fourth bars - a quaver ostinato figure in the violas alternating between C♯ and D against B♭ in the bass, with F-E and A-G♯ semiquavers in the violins - creates a development (via inversion) of the original ostinato. This suggests an almost **bitonal** approach to harmonic writing (D minor and C♯ minor combined). Semitone ostinatos are a common feature used in film music to create suspense and drama
- The inversion of the ostinato figure in bar 5 (C♯-D > A-G♯)
- The aggressive playing style, using excessive accents and down bow movement
- The conjunct violin melody with chromatic twists, suggesting a G♭ major scale and then being repeated in E minor
- The dotted rhythms separated with rests outlining augmented 4ths (D-G♯) and diminished 5th (F-C♯) over a bass B.

SETTING THE SCENE

Is the music to the opening credits effective in setting the scene for the plot that follows? Consider watching the clip without music, or with different music from another film. What impact does this have on the effect? Show your results in a table.

Listen to a similar use of semitones in the theme to *Jaws*.

The Murder (30'09"–31'12" soundtrack)

This scene is one of cinema's most famous, with Marion taking a shower and a ghostly female character emerging, silently, carrying a kitchen knife which is used to stab Marion to death. At this point in the film, we do not have any idea who is responsible for the murder. Interestingly, just before she gets in the shower, Marion flushes the toilet - a first for American film, adding to the way that the film would have shocked a 1960s audience.

MUSICAL DEVICES

Watch the scene, commenting on the action on screen and the use of music, including silence. How does the music create a sense of suspense and horror?

The music here is undoubtedly intense, using several techniques in an overall binary form.

A Section

The music starts as the murderer throws back the shower curtain, revealing the silhouette of a female character. The music is horrific, achieved by use of:

- Violins playing separate chords (each to their own part), complete with slight upward **glissando**
- The exceptionally high **tessitura** of the violins
- The dissonance achieved by this separation of parts
- Use of the flat hair of the bow played near to the bridge in a down bow fashion, creating the impression of musical stabbing
- The addition of lower string instruments

This music accompanies the physical stabbing, although the film itself does not actually show any actual stabbing. In this case, less is more, as the audience are left to contemplate the horror of the scene using their own imaginations.

B Section

As the murderer leaves Marion to die slumped over the side of the bath, the music changes in character. The high screeching of the violins is replaced by a menacing semitone figure in the cellos and double basses, again played in a heavily accented way. The stabs from the violins are now more regular, falling on the last quaver beat of the bar and outlining a diminished 7th chord with subtle use of pizzicato. While the bass moves from F to E and then from B♭ to A before settling on a C, the diminished chord does not resolve, focusing heavily on C♯ and creating a further semitone dissonance with the bass.

As Marion dies, the music fades, allowing the sound of running water and the ripped shower curtain to come to the fore; the audience is left with a scene of blood trickling down the plughole in the running water in silence.

INSTRUMENTAL TECHNIQUES

A piece that uses a similar combination of string effects is Penderecki's *Threnody to the Victims of Hiroshima* which was also written in 1960. Listen to this piece of music: is the opening more or less effective to accompany the murder scene? Give reasons for your thoughts.

'The Cellar' (57'54"–59'00" soundtrack)

Here the entire film comes to its dramatic conclusion. Mrs Bates, Norman's mother, has been wrongly blamed for the murders. Marion's sister, Lila, and Marion's boyfriend, Sam, are now at the Bates Motel to look for Marion. Suspecting Norman is not as innocent as he seems, Lila heads down to the basement of the motel where she finds Mrs Bates, sitting in a chair. As she touches her shoulder she discovers that, rather than being alive, Mrs Bates is a mummified corpse who has clearly been dead for many years. As Lila screams, a figure dressed in female clothing rushes into the cellar clutching a knife: Norman Bates.

IDENTIFYING DEVELOPMENT

Comparing different moments from the same film allows you to assess how the earlier music is changed and developed.

The use of Herrmann's music here is central to the horror and suspense of the scene. Notice how the music before Mrs Bates is revealed consists of:

- Scurrying and apparently random figures in the cello, played in quavers with much chromatic movement and some disjunct leaps
- The gradual rise in pitch as violas and violins enter
- The use of rapid bowing to create a more sinister effect
- The use of the semitone motif played in the bass, often on the first beat of the bar with accents and staccatos
- The rhythmic augmentation used in the semitone idea, where quavers are developed to crotchets
- The change of idea as Lila enters the cellar – further rhythmic augmentation in the bass with the semiquaver motif now presented as tied minims
- The descending chromatic scale as Lila walks down the stairs

As the suspense on the screen intensifies, the music actually loses the rhythmic propulsion of the earlier section, settling on an A major tonality with added 7th which is passed through the strings, ending with a high C♯. The rapid tremolo gives a true sense of suspense. The bass entirely drops out of the texture as Lila's hand approaches Mrs Bates.

Rhythmic augmentation is the process of elongating a rhythm by extending the rhythmic values.

As the mummified corpse appears on our screen, Lila's high-pitched scream moves directly into the music heard in the murder scene - which has now become a **leitmotif** for the stabbing attack. However, this time we see the murderer for who he really is - Norman Bates, dressed as his mother, complete with psychotic smile, who is stopped from killing another person by Sam. As Lila looks on, Sam and Norman wrestle to the ground, accompanied by both the A and B sections of the murder music. Rapid chromatic swirls accompany the final image of the mummified corpse before the scene changes to the County Court House.

MUSIC AND DRAMA

How does the music to 'The Cellar' support the unfolding drama? Link the use of musical elements to the action on screen.

INDEPENDENT ANALYSIS AND REVISION NOTES

There are many other films which could be used to understand the sound world Herrmann wrote in, including:

- *Vertigo*
- *Citizen Kane*
- *North by Northwest*
- *Taxi Driver*

Select two contrasting scenes from one of these films, considering how the music supports the action on screen. Complete your ideas as a table, complete with a timeline.

What musical devices characterise Herrmann's writing style? Complete the style revision sheet started for Zimmer and Newman to allow you to compare the styles of the composers.

Michael Giacchino

Giacchino has written many scores for television, film and gaming music, including the music to the television show *Lost*, the films *Up* and *The Incredibles*, and computer games including *Call of Duty*. He has won many awards for his music, including Grammy Awards, Golden Globe Award and a BAFTA.

Michael Giacchino winning an Oscar for his score of *Up!*

Up

Released in 2009, *Up* is a Pixar 3D animated film telling the story of Carl Fredricksen, including his childhood dreams of travel to Latin America, his marriage to his wife, Ellie, and his desire to carry out his dreams as a 78-year old widower.

Giacchino uses a few themes in his score which are subjected to development to change with the plot on the screen. A particularly good example of this comes from early on in the film, when Ellie and Carl get married.

'Married Life'

This scene uses one of the main themes of the film to portray the contrasting emotions of married life, from being first married to gradually getting older.

INDEPENDENT ANALYSIS

Analyse the opening theme for the scene, considering:

- The use of a descending shape
- 4-bar balanced phrasing
- The F major tonality
- The passing modulation to G major achieved via a V^7b chord
- The waltz-like accompaniment

Consider how this theme could be developed to represent two further contrasting scenes, remembering to use specific musical vocabulary to support your response.

EMOTIONAL IMPACT

Watch this scene, completing the table below for the main developments in the plot. Consider how the music is performed and how the opening theme is developed to fit with the new part of the scene. A rough guide for timings is included to aid you finding the relevant hit-points.

Time	Plot	Emotion	Musical devices and development
0'00"-0'15"	Just Married	Joy	Jazz version of Mendelssohn's 'Wedding March' to mark the end of the ceremony. Addition of swung rhythms, extended chords and runs to the main theme to create new version of an original piece
0'16"-0'36"	New House DIY		First entry of main theme
0'36"-0'50"	The Tree Part 1		
0'50"-1'06"	Zoo		
1'06"-1'28"	Cloud-gazing		
1'29"-1'58"	Hospital Part 1		
1'58"-2'35"	Savings Jar		
2'35"-3'00"	Old age		
3'00"-3'21"	Picture Frame		
3'21"-3'31"	The Tree Part 2		
3'31"-3'59"	Hospital Part 2		
3'59"-4'21"	Chapel of Rest		

Comparing different moments from the same film allows you to assess how the earlier music is changed and developed.

INDEPENDENT ANALYSIS

Other television shows, games and films that could be studied to understand more about Giacchino's style include:

- *Lost*
- *The Incredibles*
- *Mission Impossible* III
- *Star Trek into Darkness*
- *Call of Duty*

Select two scenes from two different titles listed above, completing similar tables to the one above. You should include a timing box for the scene and include references to the emotional impact and the musical devices used to help the on screen action.

REVISION NOTES

Having studied three contrasting scenes by Giacchino, complete the style revision sheet adding your thoughts to those on the composers already covered.

Nobuo Uematsu

Uematsu is best known for his video game compositions, specifically his writing for the 'Final Fantasy' series. His musical style is eclectic, ranging from sweeping orchestral landscapes to world music, electronica and techno-inspired sounds.

The 'Final Fantasy' series has, at the time of writing, released some 14 different games within the series, with Uematsu writing much of the music for each different saga. Each saga presents a plot with heroes fighting against evil while also exploring their individual characters.

Nobuo Uematsu

'Aerith's Theme'

This theme, representing Aerith Gainsborough, appears throughout *Final Fantasy* VII, acting as a character leitmotif to represent the evolving plot of the character. Several different versions exist, including an orchestral version and a solo piano version, and the various versions appear at different points in the game.

The music creates a melancholy yet epic feel from the start, achieved by use of:

- A harmonic rhythm of one chord per bar
- Alternation between D major and A minor
- Balanced phrasing - bar 1 ascends through a broken chord (F♯-A-D) with the answering phrase acting as a **retrograde** in the new chord (C-A-E)
- Use of emotive extended chords, including the initial Dsus2 chord as well as the descending bass pattern, creating subtle dissonance as it falls from the 3rd of the chord to the root
- The move to B♭ major - the flattened 6th degree of the scale

The orchestral writing here is clearly manufactured using electronic instruments, with contrast between the piano, strings and solo woodwind instruments.

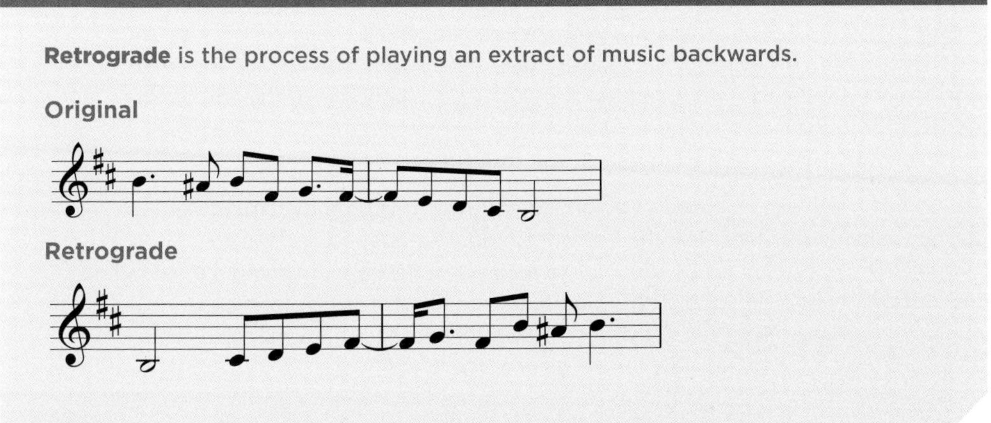

Retrograde is the process of playing an extract of music backwards.
Original
Retrograde

THEMATIC USE

Consider the use of the theme at the following points in the game:

- Elmyra Gainsborough's flashback, discussing Aerith's childhood
- The fight with Jenova-LIFE
- The sacrifice and raid

How does the theme represent the different plot lines in these contrasting scenes? Create a comparison.

'Vamo' Alla Flamenco'

In total contrast to 'Aerith's Theme', 'Vamo' Alla Flamenco' (*Final Fantasy* IX) evokes the Spanish flamenco dance style with characteristic rhythms, harmonies and use of castanets.

The main harmonic idea uses an A minor chord in root position, lasting for one full $\frac{12}{8}$ bar. The dominant note, E, is chromatically lifted to an F then an F♯ before descending back through both notes to settle back on the root position A minor chord. This essentially provides a harmonic progression of:

After this the main theme begins, forming the A section. Notice how the flamenco style is alluded to via use of:

- Regular harmonic changes – two chords per bar, often using I and V
- Use of $\frac{12}{8}$ time signature
- Characteristic use of passing notes, lower auxiliary notes and syncopation
- The increased harmonic progression at the end of the phrase: F–E–Am, allowing the passing modulation to C major to return back to the tonic A minor

The B section of the music uses rhythmic syncopation to achieve musical contrast, with the bass now appearing on every other quaver beat, interrupting the flow of the triple time meter. The passage ends with use of chord V of V (a secondary dominant chord) which uses a chromatically ascending bass to land on the dominant, which eventually adds a 7th to allow the A section to restart in the tonic key.

The C section again achieves a sense of balanced contrast, this time by exploiting increased rhythmic movement (note the use of semiquavers) as well increased chromaticism (the use of F♯ and F♮). The shift to a chord of B♭ major, forming a descending sequential pattern, gives a decidedly **Phrygian** feel to the music by exploring the Neapolitan key: the **Neapolitan** key is the key found a semitone higher than the tonic key.

STRUCTURAL OUTLINE

Create a table for the different sections of this theme, adding in your analysis of the elements of music and how repetition and contrast are balanced.

INDEPENDENT ANALYSIS

Other gaming music that could be studied to understand more about Uematsu's style includes the following titles from 'Final Fantasy':

- 'Opening Melody'
- 'Rebel Army' (I)
- 'Terra's Theme' (IV)
- 'Fragments of Memories' (VII)
- 'At Zanarkand' (X)

You could also choose different games for which Uematsu has written music, including:

- *Lost Odyssey*
- *Blue Dragon*

Select two contrasting scenes from the list above, analysing which specific musical elements are used, to gain a greater appreciation of Uematsu's musical style.

REVISION NOTES

Having studied contrasting musical works by Uematsu, complete the style revision sheet adding your thoughts to those on the composers already covered.

SAMPLE ESSAY QUESTIONS

Essay advice

Before you start, review the advice on writing essays at the end of Chapter 3.

Each essay is worth 30 marks and should take 45 minutes to write.

For AS Level

1. Choose two contrasting characters from a film/films of your choice, showing how the music represents their character.
2. Choose one of the named composers, commenting on how their musical style has changed over time. You should make reference to at least two different published pieces of music.
3. Explore the use of leitmotif to represent different characters in pieces by one named composer. What impact do these changes have on the scene?

For A Level

4. Selecting two of the named composers, comment on how each writes music that creates a sense of suspense.
5. Compare and contrast two pieces of music from two different named composers, commenting on how each uses the musical elements to create different emotions.
6. 'Music in film is secondary to the action on screen.' Discuss this opinion with reference to at least two pieces of music by different named composers.
7. Music in film is often used to enhance the sense of action on screen. How do two different named composers approach this?

Music for theatre

OVERVIEW

From Broadway in New York to the West End in London, and a whole host of theatres in between, this AoS investigates how composers have written music for a range of contrasting plots and characters on stage. The music is often dramatic, exciting and full of musical devices that help to characterise the unfolding plot.

Within this AoS there are five composers from the 20th century to study, each with different examples of their work:

- Kurt Weill
- Richard Rodgers
- Stephen Sondheim
- Claude-Michel Schönberg
- Jason Robert Brown

Bar by bar: 'Pirate Jenny'

This song was originally placed in the first act of the three-act show, but is often moved to the second act. This allows for the song to have increased gravitas owing to the developed plot.

If placed in the second act, the song is sung by Jenny, a prostitute, who has given refuge to Mackie, her lover. Jealousy soon takes over, and Jenny gives away Mackie's hiding position to the authorities, leading to his arrest and eventual execution. The song is filled with vicious venom: Jenny seems to enjoy the power of her position, imagined in an out-of-character pirate scene.

INITIAL IMPRESSIONS

Listen to the song and consider the following questions:

1. How is the song structured?
2. How does the harmony of the song link to the text?
3. Listen to three contrasting performances of the song; how do each of the performers characterise the piece?

Analysis

Having completed an initial analysis of the piece, you should have some idea of how the piece is constructed.

The piece uses an ostinato accompaniment pattern, initially based in C minor with an added D (the 9th) added on the weak beats. Once the voice has entered, the bass becomes more active, moving from a tonic pedal to quaver movement outlining both tonic and dominant. Notice how the vocal melody complements this accompaniment - initially its rhythm is reversed so that the semiquaver movement of the accompaniment does not coincide with the vocal movement.

The most interesting aspect of this verse section is the use of unrelated harmonic progressions. Notice the move to A major with added flattened 6th and 7th on the word *gawkin'*, followed by a chromatic descent to an $A\flat^{9}$ chord three bars later. This chord is then chromatically altered two bars later by adding a minor 3rd and 6th to the chord, forming an $A\flat m^{6}$ chord. As the piece progresses, the harmonic rhythm increases using a repetition of $E\flat m^{7}$ (with the D♭ in the bass) and then a Bm chord in second inversion. This is a significant journey away from the opening C minor tonality:

Cm $A^{\flat 67}$ $A\flat^{9}$ $A\flat m^{6}$ $E\flat m^{7}$ Bm

As the intensity of the lyrics continues, so does the use of **non-functional harmony**: Em^{7}, $G\sharp m^{7}$ and G^{6} are all added to the palette, further exemplifying the turbulent text.

The short chorus section, starting with the lyrics 'and the ship, a black freighter' settles in the remote key of B minor with a sudden use of diatonic **functional harmony**. Within the B minor tonality we visit the dominant, F♯, and the subdominant, E minor. Notice how the dominant chord is a **bare-5th chord**, lacking the all-important major 3rd of the triad. This has the effect of making the verses appear more anguished and gives a real sense of contrast - both musically and emotionally.

This structure is repeated three times, forming a verse-chorus structure. After this, the verse is again repeated but at a slower, more march-like tempo, aiding the ever-intensifying text. Just before the final chorus, the dramatic climax of the song is revealed with freely spoken text:

In that quiet of death I'll say 'right now'
And they pile up the bodies and I'll say 'That'll learn you'

The final repetition of the chorus reveals Jenny's desire to be on the ship with the pirates, floating away from the massacre she has just orchestrated. Of course, in this piece Jenny has stepped outside of her character and has fantasised about a very different situation.

COMPARE AND CONTRAST

Both 'Mack the Knife' and 'Pirate Jenny' tell morbid stories. Compare and contrast their use of the musical elements to show how these plots are portrayed.

FURTHER STUDY

Other contrasting pieces from *The Threepenny Opera* could also be studied. The suggested listening also identifies 'Jealousy Duet' as a suitable piece: listen to it, analysing which musical elements can be found in it. How is it similar to, and different from, 'Mack the Knife' and 'Pirate Jenny'?

INDEPENDENT ANALYSIS

The suggested listening also names two pieces from another of Weill's pieces for theatre:

- 'Alabama Song' from Rise and Fall of the City of Mahagonny
- 'Havana Song' from Rise and Fall of the City of Mahagonny

Listen to both pieces, analysing their musical elements.

REVISION AIDS

Consider creating a stylistic analysis for Weill's music, including central themes, use of the musical elements and any other points that you feel are useful.

Richard Rodgers: *Oklahoma!*

Context

Written in the early 1940s and opening on Broadway in 1943, *Oklahoma!* was the first collaboration between Richard Rodgers and Oscar Hammerstein II.

Oklahoma! set the standard for an art form where music, speech, dance and scene-changes were all integral to the central plot, rather than the music simply providing comic relief to the storyline. Rodgers also uses a recurring melodic idea or **leitmotif** to help unify the entire piece.

Leitmotif is the name given to a musical motif which represents a specific character or emotion. It was used extensively by Wagner in his operatic music, as well as being used in much film music to represent the changing fortunes of the characters onstage.

Oklahoma!

Bar by bar: 'Oh, What a Beautiful Morning'

This is the first song of the musical, presented after the orchestral overture. The piece is a solo number sung by the main character of the show, Curly, initially singing off-stage. The piece is structured in a verse-chorus form with increasingly developed orchestration helping to sustain musical interest.

SETTING THE SCENE

How does Rodgers create the impression of dawn in the opening introduction and verse of this piece? Consider the use of instrumentation, melody and harmony in your response.

From your analysis earlier you should see how Rodgers evokes the rising sun as the musical starts. This is achieved in a number of ways, including:

- The tonic pedal
- The selective use of horns, oboe, flute and clarinet
- The use of trills to mimic bird-song
- The sense of **rubato** tempo in the opening, giving a feeling of gradual awakening
- The hushed dynamics

The verse is initially presented in a monophonic vocal line; this again gives freedom to the character to add expression, as well as making the chorus that follows seem more musically complete. The verse melodic idea is often conjunct, outlining the tonic key of E major.

Divided into four phrases of four bars each, phrases 1 and 2 are symmetrical: the first phrase ends on the dominant note of B and the second on the tonic note of E, essentially giving a question and answer phrase. The third phrase starts in a similar way to the first two phrases, with a changed ending moving to the subdominant chord of A major. This is also where the string accompaniment first enters, outlining an A major triad with ♯7th and ♯4th adding expressive interest. The final phrase is essentially a dominant pedal presented in the bass and in the vocal melody, complete with an ascending line traversing through B–C♯–C𝄪–D♯.

The chorus is one of the most iconic pieces of musical theatre. This is achieved by use of:

- Triadic shapes using repeating rhythmic ideas
- Use of a D♮ on 'morning', giving an unprepared 4–3 suspension over an A major chord
- The use of balanced phrases, forming an overall four-phrase structure lasting 16 bars

INDEPENDENT ANALYSIS

Analyse the four phrases of the chorus, considering use of the following:

- Melodic shape
- Harmonic implications
- Accompaniment patterns
- Use of countermelody

VERSE AND CHORUS

The chorus and verse are repeated three times in total. Complete the table below noting any changes that occur between these repetitions.

Verse 1	
Chorus 1	
Verse 2	
Chorus 2	
Verse 3	
Chorus 3	

Bar by bar: 'Lonely Room'

In complete contrast to the opening number, 'Lonely Room' is a solo number with a very different character. Jud, a hired worker on the ranch, has been presented throughout the musical with an air of mystery and danger, and in this song he vows to convince Laurey to marry him.

Consider how the song creates this emotion in the opening A section by use of:

- B minor tonality
- Dissonance between F♯ and G throughout the first verse, played on low clarinet and viola
- The bare accompaniment, linking to the title of the song
- The quasi-recitative nature of the vocal melody, mirroring the text

The longer B section is marked by a change in accompaniment pattern: the harp plays continuous semiquavers initially outlining a Bm^9 chord over a tonic-dominant bass. This section is essentially broken into two 4-bar phrases, each employing rhyme at the end of the phrase. The second section is also divided into two 4-bar phrases; the first is identical to the music presented earlier and the second raises the emotional temperature of the music by moving towards an $E^{\sharp 7}$ chord on 'who thinks he is better 'n me!'.

A contrasting C section then follows, marked by increased disjunct melodic movement and a more independent accompaniment style. This climaxes at the line 'and her long, yeller hair, falls across my face, Jist like the rain in a storm!'

This is achieved by use of several musical devices:

- Use of orchestral tutti, initially ***mf*** but ending ***sff***
- Harp **glissando** on beats 2 to 3
- Use of crescendo
- Use of descending scaling octaves, starting after a quaver rest, in the bass
- Melodic lines that ascend using a dotted rhythm and semiquavers from dominant (F♯) to tonic (B). While this scalic idea is a popular one throughout the musical, it is specifically used in the title song 'Oklahoma!' at the end of the musical.

A return to the A section for nine bars then follows before another new idea is presented, acting as a 4-bar contrast to a repeat of the C section, which closes the piece. This includes dramatic use of an E♭ major chord with a B♮ (enharmonically the minor 6th, as found in the opening) in the bass. Such dissonance is also found in the penultimate chord - a diminished 7th chord on C♯ with an F♯ in the bass - and the final chord - a B bare-5th chord with added 9th in both the accompaniment and the voice.

COMPARE AND CONTRAST

Make notes to compare and contrast the emotions present in 'Oh, What a Beautiful Morning' and 'Lonely Room'. Reference the elements of music to give your response detail.

REVISION TIP

How does Rodgers represent contrasting emotions? Create a table to help you revise. You could add sections for the other composers explored in this chapter.

Bar by bar: 'Oklahoma!'

This piece is a rousing number for full chorus, taking place as the final number of the show before the encore, finale ultimo and exit music. As with many choruses, the piece starts off with several characters singing to set the scene before Curly introduces the main thematic idea as a solo. The main chorus enters at bar 105 (marked '2nd Special Chorus').

This chorus is very traditional in character, involving a large proportion of the characters in the musical, often singing in several different parts, and creating lush harmonies.

The structure of the chorus is rather unconventional:

A	Oklahoma, where the wind...
B	Where the wavin' wheat...
A	Oklahoma, ev'ry night...
C	We know we belong...
D	And when we say...
E	We're only saying...

COMPARISON

How does the second special chorus (bars 105–164) differ from Curly's solo (bars 45–105) heard earlier in the piece?

Rodgers cleverly divides the singers into four-part male vocals and three-part female vocals, giving a rich seven-part vocal texture. Many of these lines include ascending scales, as in bar 121, as well as more advanced chords such as diminished 7th (found on 'night my honey lamb and I'). As the piece progresses, the hoe down feel continues in earnest with a new section outlining the text 'Yippy Yi!' – a dominant pedal on A with chromatic ascending chords in the top five voices.

The excitement continues with use of an ostinato in the bass using D–C–B–A (creating a leitmotif link with music heard earlier, albeit in melodic inversion). The vocals gradually outline a tonic chord of D major, complete with added 7th, giving way to section C in the subdominant, G major, at bar 177. This is where the seven-part chorus is joined with all other characters onstage who sing the main melody.

The coda of the piece - and indeed the overall action of the musical - spells out the word 'Oklahoma', again using ascending chords and a dramatic pause before the final 'yeow'.

This is a musical that emphatically embraces the 'feel-good' factor, ensuring the audience leaves the theatre singing the main numbers.

'OKLAHOMA!' QUESTIONS

1. What is the role of the chorus in the final number, 'Oklahoma!'?
2. How does Rodgers create music to match the prairie scene of the newly-named state of Oklahoma?
3. How does Rodgers create a sense of excitement in this final number?

Answers at the back of the book

INDEPENDENT ANALYSIS

The suggested listening list also gives two other pieces from another one of Rodgers' musicals, *Carousel*:

- 'Louise's Ballet: *Pas de deux*'
- 'What's the use of Wond'rin?'

Listen to both of these pieces and complete an analysis for each.
Remember to reference specific examples from the score where possible.

STYLISTIC ANALYSIS

What are the hallmarks of Rodgers's compositional style? In your answer, consider:

- Use of instruments and voices
- Use of harmony
- Use of melody including leitmotif
- How the music matches the character and scene

Stephen Sondheim: *Sweeney Todd*

Context

Born in 1930, Sondheim is one of America's greatest composers for film and stage, winning many awards for his contributions to the genre. His compositions include the music to *A Little Night Music*, *Sweeney Todd* and *Into the Woods*, to name but a few famous productions. As well as being a highly accomplished musician, Sondheim also wrote the lyrics for *Sweeney Todd*, *West Side Story* and *Gypsy*.

Sweeney Todd: The Demon Barber of Fleet Street was completed in 1979 and is one of Sondheim's most ambitious projects. Set in a grimy London in the 19th century, the plot revolves around a barber seeking revenge on a corrupt judge who has sent him into exile. This is achieved by murdering a whole host of gentlemen seeking the barber's service at his salon, including the judge, with their bodies being used as meat for Mrs Lovett's pie shop below. It has a darkly macabre plot with some appropriately demonic music.

Bar by bar: 'The Ballad of Sweeney Todd'

Appearing after a short, chromatically intense prelude for solo organ, 'The Ballad of Sweeney Todd' is the first vocal number of the show, during which the lights slowly reveal the company and the set. Two important leitmotifs are used in this piece:

1. The use of a shrill factory whistle, often used just before Sweeney claims another victim
2. The *Dies Irae* melody from the 13th-century *Mass for the Dead* ('Day of wrath and doom impending'):

Di-es i-rae di-es il - la, Sol-vet sae - clum in fa-vil-la: Tes-te Da-vid cum Sib-y-lla

SETTING THE SCENE

Listen to the piece and comment on the following:

- How does the opening create a sense of suspense and foreboding?
- How is the *Dies Irae* motif used in the piece? Why might Sondheim have used this?
- How is the entrance of Sweeney Todd represented in the music?

Having completed this initial analysis, you should have heard and understood the effect on the audience of this number, which helps illustrate the subtitle of the musical: *A Musical Thriller*.

The mysterious and macabre nature of the piece is created from the outset by use of the following:

- F♯ minor tonality
- Repeating quavers in $\frac{6}{8}$ time creating an incessant ostinato figure
- Use of alternation between G♯ and A – the second and third degrees of the scale

'You can sleep now, you can cry now, I'm your wife now'. Both voices have been separate in this duet up to this point, singing their own musical material, but now come together at the end to sing 'until we die', echoing the marriage vows of the past and the plot to come.

'I STILL BELIEVE' QUESTIONS

1. What is an additive rhythm? How is this device employed in this piece?
2. What is a sequence? Give an example of an ascending sequence and descending sequence heard in this piece.
3. What is minor chord IV in C major? What is the effect of using such a chord?
4. Why does Schönberg modulate to E minor for the final verse? What is the effect of this?
5. Performers often alter the rhythms when performing Schönberg's music. Why do you think they do this?

Answers at the back of the book

Bar by bar: 'Bui-Doi'

The Vietnamese term 'bui-doi', as used in *Miss Saigon*, refers to the Asian-American street children who were left behind after the Vietnamese war ended, much like Kim and Chris's child, Tam. While the official meaning of the words is 'dust of life', the term was made popular by its use in *Miss Saigon*, even though the link between homeless people and young abandoned children is not clearly apparent in the Vietnamese vernacular.

Unsurprisingly, given this link to the socio-political aspect of the war, the music is the emotional heart of the musical, starting the second act.

EMOTIONAL IMPACT

How does the music convey a sense of loss, regret and hope in this piece? Listen to the number, making notes on how the various elements of music are used to achieve these emotions.

From listening to the piece, you should now have established that this number uses the following musical devices to achieve an emotive start to the second act:

- Slow tempo
- A♭ major tonality
- Harmonic rhythm in minims
- Use of the intervals of a 6th, then 7th, then octave in the chorus
- **A cappella** chorus opening the piece
- Use of E♭$^{+}$ on the word 'survivors'. A chord with a $^{+}$ symbol can be used to describe an **augmented triad** – that is a triad made up of two major thirds, for example E♭–G–B.

COMPARE AND CONTRAST

Listen to this piece, completing the table below to compare the first verse and chorus with the second. Consider the similarities and differences, especially regarding use of instruments, melody and rhythm.

	First	Second
Verse		
Chorus		

An 8-bar contrasting section follows, meaning that the overall structure could be viewed as being in developed AABA' form - a common structure in musical theatre. This form is called **popular song form**. What is interesting here is how the sections are unequal: the A sections are subdivided into a 10-bar verse and 8-bar chorus.

INDEPENDENT ANALYSIS

How does the B section (from 'These are souls in need') contrast with the A sections? In your answer, consider:

- What melodic device is employed in the vocal melody?
- How the harmony is changed - chords used, modulation and harmonic rhythm?
- The role of the chorus after five bars

The triumphant final chorus yields to a short 2-bar coda employing a subdominant pedal and final plagal cadence, complete with full harmony from the chorus.

Bar by bar: 'I'd Give My Life For You'

This piece, sung as a solo by Kim, ends the first act as she, Tam and the engineer board a boat to Bangkok. As you listen to the piece, consider the following points to aid your analysis:

Harmony and tonality:

- What is the overall tonality? How does this change as the piece progresses?
- Is the harmonic rhythm stable or changeable? How?
- Are any advanced chords used? Where and why might these be employed?

Melody and rhythm:

- Is the vocal melody conjunct or disjunct?
- Are there any memorable intervals used?
- How does the piece end? Why might it end like this?

Texture:

- Compared to other pieces in the musical, how does the accompaniment style differ?
- Does the texture change throughout the piece?

Instruments and use of voice:

- What is the range of the voice? Where it is at its extremes, can this be linked to the text?
- Which instruments support the voice?

INDEPENDENT ANALYSIS

The suggested listening list also gives the titles of two other pieces from another of Schönberg's musicals, *Les Miserables*:

- 'One Day More'
- 'Bring Him Home'

'One Day More' is a particularly interesting piece to study. It rounds off the first Act using a **simultaneous quodlibet** by having each of the main characters singing their musical motifs at the same time.

EXPLORING FURTHER

Gain an understanding of 'One Day More' and 'Bring Him Home' to further your knowledge of the genre.

STYLISTIC ANALYSIS

What are the hallmarks of Schönberg's compositional style? In your answer, consider:

- Use of instruments and voices
- Accompaniment patterns
- Use of harmony
- Use of melody including leitmotif
- How the music matches the character and scene

Jason Robert Brown: *The Last Five Years*

Context

Born in 1970s America, Brown has a distinctive approach to writing music for theatre, readily fusing elements of rock and pop within a theatrical setting. This makes his musical style significantly different from those of the other named composers.

The Last Five Years is one of Brown's most famous pieces for theatre, premiering in 2001 and subsequently touring globally. The plot shows two characters, Jamie Wellerstein and Cathy Hiatt, exploring their relationship, marriage and subsequent break-up. Rather than being told as a chronology, the musical tells the story from the break-up to first meeting through Cathy's eyes (i.e. in reverse order) and from first meeting to break-up through Jamie's eyes (i.e. chronologically). The characters often perform in isolation, only joining when their respective stories meet.

Bar by bar: 'Moving Too Fast'

Performed as the fourth piece of the musical, this is a solo song sung by Jamie, complete with orchestral backing provided by piano, two cellos, acoustic guitar, fretless bass, violin, and cymbal, tubular bells and celesta. The sound world instantly recalls a funk rock feeling, with extended chords, syncopation and complex riffs occurring throughout.

An outline of the structure of this piece is given below:

A	A	'Did I just hear an alarm start ringing?' bars 1–8	8 bars
	A	'I'm gliding smooth as a figure skater' bars 9–16	8 bars
	B	'Oh no, step on the brakes' bars 16–23	8 bars
	A	'I won't do anything' bars 24–32	8 bars
B	C	'I found a woman I love' bars 33–37	5 bars
	D	'Things might get bumpy' bars 38–55	18 bars
	E	'Oh... maybe I can't' bars 55–62	8 bars
A	A	'I dreamed of writing' bars 62–69	8 bars
	A'	'We start to take the next step together' bars 70–84	15 bars
	Link	'Oh yeah!' bars 84–87	4 bars
	B'	'And I think well, well' bars 88–92	5 bars
	A''	'I'm feeling panicked' bars 93–102	10 bars

This is a fairly complex structure which has an overall **ternary form** (ABA) with popular song form used in the outer sections. The opening A section is classic **32-bar song form** (AABA) with the A' section having a more developmental feel, disrupting these proportions. This is not an unusual form for music theatre (John Kander, for example, uses a similar form in *Cabaret*, written in 1966) but, coupled with the more adventurous harmony and virtuosic piano writing, it does show the more fusion-like nature of the piece. In some versions, a lengthy instrumental break is performed after the main B section.

Harmonically, the piece makes extensive use of complex progressions, including:

- Extended chords - 7th/9th/11th/13th
- Inversions - first, second, third and in some cases fourth where the extended 9th is in the bass
- ♭5th chords
- **Acciaccaturas** using **blue notes** from the blues scale
- Fast harmonic rhythm
- Use of augmented triads and diminished chords
- Riffs using chromaticism
- Modulations to new tonal centres - A major and F major plus a 4-bar chromatically rising passage in the final A' section (B♭–B–C each lasting four bars, then D♭–D–E♭–E in progressively quicker cycles). The piece ends in B♭ major.

This harmony is coupled with syncopation, repeating riffs in the bass and instrumental flourishes to aid the overall character of the song.

INDEPENDENT ANALYSIS

Using the structural analysis above, add in 2–3 points per section for each of the elements of music, considering how they contribute to the section in question. Focus on rhythm, melody, texture, use of instruments and voice, and specific moments of harmonic interest. Give direct links to the lyrics where possible.

Bar by bar: 'Still Hurting'

In total contrast to 'Moving Too Fast', 'Still Hurting' is the first vocal number of the show, sung by Cathy as she faces the break-up of her relationship with Jamie.

COMPARE AND CONTRAST

Compare and contrast 'Moving Too Fast' with 'Still Hurting'. How does Brown manipulate the musical elements to give contrasting emotional effects?

Based in C major, the piece makes use of a compound time signature ($\frac{9}{8}$) to create a lilting melodic line and, coupled with the slow tempo, this allows a thoughtful and somewhat subdued tone to be adopted in the voice.

The Last Five Years

The piece is in a similar structure to 'Moving Too Fast' with use of 32-bar song form; notice how the repeated A section has the title of the song in the vocal melody, acting as a refrain. Each 8-bar section is divided by a 2-bar instrumental link. The B section exploits the higher range of the vocalist, as well as a move to A minor – the relative minor.

A new central section arrives at the lyrics 'Go and hide' as the anger of the situation becomes apparent. Notice the use of rapid ascending scales and the move to a new tonal centre suggesting C minor – the tonic minor. After an expressive central instrumental break, Cathy refer to the lies in the relationship, setting the plot for the rest of the musical, before a final return to the opening idea.

The emotional impact of the song is achieved by use of several musical devices, including:

- The tonic pedal on C in the opening
- The use of a B♭ major chord (flattened 7th) which is combined with this pedal creating a $B\flat^9$ chord, giving an unresolved yearning
- The unresolved harmonic pattern – the E^7 yearns to move to A minor, the relative minor, but the required E is moved to an F, creating chord IV in first inversion rather than chord vi
- Use of suspensions
- Use of countermelodies – especially in the cello

INDEPENDENT ANALYSIS

The suggested listening list also gives the titles of two other pieces from another one of Brown's musicals, *Parade*:

- 'This is Not Over Yet'
- 'All the Wasted Time'

Listen to each piece, creating an analysis of the musical elements.

STYLISTIC ANALYSIS

Using your understanding of these four pieces, consider how you could define Brown's style and approach to writing music for theatre. Think specifically about how he fuses together different genres of music to create these effects.

SAMPLE ESSAY QUESTIONS

Essay advice
Before you start, review the advice on writing essays at the end of Chapter 3.

Each essay is worth 30 marks and should take 45 minutes to write.

For AS Level

1. Choosing one of the named composers, comment on how their musical style has changed over time.
2. How has the role of the chorus changed through the 20th century? Comment on at least two contrasting pieces referencing the different elements of music.
3. 'Musical theatre is a journey of emotions for the audience.' Using at least two published works by the same composer, comment on how contrasting emotional effects are achieved.
4. Choosing at least two contrasting pieces by the same named composer, discuss how the musical elements are used to create opposing scenes.

For A Level

5. Compare at least two of the named composers in their approach to writing songs for soloists. Comment on the use of voices, melody, harmony, structure and rhythm as appropriate.
6. Musical theatre can depict joyous optimism and the depths of despair. How have two different named composers achieved such reactions?
7. To what extent did music for theatre change during the 20th century? Reference the works of at least two named composers to help justify your argument.

Jazz

OVERVIEW

Cool, hot, funky and groovy: the vocabulary of jazz points to an area of music of infectious appeal. It is also a repertoire of considerable variety: instrumental and vocal, swing and straight, big-band and small combos.

This AoS offers not just a chance to groove and chill, but a great opportunity to develop your understanding of sophisticated rhythmic ideas, colourful complex harmony and ways to explore timbres. Featured artists are:

- Louis Armstrong
- Duke Ellington
- Charlie Parker
- Miles Davis
- Pat Metheny
- Gwilym Simcock

The named artists and recommended listening in this AoS are:

Louis Armstrong
'St. Louis Blues' (1925, Louis Armstrong and Bessie Smith)
'Muskrat Ramble' (1926, Louis Armstrong and his Hot Five)
'West End Blues' (1928, Louis Armstrong and his Hot Five)
'Stardust' (1931, Louis Armstrong and his Orchestra)
Duke Ellington
'The Mooche' (1928, Duke Ellington and his Orchestra)
'Ko-Ko' (1940, Duke Ellington and his Orchestra)
'Come Sunday', from *Black, Brown and Beige* (1943)
Charlie Parker
'Ko-Ko' (1945, Charlie Parker's Reboppers)
'A Night in Tunisia' (1946, Charlie Parker Septet)
'Bird of Paradise' (1947, Charlie Parker Quintet)
'Bird Gets the Worm' (1947, Charlie Parker All Stars)

Opposite: Charlie Parker

Miles Davis
'So What', from *Kind of Blue* (1959)
'Shhh', from *In a Silent Way* (1969)
Pat Metheny
'(Cross the) Heartland', from *American Garage* (1979)
'Are you Going With Me?', from *Offramp* (1982)
Gwilym Simcock
'Almost Moment', from *Perception* (2007)
'These Are the Good Days', from *Good Days at Schloss Elmau* (2011)

So what is this thing called jazz? Like so many musical terms, it is very difficult to create a watertight definition in a single sentence, or even a paragraph.

Three aspects can be discerned from the traditions of jazz:

- A musical tradition developed by African Americans in the early 20th century
- A view of music-making that places creativity more in the realm of performance than composition
- A compositional style characterised by certain sophisticated rhythmic, harmonic and melodic features that have evolved from the blues

These three strands are interconnected and have led to a diverse musical realm. Defining jazz today is similar to the 'duck test' (if it walks like a duck and quacks like a duck, it's probably a duck). If it sounds like jazz and feels like jazz, it's probably jazz.

It is worth emphasising 'feel': 'jazzers' talk about 'feel' far more than other musicians; it is a shortcut to referencing the character of the rhythmic groove and harmonic palette of the music, which in turn informs the melodic detail (which may well be the improvised result of how the music is making the musician feel).

It is now over a hundred years since jazz was first heard. Among the landmarks in its history are:

1895	The first known ragtime composition: 'Harlem Rag' by Tommy Turpin
1899	Scott Joplin publishes 'Maple Leaf Rag' which sells over 100,000 copies Duke Ellington born
1901	Louis Armstrong born

Here is the vocal line:

In Handy's original, recorded in 1922 as an instrumental version, the tempo is quite brisk. You can hear the brass instruments to the fore; there are multiple influences including the **habanera rhythm**, repeating triads reminiscent of tango, and a few touches of ragtime.

Listen out, too, for the clarinet, which brings much of the so-called Dixieland style to the track. Note the flattened 7th in the final tonic chord – a distinctive 'blue' sound. Here is a link to this instrumental original: http://bit.ly/StLouisBlues

The Louis Armstrong/Bessie Smith version in 1925 is much slower, giving a more lugubrious, soulful feel. There are various changes to melody and lyrics, and the track begins with the refrain section, allowing Armstrong to make a colourful contribution from the start, improvising melodic fills in the fourth bar of each phrase. The verse is then a minor key middle section.

In addition to Bessie Smith's rich-toned singing and Armstrong's florid trumpet playing, the harmonic aspect of the accompaniment is provided by Fred Longshaw on the harmonium – a type of reed organ often found in chapels.

'Satchmo' (Louis Armstrong) in action

'Muskrat Ramble' (1926)

Another famous Dixieland standard is the 'Muskrat Ramble' (1926) written by New Orleans composer Kid Ory and later performed by Louis Armstrong and his band The Hot Five. Ory also played the trombone in the Hot Five ensemble. Lyrics were written later in the 1950s but these were not penned by the original composer.

The main melody uses triadic shapes in a swing rhythm in a manner that suggests Glenn Miller's famous 1940 hit 'In the Mood'. An interesting harmonic twist is how the music, after a classic I–V: V–I progression, moves to the relative minor of the dominant for bars 6–8 before hopping onto V^7:

It is not just the swing groove that creates the cool feel here; also significant are the ties that create the mid-bar syncopations.

The two different recordings at the urls given below show vividly different interpretations. The first is performed by Armstrong and the Hot Five. Each of the 'horns' (trumpet, clarinet and trombone) have solos, in addition to the sections where all three are playing in a jazz counterpoint. Listen out for **glissandos** on Ory's trombone. In the background the banjo is injecting a rhythmic quality through its metronomic strumming. There are a few articulating moments of punctuated detached chords, again with syncopated rhythm.

The second recording is a piano solo version performed by Harry Connick Jr in the early Nineties. Despite differences, it is essentially similar in form and structure and both versions are heavily influenced by the early style of jazz know as ragtime. The comparison highlights the focus on the three contrasting 'horn' timbres of the Hot Five. There is plenty of verve to enjoy (especially **tremolandos** and glissandos) in Harry Cornick Jr's piano playing.

http://bit.ly/MuskratRumble

http://bit.ly/MuskratRumble2

Ragtime was popular in the late 1800s to early 1900s, particularly among African American communities in St Louis and New Orleans. The greatest exponent of this style was of course the famous Scott Joplin. However, ragtime was a form of dance music before it became popular as a display of virtuosity for solo pianists. The main characteristic of ragtime is syncopated rhythms and for pianists it saw the development of a style of left hand writing which later became known as **stride playing**. Essentially, this describes the movement of the left hand striding up and down the range of the piano in larger leaps. Many piano rags became so popular that they were then arranged for other solo instruments, ensembles and bands: examples include 'The Entertainer' and 'Maple Leaf Rag'.

The line-up of Armstrong's Hot Five included clarinet, trombone and banjo with Louis himself on the trumpet and his wife at the piano. As the group's popularity increased, Louis took on an increasingly soloistic role. He became well known for his displays of virtuosity, and his improvisation skills set the standard for other musicians who followed.

'West End Blues' (1928)

The 'West End Blues' is named after Lake Pontchartrain in the far west of Louisiana. This is a fine example of how Louis took a more soloistic role within the ensemble. Here, he opens the track with virtuosic trumpet solos covering a wide range of pitches:

He also sings scat later in the track, in dialogue with the clarinet solo that uses the mellow **chalumeau** register at the bottom of the instrument. Listen out for the chromatic bar at the end of this passage.

The main substance of the track is at a slow, chilled tempo. The main solos are as follows:

- The trumpet takes the tune first, the clarinet often doubling in 3rds
- The trombone solo follows with some discreet piano tremolando in the background
- The clarinet has a solo in the bottom chalumeau register with Louis responding imitatively with his characteristic scat singing
- There is a fine piano solo with a flamboyant right-hand part over a stride left hand

As the horns re-enter, there is an amazingly long top B♭ from Armstrong lasting four bars. Then a lovely moody slower cadence with chromatic inflection finishes the track.

http://bit.ly/WestEndBlues

'Stardust'

'Stardust' was originally written by Hoagy Carmichael and is known as one of the classic 20th-century jazz standards. It has since been performed and recorded by many artists. Louis's recording again features him both in solo trumpet lines and with some scat singing.

Compare and contrast the following recordings:

http://bit.ly/LouisArmstrongStardust

http://bit.ly/NatKingColeStardust2

The first is the 1931 Louis Armstrong version and the second is performed by Nat 'King' Cole from the album *Love is the Thing / After midnight.*

The basic structure of the music is a 32-bar melody in ABAC form. The Nat King Cole version has a stricter feel to the pulse and greater clarity of diction, while the Louis Armstrong version has greater freedom of pulse, bending of pitches and use of **blue notes**.

Duke Ellington

The artist and his context

Edward Kennedy Ellington was born in 1899 to musical parents in Washington DC. Encouraged by his aspirational mother to dress in dapper fashion from boyhood, Ellington was nicknamed 'Duke' early in life; it is as 'Duke Ellington' that he is known – one of the most successful jazz musicians of all time. He was one of the first to focus on composition in jazz as distinct from tune-writing, improvisation and arrangement.

After a diffident start to taking piano lessons, he began to visit the local pool-room in order to hear the pianists who regularly played there. He soon wrote his first piece, the 'Soda Fountain Rag', in 1914, and invented one-step, two-step, waltz, tango and foxtrot versions of it, all by ear.

At 18 he began to work as a freelance sign-painter, but was also playing the piano for dances. In 1919 he met drummer Sonny Greer whom he included in his first band, The Duke's Serenaders. When Greer decided to move to New York to join the Walter Sweatman Orchestra, Ellington followed, becoming part of the 'Harlem Renaissance'.

In New York, Ellington founded his 'orchestra' in 1923, initially playing at the Kentucky Club. In 1927 Ellington had his big break, being invited to take his band to the prestigious Cotton Club, whose clientele were exclusive, white and wealthy. Here they played for the weekly revue, which combined comedy, dance, vaudeville, burlesque and music,

Duke Ellington (at the piano) and his orchestra

as well as illicit alcohol (it was the time of prohibition in America). In order to meet the management's requirements, Ellington increased his band from 6 to 11 players, directing from the piano. Weekly radio broadcasts from the club gave the band national exposure.

For over 50 years Ellington led his band through good times and bad. In the 1930s, although the Great Depression affected the recording industry badly, he produced a string of big hits including 'Mood Indigo' (1930), 'It Don't Mean a Thing (If It Ain't Got That Swing)' (1932), and 'In a Sentimental Mood' (1935).

The Band also toured Europe, where Ellington gained encouragement for his ambition of writing longer pieces from British composer, Constant Lambert. The first of these was *Black, Brown and Beige* in 1943.

Leaner times followed after the Second World War, but Ellington's central place in jazz history was cemented when Ella Fitzgerald recorded her *Duke Ellington Songbook* with his band in 1957 as part of what had by then been recognised as a cultural icon and named 'The Great American Songbook'. In the 1960s he recorded with many of the greats, including Louis Armstrong, Count Basie, John Coltrane and Charles Mingus. He also composed various suites, film scores and works for theatre including a score for Shakespeare's *Timon of Athens.*

In his final decade, Ellington mostly wrote sacred music. *In the Beginning God* for jazz orchestra, narrator, two solo singers, chorus and dancer, was performed in Grace Cathedral, San Francisco in 1965. The Duke gave his final concert in March 1974; he died two months later.

'The Mooche'

Ellington recorded 'The Mooche' with his orchestra in 1928. The piece is in 'jungle style' – a deliberate attempt to give music an exotic colour. Often this is achieved through mutes on the brass instruments – the trumpet uses a wah-wah (or Harmon) mute here in the interjections at the end of each main phrase.

However, a large part of the exoticism is in the use of harmonic chromaticism:

The significant part of the chromaticism here is a jazz feature known as **tritone substitution**. The chord in bar 1 is clearly the tonic (C minor) in root position. In bar 2 the right hand alone has a version of dominant 7th (V^7): the dominant itself (G) is at the top of the chord, and in the tenor register we have the all-important raised leading note (B♮) and the 7th degree of the chord (F); the E♭ is the 13th – a common **extension** to the dominant chord in the jazz world. What is so surprising is the C♯ in the bass. This note is the tritone substitution – it is a tritone (three tones) away from the expected root of the chord – G♮.

A similar logic pertains to the chord in bar 7. It does not appear so, but this is essentially a chord built on the subdominant (F). In the right hand are three critical notes of such a chord: the 3rd (A), 5th (C) and 7th (E♭). The F♯ is enharmonically a minor 9th – another possible extension to a jazz chord. Then, in the bass, instead of the actual root (F♮) there is a B which is, again, a tritone away.

Once you factor in all these substitutions and extensions, the harmony is as straightforward as could be:

	Intro										
Bar	bar 1	bar 2	bar 3	bar 4	bar 5	bar 6	bar 7	bar 8	bar 9	bar 10	bar 11
Chord	I	V	I	V	I	I	IV	IV	V	V	I
Substitution		Yes		Yes			Yes	Yes	Yes	Yes	
Extension		13th		13th			m9th	m9th	13th		

ANALYSING JAZZ

Using chord charts like this one can be a very handy way of practising your harmonic analysis and helping you to remember each piece. The chart could also provide a blueprint for your own jazz improvisations.

This use of alternative roots a tritone apart in the bass was not only known to jazz musicians. A similar harmonic twist was used by late Romantic composers. Here, for example, is Grieg in the second of his Symphonic Dances Op. 64 (in his own piano duet version):

In 1928 recording technology only allowed for three-minute tracks. This probably accounts for why the introductory four bars do not appear here (unlike subsequent Ellington recordings – his 1953 'Mooche' lasts over 6½ minutes!).

The table shows a timeline for the track:

0'00"	A section	Uses bars 5–12 of the short score printed on page 282, played twice The woodwinds play the melody in parallel triads Muted trumpet interjections
0'31"	Link	Two similar 4-bar phrases with similar scoring to A section The first has two bars on A♭^{7} followed by two bars on C minor The second has the same two bars on A♭^{7} followed by two bars on B♭^{7} Listen for the twist in the final bar of the dominant 7th gaining an augmented 5th
0'46"	B section	The brass now come to the fore in homophonic texture. The harmony is built on a sophisticated variant of the 12-bar blues:

1	2	3	4	5	6
E♭>B♭	E♭>B♭	E♭	E♭	A♭	A♭m
I-V	I-V	I	I	IV	iv

7	8	9	10	11	12
E♭	C^7	Fm>B♭	Fm>B♭	E♭	E♭
I	V^7 of ii	ii-V	ii-V	I	I

Note in particular the use of the subdominant minor in the 6th bar and the secondary dominant 7th in the 8th bar - both chromatic chords

1'10"	Clarinet solo	This improvised solo in the chalumeau register of the clarinet is essentially underpinned by an E♭ minor chord, darkening the sunny mood of the previous section (echoing the A section) There are some guitar injections
1'33"	Scat solo	The music reverts to E♭ major, and the singer improvises over the chord progression of the B section; the guitar continues to have the secondary role
1'56"	Trumpet solo	A muted trumpet solo over E♭ minor, which balances the previous clarinet solo
2'19"	A section	Similar to the original A section, returns the music to C minor
2'50"	Coda	This uses the first 4-bar phrase from the Link section, which is played twice

'Ko-Ko' (Duke Ellington version)

'Ko-Ko' was recorded in 1940. Ellington used a 15-piece orchestra for the track:

- **Ellington**: Piano
- **Wallace Jones, Cootie Williams**: Trumpets
- **Rec Stewart**: Cornet
- **Joe 'Tricky Sam' Nanton, Laurence Brown**: Trombones
- **Juan Tizol**: Valve trombone
- **Barney Bigard (doubling tenor sax)**: Clarinet
- **Otto Hardwick, Johnny Hodges**: Alto saxes
- **Ben Webster**: Tenor sax
- **Harry Carney**: Baritone sax
- **Fred Guy**: Guitar
- **Jimmy Blanton**: Bass
- **Sonny Greer**: Drums

The opening features low pedal notes in the baritone sax, and trombones moving in parallel, syncopated triads:

Much of the track is built around this kind of call-and-response between sections of the orchestra and between registers (see timeline in the table).

0'00"	8 bars	Low, articulated tonic pedal in baritone sax, answer by trombones in parallel triads; pattern played four times and gradually getting higher
0'13"	12 bars	The rhythm of the baritone sax in the intro becomes 4-note melodic motif (the 'call figure') played by valve trombone and answered by saxes
0'32"	12 bars	An improvised high trombone solo over a punctuated, offbeat chordal accompaniment on muted brass

0'50"	12 bars	A similar passage, but the improvised muted solo is more wide-ranging in pitch
1'08"	12 bars	Call-and-response continues in modified form (trombones not playing); Ellington improvises a solo that uses both flamboyant runs and punchy chords with dissonant verve
1'26"	12 bars	The 'call' role is taken over by trumpet with plunger mute, which is answered by saxes and trombones
1'44"	12 bars	A series of chords is built up across the whole orchestra; these are articulated by solo **breaks** on the double bass
2'03"	12 bars	Chords now in the brass and answered by descending pattern in the saxes
2'21"	8 bars	A reprise of the intro
2'34"	4 bars	A final chord is built up using the call figure for each section in turn

'Come Sunday' from *Black, Brown and Beige*

Duke Ellington was the master of composing three-minute pieces for the recording industry, but he aspired to write more substantial works. *Black, Brown and Beige* is a jazz symphony intended to be a musical allegory of the history of the negro in America. Composed for Ellington's first concert in New York's prestigious Carnegie Hall on 23 January 1943, it is his longest and most ambitious piece. It received its second performance five nights later in Boston, and still awaits its third complete performance.

There are three movements:

I. 'Black' which subdivides into three – i. 'Work Song', ii. 'Come Sunday', iii. 'Light'

II. 'Brown' which also subdivides into three – i. 'West Indian Dance 'or 'Influence', ii. 'Emancipation Celebration', iii. 'The Blues'

III. 'Beige' which depicts America in the Twenties, the Thirties, and during the Second World War

Sadly, the work was not well received; some have accused the critics of a racially motivated, musically unjustified response. Ellington was very downcast, but in time he made various other arrangements (including a *Black, Brown and Beige* suite providing a selection of the music) and recorded a number of excerpts at different times.

As a result, available recordings are somewhat confusing. They include a more recent recording of the 'Black' movement in an orchestral arrangement available at **http://bit.ly/DukeEllingtonBBB**

and a version of the 'Come Sunday' section with Mahalia Jackson singing and The Duke at the piano, available at **http://bit.ly/MahaliaJackson**

In the original concert version the 'Come Sunday' melody was played by alto saxophonist Johnny Hodges.

Charlie Parker

The artist and his context

Alto saxophonist Charlie Parker – famously nicknamed 'Yardbird' or just 'Bird' – was one of the most influential jazz artists in the mid-20th century. He was a leading figure in the development of a new concept or style in jazz called bebop, characterised by fast tempos, an advanced harmonic vocabulary and dazzling improvisation.

Parker was born in Kansas City, Kansas, in 1920; in 1927 his parents moved to the city of the same name in Missouri, an important centre for African American music at the time. He took up the saxophone at the age of 11, once saying that he spent the next four years practising for up to 15 hours a day.

Parker moved to New York in 1939 and, frustrated by the stereotyped harmonic patterns of the music he found there, developed new ideas about the harmonic underpinning to his improvisations. In 1942 he joined Earl Hines's big band where he first met trumpeter Dizzy Gillespie. After hours, Parker and Gillespie would indulge in jam sessions at Minton's Playhouse with other prodigious young talents such as pianist Thelonious Monk and drummer Kenny Clark. It was said that these young musicians were searching for 'a music that *they* couldn't play'; 'they' being the white bandleaders who had profited from adopting big-band music.

For a while the developments happened under the radar: a strike by the American Federation of Musicians in 1942–1944 caused little recording to happen. When Parker entered a recording studio on 26 November 1945 with Miles Davis and Dizzy Gillespie and others it led to 'the greatest jazz session ever' according to the marketing team at the record label, Savoy. Among the tracks recorded were his version of 'Ko-Ko' and 'Now's the Time'.

The period 1947–1951 was the high point of Parker's career. Over half of his recorded legacy was produced in these years. He worked for night clubs, radio, live concerts and recording studios, and collaborated with a string orchestra, Afro-Cuban bands and his own small ensembles. He twice toured Europe. He was a keen student of classical music, in particular the innovations of Igor Stravinsky.

Addiction to heroin and alcohol was Parker's nemesis. It caused him to miss performances, and he even pawned his instruments in order to buy drugs. In the Fifties he was considered by some to be unemployable, and he was badly in debt. He twice attempted suicide. His final performance was at Birdland – a New York night club named in his honour – on 5 March 1955. He died a week later.

Miles Davis (see page 292) said that the history of jazz could be told in four words: 'Louis Armstrong. Charlie Parker.'

Musical ideas

Harmony

Parker often added new melodies to an existing chord progression. For example, 'Ornithology' (with its punning title) builds a new melody over the chord progression of the jazz standard 'How high the moon.' This process is known as **contrafact**.

Some pieces – including 'Now's the Time', 'Billie's Bounce', 'Bloomdido' and 'Cool Blues' – are based on standard patterns of the 12-bar blues pattern. 'Barbados' is a standard 12-bar blues in a **mambo rhythm**.

Chord patterns you might encounter (defined in C major) include:

	bar 1	bar 2	bar 3	bar 4	bar 5	bar 6	bar 7	bar 8	bar 9	bar 10	bar 11	bar 12
Basic	C	C	C	C	F	F	C	C	G	F	C	C
Variant	C^7	F^7	C^7	C^7	F^7	F^7	V^7	Em^7 >A^7	Dm^7	G^7	C^7 >A^7	D^7 >G^7

BE PREPARED

Research other variants of the 12-bar blues pattern and make chord charts of the different options. If you play the piano or guitar, try playing them *and* in a range of different keys!

Parker developed a far more elaborate 12-bar pattern which often includes a pair of chords in a single bar that have a supertonic to dominant 7th relationship. Chord ii^7b in a minor context then appears as a half-diminished 7th.

This enhanced progression is known as 'Bird Changes' and appears in various tracks including 'Blues for Alice', 'Laird Baird' and 'Si Si'.

The following chart indicates the chords for 'Bird Changes':

bar 1	bar 2	bar 3	bar 4	bar 5	bar 6	bar 7	bar 8	bar 9	bar 10	bar 11	bar 12
$Cmaj^7$	$Bm^{7\flat5}$ >E^7	Am^7 >D^7	Gm^7 >C^7	F^7	Fm^7 >$B\flat^7$	Em^7 >A^7	$E\flat m^7$ >$A\flat^7$	Dm^7	G^7	$Cmaj^7$ >A^7	Dm^7 >G^7

Melodic pitch and rhythm

This fast-moving harmonic palette allowed Parker to have a far wider vocabulary for his melodic improvisations. In addition, he saw potential for all chords to be extended beyond the customary 7th of earlier jazz. In particular, he made use of the flattened 9th and raised 11th; he also interchanged major, minor, augmented and diminished chords, and could anticipate or prolong chords of the progression within the melodic line.

The rhythmic detail in Parker's improvisations can relate only obliquely to the fundamentals of pulse and metre. Coupled with the often rapid tempo, the effect can be very exciting and airborne.

Parker was fond of using quotes within his melodic improvisation. The range of sources include popular songs and heavyweight classical composers including Wagner and Bizet, as well as jazz artists such as Louis Armstrong.

In 1955 Davis formed a group now referred to as his First Great Quintet with John Coltrane on tenor sax. In 1959 he brought pianist Bill Evans into the group and made the album *Kind of Blue*, possibly the most successful jazz album of all time. A Second Great Quintet was founded in 1964 with Herbie Hancock at the piano. Davis's music then became more influenced by rock and funk artists such as James Brown and Jimi Hendrix. A fusion period using electronic instruments followed, starting with the album *In a Silent Way* in 1969.

Miles Davis retired in 1975, but re-emerged in 1979 to make further albums starting with *The Man with the Horn* in 1981. His final album, *Doo-Bop*, featuring hip-hop influences, was released after his death on 28 September 1991.

'So What'

'So What' appears on the album *Kind of Blue*, and has become a classic jazz standard in its own right. Over the years this has been performed in various arrangements by many different artists and ensembles.

The track can be found here: **http://bit.ly/MilesDavisSoWhat**

An interesting comparison can be made with Marcus Miller's performance: **http://bit.ly/MarcusMillerSoWhat**

'So What' is an excellent example of what was known as modal jazz and is chiefly based upon two modes, Dorian on D and Dorian on E♭, before a return to Dorian on D to finish. The Dorian mode is a 'light and shade' scale, with a dark minor 3rd and a bright major 6th.

The piece follows a typical 32-bar structure (AABA) as follows:

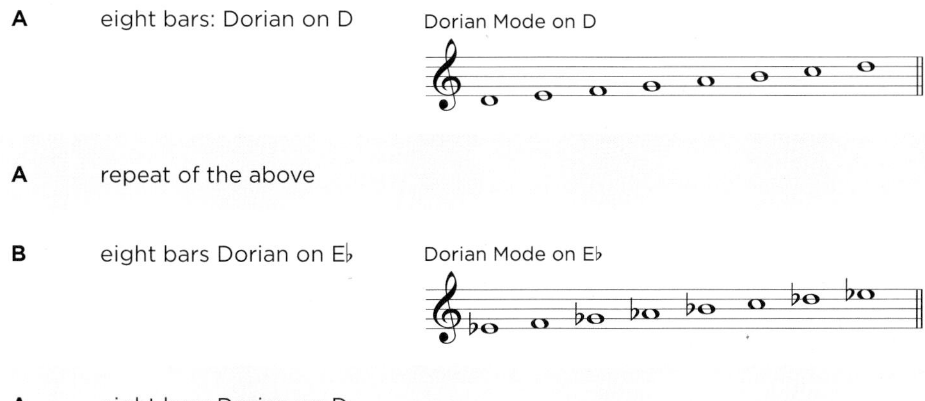

Interestingly, the main ascending theme is played by the double bass, which is then answered by a dotted crotchet-quaver response from the trumpet accompanied by the other instruments. This is then extended and improvised upon by the remaining band members.

It is this dotted crotchet-quaver response that characterises the whole piece and provides its harmonic centre point. Mark Levine, jazz musician and author, described the persistent use of this five note chord (Em^{7sus4}) as being the 'So What' chord, as it is prevalent throughout the piece and became a very influential chord in jazz music for years to come. It can be defined as Em^{7sus4}, but is built from three perfect 4ths topped with a major 3rd.

A simple timeline for the track is as follows:

0'00"	Intro for piano and bass
0'32"	The main riff starts on bass with the A section using Dorian on D (drums join in)
0'48"	Repeat of A (horns join in softly on the chords)
1'02"	B section with Dorian on E
1'16"	Final A section of first statement
1'30"	An improvised trumpet solo over two statements of the chord progression
3'25"	The first of two improvised sax solos over the next two statements
5'17"	A change to the other saxophonist for a further solo
7'10"	The piano is more to the fore with the horns replying on the chord pattern

JAZZ STRUCTURE

Changing tonal centre or instrumentation are clear ways of creating structural articulation in a jazz piece, but listen behind this for how the accompaniment texture and patters can change at these moments too.

'Shhh'

'Shhh' from the album *In a Silent Way* (1969), is another of Davis's most influential works. It comes from a time in his musical output also known as the electric era (c.1967–1991) when many jazz musicians experimented with the fusing together of different musical styles and exploring the different combinations of electronic and acoustic instruments.

This type of jazz music is far removed from the harmonic idiom of 'So What'. *In a Silent Way* is the first album Miles Davis recorded that shows his music leaning towards a jazz fusion style. The line-up consists of trumpet, soprano saxophone, electric guitar, electric piano, organ, double bass and drums. The recording was met with mixed reviews from critics, with tracks on this album showing a wide range of influences from rock music and the use of electric instruments to the use of the classical sonata form structure.
In fact, 'Shhh' lends itself to this form and, loosely, consists of an exposition-development-recapitulation format.

The track can be found here: **http://bit.ly/SilentWay**

That said, it is highly improvisatory and rather experimental in style, pointing towards characteristics that are more in common with **free** or **avant-garde jazz**. The melodic shapes are short and lack a distinctive framework. The music is harmonically challenging with a wide tonal compass and use of dissonance. It is rhythmically temperamental and lacks the predictability associated with the harmonic and melodic structures of earlier kinds of jazz.

Pat Metheny

The artist and his context

Pat Metheny was born in Illinois in 1954 and has become a very significant guitarist in the jazz world, winning numerous Grammy awards for his music, which combines various traditions including bop and Latin in a jazz fusion.

Metheny's first significant position was as guitarist in the band of Gary Burton, a famous vibraphonist (who worked with Astor Piazzolla among others). He soon had enough original material to release his first solo album *Bright Size Life* in 1976 on the renowned ECM label. The following year he released *Watercolours* with pianist Lyle Mays, who has become Metheny's most frequent collaborator.

Metheny has subsequently worked with many famous musicians including Chick Corea, Herbie Hancock, Santana, Joni Mitchell and Silje Nergaard. He has his own group, who in 1982 released their third album, *Offramp*, which won the Grammy award for Best Jazz Fusion Performance.

In 2016 Pat Metheny undertook a world tour supported by British jazz pianist Gwilym Simcock that included gigs in Japan, Ronnie Scott's in London and the Copenhagen Jazz Festival.

Pat Metheny: one of the great guitarists of jazz

'(Cross the) Heartland'

This is the first track on the album *American Garage*, which was the so-called 'breakout' second album for Pat Metheny Group, reaching No. 1 in the jazz charts.

The track can be heard at: **http://bit.ly/PatMethenyHeartland**

The musicians on the album are:

- **Pat Metheny**: 6- and 12-string electric and acoustic guitars
- **Lyle Mays**: Piano, Oberheim synthesiser, Autoharp and electric organ
- **Mark Egan**: Electric bass
- **Dan Gottlieb**: Drums

The 6'50" track has an overall intro + ABA structure, though its contrasts are finely nuanced, largely through harmonic palette (rather than tonal centres) and timbral blend. Much of the track is built around an energised tonic pedal on G which is heard in both bass and treble registers.

A timeline for the track is as follows:

0'00"	The intro starts with an ostinato built on tonic (G) and dominant (D) pitches at an upbeat tempo
0'10"	The main melodic ideas in the intro are fashioned from a major **pentatonic scale** that avoids subdominant and leading-note degrees of the scale, for example: 
1'12"	The sharpened leading note is heard for the first time as the intro ends with chords of G^{maj7} and C
1'19"	The beginning of the A section gains a bluesy funk feel, especially in the piano writing. The G pedal is largely continued, but there are some inflections in the harmony including the **mixolydian** F♮ at 1'22" and V of V with its C♯ at 1'31"
2'00"	A distinctive chord pattern of I–III–VI occurs twice from this point
2'18"	There is a sense of coda to the A section here with a descending chromatic chord progression in a fast and syncopated harmonic rhythm of G–F–C / E–E♭–B♭ / D–G, which is played twice
2'36"	The B section has a slower feel and synthesised timbres are more apparent in a lighter texture; mixolydian flavours are involved with F major harmonies over G pedals
3'30"	The harmonic palette begins to explore the flat side with C minor in use and melodic ideas using a natural minor mode

4'55"	A piano glissando leads into the final section, a variant of the first A section. The use of I-III-VI provides a connection; there are some boogie hints in the piano writing as well as some Hammond organ sounds
6'29"	The coda formula returns to close the piece

'Are you going with me?'

'Are you going with me?' from the 1982 album *Offramp* has been described as Metheny's signature tune. It has a strong Brazilian influence reminiscent of the Bossa Nova; significantly, Brazilian musician Naná Vasconcelos was brought into the group to play percussion on the track.

The track can be found at: **http://bit.ly/PatMethenyGoing**

The track has a regular bass vamp with a syncopated groove, over which a number of synthesised layers are laid, including a synthesised harmonica melody. The album captures Metheny's first use of a guitar synthesiser, the Roland GR-300, and this track includes a long solo on it starting at 3'45".

Gwilym Simcock

The artist and his context

Classically-trained, Welsh-born pianist and composer Gwilym Simcock (b. 1981) studied first at the world-famous Chetham's School of Music in Manchester and latterly at the Royal Academy of Music in London.

He is the winner of several awards for his contributions to jazz music and is a prolific recording artist and performer. Simcock is a significant 21st-century jazz musician often crossing boundaries between jazz and contemporary classical music. In his compositions can be heard a wide range of influences from Ravel and Turnage to Chick Corea and Keith Jarrett. He has been commissioned to write several important works, chief among them a piano concerto, which was first performed with Simcock as the soloist alongside the BBC Concert Orchestra at the 2008 BBC Proms.

'These are the Good Days'

'These Are the Good Days' (2011), a short piano solo, is one of a set of eight original compositions from a series of works recorded at Schloss Elmau in Germany. The album that resulted from this recording, *Good Days at Schloss Elmau*, was shortlisted for the Mercury prize in the same year.

CROSS-OVER STYLES

Musicians working today have easy access to recordings of all musical styles, and can therefore draw on very diverse ideas to create their own new sounds. Old-fashioned 'walls' between musical traditions (e.g. jazz and classical) have been dismantled by such musicians who are sometimes called cross-over artists.

One of the most exciting jazz musicians to emerge in recent years: Gwilym Simcock

Essentially the form of this short piece falls into three distinct sections: energetic, repeated rhythmic sequences and parallel moving chords characterise the opening and first section, revealing influences of the harmonic and rhythmic style of Russian composer Nicolai Kapustin (b. 1937). Kapustin himself is often described as a cross-over musician and is particularly well known for compositions that display virtuoso piano techniques within the idioms of an improvisatory jazz style. His eight Concert Studies Op. 40 provide a good example: **http://bit.ly/KapustinPrelude**

While Simcock writes colourful and texturally complex music, in this particular composition his style is arguably economical, perhaps even minimalistic in terms of its rhythmic and melodic structures. The recurring riff is the driving force behind the music, with the left hand part mimicking a double bass and bass drum of the rhythm section of a jazz ensemble. This provides a syncopated effect playing on beats 1 and 3 against the right hand, which plays on beats 2 and 4 taking the role of the snare drum. The first section contains little deviation from this idea, with the strong bass line and accompanying chordal groove acting as a focal point. Melodic shapes are short and interject with the repeated, percussive chords that mimic the bass and drums.

The key of this groove is predominantly D major but to add harmonic colour and interest, two scales (C major and D major) are used and act as links between each repetition of the groove. Tension created by the **false relation** between the C♯ found in D major and the C♮ of C major is cleverly timed and creates effective blends of sounds between the clashing notes.

The second, more freely moving section has a simpler bass part alongside a building ostinato in the right hand. The key of D♭ major here provides a rich harmonic tone before a transition back to the first groove in D major.

The capabilities of the modern piano are displayed to good effect in this work, with the final section of the music using the piano as a percussion instrument. The sostenuto pedal (middle pedal) is used in order to hold over certain notes while the artist strums strings inside the piano, an effective device that ensures only the desired notes continue to sound while others are played. This technique was often used in the impressionistic piano music of Debussy. Rhythms are also drummed on the casing and the inner frame of the instrument while the pianist plucks/strums and plays glissandi on the strings inside the piano.

Simcock is not unique in exploring the sonorities of the piano in this way. The piano duo Anderson and Roe are also well known for such techniques (**http://bit.ly/AndersonRoeMambo**) and it has become increasingly common in piano music written during the 20th and 21st centuries.

The American composer Henry Cowell (1897–1965) coined the phrase 'string piano' in an attempt to describe extended pianistic techniques that involve using the strings of the piano in new and unusual ways. His composition entitled 'Aeolian Harp' (1923) is one such example: (**http://bit.ly/AeolianHarp**).

Australian composer Percy Grainger (1882–1961) and later Crumb (b. 1929), Gubaidulina (b. 1931), Takemitsu (1930–1996) and Stockhausen (1928–2007) explored similar techniques that paved the way for the 'prepared piano', where the sounds it was possible to make on a piano were altered by attaching objects to the strings, as for example in 'Bacchanale' (1940) by John Cage. (**http://bit.ly/JohnCageBacchanale**)

SAMPLE ESSAY QUESTIONS

Essay advice

Before you start, review the advice on writing essays at the end of Chapter 3.

Each essay is worth 30 marks and should take 45 minutes to write.

For AS Level

1. Choosing one of the named artists, write an essay analysing their contribution to the genre. You should reference at least two contrasting pieces of music in detail.

For A Level

2. Choose pieces by two named artists you have studied, and explain their contrasting approaches to melody, rhythm and harmony.
3. 'Jazz is not composed; it's performed.' Discuss this viewpoint with reference to two pieces by two different named artists.
4. How has Jazz changed in the music of the named artists? Refer to detailed passages of music by at least two different named artists to illustrate your argument.
5. 'The 12-bar blues is the foundation of Jazz.' How has this harmonic framework been used by different named artists? Reference at least two different named artists in your response.

Contemporary traditional music

OVERVIEW

This is an exciting and adventurous AoS: more than any of the others it presents a diversity of music that will stretch your listening repertoire across four continents.

Artists include:

- Astor Piazzolla
- Toumani Diabaté
- Anoushka Shankar
- Mariza
- Bellowhead

The named artists and recommended listening in this AoS are:

Astor Piazzolla
'Libertango', from the album *Libertango*
'Knife Fight', from *Rough Dancer and the Cyclical Night*
'Milonga del Ángel', from *Tango: Zero Hour*
'Yo soy Maria', from *Maria de Buenos Aires*
'Fear', no.5 from *Tango Sensations*
Toumani Diabaté
'Bi Lamban', from *New Ancient Strings*
'Jarabi', from *Songhai*
'Ali Farka Touré', from *Mandé Variations*
'Kala', from *In the Heart of the Moon*
'Africa Challenge', from *Boulevard de l'Indépendence*
Anoushka Shankar
'Swarna Jayanti' (Golden Jubilee) from *Anourag*
'Prayer in Passing', from *Rise*
'Oceanic, Part 1', from *Breathing under Water*
'The Sun Won't Set', from *Traces of You*

Opposite: Toumani Diabaté, kora player from Mali

Mariza
'Loucura', from *Fado em Mim*
'Oiça lá ó Senhor Vinho', from *Fado em Mim*
'Retrato', from *Fado Curvo*
'Beijo de Saudade', from *Terra*
'Mais Uma Lua', from *Fado Tradicional*
Bellowhead
'Sloe Gin', from *Burlesque*
'The Outlandish Knight', from *Burlesque*
'New York Girls', from *Hedonism*
'Roll the Woodpile Down', from *Broadside*
'Roll Alabama', from *Revival*

What do these artists have in common? In each case, theirs is a very distinctive creativity that starts with a well-defined musical tradition and, in a clear case of 'thinking outside the box', takes that tradition into new pastures. In each case, this process both breathes new life into a tradition, and also knocks down various perceived walls between styles of music.

For instance:

- Astor Piazzolla took the tradition of Argentine tango and created music that uses ideas from jazz and classical music while retaining the essence of tango at its core
- Toumani Diabaté followed many generations of his family in learning to play the kora, and then reached out to jazz and blues styles, working with musicians such as Ali Farka Touré and Björk
- Anoushka Shankar learned classical Indian music from her father, a famous sitar player, and has combined its sounds with a range of western influences from electronica beats to duets with classical stars such as Joshua Bell (violin) and Mstislav Rostropovich (cello)
- Mariza has taken the traditional Portuguese song style of fado and given it a global reach through collaborations with musicians such as Jools Holland and Sting, and ideas from jazz, flamenco, Latin and African musical influences
- Bellowhead have given new energy and colour to English folk music through the flair and imagination of their arrangements that embrace everything from lush strings to marching brass bands

Astor Piazzolla: Argentine tango

The artist

Astor Piazzolla was born in Argentina in 1921, the son of immigrant Italian parents. Although part of his childhood was spent in New York - another city of immigrants - he was soon mastering the iconic instrument of the music of Argentine tango: the bandoneon.

Returning to Argentina, Piazzolla worked as a tango musician in Buenos Aires, both as a bandoneonist and an arranger. He studied composition with Alberto Ginastera (Argentina's foremost classical composer of the day) and then, in 1954, in Paris with Nadia Boulanger, a renowned composition teacher. When Boulanger, having initially focused on his classical works, heard Piazzolla play one of his tangos, she recognised an authentic, original compositional voice. Piazzolla returned to Argentina and pursued a highly successful (if sometimes volatile) career as the pre-eminent tango musician of his generation, developing a worldwide reputation.

Astor Piazzolla was a brilliant bandoneonist as well as composer

Piazzolla's creativity was inextricably linked to his life as a performer. There were a number of different ensembles he formed to pursue new directions in his composing: an octet in 1955 that took tango away from a song-based style into something rather akin to chamber music; his first quintet in 1960 (bandoneon, violin, guitar, piano and string bass); *Conjunto 9* in 1970, an electronic octet in 1975; and his second quintet in 1978 - possibly his most successful group. His final ensemble was the *Sexteto Nuevo Tango* in 1989.

Piazzolla worked with renowned musicians of diverse styles, including the jazz vibraphonist Gary Burton, and classical cellist Mstislav Rostropovich, for whom he wrote his virtuoso piece for cello and piano *Le Grand Tango*. He also wrote film scores and substantial orchestral works.

Piazzolla suffered a cerebral haemorrhage in 1990 and died two years later without regaining consciousness. Since his death, his music has only increased in popularity. His style - called nuevo tango - has been pursued further by Pablo Ziegler (who played piano in Piazzolla's second quintet) and the eclectic Argentine-Jewish composer Osvaldo Golijov.

The tango tradition

Just as the waltz is associated with Vienna and, although danced the world over, there is a specifically Viennese style to the music and dance of waltz as done in that city, so the tango has its home in the Argentine capital city of Buenos Aires.

The dance has its somewhat murky origins in the late 19th century when the young city was an important port of immigrants from Europe, with an imbalance of men to women. In such a place, the brothels were popular, and here men would learn to dance tango. It was not long before the dance and its music was being taken to more salubrious quarters of the city.

In 1910 an instrument arrived in Buenos Aires from Germany that forever changed the sound of tango: the bandoneon. It is one of the marvellous quirks in musical history that this particular type of accordion, which had been intended as a portable substitute for a church organ in the playing of hymns in church, became the iconic sound of the tango. Somehow its unique timbre, almost whining in character, captures the heartache that is at the centre of this most sensuous of dances.

The bandoneon is the classic sound of Argentine tango

A second important development in tango was the recording industry, which found in Carlos Gardel (1890–1935) the pop idol of his day. Gardel recorded many tango songs (look out for 'Por una cabeza' and 'Mi Buenos Aires querido'), appeared in Hollywood films, and – in an early example of celebrity tragedy – died in a plane crash during one of his tours. As a young teenager, Piazzolla met Gardel; he had been invited on the fateful tour, but had been forbidden to go by his father.

The 20 years following the death of Gardel were the golden age for tango; the tango band, or *orquesta típica*, was all the rage in Buenos Aires and provided the foundations for Piazzolla's music. You should listen to some music of this era in order to gain a perspective on Piazzolla's achievement in moving tango forward to a new style, which he called **nuevo tango**.

A good example of how things were done is the old film footage of Juan d'Arienzo and his *orquesta* playing 'La Cumparsita', possibly the best known tango tune of all time. This can be seen at **http://bit.ly/LaCumparsitaTango**

'Libertango'

'Libertango' is characteristic Piazzolla: a taut, energetic and spiky piece into which is woven a yearning, lyrical melody. There are numerous recordings, some by Piazzolla himself, and many more in all sorts of arrangements by other musicians.

The main recording Piazzolla made of the piece is on the album of the same name and can be found here: **http://bit.ly/LibertangoAlbum**

Piazzolla made this album in 1974 in Milan, and it is distinctive because of its large-scale instrumental forces, including Hammond organ, guitars, string section and drums.

The driving rhythmic quality of the piece comes from the ostinato-like figure heard from the start on the bandoneon.

This is essentially a decoration of a triadic melody using **auxiliary notes** a semitone away:

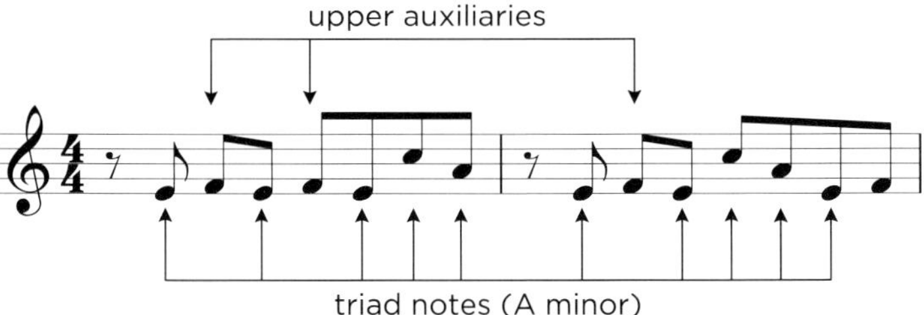

These semitonal auxiliaries are a strong feature of tango melodies – they can be heard in the famous 'La Cumparsita' tune. A significant feature of the **ostinato** is the tweak to the shape in the second bar where the high note comes a beat earlier.

As the chords change, the ostinato adapts to fit each chord. It is not unlike the famous First Prelude from Bach's *Well-Tempered Clavier* in this regard – the two pieces make an interesting comparison. Initially there is a tonic pedal (A), and then the bass moves downwards by step, including some chromaticism to the dominant: A (x8), G (x2), F♯ (x2), F (x2), E (x2).

Listen for how the bass uses the **Latin rhythm** of two dotted crotchets and a crotchet for each bar (3 + 3 + 2 in quavers). There is also some colourful drumming using closed and open hi-hat and a short drum fill at the end of the intro. Traditionally tango does not use drums, but derives its percussiveness from its strong articulation, so this is an area in which Piazzolla is being a pioneer with his nuevo tango.

At bar 17 (0'28") the main melody enters in octaves on flute and alto flute, it is played over the same chord progression as the intro, and starts with two conjunct falling phrases, the second of which is a sequence of the first. The melody is immediately played a second time on the Hammond organ (from 0'55").

A **middle 8** to the melody starts at 1'23" with a very colourful change of harmony to a chord not heard before (and outside the home key of A minor). This is G minor, and its unexpected character also comes from being heard in first inversion. This 8-bar section comprises a 4-bar sequence over the following chord progression:

Gm/B♭–A^7–Dm–Dm ; Fm/A♭–G^7–C–E^7/B

The E^7 chord naturally returns to A minor whereupon the first half of the main melody is heard again at 1'37", somewhat disguised through being decorated and shared between Hammond organ and bandoneon.

At 1'51" a long outro begins, based on the harmonic progression of the first half of the intro and all over a tonic pedal. Listen out for:

- The sustained chromatic chord progression on the Hammond organ
- The ostinato pattern on the flutes and string section
- Staccato 'stab' chords on the bandoneon
- Some fascinating **cross-rhythms** towards the end

'Libertango' is often known in a version for smaller forces such as the recording featuring cellist Yo Yo Ma (**http://bit.ly/YoYoMaTango**) in which the violinist can be clearly heard playing with the **chicharra** technique. In chicharra, the player grates the bow on the strings *behind* the bridge. 'Chicharra' translates as 'cricket' or 'cicada' and the sound is reminiscent of their noise. This is one of several specialist techniques required from violinists in tango, and especially nuevo tango. You can find excellent explanations and demonstrations at **http://bit.ly/TangoTechnique**

'Milonga del Ángel'

This beautiful, slow and moody piece appears on the album *Tango: Zero Hour*, which was made in 1986. Piazzolla considered it to be his best album. It featured his so-called 'second quintet'; the pianist, Pablo Ziegler, is still creating new tango music today.

Milonga is a significant tango word with several meanings. It is the word used to describe a specialist tango venue, and an event where tango is danced. Milonga is also a specific type of piece within tango: a fast, exuberant dance in $\frac{2}{4}$ time. And then, just to confuse things, there is an alternative type of slow Milonga; *Milonga del Ángel* is one of these.

The piece essentially has a ternary structure, but with a free approach to key scheme:

Introduction	A section	B section	A section
0'00–0'27" B minor	0'27"–2'26" B minor	2'26"–4'00" E minor, F♯ minor, and then – mostly – C minor	4'00–end C♯ minor, F minor

Among the features to listen out for are:

- The **habanera rhythm** and shape to the bass part in the introduction:

- The persistent dissonant C♯ through the introduction on the violin which is treated to some **pitch-bending**
- The very long crescendo from almost nothing on the first bandoneon note as it turns into the first melodic phrase
- The characteristic use of *sul G* on the violin (playing only on the G string) for the countermelody to the initial bandoneon melody, and then – equally characteristic – the contrast of very high violin register on the repeat of the melody
- Prominent use of rubato by Piazzolla on the bandoneon (for example around 1'25") and other apparently improvised melodic flourishes
- Shimmering on the bandoneon chords from 3'00" achieved through a vibrato on the bellows
- The transfer of a long note from violin to bandoneon around 3'50"
- The syncopated repeating chords at 5'46"
- The **glissando** in the bowed double bass at 6'04"

Other pieces

On the AQA recommended listening list are three other pieces by Piazzolla:

'Knife Fight' is an astringent portrayal of a violent confrontation. Note the dissonant tremolo chords and glissandos on the piano, and the ***latigo*** playing (meaning 'whip' – a type of glissando) on the violin.

'Yo soy Maria' is a song from his operita *Maria de Buenos Aires*. There is a fast habanera rhythm at the start and then a clear 3 + 3 + 2 rhythm through much of the song. Listen also for the circle of 5ths progressions and the rising chromatic counterpoint melody in the strings at 1'10". Piano glissandos mark some of the key changes and a sung **portamento** over an octave at the end. There is a bandoneon solo when the singer is silent in the second half.

'Fear' comes from *Five Tango Sensations* which was written late in Piazzolla's life for the renowned Kronos Quartet, based in San Francisco. 'Fear' is the final movement and is an exciting fugue written in a tango style with a heavily syncopated fugue subject. Much of the music - especially the countersubject - is based on a descending chromatic scale. Listen out for the pedal notes used from 2 minutes onwards and the double-stopped glissandos on all four string instruments just before the end. Many of these features suggest Baroque music put into a new fashion.

The Kronos Quartet, a string quartet founded in 1973, has worked with many major composers including Steve Reich (see page 350, *Different Trains*).

There is plenty of other music by Piazzolla for you to explore further, ranging from 'Etudes' for unaccompanied violin to a full bandoneon concerto. Flautists and guitarists should look out for 'Histoire du Tango'. Perhaps his signature tune, however, is 'Adiós Nonino', written in memory of his father.

Toumani Diabaté: kora music from Mali

The artist

Toumani Diabaté was born in Mali (West Africa) in 1965 into a family of musicians. His father, Sidike Diabaté, played the kora - a type of African harp; indeed, the family oral tradition relays that 70 generations of his family have been musicians. His cousin, Sona Jobarteh, is the first female kora player to have come from a so-called griot family. Griot is the name given to a traditional West African storyteller, historian, poet or musician - a role that is usually part of a family identity.

Toumani Diabaté's first recordings appeared in 1987, initially with his father on *Ba Togoma,* and then by himself with *Kaira*. More significant was the release of *New Ancient Strings* in 1999, an album of traditional African kora music played by Diabaté and Ballaké Sissoko. Another collaboration with the guitarist Ali Farka Touré, one of Africa's most famous musicians, led to a Grammy award in 2006 for their album *In the Heart of the Moon.*

Toumani Diabaté with his kora, a traditional West African instrument

Also in 2006, Diabaté released his album *Boulevard de l'Indépendence* (named after a landmark in the Malian capital, Bamako) with his own Symmetric Orchestra comprising griot musicians playing a range of traditional instruments:

- Kora – Diabaté's own instrument: a 21-stringed harp-cum-lute which uses a calabash or gourd, cut in half and covered with a cow's hide, to make a resonator
- Djembe – the traditional African rope-tuned drum
- Balafon – a type of xylophone with 16–27 notes, again using calabash as resonators, which dates back to the 14th century
- Bolombatto – an African string instrument with the additional percussive element of a tin rattle, traditionally used to frighten away wild animals

In addition to his traditional music, Toumani Diabaté has also worked with musicians from other backgrounds including the Icelandic musician Björk on her 2007 album *Volta*, the flamenco group Ketama, and American jazz trombonist Roswell Rudd.

Diabaté now has an international profile and travels the world. He played at the Glastonbury Festival in 2007; he came to the UK again in 2010, and played at the Barbican in 2014.

'Bi Lamban'

This track comes from the album *New Ancient Strings* and is a kora duet.

The most significant pitches in this piece are F, G and C. There is a short intro of four separated solo phrases in the treble register which signposts these important pitches:

- The first phrase, a 'V'-shaped phrase of conjunct motion, ends on C
- The answering second phrase finishes on F
- The third phrase is similar to the first, but climbs further to end on high E
- The fourth phrase has more twists and turns and ends on G, having initially leapt to high G

At 0'18", the second player joins in with the **kumbengo riff pattern** that underpins the main piece. This provides F as the most important bass note. Under the mesmeric weaving of intricate melodic ideas from the first player, the sense of metre is subtle, but the F is present for six beats and it then gives way for two beats:

- From 0'18" to 0'41" the bass note of secondary importance is G (5 patterns)
- From 0'41" to 1'09" the bass note of secondary importance is D (6 patterns)
- From 1'09" to 1'56" the bass note of secondary importance reverts to G (10 patterns)
- After 1'56" there is a mix of patterns from F to G and F to D

Subtle, short inflections to E decorate the kumbengo riffs and disguise any potential for rigid, four-squareness.

The intricacies of the melodic playing, including the **birimintingo** improvised runs, provide a kaleidoscope of ideas, with differing phrase lengths, registers and dynamics explored. Fragmentary ideas occur from 1'50", a busier melodic energy occurs after 3'00" and then some extraordinary, insistent top As with a strumming effect from 3'30".

There is a sense of the kumbengo pattern disintegrating from around 4'30" as the piece comes to a close.

'Jarabi'

This is the first track from Diabaté's 1988 album *Songhai,* made in conjunction with the flamenco group Ketama and Danny Thompson, the British bass player. The same team produced *Songhai 2* in 1994.

The track begins with an enervated introduction with syncopated strummed chords that make chromatic juxtaposition between G major and F♯ major and F♯ minor and F minor in flamenco **rasgueado** style. Rasgueado is a finger-strumming technique on the guitar, of precise, rapid strumming patterns, and is typical of flamenco guitar music.

At 0'18" the music settles into E minor and a mellow modal mood is created from the broken chord figuration on the guitar alternating between E minor root position and B minor 2nd inversion with resonant bass notes from Thompson's string bass. There is some pitch-bending of the upper tonic.

The kora enters at 0'47" with a conjunct rapid flourish, which is the lead into a series of short phrases in quavers that announce each chord change in the guitar.

A point of structural articulation is reached at 1'10" with a short silence and another kora flourish into a second 'verse', which commences with a tremolo guitar chord of E minor. This second verse is characterised by a percussive effect on the guitar on the 4th beat of the bar and more filigree melodic flourishes on the kora.

The guitar becomes more active as a melodic instrument in dialogue with the kora after 2'00". There is another point of articulation at 2'35". After this there is a rapid rhythmic clapping effect, another hallmark of the flamenco tradition, before a succinct final cadence.

The whole track has a mellow flavour of **Dorian** mode on E as a scale (there are C♯s) and an infectious sense of momentum, skilfully articulated through the momentary pauses in action. The harmonic content, beyond the introduction, is very limited, but the intricacies of the melodic lines and interplay of subtly differing plucked string timbres create a very attractive sound world.

Other pieces

On the AQA list of recommended listening are tracks from three other albums from Diabaté's discography:

'Ali Farka Touré' is a portrayal of the other great Malian musician of Diabaté's generation who has gained international renown, in the form of a beautiful kora solo.

'Kala' is a duet with guitarist Ali Farka Touré from the album *In the Heart of the Moon,* built over a kumbengo riff centred on twin poles of F and C.

'Africa Challenge' is an upbeat track from Diabaté's album *Boulevard de l'Indépendence* which places his kora in the context of a large group of instruments including brass, balafon and singers. Some of the melodic shapes - especially on the balafon after 2'50" - suggest the **guajeo** piano patterns of Cuban styles such as **son** and **salsa**, pointing to the African roots of Latin music. There is a prominent kora solo at 3'45". A guajeo is a Cuban ostinato melody, often made up of arpeggiated chords played in syncopated patterns.

More recent recordings from Toumani Diabaté include *A Curva da Cintura* (2011) which is an African-Brazilian **fusion** album, and *Toumani & Sidiki* (2014) - an album of kora duets with his son, the next generation in this great griot family, who, in addition to the family traditional of playing the kora, is also a hip-hop artist.

Anoushka Shankar: Indian classical music and fusions

The artist

Anoushka Shankar is a British-born (1981) Indian musician whose father, Ravi Shankar, was a world-famous sitar player in the second half of the 20th century. Anoushka followed her father's example and gave her first public performance on the sitar aged 13 in New Delhi. She is also half-sister to the singer Norah Jones.

Anoushka Shankar: the foremost sitar player of her generation

At the age of 15, Anoushka played on her father's album *Chants of India*, a collection of Hindu prayers set to music that was produced by George Harrison (of Beatles fame). She then signed her first exclusive recording contract with EMI aged 16. Her first album, *Anoushka,* was released in 1998, and is a collection of classical Indian sitar music.

Each piece (there are five on the album, the longest 20 minutes in duration) is based on a scale or **raga**. 'Raga' means 'colour', as well as 'melody' and 'beauty'. A raga can have between five and nine notes which provide the basis for the melodic invention in a piece. The 'colour' of each raga is often associated with its mood and considered as appropriate to a time of day or season. A piece begins with a slow introduction known as the **alap** which is characterised by fluid rhythms and little sense of metre. The tabla (hand drums) then enters to establish pulse. Gradually the tempo increases, and with it the virtuosity of the sitar playing.

Shankar released a second album of classical Indian sitar music in 2000, called *Anourag*, with six further raga-based pieces. Her third album, *Live at Carnegie Hall*, was released the following year and won her a Grammy for Best Contemporary World Music. A busy period of touring and performing as a solo artist followed, that led her to explore new paths for her Indian musical roots within a more global context.

The result has been a series of albums that combine Shankar's virtuosity as a sitar player with musical ideas from jazz and pop traditions:

- *Rise* (2005) which uses a wide range of Indian instruments including the veena (a type of lute) bansuri (a flute), shehnai (an Indian oboe), the Armenian duduk (a flute) and the African djembe (drum)
- *Breathing Under Water* (2007), in collaboration with Indian/American music producer Karsh Kale, is a mix of classical sitar and electronica beats and melodies, with contributions from Anoushka's father, Ravi, half-sister, Norah Jones, and singer Sting
- *Traveller* (2011) is an exploration of connections between Indian Sitar music and Spanish flamenco
- *Traces of You* (2013) was produced partly in collaboration with her half-sister, Norah Jones, after their father's death

In addition to being a creative musician, Anoushka Shankar continues to be an important performer, championing her father's three concertos for sitar and orchestra, and working in conjunction with other classical musicians including violinist Joshua Bell.

Context: The sitar

The sitar is the iconic instrument in Indian classical music; it is a plucked string instrument with a long, ornate neck and bulbous body. The sitar flourished in 16th- and 17th-century India, and remains the central instrument in Hindustani music.

The sitar has between 18 and 21 strings, six or seven of which are actually played - plucked and stopped on the fretted fingerboard, rather as on a guitar. The remaining strings are **sympathetic strings** that resonate in response to the other notes being played, thereby producing the characteristic **drone** effect.

'Swarna Jayanti' ('Golden Jubilee')

This piece celebrates the 50th anniversary of India's independence. Many of the structural aspects of the piece reflect this. The tala (akin to metre in Indian music) comprises 50 matras (beats) which are organised in ascending and then descending groups: 3 + 4 + 5 + 6 + 7 and 7 + 6 + 5+ 4 + 3.

The raga for this piece is heard soon after the drone begins, with its characterful augmented 2nd followed by a semitone at the bottom:

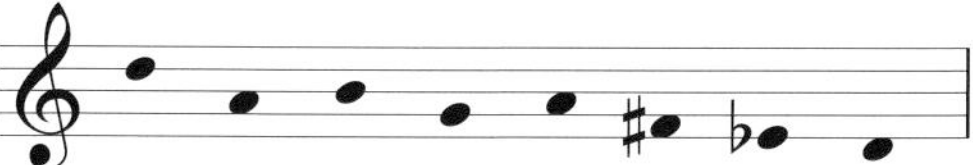

There is a lengthy alap section with some pitch-bending between the E♭ - D semitone at 0'27". The lowest degrees of the raga are heard an octave down at 0'46" and then two octaves higher at 1'40". The top half of the raga is then played, with a little more pace, at 1'44", and the complete raga at 1'55".

At 2'10" the sitar gathers a sense of fast pulse, but this is not confirmed until the tabla enters at 2'35". There is some interplay of percussive rhythms while the sitar is limited to just the note D at various octaves. Then, at 3'05", it resumes the raga in a more metrical manner to the accompaniment of the tabla.

The sitar melody has various fascinating twists and turns and some intricate rhythmic features, including some triplet units (or a cross-rhythm compound effect) around 3'40" and again at 3'55". The E♭-D semitone is frequently present, and is a strong colour in the music where it does occur. The momentum increases with some syncopation in the melodic line at 5'15" and a quickening tempo. The tabla is more frenzied from 5'35" as the ending nears.

'Prayer in Passing'

This slow, dreamy piece has quite a hypnotic quality. It is based on a particularly beautiful raga which is notable for being symmetrical:

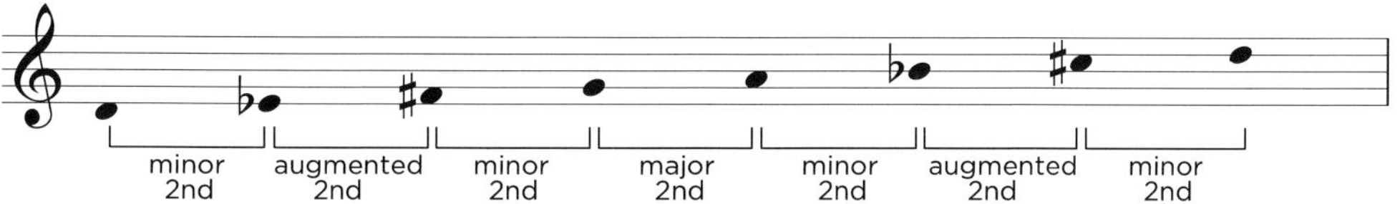

This raga affords some very interesting potential. There are four semitones to explore that give a dark colour, and these provide emphasis to the notes of a D major chord by the semitone above. The 'tonic' note is the only one of these that is also emphasised by the semitone below as well. There are two augmented 2nds that give an exotic flavour, and these are complemented by the interval of a diminished 4th which is heard frequently as Shankar explores the middle portion of the raga between F♯ and B♭.

The whole piece is underpinned by a drone on D played in a soft timbre on keyboard. Over the course of the piece (nearly six and a half minutes) there is a wonderful weaving of varied timbres, all exploring in intricate detail the various segments of the raga and relationships between its constituent notes. Among the details to notice are:

0'00"	The drone begins on D, with A often in the mix too
0'06"	The piano presents the raga for the first time in descending arabesque-like flourishes
0'18"	First entry of the sitar with an ascending version of the raga
0'24"	The mellow veena enters with a longer solo, which initially explores the first three rising notes of the raga (D–E♭–F♯) and then the first four falling notes (D–C♯–B♭–A)
1'05"	The first clear chance to hear the dripping water sample, which adds to the hypnotic mood
1'10"	The piano now playing the raga in tremolo octaves, initially with ascending patterns from the raga; E♭ is sometimes used in the background as a sustained dissonant harmony against the drone, resolving after a while to the consonant D–A open 5th
1'44"	The low bansuri is now apparent in the musical tapestry
1'53"	A percussive shaker is first heard
2'10"	The tabla starts to play
2'35"	The sitar explores the middle part of the raga from F♯ to B♭; meanwhile, the bass guitar joins in, sometimes alternating between D and E♭, and sometimes exploring the top of the raga – D, (C♯), B♭, A
3'02"	The piano takes over exploring the middle part of the raga
3'28"	The bansuri (now in higher register) and veena are in dialogue for some time from this point, with the sitar joining with the veena from 4'02"
4'02"	The sitar joins the veena, playing together in octaves, as the texture and dynamic of the piece begin to build

4'23"	The bass guitar twice descends the raga from D to F♯ in slow notes
4'51"	A quieter section begins
5'28"	A final phrase from the veena
5'44"	The piano takes the melodic interest with the hands doubling two octaves apart
6'12"	The closing moments are essentially on the note D, with some pitch-bending on the stringed instruments

Other pieces

On the AQA recommended listening list are two other pieces by Anoushka Shankar:

'Oceanic, part 1' comes from the album *Breathing under Water* which Shankar released in 2007 in conjunction with Karsh Kale, a pioneering music producer in the Asian underground. From the outset, the Indian sound of Shankar's sitar is set in an opulent background of lush synthesised strings that give more of a harmonic cloak to the Indian melodies. The faster 'Oceanic part 2' arrives with more rhythmic momentum; the tabla is often involved.

'The Sun Won't Set' from the 2013 album *Traces of You*, features Norah Jones as vocalist and incorporates some beautiful melodic ideas from Shankar as a counterpoint to a more western ballad. There is an entrancing sitar instrumental from 2'30".

There are some other albums in Anoushka Shankar's discography, including *Traveller* (2011), which is an exploration of connections between Indian classical music and Spanish flamenco. In 2015 she brought out a new album of Indian classical music called *Home*.

Mariza: Portuguese fado

The artist

Mariza was born Marisa dos Reis Nunes in 1973 in Mozambique – one of Portugal's former African colonies. Indeed, her father was Portuguese, and when she was three the family moved to Lisbon, capital of Portugal.

In Portugal the star **fado** singer of the time was Amália Rodrigues. You can see her performing here: **http://bit.ly/AmaliaRodriguesFado**

When Rodrigues died in 1999, Mariza was invited to perform a tribute to the great singer that was broadcast. This led to a subsequent album of fado songs, *Fado em Mim,* which was a huge success – over 100,000 copies were sold. Her career has flourished ever since. Her music has ranged from the traditional approach of *Fado Tradicional* (2010) to songs influenced by African, Latin and Flamenco sounds in *Concerto em Lisboa* (2007).

Mariza now has an international profile and has sung in many of the world's top music venues including New York's Carnegie Hall and the Sydney Opera House. She is *the* 'fadista' (fado singer) of her generation.

Context: The fado tradition

Fado is to Portugal what tango is to Argentina or flamenco is to Spain. It has been called the Portuguese expression of the blues.

Fado has its roots in the first half of the 19th century in Lisbon where a tradition of singing about the harsh realities of life took hold in public spaces such as in gardens, at bullfights or in taverns. This gave fado its melancholic, resigned character, which sometimes goes on to embrace hope in resolution of current woes.

The name 'fado' is believed to have come from the Latin *fatum* meaning 'fate'. It is sung by a solo singer (male or female), traditionally to the accompaniment of one or two guitars. Originally the songs were danced to, but this custom died out.

The first fado singer of renown was Maria Severa, who was born in 1820 and was a tavern singer until her death at the age of just 26. Severa always sang wearing a black shawl - something which remains a common accoutrement of female fado singers today. Early fado included a strong element of improvisation.

Fado grew in popularity cross Portugal in the 20th century with the rise of theatre (in the 1920s it had a place in Portuguese vaudeville), cinema and radio. It was carefully nurtured by the *Estado Novo* authoritarian regime (often considered to be a dictatorship) that ruled the country between 1933 and 1974. However, in this time the tradition of improvisation was discouraged and largely lost. The poetry of fado songs became more sophisticated. In 1953 there was the first *Grande Noite do Fado* contest, which runs annually to this day.

Having been supported by the regime, the popularity of fado waned for a while after the revolution of 1974 that brought democracy to Portugal. For a time Amália Rodrigues, called the queen of fado, was suspected (wrongly) of having been a covert agent for the regime. As the new democracy took root, however, interest in fado returned; when Rodrigues died, the government declared three days of national mourning.

Musical aspects

Fado traditionally uses the Dorian mode (or natural minor scale) for its melodies, turning sometimes to the **Ionian** mode (major scale) for more optimistic phrases or sections. More recently some fado songs have used the **Phrygian** mode, bringing a middle Eastern or flamenco colour.

Fado is traditionally in 4-time, though - as with tango - there is a waltz possibility in 3-time.

The lyrics of fado are expected to be in quatrains (stanzas four lines long, often with rhyming alternate lines).

Mariza

'Loucura' ('Madness')

Typical of fado, the lyrics (by Joaquím Frederico de Brito) are structured in eight four-line stanzas. Like many fado songs, the poem refers to fado itself (many tango lyrics are similarly self-referential).

1	Sou do fado Como sei Vivo um poema cantado De um fado que eu inventei	I belong to fado The one I know I live a sung poem A fado that I invented
2	A falar Não posso dar-me Mas ponho a alma a cantar E as almas sabem escutar-me	Speaking I can't express myself But I make my soul sing And souls know how to listen
3	Chorai, chorai Poetas do meu país Troncos da mesma raíz Da vida que nos juntou	Cry, cry Poets of my country Trunks of the same root Of the life that put us together
4	E se vocés Não estivessem a meu lado Então não havia fado Nem fadistas como eu sou	And if you Were not by my side There would be no fado Nor fadistas such as I
5	Esta voz tão dolorida É culpa de todos vós Poetas da minha vida	In this voice So painful Is the fault of all of you Poets of my life
6	É loucura, oiçu dizer Mas bendita esta loucura de cantar e de sofrer	It is madness I hear them say, But blessed is this madness Of singing and suffering
7	Chorai, chorai Poetas do meu país Troncos da mesma raíz Da vida que nos juntou	Cry, cry Poets of my country Trunks of the same root Of the life that put us together
8	E se vocés não estivessem a meu lado Então não havia fado Nem fadistas como eu sou	And if you Were not by my side There would be no fado Nor fadistas such as I

The music of the song is in $\frac{4}{4}$ time, with the voice accompanied in the traditional manner by two guitars. The accompaniment comprises three different chord progressions:

Stanzas 1, 2, 5 and 6 are the most straightforward with two bars of a single chord per bar:

Line 1: E minor (I) **Line 2: B major (V)** **Line 3: B^7 (V^7)** **Line 4: E minor (I)**

Listen for how the guitarist responsible for the bass line emphasises beats 1 and 3, creating a variety of chord inversion (especially in the chord V bars), sometimes providing extra decorative detail

Also listen for the attractive melodic lines provided in the treble register by the other guitarist and the way these often dovetail with Mariza's singing. The vocal line avoids the 6th degree of the scale (C); the guitar sometimes has a passing C natural, but in the 6th stanza plays a more noticeable C♯ - thereby creating the traditional Dorian mode of fado

Stanzas 3 and 7 - which can be seen as the first half of the chorus - have a more elaborate harmonic scheme, which starts from the chord of A minor (IV). This is a classic way to balance the predominance of the common I-V harmonic axis at the forefront of much tonal music

From A, the bass moves down chromatically (A–G♯–G–F–E) in a manner that colours the lyric ('cry, cry') and adds to the sorrow and soul of the song

Stanzas 4 and 8 - the second half of the chorus - also start on A minor but this lasts for two bars and then moves (via a striking diminished 5th in the bass to D♯) to E minor. There is then a telling moment of significant rubato - a classic feature of fado - halfway through the stanza, which is followed by colourful VI-V progression and from there to a perfect cadence

The song ends with an instrumental section over the first of these chord patterns, which is then followed by a condensed chorus comprising the first half of the music from stanza 2 and the second half of the music from stanza 4

'Retrato'

By the time *Fado Curvo*, Mariza's second album, was released she was associated with the 'new fado' movement. In this song from the album, you can hear the blend of the old and new. The vocal element has the same recognisable sense of 'soul' as in 'Loucura' and the poem again has stanzas of four lines, which allows for quite short vocal phrases.

However, in the accompaniment one hears a different approach, not just in the obvious move away from guitars to piano and cello, but in the imaginative way these instruments are used - exploring rich sonorities and use of dissonance. The pianist is Tiago Machado, and the cellist is Davide Zaccaria.

The lyrics are:

1	No teu rosto começa a madrugada Luz abrindo De rosa em rosa Transparente e molhada	The dawn in your face begins Light that opens From rose to rose Transparent and wet

2	Melodia Distante mas segura; Irrompendo da terra, Quente, redonda, madura	Melody Distant but safe Springing from the earth, Hot, round and ripe
3	Mar imenso, Praia deserta, horizontal e calma. Sabor agreste. Rosto da minha alma.	Immense sea Desert beach, horizontal and calm Rustical flavour Face of my soul

The song is in B minor/major; a timeline for the track is:

0'00"	The introduction is for piano only in B minor Note use of the Neapolitan C natural at 0'12"
0'17"	The first stanza, accompanied by piano Note the colourful chromatic chord (G minor) at 0'24"
0'41"	Start of the second stanza which has a much more expansive piano sonority, exploring wide registers and a flurry of notes of including various piquant dissonances
1'01"	End of the second stanza, with a tierce de Picardie that turns the music to B major
1'05"	The third stanza, which paints a musical picture of the words through use of a tonic pedal; it also marks the entry of the solo cello
1'36"	At the end of the third stanza, the piano and cello return to the music of the introduction and B minor The cello (in tenor register) plays a version of the music for the first stanza while the singer is silent, which ends in tremolo at 2'06"
2'12"	A repeat of the second stanza, but now with the cello involved as well, which again ends in a tierce de Picardie at 2'32"
2'35"	A reprise of the third stanza. This ends on a B^7 chord, which means that when the third stanza is sung one last time from 3'03" it starts from a E major chord. Note the colourful version of the dominant chord, including minor 9th and 11th in the final cadence at 3'31"
3'39"	A brief codetta on B major

Other pieces

On the AQA recommended listening list are three other songs of Mariza's:

'Oiça lá ó Senhor Vinho', from *Fado em Mim* – a faster, major key example of fado music, which is a song to 'Mr Wine'.

'Beijo de Saudade', from *Terra* is a duet with Tito Paris which discreetly adopts some traits from Latin music, including instrumentation such as trumpet (muted) and drums. The title (meaning 'Kiss of Yearning') uses a Portuguese word *saudade* that is often used to pinpoint the strong flavour that pervades the music of fado.

'Mais Uma Lua', from *Fado Tradicional* is a more recent example of traditional fado from Mariza's 2011 album.

In 2015 Mariza released her latest album *Mundo*, which is a fascinating blend of fado with Iberian pop music.

Bellowhead

Bellowhead

The artists and their context

Bellowhead is an English group of musicians who have explored and re-cast English folk music, including songs, jigs and shanties, with enormous verve and imagination. Their 11-piece band includes vocalist, strings and brass section. Between them they play more than 20 instruments, making their music kaleidoscopic in colour.

The band's first appearance was at the Oxford Folk Festival in 2004; their debut album, *Burlesque*, was released in 2006, an eclectic mix of music from the Napoleonic Wars, the American minstrel movement and sea shanties. Their second album, *Matachin*, was released in 2008; also that year they played at the Proms in London. When *Hedonism*, their third album, appeared in 2010 it became the best-selling independently-released folk album of all time.

A diverse range of work has come their way, including recording the theme tune for the spin-off to the famous radio programme *The Archers*, called *Ambridge Extra*, and playing for the opening of the restored Cardigan Castle in 2015. They have played in many of the UK's main concert halls, including Manchester's Bridgewater Hall, and toured Europe.

The full line-up

- **Jon Boden**: lead vocals, fiddle, tambourine, shaky egg, thunder tube, kazoo, whistle
- **Pete Flood**: percussion (including frying pan, glockenspiel, knives and forks, clockwork toys, megaphone scratching, stomp box, coal scuttle, party blowers, broomsticks, ratchet, shakers and tambourine), vocals
- **Brendan Kelly**: saxophone, bass clarinet, vocals
- **Benji Kirkpatrick**: guitar, bouzouki, mandolin, tenor banjo, vocals, kazoo
- **Rachael McShane**: cello, fiddle, kazoo, vocals
- **Andy Mellon**: trumpet, vocals
- **Ed Neuhauser**: sousaphone, helicon, tuba, vocals
- **Paul Sartin**: fiddle, oboe, slide whistle, kazoo, vocals
- **John Spiers**: melodeons, Anglo concertina, Claviola, kazoo, vocals, tambourine
- **Sam Sweeney**: fiddle, English bagpipes, kazoo, vocals, whistle
- **Justin Thurgur**: trombone, vocals

In late 2015 Bellowhead started their farewell tour, after a decision by Jon Boden to leave the band. Their last concert was in Oxford - where it all began - on 1 May 2016. The album of the tour was released in April 2016.

'Sloe Gin'

This instrumental track is a mixture of English folk dance tunes, richly and playfully arranged in the Bellowhead manner.

The music starts with concertina supported by some energetic brass bass notes and some shaker sounds from the percussion section. There is a simple harmonic basis to the opening section, which is mostly tonic harmony with occasional dominant chords creating cadences that articulate the phrase structure.

The second half of the tune for this section (0'24") continues with similar musical material, but phrases now start on chord V rather than chord I. The final cadence is prefaced by new harmony with chords VI and IV at 0'42".

This expanded harmonic palette is then adopted for the next section starting at 0'45" which has a richer instrumentation.

At 2'00" an episode for solo fiddle accompanied by concertina begins. This is a good example of folk fiddling with a filigree, energetic melodic line while open strings (in this case the D) are frequently made to ring underneath. The harmonic underpinning here begins as I-V-IV-I; it then changes at 2'17" to half-speed harmonic rhythm using IV and V, which makes all the more effective the next change to a busy, syncopated IV-II-V-VI from 2'24". This is the first time the supertonic chord has been heard in the piece - its mellow minor character stands out as a fresh colour in the music.

The full band play again from 2'32". There is some playful rhythmic interplay with triple-time cross-rhythms from 2'49", before another fiddle episode starts at 3'30".

For the final portion of the track, starting at 3'44", there is a distinct change to new material that starts with the melodic instruments in unison over an active bass line and an upscaling of percussion for increased energy. The brass instruments are initially to the fore, the fiddles join in from 3'59".

'New York Girls'

This song from Bellowhead's best-selling album, *Hedonism*, is a ballad told with a verse – refrain structure which the band articulates with instrumental sections. The final verse has different music which adds to the drama of the tale being narrated.

Here is a listening guide to the song:

Lyrics	Commentary
Introduction	The introduction starts as a fiddle solo over a tonic pedal (D) with drum accompaniment The tonic pedal is reiterated in a syncopated rhythm: At 0'20" a bass **riff** appears underneath the repeating D using this shape: The introduction ends loudly with the full band playing
Verse 1: As I walked down to New York town, a fair maid I did meet She asked me back to see her place; she lived on Barrack Street	The verse is accompanied with just the string section There is a legato cello bass line in crotchets (starting high D-G-A-low D) Backbeats (off-beats) are emphasised
Chorus: And away, Santy, my dear Annie Oh you New York girls, can't you dance the polka?	The melody for the chorus is:  The two rising major 3rds at the start give it a positive character There are some backing vocals

Short instrumental	The fiddle is again to the fore The bass drum marks out the crotchet beats

Verse 2:
And when we got to Barrack Street, we stopped at forty-four
Her mother and her sister were waiting at the door

Chorus:
And away, Santy, my dear Annie
Oh you New York girls, can't you dance the polka?

Instrumental	Initially this is like the previous instrumental... ...however, after a surprise silence at 1'38" the bass riff from the intro returns, the full band is then involved in an exuberant tutti
Verse 3: And when I got inside the house, the drinks were passed around The liquor was so awful strong, my head went round and round	Listen out for the flamboyant percussion here
Verse 4: And then we had another drink before we sat to eat The liquor was so awful strong, I quickly fell asleep	This verse – the second of a pair – starts verse 4 on chord VI rather than I An instrumental countermelody / descant is heard above the vocal line

Chorus:
And away, Santy, my dear Annie
Oh you New York girls, can't you dance the polka?

Verse 5: When I awoke next morning, I had an aching head And there was I Jack all alone, stark naked in me bed	The concertina provides a more sustained harmonic backing here

Verse 6:
My gold watch and my money and my lady friend were gone

And there was I Jack all alone, stark naked in the room

Chorus:
And away, Santy, my dear Annie

Oh you New York girls, can't you dance the polka?

Instrumental	Shorter than the last instrumental, using only its first section Fiddles again to the fore
Verse 7: Oh looking round that little room, there's nothing I could see But a woman's shift and apron that were no use to me	There is a sense of tension as the accompaniment changes to being a reiterated subdominant G There are fragments of instrumental melody in the background
With a barrel for a suit of clothes, down Cherry Street forlorn Where Martin Churchill took me in and he sent me round Cape Horn	Still the G sounds, getting louder and more insistent…
So sailor lads, take warning when you land on New York shore You'll have to get up early to be smarter than a whore	In the second half of this couplet, the G moves to the dominant A, pointing to the return to D

Chorus:
And away, Santy, my dear Annie

Oh you New York girls, can't you dance the polka?

And away, Santy, my dear Annie

Oh you New York girls, can't you dance the polka?

Instrumental	Another exuberant instrument solo, initially similar to earlier ones At 4'11" a new descending bass pattern is heard, that passes through a mixolydian flattened 7th

Other pieces

On the AQA recommended listening list are three other songs from the Bellowhead catalogue:

'The Outlandish Knight' starts with a wonderfully plaintive fiddle solo over drone on A: listen out for the colourful use of the flattened 5th. The instrumental richness of the Bellowhead sounds is captured in a few phrases in the instrumental section from 2'05".

'Roll the woodpile down' is a terrific 'feel-good' song; it ends with a big choral sound from 2'40".

'Roll Alabama' is another song with a fiddle solo at the start, but listen out for the oboe as well.

And look out for *Bellowhead Live: The Farewell Tour* album released in April 2016.

SAMPLE ESSAY QUESTIONS

Essay advice

Before you start, review the advice on writing essays at the end of Chapter 3.

Each essay is worth 30 marks and should take 45 minutes to write.

For AS Level

1. Selecting one of the named artists, comment on how they have made music that is contemporary, building on older traditions. You should reference at least two different pieces of music in your response.
2. Compare and contrast the traditions of two of the named artists, using at least one piece by each to illustrate your answer.

For A Level

3. 'Contemporary musicians often think outside the box.' To what extent do you agree with this statement? Select at least two contrasting pieces by two different artists to illustrate your answer.
4. Choosing one of the named artists, write an essay analysing their contribution to the genre. You should reference at least two contrasting pieces of music in detail.
5. Choose pieces by two named artists you have studied, and explain their contrasting approaches to rhythm and texture.

Art music since 1910

OVERVIEW

This AoS will introduce you to some of the most fascinating and profound music written in the last hundred years or so.

Art, and music in particular, is a mirror on the creative individual, and on society in general: with this topic you can study composers and music that have something important to say about the journey of our society through the challenges of the 20th century and the world we live in today. Here you will find music that will make you think. The featured composers are:

- **Dmitri Shostakovich**
- **Olivier Messiaen**
- **Steve Reich**
- **James MacMillan**

THIS AOS IS FOR A LEVEL ONLY

The named composers and recommended listening in this AoS are:

Dmitri Shostakovich
Symphony no. 5 in D minor, 1st movement
Piano Concerto no. 2 in F major, 2nd movement
String Quartet no. 8 in C minor, 1st movement
Jazz Suite no. 2, 'Waltz' no. 2
Olivier Messiaen
L'ascension, Part 1 – in the version for solo organ
Quatuor pour la fin du temps, 2nd movement
Turangalîla-Symphonie, 1st movement
'L'alouette calandrelle' from Book 5 of *Catalogue d'Oiseaux*
Steve Reich
Music for 18 Musicians, 1st movement: 'Pulses'
Tehillim, 2nd movement
Different Trains, 1st movement

Opposite: Steve Reich

James MacMillan
Veni, Veni, Emmanuel, 3rd movement: 'Dance'
Memento for string quartet
Strathclyde Motets, no. 5: 'O Radiant Dawn'
Seraph for trumpet and string orchestra, 1st movement

Why is the music of these composers referred to as 'art music'? It can be a difficult term, but it attempts to differentiate music where the primary catalyst for its creation is neither popular appeal (music for commercial purpose or instant entertainment) or a folk tradition (music that is orally handed down in a society, such as music for nursery rhymes or traditional dance). Sometimes the word 'classical' is used, but this is also a tricky word and is best used to describe music of the Classical period in Western music (represented by the music of Haydn and Mozart).

One aspect of this third category - art music - is that it is likely to be more complex and intellectually involved than popular or folk music. Indeed, one could define art music as a kind of music that requires commitment and concentration from the listener.

WIDENING THE FOCUS

Some of the more complex examples of jazz and rock music might also be considered as art music.

When we consider the history of Western music, much of the repertoire was written before the notion was around of 'music as art'. Indeed, Bach included types of dance music - sarabandes and gigues - in his compositions, and others were not averse to borrowing traditional musical flavours, such as in Haydn's 'Gypsy Rondo' Piano Trio, Schubert's numerous *Ländler* for piano solo or Brahms's 21 Hungarian Dances for piano duet. Some composers rode the crest of a wave of popularity for particular types of piece: Handel with his Italian operas, which were all the rage in London in the 1710s and 1720s, for example, or Johann Strauss with his waltzes and polkas for dance-crazy 19th-century Vienna. To view all these 'classical' pieces as 'art music' is, at best, a posthumous evaluation - saying that, with hindsight, the music represents the values of their age - and is possibly a misuse of the term.

If we examine the history of painting, we can see that for much of the last millennium (approximately the length of the whole history of our European musical tradition), painting was undertaken in response to patronage from church or prince (hence the large number of biblical scenes and portraits of kings and nobility) and gradually for decorative purposes (especially in the landscape painting of the Romantic artists). However, any brief tour of a modern art gallery - for instance the Tate in London - will show that artists in the 20th century were inspired by a far wider range of motivations: political statement, technical experimentation, aesthetic creed and parody, among others. Consider the following four canvases, for instance:

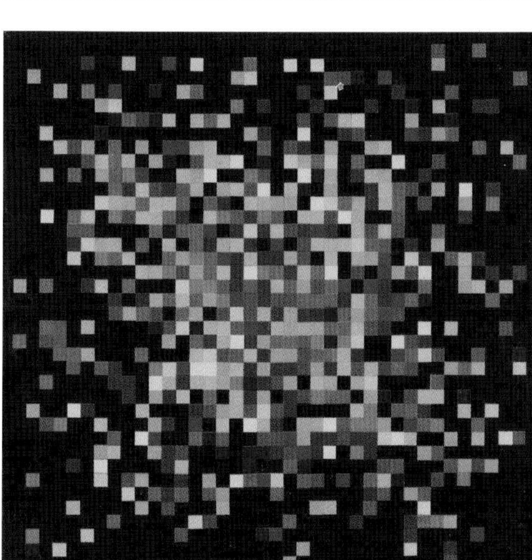

Top left: Kazimir Malevich: Portrait of MV Matyushin (1913)

Top right: Pablo Picasso: Le Rêve (1932)

Above: Ellsworth Kelly: Spectrum Colors Arranged by Chance IV (1951)

Right: Jack Vettriano: Just another day (2005)

These paintings represent a more conscious attempt to explore the wide-ranging potential of the art of painting. So it is with music of the last 100 years or so. The four composers chosen by AQA to represent the diversity of art music since 1910 have all seen music as a means of creating profound statements that, in each case, reflect a unique synthesis of personal beliefs (spiritual and otherwise) and interests, social and political context, and a fascination with exploring complex compositional techniques.

Dmitri Shostakovich

The composer

Dmitri Shostakovich (1906–1975) is one of the most significant of all 20th-century composers; in the words of the *New Grove Dictionary of Music and Musicians* (2nd edition, 2001), he 'is generally regarded as the greatest symphonist of the mid-20th century'. He is the voice of the individual in Soviet Russia, who for his entire adult life had a tortuous path to tread, expressing the experience of living under the oppression of the Communist regime (above all, under the fearsome dictator Joseph Stalin who was responsible for the deaths of over 10 million Russians), while avoiding confrontation with that regime.

Dmitri Shostakovich: the greatest Russian composer of the Soviet era

To us in 21st-century Britain, such a thought seems very strange, but the Communists would take considerable interest in the work of artists, and were quick to condemn any artistic expression that they considered critical of the regime, or 'infiltrated' by ideas from the 'decadent West'. For an artist, condemnation could easily and quickly lead to long-term imprisonment in a Siberian gulag, or even assassination. Ironically, it was working under this intense personal pressure that led Shostakovich to write his greatest music.

Shostakovich was born in St Petersburg. He began piano lessons with his mother at the age of 9, and joined the renowned Conservatory in St Petersburg when he was 13. Here he studied piano and composition; his graduation work (at the age of 19) was his 1st Symphony. By 1928 it had been performed in America; meanwhile Shostakovich had written his 2nd and 3rd Symphonies and his first opera, *The Nose*.

In 1931 Shostakovich began work on a new opera, *Lady Macbeth of the Mtsensk District*. When it was first performed in 1934, the composer was very much under the spotlight. Initially, critical reception was favourable; however, in January 1936 Stalin himself attended a performance. Eleven days later an article appeared in the Communist Party's newspaper *Pravda* (which translates as 'Truth') entitled 'Muddle instead of Music'. This was unsigned, but had obviously been ordered by Stalin, and it castigated Shostakovich for his new work. Performance of the opera was soon banned.

Shostakovich was facing an extreme crisis. Overnight he had had lost his place as the leading voice in Soviet music. Friends would not return his calls; people crossed the street to avoid him. He had already written his 4th Symphony - the most challenging piece he had yet written - and it was due for its first performance at the end of the year. After many rehearsals, Shostakovich withdrew the piece; it is unclear under what pressure. It finally received its premiere in 1961, long after Stalin's death.

Somehow Shostakovich avoided arrest, and in 1937 took the remarkably courageous path of writing a new symphony: his 5th. The intensity of the premiere on November 21 of that year, and the stress of waiting for a verdict from those in authority, were immense. In the event the hall was packed; many people broke down and wept during the slow movement,

Fifth section: figures 27–29

A dynamic entry of the percussion marks a strong change of mood as a grotesque parody of a march erupts in the trumpets.

There are various martial trappings:

- The 'left-right' effect of alternating bass notes on the timpani, tuba and double basses
- The motor rhythm now played incessantly on the snare drum
- The dotted rhythms in the trumpet melody from the third bar of figure 27 which give a rather pompous quality

Despite these features, the march tune starts with a variant of the first subject theme; it has been subverted from being a haunting, mournful theme, and is now an ostentatious, militaristic anthem. This transformation involves changing the original Phrygian mode (with its dark flattened 2nd) for the Lydian mode – the brightest of all modes with its sharpened 4th.

1st violins at fig. 1 (Exposition)

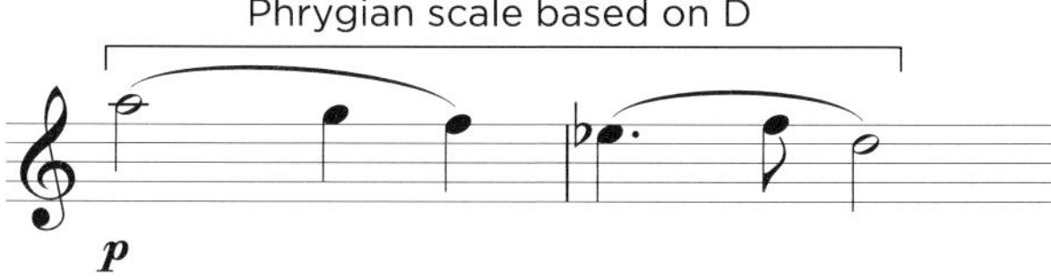

1st trumpet at fig. 27 (Development)

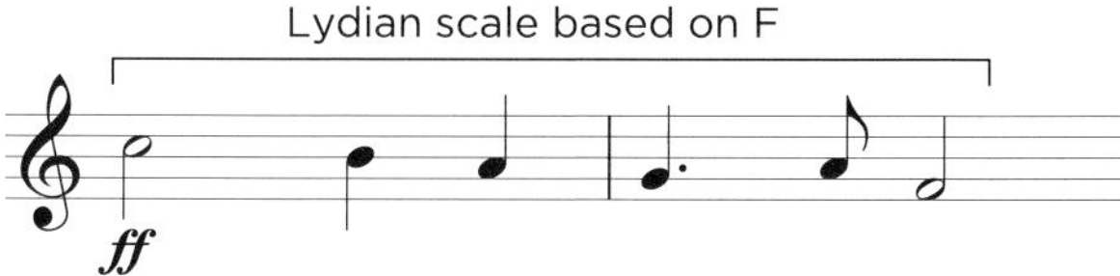

After figure 28 Shostakovich adds various wind instruments to the parade, carefully selecting timbres that will add to the shrill quality: piccolo, high flute and oboe, and the E♭ clarinet.

Sixth section: figures 29–32

The marching F–C timpani continues for two more bars; the momentum is then propelled by a long chain of As played on the brittle xylophone, winds and violins in support, in the insistent two semiquavers + quaver pattern.

Under this, the bass instruments of the orchestra, led by trombones, blast out a rhythmically augmented version of the opening dotted rhythm canon. As this continues, trumpets and horns add the main first subject theme at figure 30 in a turbulent mêlée. With the ***ff*** entry of timpani and snare drum on the motor rhythm, the whole texture descends with dissonant chords, while another *stringendo* gives the music a sense of headlong descent into terror.

Seventh section: figures 32–36

The music reaches its fastest tempo (♪ = 138) and the winds and strings engage in a furious version of the symphony's opening dotted rhythms, played ***ff***. Meanwhile, the second subject is transformed into a tyrannically monstrous melody played ***ff*** by trombones and tuba, and then in canon by horns (and from figure 34 by trumpets).

Four bars after figure 35, the trombones drop out and there is an intense build-up on A (the movement's dominant) with the dotted rhythm figure. There is a sense of a void in the bass, waiting to be filled, almost like the sea retreating before a tsunami strikes.

Recapitulation

At figure 36 the void is emphatically filled by the return of the bass instruments and a massive bass D. A cymbal crash reinforces the moment. This all suggests the point of recapitulation with the return of the tonic tonality.

We are, however, a world away from the start of the symphony and Shostakovich boldly ignores the main first subject theme. Instead, in a remarkable passage that sustains rather than releases the great intensity built up in the development, he uses the subsidiary willowy melody first heard either side of figure 4. By having nearly the whole orchestra playing this in a four octaves texture, he generates both power and a tense constraint. Only occasional blasts of D in the heavy brass and timpani punctuate the effect, and never with a 3rd sounding.

Eventually the fury passes, the tempo slows and the dynamic melts away to ***pp***. At figure 39, the second subject returns in its original soft, floating guise and for a while at least, in the peaceful context of D major, which sounds wonderfully beautiful at this point. After figure 41 the tonality returns to more minor modes.

Coda

Only now does Shostakovich return to the main first subject theme; however, he does so in enigmatic fashion, treating it to inversion while maintaining its cold Phrygian character. The movement ends sombrely with lonely solos on the piccolo and first violin, a distant echo of the opening leaping dotted rhythms in the cello and basses, and eerie chromatic scales on the celesta.

GET TO KNOW IT

You will be rewarded for your commitment in getting to know this symphony. It is rightly frequently played, and nothing beats hearing it in the concert hall.

Undoubtedly the composer was under intense strain at the time of writing this stunning symphony, and there are deep personal aspects to the music.

As you listen to the whole work, look out for the following:

- Unusual twists in the melodic shapes
- The use of both consonant and dissonant harmony
- Distinct changes of texture that articulate the structure
- The brilliance of the orchestration, especially in making use of the extremes of each instrument's range

Other pieces

Shostakovich was enormously prolific. His symphonies, concertos and string quartets contain a lot of very fine music. The more you explore, the more you will become familiar with his unique sound.

Piano Concerto No. 2

Shostakovich wrote six concertos: two each for piano, violin and cello. The second piano concerto was written in 1957 for his son Maxim as a 19th birthday present; Maxim gave its premiere as part of his graduation recital at Moscow Conservatoire. It uses quite a small orchestra: double wind plus piccolo, horns, timpani, snare drum and strings.

The outer movements have a positive spirit, at times quirky, sparkling and witty (some of the piano writing is reminiscent of technical exercises - appropriate for a graduation piece maybe) and sometimes stirring and bold. In the finale there is considerable use of pizzicato strings, suggestive of the traditional Russian balalaika orchestra.

The balalaika is a Russian folk stringed instrument plucked or strummed like a guitar, and when grouped into a balalaika orchestra with various percussion instruments, has a very distinctive folk sound which is quite different to most Western European music. It was much encouraged during the Soviet era as an instrument of the 'proletariat'.

The slow movement is lyrical and romantic, contrasting tonic minor and major. The strings start in C minor with an idea that suggests the Baroque sarabande by the emphasis on second beats. Note the modal take on the key (no raised 7ths) and the rich root position Neapolitan chord in the 9th bar:

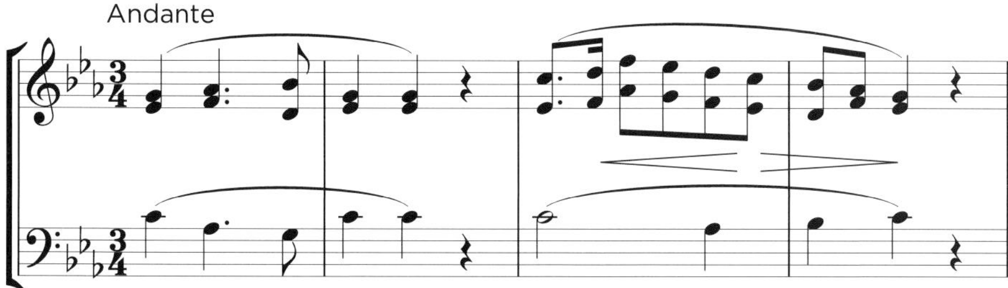

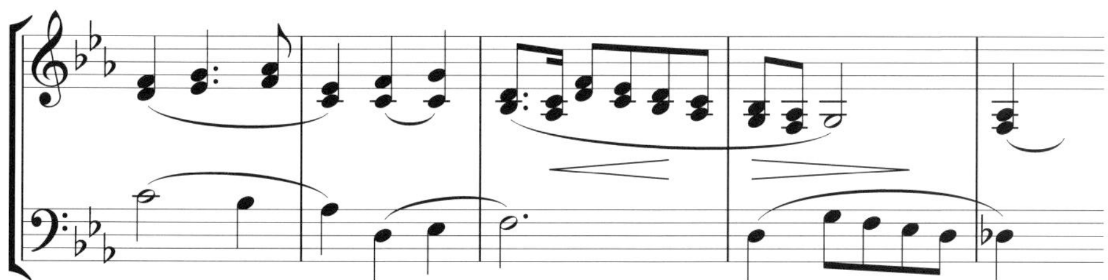

The introduction concludes with a melting tierce de Picardie as the piano enters with a beautiful melody that makes considerable use of hemiola:

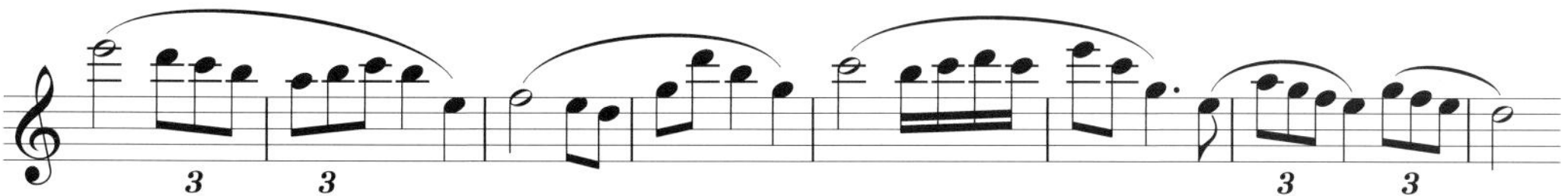

Under this the left hand of the piano has gentle triplet quavers creating various cross rhythms, and the strings provide a sustained accompaniment. The harmony is diatonic in the first four bars (the move to chord III in the second bar adds unexpected minor colour and sets up a 9–8 suspension on chord II on the downbeat of the third bar); the second half of the theme is harmonised with descending chromatic lines in the orchestra.

For all the beauty of this C major theme, when it is recapitulated (figure 32), Shostakovich chooses to do so in C minor. This makes for a more poignant mood, and sets up a strong contrast when the music moves straight into the vibrant third movement (*'attacca'*).

String Quartet No. 8

Shostakovich's 15 string quartets are the most significant contribution to the genre made by any composer in the 20th century. The eighth was written in 1960 at another point of crisis in Shostakovich's life that involved ill health, divorce and finally yielding to great pressure from the authorities to join the Communist Party. The work is in five interconnected movements, and lasts around 20 minutes.

The quartet uses numerous self-quotations, each acquiring either a sadder or more violent character than it had in its original setting. The most painful is in the fourth movement when the composer quotes from an aria in his opera *Lady Macbeth* in which the character Katerina sings of her longing for her lover.

The first movement, a Largo, opens with the most significant motif of the whole work: a four-note pattern - D, E♭, C, B - which is a musical signature. In German musical notation, *Es* is E♭ and *H* is B♮: Bach was known to have spelt his name in music notation as B♭ A C B♮, so these four pitches can be seen to spell out DSCH and are therefore self-referential as the start of D(mitri) Schostakovich (as it can be transliterated from the Russian Cyrillic alphabet).

This mournful melodic shape is given a mysterious fugal treatment at the start, each player entering in turn:

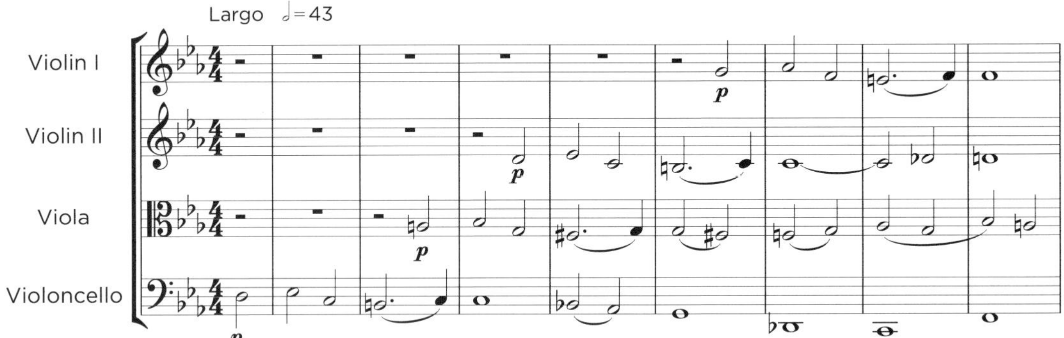

Once the fugal introduction is complete, the first main section starts halfway through bar 11 where the motif is heard in three octaves. By bar 16 Shostakovich is making the first self-quote which is based on the opening to his 1st Symphony:

1st Symphony, opening:

String Quartet No. 8, bar 16:

From bar 28 there is a second section with a strange chromatic melodic line in the first violin over a sustained drone in the other instruments. This section ends with a new statement of the DSCH motif in the cello at bars 46–49.

A third section then starts at bar 50 with the drone still present. When the 1st violin enters at bar 55, the melody seems to be deliberately reminiscent of the first subject of the 5th Symphony:

Symphony No.5, 1st movement b.6

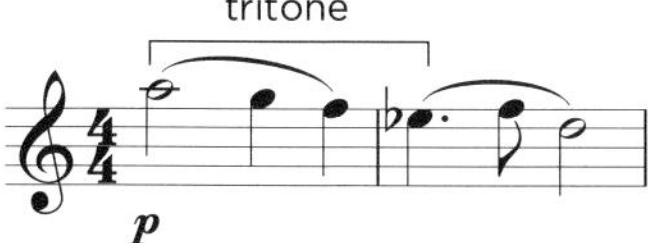

String Quartet No.8, 1st movement b.55

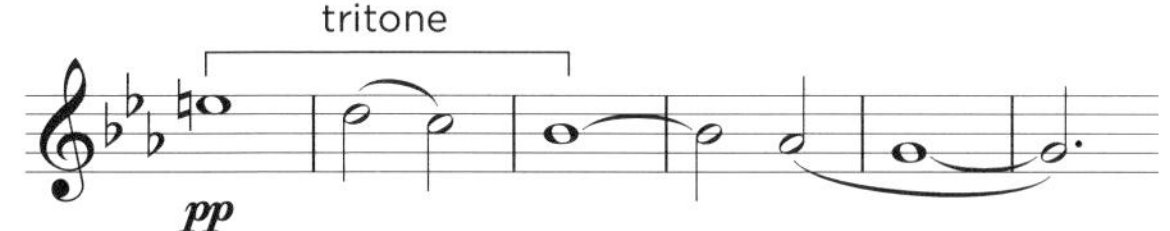

Music of the second section returns from bar 85, but in a varied manner, without the drone and with the chromatic line in the cello. The return of the DSCH motif at bar 104 returns the movement to its first main section and the quote from the 1st Symphony. The surprising final G♯ prepares the way for the second movement.

Jazz Suite No. 2, 'Waltz' No. 2

This *Jazz Suite* (in some places called *Suite for Variety Orchestra*) may not sound particularly infused by jazz idioms, but one must appreciate that American jazz was considered 'degenerate' by the Soviet authorities and banned from Russia. It does, however, find Shostakovich in a lighter mood.

The waltz mood is unmistakable (there is a clear 'um-cha-cha' pattern). The opening theme is heard on saxophone – a nod to the jazz world – and is a classically balanced melody in 4-bar phrases. The chromatic lower appoggiatura in bar 15 is a colourful twist:

When the tune is repeated in a full orchestration the effect is more fairground than jazz club. Listen out for use of the glockenspiel – a Shostakovich favourite. The movement is in ternary form, and the trombone takes the role of the saxophone on the reprise of the main melody.

EXPLORING FURTHER

Shostakovich was a very prolific composer, and there is a huge amount of fascinating music to explore, including his music for solo piano. This will help you become better acquainted with his style and prepare you for the listening part of the examination paper.

Olivier Messiaen

The composer

Olivier Messiaen (1908–1992) is the major French composer of the 20th century. He was still an infant when Stravinsky took Paris by storm in 1913 with his revolutionary ballet score *The Rite of Spring*, and, as a young boy of prodigious musical talent, Messiaen was the first great French composer to grow up in a musical world that was free of the tradition of tonality-dominated Western Classical music (though late in life he expressed admiration for Mozart).

Olivier Messiaen: in addition to being a great composer, he was a fine organist

Among his influences, which included birdsong, oriental music and a fascination with **modality**, his Roman Catholic faith was central. He was a wonderful organist and – in the renowned French tradition – improviser on the instrument. In 1931 he was appointed organist at the church of La Trinité in Paris, a post he held until his death over 60 years later.

As a boy, Messiaen would ask for opera scores as presents; the gift of Debussy's *Pelléas et Mélisande* in 1918 had a profound effect: 'probably the most decisive influence on me' he later said.

Remarkably, Messiaen entered the Paris Conservatoire at the age of 11 where he won numerous prizes over the next decade. He studied organ with the legendary Marcel Dupré, but it was Maurice Emmanuel, an expert in ancient Greek modes, who was the most significant to Messiaen's development as a composer. He soon had his first published works, the eight *Préludes* for solo piano and an unusually slow piece for solo organ called *Le Banquet Céleste*. Early though this was in his career, these pieces already reveal a unique approach to modality and preference for the tritone over the perfect 4th and perfect 5th of conventional cadences.

Modes of limited transposition

As an organist in the Catholic tradition, Messiaen inherited an instinct for the traditional modes of medieval music. These are often defined as white note scales beginning on different notes, but a clearer way to understand them is as patterns of tones and semitones:

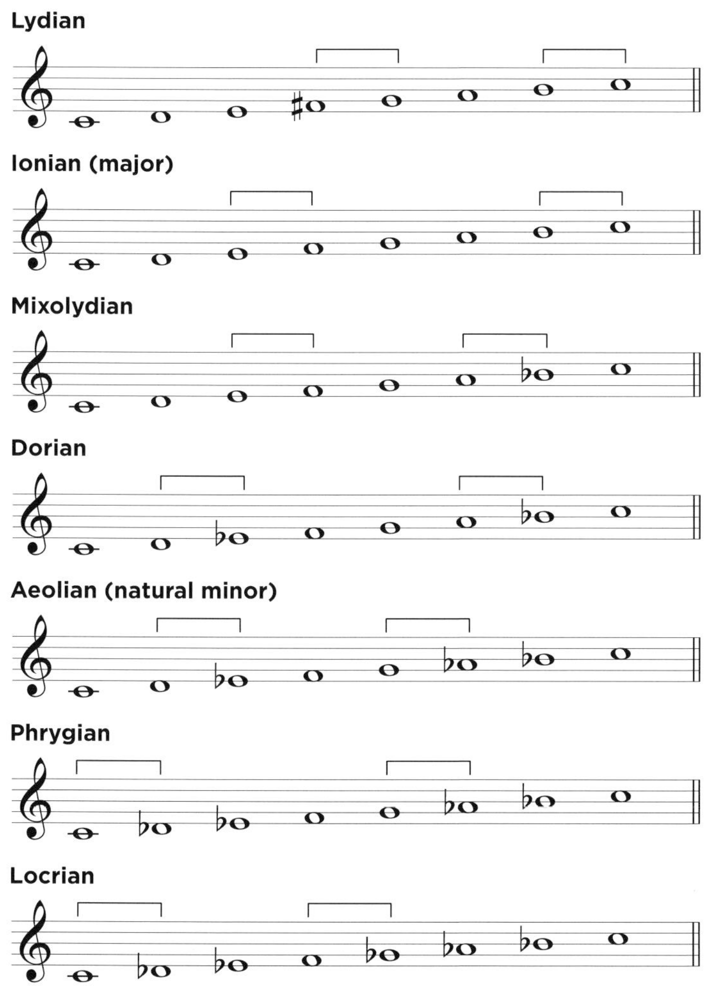

All these have the potential to generate 12 unique scales by transposing the pattern to begin on any of the notes of the chromatic scale. For instance, the Ionian mode - which is recognised today as the major scale - is the basis for 12 different major scales.

In medieval days, these modes provided the basis for chants. The choice of mode would lock the music into a particular mood. The brightest mood came with the Lydian mode, where the semitones are in the highest positions of the scale; the darkest mood came with the Phrygian mode where the semitones are at the (almost) lowest positions. The Locrian was not used. All the other six allow for a perfect 5th between tonic and dominant; the Locrian has a diminished 5th - a tritone - at this point, and the tritone was considered to be *diabolus in musica* - the devil in music.

Messiaen was fascinated by other possibilities. He was a great admirer of the music of his compatriot Debussy who often used the **whole-tone scale** in his impressionist style.

An interesting fact about whole-tone scales is that there are only two:

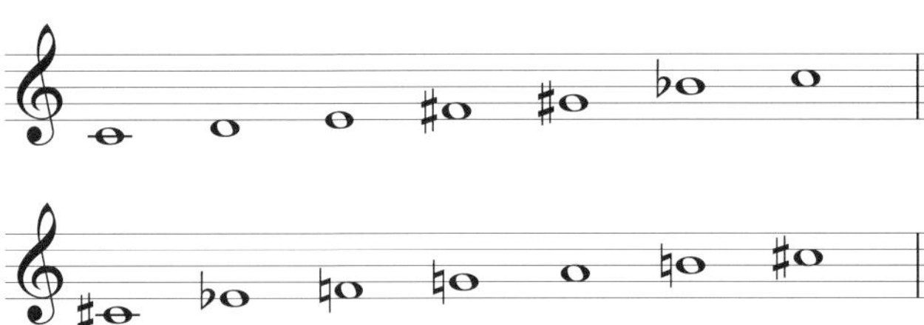

However you choose to transpose either of these two scales, you will end up with one or other of the two sets of notes. This means that they are modes of limited transposition.

Messiaen's modes of limited transposition

Messiaen tended to avoid the whole-tone scale, maybe out of deference to Debussy; instead he designed other modes of limited transposition for himself. The full set is:

The first mode (whole tone scale): All intervals are tones. There are 2 transpositions.

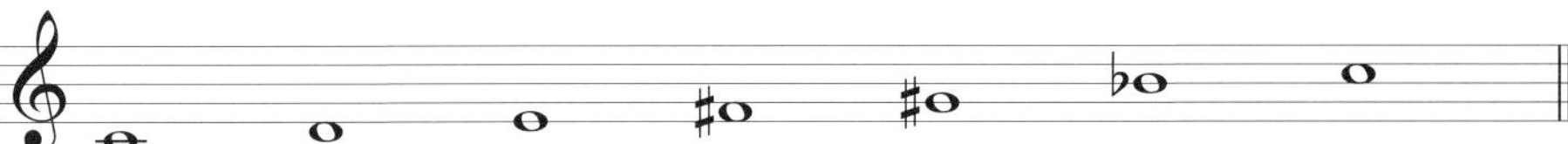

The second mode (octatonic scale): alternate tones and semitones. It has three transpositions and two versions (the other starts on D♭, E, G or B♭).

The third mode: based on tone, semitone, semitone. It has four transpositions and three versions (the others start on D, F♯, or B♭ and E♭, G or B).

The fourth mode: based on semitone, semitone, minor 3rd, semitone. It has six transpositions and four versions (the others start on D♭ or G, D or A♭, and F or B).

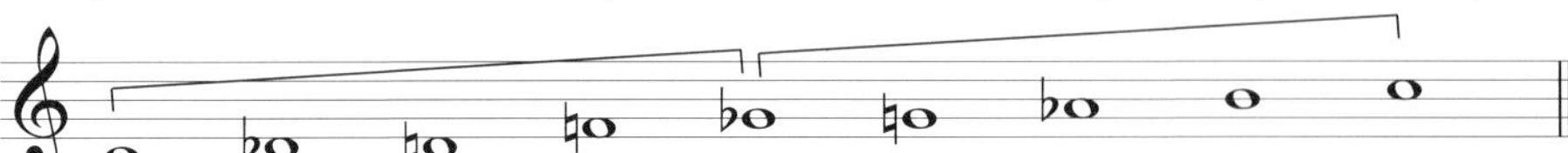

The fifth mode: based on semitone, major 3rd, semitone. It has six transpositions and three versions (the others start on D♭ or G, and F or B)

The sixth mode: based on tone, tone, semitone, semitone. It has six transpositions and four versions (the others start on D or G♯, E or A♯, and F or B)

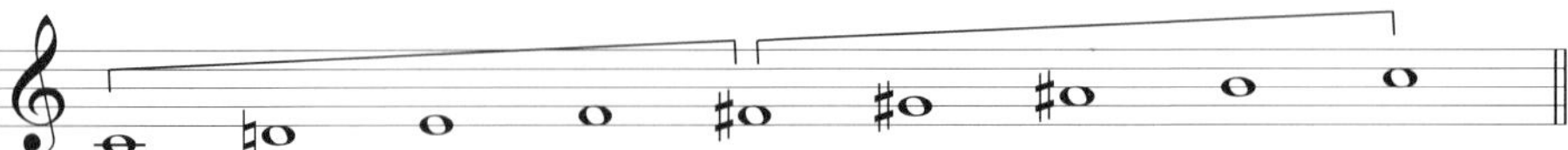

The seventh mode: based on semitone, semitone, semitone, tone, semitone. It has six transpositions and five versions (the others start on D♭ or G, D or A♭, E♭ or A and F or B)

The essence of these modes is their internal symmetry. This is unlike the familiar scales of the tonal system which, like the piano keyboard with its pattern of two and three black notes, do not have a symmetrical approach to the octave scale. As a result, all but one of Messiaen's modes split the octave exactly in half, thereby emphasising the interval of a tritone instead of the tonal system's preference for the perfect 5th and perfect 4th. The exception is the third mode which is based on a division of the octave into equal 3rds and therefore emphasises the equally exotic sounding augmented triad.

Non-retrogradable rhythms

In a parallel approach to rhythm, Messiaen was also fascinated by symmetry in his approach to rhythm, sometimes using rhythms that are identical when played in reverse (that is, they are *palindromic*, like the word 'level') and therefore cannot knowingly be used backwards.

This bar from the early *Préludes* (*Instants défunts*) shows the principle in the left hand:

Later life and career

During the 1930s Messiaen wrote several substantial cycles of pieces for the organ, including *L'ascension* (which existed first as an orchestral version) and *La Nativité du Seigneur*. He also became interested in a new electronic instrument - the **ondes Martenot** - which was demonstrated at the Paris Exposition in 1937. The ondes Martenot is an early electronic instrument, played with a keyboard, and producing eerie, wavering notes. Messiaen is one of the most notable composers for the instrument.

In 1940 he was captured by the advancing German army and was held prisoner at Görlitz, where he wrote his amazing *Quatuor pour la fin du temps* (*Quartet for the end of time*), which was first performed by fellow prisoners at the camp. He was released by the Germans in 1941 and returned to the Paris Conservatoire where he continued to teach until his retirement in 1978. There he taught many significant composers, including Boulez, Stockhausen and Xenakis.

In the 1940s he wrote some significant piano works, including *Vingt regards sur l'enfant-Jésus*, and then embarked on three works inspired by the legend of Tristan and Isolde (memorably set as an opera by Wagner in 1857–1859). The second of these is the *Turangalîla-Symphonie*.

MESSIAEN'S INSPIRATION

His religious faith remained Messiaen's primary inspiration, but he also became interested in birdsong and the Orient.

In the 1950s Messiaen became fascinated by birdsong and this led to a number of related works, starting with *Le merle noir (The blackbird)* for solo flute and piano in 1952.

Musicologist Paul Griffiths has said Messiaen was a more conscientious ornithologist than any previous composer, and a more musical observer of birdsong than any previous ornithologist (*Olivier Messiaen and the Music of Time*, Cornell University Press, 1985). Another influence was music from the Orient, especially following a trip to Japan in 1962.

Most of his later works are on an enormous scale, including *La Transfiguration de Notre Seigneur Jésus-Christ* for large chorus and orchestra, an opera (or, as he preferred to call it, 'spectacle') *Saint François d'Assise*, and his final work (completed months before his death), *Eclairs sur l'au-delà* ('Illuminations of the beyond') commissioned by the New York Philharmonic Orchestra. This final piece is a summation of the composer and his ideas, using modes of limited transposition, birdsong and theological ideas from the Catholic faith in an often ecstatic synthesis.

Bar by bar: *L'ascension*, first movement

***L'ascension* was composed in 1932/33 as an orchestral suite of four movements. The composer described it as 'four meditations for orchestra'. The movements are as follows:**

1. *Majesté du Christ demandant sa gloire à son Père* ('The majesty of Christ demanding his glory from the Father')
2. *Alleluias sereins d'une âme qui désire le ciel* ('Serene alleluias of a soul that longs for heaven')
3. *Alleluia sur la trompette, alleluia sur la cymbale* ('Alleluia on the trumpet, alleluia on the cymbal')
4. *Prière du Christ montant vers son Père* ('Prayer of Christ ascending towards his Father')

Soon after Messiaen produced a version for solo organ, which has a completely different third movement called *Transports de joie d'une âme devant la gloire du Christ qui est la sienne* ('Outbursts of joy from a soul before the glory of Christ which is its own glory'). AQA has recommended listening to the later organ version for the first movement, though the comparison with the orchestral edition is fascinating.

The opening movement is marked *Très lent et majestueux* (very slow and majestic) and there is immediately a sense of spiritual mystery.

The movement has a ternary shape:

- A section bar 1–6
- B section bar 7–14
- A section bar 15–22

A section

There is in the first bar a sense of a dominant 7th chord resolving to its tonic chord of E major, yet this is no commonplace cadential progression:

- The dominant 7th harmony is heard in the left hand in third inversion; in most classical music this would see the bass fall to a Ic chord, but here not only does the bass rise, but the whole progression is infused with a sense of ascent
- The melody enriches the dominant 7th harmony by beginning with a dominant 13th (G♯) and then an augmented 4th (E♯) as might be found in a French augmented 6th chord, but neither of these notes resolves in the way that such functional tonal notes usually would
- The resolution onto the E major chord is further coloured by passing dissonant harmonies, especially the F major-like chord on the 6th quaver

If we collect and order the pitches being used in this bar, we find a scale typical of Messiaen:

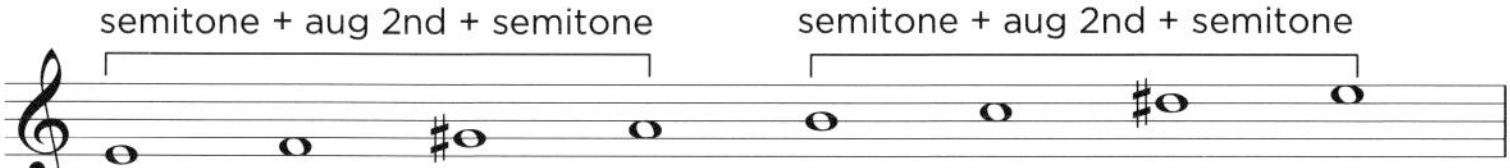

Bars 2–3 provide a longer second phrase with a twisting melodic line in the right hand that includes Messiaen's favoured tritone (F♮ to B♮). Here the composer is using a very interesting pitch set which is reflective about the home note ('tonic') of E:

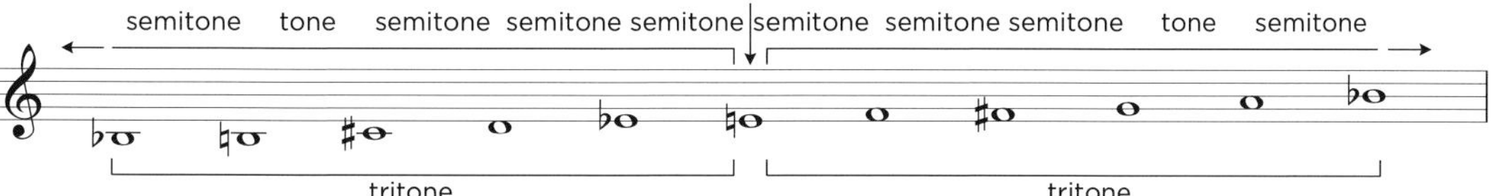

Bars 4–6 contain essentially the same music as bars 1–3 with a few small adjustments.

The sense of metre is opaque throughout. The music is notated in $\frac{12}{8}$, but the very slow tempo and various ties disguise the sense of pulse. This is heavenly music, not earthly.

B section

These eight bars are a mosaic of melodic and harmonic ideas, most of which are shorter than a bar long, allowing Messiaen to hide both the pulse and the downbeat.

The first idea is a new melodic shape that starts with a rising tritone. This is soon followed by a triadic shape that rhythmically floats in space, disregarding the pulse. Both ideas recur during the next few bars.

The harmonic colours become increasingly vivid as the music becomes more chromatic in the second half of the section. The music seems to be in search of a route back to where it started, and Messiaen finds an extraordinary chord progression to end the passage, approaching the helpful B^7 chord from F major – a tritone away.

A section

This begins in the same way as the start of the piece but takes a change of direction in the third bar (bar 17), where the composer adopts a more homophonic texture (perhaps reminiscent of the end of the B section) as a chord sequence of G minor–A minor–B minor–E major occurs with a marked crescendo.

Bar 19 correlates to bar 5 but this is then extended by a bar. The final phrase takes the form of another homophonic progression of rising chords that pass from ***pp*** to reach ***ff*** on the final triumphant E major chord.

Turangalîla-Symphonie

Messiaen composed this huge work in 1946–1948 to a commission from the conductor of the Boston Symphony Orchestra, Serge Koussevitzky. Unfortunately, Koussevitzky fell ill, and the premiere was conducted by Leonard Bernstein.

The work was inspired by the great romantic legend of Tristan and Isolde, and Messiaen described it as a love song. The title comes from two Sanskrit words *Turanga*, meaning time, and *lîla*, which is more difficult to translate: it means love but also the play that is life and death.

The piece lasts for about 80 minutes and is scored for a large orchestra, including triple wind, 12 brass players, 11 percussionists and strings. In addition, there is a very demanding solo piano part and a part for the ondes Martenot.

There are ten movements:

1. 'Introduction', *Modéré, un peu vif*
2. 'Chant d'amour 1', *Modéré, lourd*
3. 'Turangalîla 1', *Presque lent, rêveur*
4. 'Chant d'amour 2', *Bien modéré*
5. 'Joie du sang des étoiles' (Joy of the blood of the stars), *Vif, passionné avec joie*
6. 'Jardin du sommeil d'amour' (Garden of love's sleep), *Très modéré, très tendre*
7. 'Turangalîla 2', *Un peu vif, bien modéré*
8. 'Développement d'amour' (Development of love), *Bien modéré*
9. 'Turangalîla 3', *Un peu vif, bien modéré*
10. 'Final', *Modéré, presque vif, avec une grande joie*

There is a super short film introducing the symphony with commentary by the charismatic Venezuelan conductor, Gustavo Dudamel, available at **http://bit.ly/Turangalila**. You can find a complete performance of this work by the National Youth Orchestra at **http://bit.ly/MessiaenNYO**

Important motifs

Turangalîla is not symphonic in the traditional sense. To bring cohesion to its ten movement structure, there are four themes or motifs which recur throughout the work. These are:

1. The statue theme. This is loud and slow, oppressive and brutal:

2. The flower theme:

3. The love theme. This is the most important of all and has many different guises from being played quietly by the strings in movement 6 to a full orchestral climax in the Final:

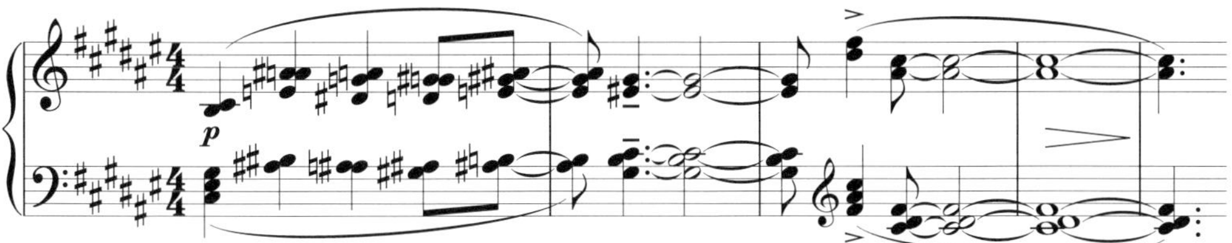

4. A simple chain of complex chords:

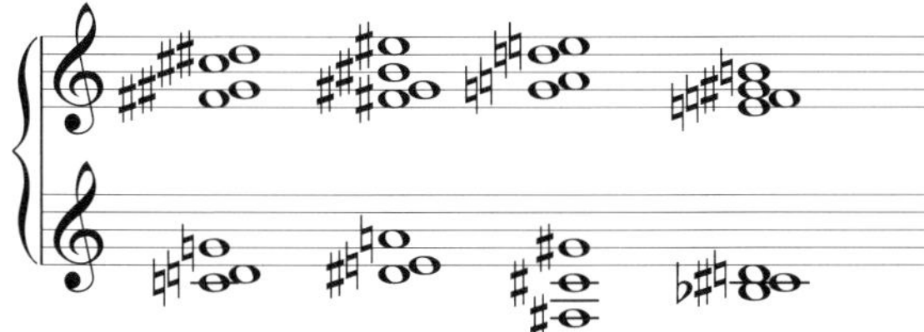

Bar by bar: First movement: 'Introduction'

Opening to figure 2

There is an immediately vigorous energy with angular semiquavers played *ff* by strings, and destinations to each short phrase marked by wind and brass notes that occur in rhythmically unpredictable places, giving a sense of urgency. The very first melodic interval is a tritone.

The bar before figure 2 has a sense of manic fanfare with a rapid descent of tritones in the winds and piano and a cymbal crash just before the energy breaks off into a moment of silence.

Figure 2 to figure 4

There is a series of statements of different lengths of the statue motif in the trombones and other instruments underneath a mêlée of high tremolo cluster chords on the piano, high trills in strings and piccolo, and a shimmering roll on a suspended cymbal.

Figure 4 to figure 7

This is a highly coloristic passage, starting a little tentatively and gathering momentum.

Among the techniques used are:

- Contrary motion arpeggio figures using complex and juxtaposed chords in the piano
- Arabesque-like woodwind figures
- High string **harmonics**
- Splashes of exotic chords on the celesta

From figure 6 there is a rapid descent throughout the orchestra, not least with a glissando on the ondes Martenot.

Figure 7 to figure 10

A second descent is made across the orchestra at figure 7, this time declamatory and angular with a series of tritones: D–G♯, D♯–A, E–B♭, F–B and finally G–D♭. Note values get progressively shorter: in quavers – 3, 2½, 2, 1½, 1 and ½. This is followed by some increasingly eerie music with alternating chords using semiquaver and quaver alternately across the beat, and skilfully scored to reduce the intensity of the sound incrementally.

At figure 9 the flower motif is introduced for the first time on the clarinets and there is a sense of delicacy with two bars scored for celesta, vibraphone and piano over sustained ***pp*** cellos and basses.

Figure 10 to figure 12

The tranquillity is suddenly broken off and the piano then embarks on a virtuoso **cadenza** that traverses the whole compass of the instrument. There are brief allusions to both the flower and statue figures midway through.

Figure 12 to figure 21

This extraordinary and substantial section creates a sound world related to the Balinese Gamelan orchestra that fascinated Messiaen.

This is achieved by:

- Ostinato-like melodic shapes - for example the flutes and 'inside' 1st violin line at figure 12
- Indulgent use of percussion including 'cloches' (bells)
- Polarised texture in the solo piano part
- Control of complex cross rhythms through fascinating number patterns. For instance, the 'caisse claire' (snare drum) has notes - measured in semiquaver lengths - as follows:

2 + 1-1-1 + 2-3-2 + 1-1-1 + 2-4-2 + 1-1-1 + 2-3-2 + 1-1-1 (etc.)

Amid all the intertwining jingling patterns, there is a dreamy legato strand in the elaborate texture provided by 2nd violins and violas, both *divisi*, playing exotic chords. Rhythmically, these too are controlled by number pattern. Measured in quavers, the pattern is

2 + 2 + 2 + 1 + 1½ + 1

repeated many times over, as this element of the texture roams freely across a wide compass. It is as though the 2nd violins and violas are the wind blowing in a garden of wind chimes, which are represented by the percussion and other instruments.

The passage is given further articulation by moments where the piano has a complex chord repeating in semiquavers with a crescendo, and by chromatically descending chords in the brass.

Figure 21 to end

The gamelan-like passage breaks off and the movement's conclusion starts with a passage similar to that which occurred at figure 7 (though there are differences). Two bars of the chords alternating in semiquaver + quaver rhythm lead into a final rapid descent across the orchestra, which includes another glissando on the ondes Martenot, and the movement ends with a loud thud on the bass drum.

Quatuor pour la fin du temps

The *Quartet for the end of time* was written in 1940 while Messiaen was a prisoner of war at Görlitz (now in Poland and known as Zgorzelec).

It was composed for three other professional musicians in the camp to play, with the composer himself, and is scored for clarinet, violin, cello and piano - the combination of instruments the composer happened to have available to him. The first performance was in the camp on January 15, 1941 in the rain, listened to by about 400 fellow prisoners; Messiaen later said 'Never was I listened to with such rapt attention and comprehension'.

Inspired by the Book of Revelation, the work is in eight movements:

1. 'Crystal Liturgy' for the full quartet – a movement that includes imitations of blackbird and nightingale song
2. 'Vocalise for the Angel who announces the end of time' for all four players
3. 'Abyss of birds' for solo clarinet
4. 'Interlude' for violin, cello and clarinet
5. 'Praise to the eternity of Jesus' for cello and piano
6. 'Dance of fury, for the seven trumpets' for all four players
7. 'Tangle of Rainbows, for the Angel who announces the end of time' for all four players
8. 'Praise to the immortality of Jesus' for violin and piano

A performance of the full quartet lasts around 50 minutes.

In the second movement, after a short and stirring introduction for all four players, the main substance is a ghostly musical landscape which keeps to the same eerie texture. Violin and cello, both muted, play a strange, sinewy melodic line that has a rhythmic profile typical of Messiaen in which there is no obvious awareness of the pulse due to the use of single semiquavers and various ties in the continual line. Meanwhile the piano has constant complex chords in semiquavers that produce lots of falling phrases. It is music that seems to capture the expression 'frozen in time'.

Catalogue d'oiseaux

The *Catalogue of Birds* for solo piano was published in 1958 at the end of a decade of working on pieces based on birdsong. There are 13 pieces in total, published in seven books in a symmetrical pattern typical of the composer:

Book 1

I 'Le chocard des Alpes' (Alpine chough)

II 'Le loriet' (golden oriole)

III 'Le merle bleu' (blue rock thrush)

Book 2

IV 'Le traquet stapazin' (black-eared wheatear)

Book 3

V 'La chouette hulotte' (tawny owl)

VI 'L'alouette lulu' (wood lark)

Book 4

VII 'La rousserolle effarvatte' (reed warbler)

Book 5

VIII 'L'alouette calandrelle' (short-toed lark)

IX 'La bouscarle' (Cetti's warbler)

Book 6

X 'Le merle de roche' (rock thrush)

Book 7

XI 'La buse variable' (buzzard)

XII 'Le traquet rieur' (black wheatear)

XIII 'Le courlis cendré' (curlew)

Although most prominent in each piece is the bird of its title, others also appear. In all, 77 songbirds are referenced. Messiaen marks these in the music, so it is important to follow a score as you study this music. There is also non-birdsong content to give a setting for each piece.

Bar by bar: 'L'alouette calandrelle'

'L'alouette calandrelle' (short-toed lark) is set in the Crau region of Provence in the south of France. The piece has three sections plus a coda. The focal point of the piece is actually the appearance of the skylark in the coda, which is marked '*jubilation véhémente*'. The order of the appearance of the birds is as follows:

Section 1	Bars 1-26	Introductory chords (= setting), short-toed lark (bar 2), chorus of cicadas (bar 9), kestrel (bar 12), quail (bar 14), short-toed lark (bar 16)
Section 2	Bars 27-57	Short-toed lark and crested lark in counterpoint (bar 27), short-toed lark (bar 44)
Section 3	Bars 58-79	Chorus of cicadas (bar 58), kestrel (bar 64), quail (bar 68), introductory chords and short-toed lark (from bar 70)
Coda	Bars 80-end	Quail (bar 80), skylark (bar 81), quail (bar 95), introductory chords (bar 96), short-toed lark (bar 97)

Steve Reich

The Composer

Steve Reich (b. 1936) is an American composer who was at the forefront of pioneering a new style in the Sixties that has become known as Minimalism. He is particularly associated with compositions that explore the use of the phasing of repetitive patterns and the use of combining live performers and recorded tape.

Reich's childhood was musical, but unexceptionally so. He was born in New York and took piano lessons as a boy and has described growing up with a listening repertoire of 'middle-class favourites'. He also learned the drums. At university he majored in Philosophy and only began to study composition after graduation, before enrolling at the Juilliard School.

Initially Reich explored 12-tone music in his composition, but he was soon strongly influenced by Terry Riley's 1964 piece *In C* which is often thought of (not altogether accurately) as the first minimalist composition. Reich's first major work *It's Gonna Rain* shows a similar approach to shifting patterns; it also uses a fragment from a sermon given by a Pentecostal street-preacher, which is multi-layered on multiple tape loops that gradually move out of phase with each other.

A more famous early piece is *Clapping Music* written in 1972. Here a pattern 12 quavers long is clapped by two people, with one of the clappers shifting the start of the pattern by one quaver every 12th bar until, after 144 bars, both are in unison again. Further 'phase-shifting' pieces followed, including *Music for Mallet Instruments, Voices and Organ* and *Six Pianos*, both written in 1973.

Reich continues to be an innovative musical creator. He has drawn on his Jewish roots, especially in *Tehillim* (1981) and his Grammy-award-winning *Different Trains* of 1988, which contrasts the train journeys he was making during World War II with the train journeys other Jews in Europe were being forced to take to the Nazi death camps.

In the 1990s Reich turned to opera in collaboration with his wife, video artist Beryl Korot. Together they created *The Cave*, which explores the origins of Judaism, Christianity and

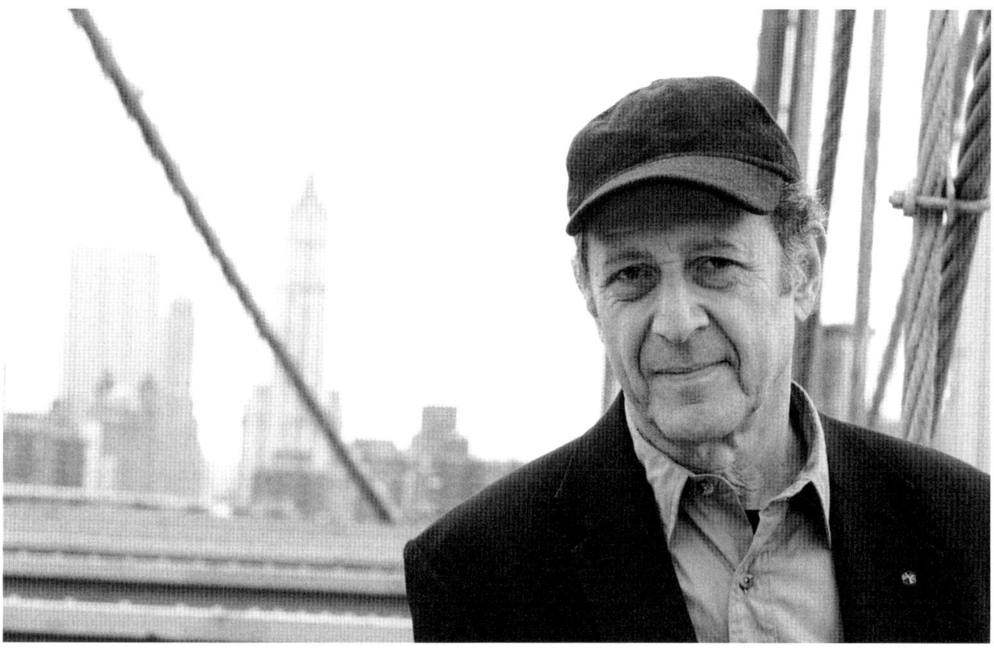

Steve Reich: minimalist composer of maximum significance

Islam, and *Three Tales*, in which Reich used **sampling** techniques. Meanwhile, for the concert hall he composed *Triple Quartet* which can be performed by three quartets, or one quartet and tape. Reich has said that the piece is influenced by Bartók and Schnittke.

More recent pieces have included the *Double Sextet* of 2007 and *WTC 9/11* in response to the terrorist attack on the World Trade Centre. In 2013 he produced *Radio Rewrite* for 11 players, which is inspired by the music of Radiohead.

Reich has inspired a wide range of musicians, from fellow minimalist composers such as John Adams to electronic musician Brian Eno and ambient techno band The Orb. In 2003, David Bowie included Reich's *Music for 18 Musicians* on his list of 25 favourite albums.

Music for 18 Musicians

This work was written in 1974, three years after Reich had spent time in Ghana studying African drumming techniques. *Music for 18 Musicians* was his first attempt to compose for a large ensemble, and is a substantial work, lasting nearly an hour in performance; it has been called a seminal masterpiece.

The 18 musicians play the flowing combination of instruments:

1. Violin
2. Cello
3. Female voice
4. Female voice
5. Female voice
6. Piano
7. Piano
8. Piano and maracas
9. Marimba and maracas
10. Marimba and xylophone
11. Marimba and xylophone
12. Marimba and xylophone
13. Metallophone and piano
14. Piano and marimba
15. Marimba, xylophone and piano
16. Clarinet and bass clarinet
17. Clarinet and bass clarinet
18. Female voice and piano

The piece is based on a series of 11 chords which are presented in the first section called 'Pulses':

All players and vocalists play or sing pulsating notes in each chord. Notes crescendo and fade according to the breath of the musicians (strings being guided by the bass clarinet) and different notes pulsate at different speeds. Each chord lasts for two breaths of the players. The listener, as a result, perceives the presence of different notes of the same chord at different times in the duration of the chord. This aspect is called psycho-acoustics, and fascinates the composer.

Try listening to a recording following the chords printed above, listening out for each of the notes in a chord.

After 'Pulses' there are 11 'Sections' – each focused on just one of the chords. The work ends with a reprise of 'Pulses'.

Tehillim

Tehillim **was written in 1981 and takes its title from the Hebrew for 'Psalms'. Reich studied Hebrew in the mid-Seventies and visited Israel to research Sephardic singing traditions. There are four movements, which use verses from Psalms 19, 34, 18 and 150. The piece is scored for four women's voices (it was Reich's first major composition to use live singing) and a varied chamber orchestra including six percussionists and two electric organs.**

It is a substantial piece, lasting about half an hour. There is an echo of a symphonic structure: the four movements include first, the most substantial and quite fast movement; second, a faster and shorter movement; third, a slow movement; and last, another fast movement. However, the changing metres, prominent unpitched rhythmic ostinatos (including clapping), and use of canons clearly point to this being Reich's voice.

The second movement begins with a two-part contrapuntal texture with clapping ostinatos in support. Extraordinary demands are made of the singers, especially the top soprano who has several top Cs. There is a fascinating combination of quite slow, sustained instrumental lines in the strings and winds, agile and angular vocal lines (often with an impression of syncopation caused by the metre changes) and crisp, staccato percussion ostinatos, often played through hand-clapping. It is as though the sung lines energise the instrumental harmony, and the percussive detail further energises the sung layer.

Different Trains

Different Trains **was composed in 1988 for string quartet and tape. It was first recorded by the Kronos Quartet, a recording that won a Grammy for Best Contemporary Classical**

Composition in 1989. The concept at the heart of the work is to contrast journeys that Reich made as a child between New York and Los Angeles to visit his parents who had separated, and journeys made by other Jewish children at the time in Europe on Holocaust trains.

There are three movements:

1. America - Before the War
2. Europe - During the War
3. America - After the War

The settings can be distinguished by their train whistle sounds: sustained open 4ths and 5ths for American trains, short triadic shrieks for European trains.

A fascinating aspect of the work is the spoken parts of the tape, which were made through interviews with people in the United States and Europe. In the opening movement we hear Reich's governess, Virginia, and an American railway porter called Lawrence Davis reminisce about train travel before the war. In the second movement, there are recordings of three Holocaust survivors talking about their wartime experiences. In the final movement, all five voices are heard.

Much of the musical backdrop for this is a minimalist canvas of repeating patterns that evoke the mechanical momentum of the trains. Listen out, however, for the melodic ideas, which are often directly suggested by the natural speech rhythms and intonations of the speaking voices. A very clever aspect of this is that Reich allows the instruments to take these melodic shapes first, so the spoken samples appear to grow organically out of the musical substance.

For example, here is the first spoken moment in the whole work, 'From Chicago', which is prefaced by the cello (on the tape). Note how the recorded track (top stave) is actually in $\frac{7}{8}$ while the quartet have a regularly repeating pattern in $\frac{2}{4}$ (though with its own cross-rhythm against the metre):

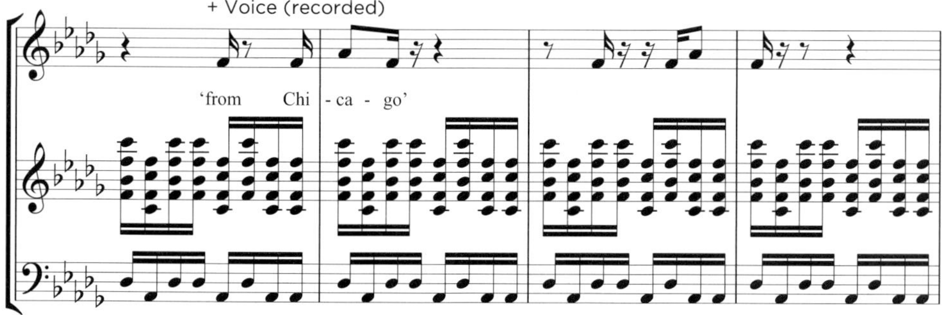

Other works

Other works by Reich that you could explore include *New York Counterpoint* for amplified clarinet and tape, or 11 clarinets and bass clarinet (1985), *Electric Counterpoint* for electric guitar and tape, which was written for Pat Metheny (see pages 295-297) and *Proverb* (1995).

This latter piece is a further development of the 'speech melody' found in *Different Trains*, and sets a text by philosopher Ludwig Wittgenstein. Written for early music specialist Paul Hillier, it has various medieval elements in homage to the monastic composer Perotin who flourished around 1200 and belongs to the 'Notre Dame School'. The text is 'How small a thought it takes to fill a whole life', words curiously appropriate to Reich's career and musical idiom.

Significant works since the millennium include the *Double Sextet* of 2007, and *Radio Rewrite* in 2012.

James MacMillan

The composer

James MacMillan was born in Ayrshire, Scotland, in 1959. He studied Music at Edinburgh University and then specialised in composition for a PhD at the University of Durham in 1987. Up to this point, he was following a 'modernist' path, influenced by Polish composers Lutosławski and Penderecki.

Returning to Scotland, he was drawn to the influences of his roots: national and religious identities. Much of his music since has explored ways in which his Roman Catholic faith and Scottish heritage can be brought together.

James MacMillan

Two works in particular announced MacMillan's arrival on the UK musical scene as a composer of considerable significance. Firstly, *The Confession of Isobel Gowdie*, which was premiered at the BBC Proms in 1990. Though he wrote it purely as an orchestral piece, the composer considers the piece a Requiem for Isobel Gowdie, who was burnt as a witch in 17th-century Scotland. According to the critic Stephen Johnson, the first performance received an ovation 'the like of which had rarely been seen at a British premiere since the death of Benjamin Britten'. The work's acclaim attracted further commissions, including a percussion concerto for Evelyn Glennie, which led to *Veni, Veni Emmanuel*, performed by Glennie in 1992; it has since become MacMillan's most-performed piece.

MacMillan has been very prolific in the years since. Major works have included four symphonies, three piano concertos and other concertos for violin, cello and oboe, and an opera, *The Sacrifice*, premiered by Welsh National Opera in 2007. He has also written a large amount of choral music, including both large-scale works such as Passion settings, and smaller pieces for church choirs such as the *Strathclyde Motets*.

MacMillan was knighted in 2015. His music makes for a fascinating study, combining a wide range of influences. Uncompromising forceful **atonality** can sit alongside passages of tonal or modal beauty, but whether writing for virtuoso soloists or amateur choirs, his music is characterised by intensity and authenticity.

Veni, Veni Emmanuel

Written in 1991/92, and the best-known of MacMillan's works, *Veni, Veni Emmanuel* (O come, o come Emmanuel) is the most often performed of any concerto written in the Nineties; its 300th performance came just over ten years after its premiere. The structure of the piece follows the annual cycle of the Christian Church, reflecting the fact that the composer began work on the piece on Advent Sunday and finished it on Easter Sunday.

The work has a single movement lasting around 25 minutes, within which there are five main sections and some linking passages:

Introit - Advent

Heartbeats

Danece - Hocket

Transition: Sequence I

Gaude, Gaude

Transition: Sequence II

Dance - Chorale

Coda - Easter

The unusual title of this concerto is due to the fact the music draws on the traditional Advent **plainsong** chant of the same name, still used as a hymn tune today:

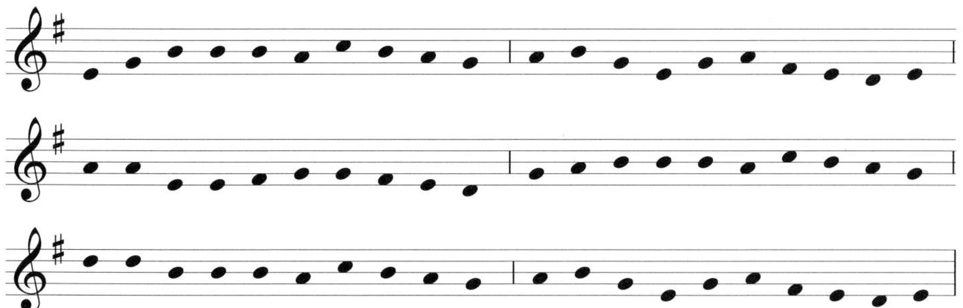

MacMillan deconstructs this chant: small fragments permeate the orchestral texture at many points. It gradually becomes more apparent with longer legato lines heard on the wind instruments. At the climax of the work the plainsong is presented as 'the human presence of Christ' (MacMillan's description).

The soloist requires an impressive array of instruments: two tam-tams, two snare drums, six tom-toms, two timbales, pedal bass drum, six Chinese gongs, six temple blocks, log drum, two wood blocks, marimba, large cymbal, sizzle cymbal, tubular bells.

The Dance section begins with the soloist playing the timbales and tom-toms, providing the playful detail to the homophonic texture of the orchestra in which alternate chords are scored differently to make the music pulsate. The soloist has a rest in the following orchestral passage, which has a fascinating scoring in which loud brass notes are sustained quietly while the strings play with a dancing melodic idea of repeating anacrusis notes that fall by leap after the downbeat.

When the soloist re-enters, there is an elaborate passage requiring not just the skinned instruments (including pedal bass drum) but metallic sounds too. Underneath this the orchestral material begins to evoke something of a renaissance dance feel with syncopated chordal writing; midway through there are also some wide textured spectral woodwind chords that hang in mid-air, and some rapidly reiterated brass interjections.

In a memorable conclusion to the concerto all the orchestral players become percussionists, playing rhythms on their own metal chimes while the soloist plays an ostinato on the tubular bells with increasing tempo and sense of fervour. When the conductor directs everyone to stop abruptly, the ringing of all the chimes and bells takes a long time to fade into the distance.

Memento for string quartet

After all the energy and dance of *Veni, Veni Emmanuel* this short piece for string quartet creates a very different atmosphere for the listener. The composer's note of the piece is as follows:

> **A brief movement for string quartet, *Memento* was written in memory of a friend, David Huntley, the representative of Boosey & Hawkes in the USA, who died in 1994. It was premiered at his memorial concert in New York by the Kronos Quartet. The music is slow, delicate and tentative and is based on the modality of Gaelic lament music and the Gaelic heterophony of psalm-singing in the Hebrides.**

There is an intimate beauty to the piece. Considerable use is made of string harmonics that add to the atmosphere of stillness and timelessness; there is a sense of the miniscule amid the immense.

'O Radiant Dawn'

The *Strathclyde Motets* are a series of 14 Communion motets composed for church choirs, all but two of which are a cappella.

'O Radiant Dawn' takes the text of one of the ancient Advent antiphons ('O oriens, splendor lucis aeternae') in an English translation, and, according to Catholic practice, should be sung on 21st December.

MacMillan uses a simple four-part homophonic texture in a ternary structure. The middle section is for sopranos and altos only. There is a *da capo* of the opening section, and then a short coda to accommodate six 'Amen's.

The composer's Scottish identity is apparent in the opening two phrases in which the final chord (on 'Dawn') features acciaccaturas in soprano and tenor which he requests to be sung on the beat. The effect is reminiscent of the **Scotch snap**. Towards the end of the opening section, the word 'come' is set six times to a rising Phrygian scale (on G) in the soprano line:

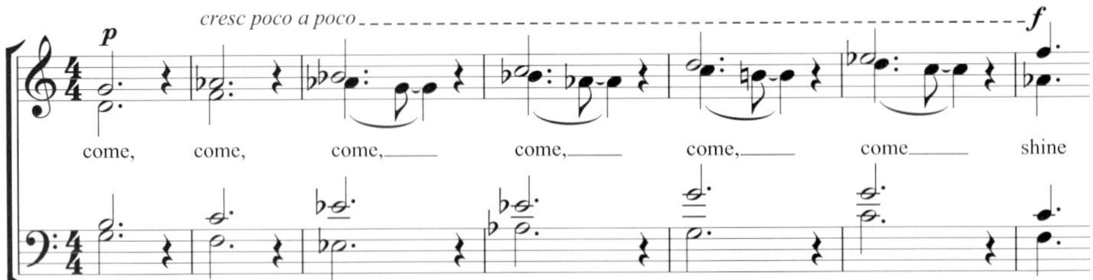

The combination of the dark Phrygian mode with a rising scale creates an increasing intensity to the invocatory nature of this text. The concluding six 'Amen's connect to this, but here the sopranos stay on the low tonic G throughout, suggesting a spirit of acceptance.

Seraph

***Seraph* is a concertante piece for solo trumpet and strings in three movements. It was composed in 2010 and first performed by Alison Balsom and the Scottish Ensemble at the Wigmore Hall in 2011. The whole work last about 15 minutes. A seraph is an angelic figure who is often portrayed playing a trumpet.**

The opening movement uses a sonata form plan. The piece opens with gutsy repetitions of a doubly dissonant chord in the strings (E and F, C and B) and the trumpet enters with a jaunty first theme that starts with four notes reminiscent of the final movement from Haydn's famous trumpet concerto, and then heads in a different direction to incorporate running semiquavers, syncopation and repeated notes:

The opening motif of this theme also appears in the 1st violins at bar 13 and in the cellos and bass in bars 15 and 16.

A second idea appears at figure A (bar 18) which is more lyrical in character and features rising 4ths and falling 3rds in the trumpet line:

Also contrasting in this passage is the accompaniment which is reduced to just 2nd violins, violas and cellos and has a more sustained hue with chord changes often on the half-beat. The passage ends with a crescendo on a tremolando chord and a return of the opening acerbic chords.

Something of a development section follows. Shortly, after a sudden silence, the two main ideas are played simultaneously by violas, cellos and basses (first idea) and 1st violins (second idea) in 6ths:

Much of this middle section is a little subdued and serene. The texture is relatively sustained in the lower strings with long lines of semiquavers, often arpeggio in contour, in the violin lines. A significant crescendo over four bars leads to a recapitulation at figure E (bar 70). The return of the second theme is transposed by a tritone but has a similar contrast of texture. The detached dissonant chords return at figure H (bar 96) to mark the start of the codetta. The movement ends in a flurry of semiquavers in all instruments, which end abruptly in silence halfway through the 2nd beat of the bar.

Of the remaining two movements of the piece, the composer writes:

> **The second movement, an Adagio, has its leading cantabile melodic material on solo violin or tutti strings, while the solo trumpet seems to ruminate introspectively with oppositional and contrary lines. The movement subsides in a quasi-improvisatory duet between solo trumpet and violin.**
>
> **The last movement, marcato e ritmico, is based on a closely worked canonic idea, which first appears on low strings, giving a somewhat 'ungainly' sensation at the outset, and a more fulsome arching melody marked cantabile e sonore. The trumpet part is peppered with little military fanfares. Eventually the music settles down to a cadenza-like passage, where the soloist is accompanied by tremolando strings, before the principal canonic theme is recapitulated on the violins and violas.**

SAMPLE ESSAY QUESTIONS

Essay advice

Before you start, review the advice on writing essays at the end of Chapter 3.

Each essay is worth 30 marks and should take 45 minutes to write.

For A Level

1. 'Art music is a kind of music that requires commitment and concentration from the listener.' Selecting two contrasting passages of music from two different artists, consider this view, discussing the music in detail.
2. Compare chamber music by two named artists from 1910 onwards and discuss their contrasting approaches to harmony and structure.
3. Choose pieces by two named artists you have studied, and explain their contrasting approaches to melody and rhythm.
4. 'Composers of this period have explored the capabilities of instruments to the full.' Consider this point, selecting at least two contrasting pieces by two different named artists to give your response musical detail.

Answers

Pages 24-25: Listening exercise 1

First angle of approach:

a. There are recordings at various tempi available; most are very slow

b. This will depend on how 'romantic' the interpretation is; most will only slow at the end

c. Peaceful

d. This can vary; most likely is bowed strings and harpsichord

e. AABB (binary)

Second angle of approach:

a. True

b. False

c. True

d. True

e. False

f. True

g. False

Third angle of approach:

The following are features of the bass line:

Rising octave scales, falling octave scales, descending scale, rising scale, passing note, even rhythm, chromatic notes

The playing technique depends on the recording; most likely is pizzicato with arco in the last bar of each half

Dynamic features will depend on the recording

Fourth angle of approach:

Pages 26-28: Listening exercise 2

The instrumental sections

a. 4½ beats

b. Bar 3^1

c. Major 6th

d. Perfect 4th

e. iii

f. Eight steps down to the lower tonic

g. Bars 2 and 8

h.

	bar 1	bar 2	bar 3	bar 4	bar 5	bar 6	bar 7	bar 8
A major chord on the downbeat	Y		Y		Y	Y	Y	Y
A minor chord on the downbeat		Y		Y				
The melody note is a compound 3rd above the bass note on the downbeat	Y		Y	Y	Y	Y		
The 2nd beat of the bar is a first inversion							Y	
The bar uses three different chords leading to a faster harmonic rhythm								Y

The vocal sections

a. 12 bars

b. 12 bars

c. 8 bars

d. 16 bars

e.

verse or chorus?	section	phrase	verse 1	verse 2
verse	A1 section	first phrase	3	2
		second phrase	2	2
		third phrase	X	X
	A2 section	first phrase	X	3
		second phrase	X	X
		third phrase	2	2
chorus	B1 section	first phrase	3	X
		second phrase	2	2
	B2 section	first phrase	2	3
		second phrase	2	2
		third phrase	X	X
		fourth phrase	3	3

f. Glissando

g. Plagal cadence

Overall impression

a. Similarities: metre, tonality (major), tempo, texture (melody at top), use of descending scale in bass line, some aspects of melody (long notes a 3rd above bass, rhythmic character)

b. Differences: instrumentation, key, structure, texture (contrapuntal aspects of Bach's 'Air' are not present in 'A Whiter Shade Of Pale'), final cadence

Page 107: Interval questions on 'Melodic Featurefest 1'

1. Minor 2nd: C to B, bar 2
Major 2nd: C to D, bar 2
Minor 3rd: G to E, bar 2
Major 3rd: E to C, bar 1
Perfect 4th: C to G, bar 1
Perfect 5th: C to G, bar 1
Minor 6th: E to C, bars 1-2
Major 6th: G to C, bar 1

2. Diminished 5th

3. A to B at end of bar 7: minor 7th

Pages 108-9: Questions on 'Melodic Featurefest 2'

1. Motif
2. Rising sequence
3. Descending, scalic (conjunct also true, but less precise than scalic)
4. Intervallic augmentation
5. Ascending arpeggio
6. Note of anticipation
7. Descending sequence
8. Turn
9. Appoggiatura
10. Accented passing note
11. Conjunct
12. Ascending arpeggio
13. Repetition
14. Acciaccatura
15. Echappée
16. **a.** minor 3rd
b. major 3rd
c. perfect 4th
d. perfect 5th
e. major 10th (or compound major 3rd)

Pages 116-117: Questions on 'Harmonic Featurefest 2'

1. B major
2. Diatonic
3. I-Vc-Ib
4. 7-6
5. Perfect
6. Plagal
7. Secondary dominant 7th
8. Relative minor of the dominant
9. 8 bars
10. 9-8
11. Neapolitan 6th
12. Interrupted
13. Third inversion
14. German
15. Dominant pedal
16. Interrupted
17. Descending chromatic scale
18. Major 10th
19. Phrygian
20. French

Page 121: Questions on 'Texture Melange'

1. Monophonic
2. Unison
3. Parallel 3rds
4. Homophonic
5. Melody and accompaniment
6. Contrapuntal
7. Antiphonal
8. Fugal
9. Solo
10. Octaves (3 octaves)
11. Canon

Page 201: 'Superstition' questions

1. Key points might include:
   - **a.** Use of G♭s in the clavinet part, pentatonic writing, use of riffs
   - **b.** The opening drum pattern, propelling the music forward, use of syncopation, riffs, sextuplets
   - **c.** Layered textures with riff, bass, drums, vocals, use and effect of no chord bars
2. Comparisons might include melodic embellishment on repeated verses, contrast between verse, chorus and bridge in terms of harmonic rate of change, drum pattern and melodic shape
3. **a.** Riff: repeated ostinato pattern used in pop music having rhythmic and/or melodic features (opening bars)
   - **b.** Glissando: a slide between two notes (on an instrument) or portamento (in vocals during the bridge)
   - **c.** Breakdown: a literal 'break' in the flow of the music, often achieved by a No Chord bar (end of bridge)
   - **d.** Pentatonic scale: a scale of five notes (used throughout the vocal line)
   - **e.** Drum fill: often found at the end of a phrase to 'fill' the texture during melodic gaps (end of each 4-bar phrase, for example in the instrumental introduction)
   - **f.** Fade out: a music technological process used to reduce the volume of the track to nothing (final bar)

Page 205: 'Big Yellow Taxi' questions

1.
   a. 

   b. C major:

   c. A major:

2. Textural variety is achieved by varied use of instrumentation, changes in strumming patterns and the use of three-part vocal harmony at the end of the chorus
3. Your revision note should discuss each of the elements of music and how they are used within the piece. Consider:
   - Structure: verse chorus form, introduction, verses, chorus, breakdown
   - Instruments: use of guitar, percussion, vocals (including backing vocals), strumming patterns
   - Harmony/tonality: A major tonality, use of extended chords, bare-5th chords, the chord sequence, the use of primary triads and secondary dominant chords
   - Melody: use of conjunct and disjunct melodic lines, the differences between verse and chorus patterns
   - Rhythm: regular $\frac{4}{4}$ time with syncopation often at the end of a section
   - Texture: see answer to 2

Page 209: 'Supermassive Black Hole' questions

1. Guitar distortion is a gain effect used to alter the sound of an electronic instrument, often electric guitars. It is used throughout the piece to effect the sound quality and create a significantly denser sound than a clean effect would achieve. This is integral to Muse's soundworld.
2. A blue note is a chromatic note, often used to provide harmonic interest. These often include flattened 7ths, raised 4ths/flattened 5ths and major/minor 3rds. For example, the B♭s found in the introduction to this piece are a flattened 5th.
3. Verses are characterised by melodic lines with a narrow range, often alternating between three different notes in a conjunct fashion. Quavers are used which are sometimes tied over the second and third beats. The verse often features only the bass in these sections. However, in choruses the texture is thickened with the vocal melody joined by homophonic backing vocals in 3rds, complete with constant bass quavers using blue notes.

Page 212: 'Harder, Better, Stronger, Faster' questions

1. Vocoder refers to an effect which can be applied to vocals to transform the vocal sound from sounding live and acoustic to a more computerised effect.
2. Sampling is the process of using a pre-existing piece of music, speech or other sound in a new piece. This is a common practice in much music, where riffs and ideas from older pieces are reused in a new way. An artist might choose to do this for a number of reasons, including paying homage to the older piece or alluding to the themes present in the older piece.
3. Repetition and change are balanced by developments in the verses and choruses as they progress. The vocals are subjected to changes in instrumental and backing vocal accompaniment to give a sense of musical development by varying the musical texture.

Page 212: 'Get Lucky' questions

1. B Dorian is the use of the Dorian mode transposed to B. The Dorian mode is the white notes from D-D (D E F G A B C D), giving a minor scale with a sharpened 6th and flattened 7th. When transposed to B this gives the following scale: B C♯ D E F♯ G♯ A B.
2. The essay could discuss any number of points, but must make reference to the musical features which have helped to contribute to the popularity of the song. These might include: the repetitive chord sequence, the singable melodic lines, the groove tempo, accompaniment and changes via syncopation, use of vocoder effects.

Page 214: 'Single Ladies' questions

1. This allows the texture to develop and thicken for the chorus, as well as providing a more original start to the piece.
2. The C natural is a chromatic note to the E major harmony, suggesting a flattened 6th and a tertiary chord of C major (no third, added 6th). This unrelated chord helps to give a sense of harmonic venture, especially important given the N.C. bars which precede it.
3. Any musical element could be argued here, with sufficient evidence from the score to help justify the response.

Page 255: 'Oklahoma!' questions

1. The chorus are all on stage in this exciting number, helping to give the sense of closure to the show. The piece starts with many soloists, helping the story to move, before a lengthy solo by Curly. On the second special chorus the chorus enter, divided into seven parts (four tenor/bass roles and three soprano/alto roles) allowing them to reinforce the main melody, develop the ideas by adding new material and to raise the emotional temperature of the song.
2. The piece sounds rustic in nature - bare 5ths on open strings from the strings at the opening to the simple melodic ideas, complete with 'yippee' lyrics which help to evoke a hoe down - an American folk dance in duple time.
3. Aside from the use of full chorus, the sense of excitement is achieved by the way the voices are layered (especially in the gradually added chord on 'Okla-homa' complete with minor 7th), the use of a fast tempo, major tonality and the final chords with added pause.

Page 263: 'I Still Believe' questions

1. An additive rhythm is a rhythm where the usual stresses of the bar are changed - for example by playing 3+3+2 quavers in a bar of $\frac{4}{4}$, changing the emphasis. The harmony quavers use this rhythm but displaced by a quaver (see opening introduction).
2. A sequence is a repetition of a musical idea which is either higher (ascending) or lower (descending). An ascending sequence is found on the line 'I still believe/you will return/I know you will'). A descending sequence is found at 'You will return/you will return'.
3. F minor: this enlivens the harmonic palette and is a commonly used device in musical theatre pieces.
4. Modulating up a semitone is a device often found in pop or musical pieces, allowing the music to gain a sense of excitement and development. By raising the piece by a tone, this effect is heightened. Notice how the piece still ends in D minor, helping to reflect the text and plot.
5. Many different reasons could be given for this including the desire to add character expression. Much of the music would sound robotic if sung exactly to the notated rhythms, lacking the characterisation required for this type of music.

Page 275: Test yourself

Glossary

12-bar blues One of the most prominent chord progressions in popular music, starting in blues music and spreading to jazz, rock, R&B, etc.

The standard pattern is:

1	2	3	4	5	6
I^7	I^7	I^7	I^7	IV^7	IV^7
7	**8**	**9**	**10**	**11**	**12**
I^7	I^7	V^7	IV^7	I^7	I^7

This is only a basis for many variants, of which common versions are:

- **Quick change**: uses IV^7in bar 2
- **Turnaround**: uses V^7in bar 12 to lead back to the tonic at the start of the next 12 bars
- **Minor blues**: in addition to using i^7 and iv^7, this can use $\flat VI^7$ in bar 9
- **Bebop blues**: among many elaborate options, common changes made in bebop include using a diminished 7th ($\sharp IV^{o7}$) in bar 6, and ii^7 in bar 9

An excellent interactive resource for further information is the iReal Pro app.

32-bar song form A name sometimes used for **popular song form** when each phrase is eight bars long.

A cappella Unaccompanied singing; from the Italian meaning 'in the chapel style', this term originally applied to church music, but is now used in contemporary vocal music.

Acciaccatura An ornament printed as a small note with a slash through its tail, which is played as quickly as possible before the main note that follows it; also known as a grace note.

Additive rhythm A rhythm where the bar is divided into beats of unequal length, e.g. 3+3+2.

Aeolian mode A natural minor scale: see example on p257.

Affect The emotion aroused by a piece of music.

Alap The opening section of a piece of Indian classical music, usually with melodic improvisation and free rhythm, developing into a **raga**.

Anacrusis One or more weak-beat notes before the first strong beat of a phrase, which is often called a 'pick up' in pop music (plural: anacruses).

Antecedent and consequent phrases Used to describe a pairing of phrases, typically found in **periodic phrasing**. Alternatively, the second phrase may be called an answering phrase. The two phrases will match in length, usually in rhythm, and sometimes in contour.

Antiphony, antiphonal A musical texture where two groups of musicians take it in turns to play; can also refer to sections of alternating registers.

Appoggiatura A melodic ornament where a neighbouring note (that sounds dissonant) is sounded for a measured period of time before the main note of the melody. In the Romantic era appoggiaturas are also found in the accompanying harmonic texture.

Arco An instruction for string players to use the bow, after playing pizzicato.

Aria An extended vocal solo in an opera, oratorio or cantata.

Arpeggio The notes of a standard triad played one after another, in ascending or descending order, that is, the 1st, 3rd, 5th and 8th notes of a scale.

Arrastre From Spanish, meaning 'drag', a specialist bow stroke that changes the bow speed from slow to fast, usually onto the downbeat. Often heard in the double bass part of an **orquesta típica**.

Articulation How smoothly or otherwise the notes are played, e.g. very detached (**staccato**), or joined together (**legato**) are types of articulation.

Atonal, atonality Western music without an obvious home key. Atonal music avoids major and minor keys (and also **modes**).

Augmentation Literally means 'expanded'. The opposite of **diminution**. It can refer to various features:

- **Interval**: an augmented interval is a semitone wider than a major or perfect interval, e.g. C-D♯, C-F♯
- **Chord**: a triad made up of two major 3rds, e.g. C-E-G♯
- **Rhythm**: a proportionate increase in the note lengths of a melody, for example, when two quavers and a crotchet are augmented they become two crotchets and a minim: see example p237.

Auxiliary note A melodic decoration and non-harmony note one step away from the chord onto which it resolves, creating **dissonance.** They can be higher or lower than the chord, and so described as upper or lower auxiliary notes respectively. Where an accidental is used to create an auxiliary note that is a semitone away from the harmony note, this is called a **chromatic auxiliary note**.

Avant-garde jazz A late-1950s and 1960s style of jazz that rejected the conventions of **bebop** and favoured shifting rhythms and tonalities, with much improvisation.

Bare 5ths A texture where a melodic line is simultaneously played (doubled) a 5th higher or lower, thus creating a sparse, hollow effect, sometimes reminiscent of medieval organum (a style associated with monastic singing): see also open 5ths.

Basso continuo The fundamental basis of most orchestral and ensemble music in the Baroque period, represented in the score by the bass line that includes **figured bass** notation. This is played by a bass instrument (typically a cello, possibly a bassoon or other options) and a harmony instrument (harpsichord, organ or lute).

Bebop A style of jazz developed in the 1940s, notable for fast tempos, complex harmonies, virtuosic playing and much use of improvisation.

Belt A style of singing sometimes found in music theatre and pop music in which the singer uses their chest voice (usually a low register sound) above its natural range with a very loud dynamic.

Binary form A musical structure of two sections each of which is repeated to give ||: A :||: B :||. The A section usually modulates to the dominant (or relative major); the B section starts in the dominant (or relative major) and returns to the tonic. Sometimes the B section refers to the opening tune of the A section to mark the return to the tonic key; this is known as **rounded binary form**.

Birimintingo Improvised solo melodic runs in kora playing.

Bitonal Music which is in two keys simultaneously.

Blue note In blues music, notes used in the melodic line which do not belong to the fundamental major key of the music, e.g. a flattened 3rd or flattened 7th.

Break A short instrumental solo, often improvised, in pop and jazz.

Breakdown A section of a song where various instrumentalists all have solo **breaks**.

Bridge A contrasting section in a pop song which usually joins the verse to the chorus, or is heard after twice through the verse and chorus.

Cadence A pair of chords which mark the end of a musical statement. Perfect, imperfect, plagal and interrupted cadences are all explained in detail on pp80-83. See also:

- **Half-close** A type of imperfect cadence, Ic-V
- **Phrygian** ivb-V in a minor key, where the bass line moves down a semitone and the top line moves up a tone; common in Baroque music, and another type of imperfect cadence
- **Cadential 6/4** A second inversion chord resolving to the dominant, so Ic-V, another type of imperfect cadence

Cadenza An extended passage for the soloist in a concerto, usually unaccompanied and requiring virtuoso playing, it is intended to show off the instrument's capabilities and the player's skill.

Canon A contrapuntal device in which a melody in one part is repeated note for note in another part starting a few beats later (and possibly at a different pitch), while the melody in the first pat continues to unfold.

Chalumeau register The lowest range of a clarinet, with a rich, dark tone.

Chicharra In tango music, a technique where the violinist plays the strings *behind* the bridge, with heavy downward pressure on the bow, to emulate the sound of a cicada or cricket. See also p305.

Chromatic Notes that don't belong to the current key; the opposite of **diatonic.**

Circle of 5ths progression A series of chords whose roots are each a perfect 5th lower than the previous chord.

Cluster chord A chord of at least three adjacent notes (probably semitones).

Coda The final section of a composition; where following repeated sections, such as in **32-bar song form**, the coda will be different from earlier sections.

Codetta A coda to a section of music, e.g. in sonata form, the close of an exposition section before the development starts.

Col legno Played with the wood of a bow, rather than the hair, producing a dry sound.

Compound interval Intervals which are greater than an octave, so compound 5th describes an octave (or even two octaves) plus a 5th.

Compound time A metre in which the main beat can be subdivided into three. Common time signatures are $\frac{6}{8}$, $\frac{12}{8}$, $\frac{6}{4}$. The opposite of **Simple time**.

Compression In music technology, the automatic reduction of the dynamic range of a sound.

Conjunct A style of melodic writing in which each note is a step away from the previous one.

Consonant (harmony) A combination of notes providing a pleasing sound when played together, the opposite of **dissonant**. This is generally achieved by avoiding notes that are a semitone, tone or tritone apart.

Con sordino Played with a mute on the instrument thereby altering the timbre (on bowed string instruments and brass instruments).

Contour As contours on a map indicate the ups and downs of a landscape, this term is used to describe the rise and fall (or shape) of a melody line, such as ascending, descending, scalic, arpeggio, conjunct, disjunct.

Contrafact In jazz, a new melody line laid over an existing or standard harmonic progression.

Contrapuntal Music that uses **counterpoint**, a texture where two or more melodic lines are played together at the same time.

Cool jazz A lighter style of jazz, with a laid-back style of relaxed tempos, contrasting with the earlier **bebop** style.

Countermelody An independent melody sounding against another melody which has already been heard.

Counterpoint The simultaneous combination of two or more melodies with independent rhythms. There may be some imitation between parts, but counterpoint can also be non-imitative. A whole movement may be contrapuntal, or the music may alternate between contrapuntal and other textures. This term is often used interchangeably with **polyphony,** but is more commonly used for instrumental music.

Cross-rhythm A pattern in which the rhythmic detail of the music is out of phase with the underlying pulse (as in a **hemiola**), or where different subdivisions of the beat are used simultaneously (as in duple and triplet quavers).

Da capo Literally 'from the head', this term directs the player to repeat from the beginning.

Delay Guitar device which records a sound and repeats it at a given time, or multiple times, often with a diminuendo. Not to be confused with an echo, which does not repeat the sound.

Descant A counter melody sung above the main melody line.

Diatonic Music using just the notes of the home key; the opposite of **chromatic**.

Diegetic music Music that is heard in a film, the source of which is part of the film, such as the band in the saloon, the busker on the street, the organ in the church.

Diminished chord A triad made up of two minor 3rds, e.g. C-E♭-G♭. A diminished 7th is made up of three minor 3rds.

Diminution Literally means 'reduced'. The opposite of **augmentation**. It can refer to various features:

- **Interval**: a diminished interval is a semitone narrower than a major or perfect interval, e.g. C-D♭, C-G♭
- **Chord**: a triad made up of two minor 3rds, e.g. C-E♭-G♭
- **Rhythm**: a proportionate reduction in the note lengths of a melody, for example, when two quavers and a crotchet are diminished they become two semiquavers and a quaver.

Disjunct A style of melodic writing including many leaps between one note and the next; opposite of **conjunct**.

Dissonant, dissonance A combination of notes producing a clashing sound when played together; opposite of **consonant.**

Distortion A technological effect used to alter the sound of an amplified instrument, usually creating a 'dirty' or 'clipped' version of the same sound.

Dominant 7th Literally the note that is a 7th above the dominant; however, it is usually used to describe the dominant chord when the 7th note is included. The result is very direction-inducing, usually requiring resolution onto the tonic chord.

Dorian mode A modal scale with a minor 3rd and a minor 7th: see example p211.

Doubled, doubling More than one part playing the same line, either in unison or an octave apart. Doubling of a melody can also occur at other intervals, e.g. at a 3rd for a consonant effect, or at a 4th for a more spikey, aggressive effect.

Double stopping Two notes played at the same time on a stringed instrument on two adjacent strings.

Double time In jazz, an instruction to change to using notes of double speed (e.g. semiquavers instead of quavers) without changing the underlying tempo of the chord progression. Often used in improvised solos.

Downbeat The first beat of a bar.

Drone One or more notes held or repeated throughout an extended passage of music. Some instruments, such as bagpipes and sitar, have an inbuilt drone.

Echappée note An unaccented, dissonant melodic decoration note, that is one step higher or lower than the essential note, and then resolves by a leap back to the harmony note.

Enharmonic Two notes or keys which sound the same but are written differently, such as C♯ and D♭.

Episode A solo passage occurring in a **ritornello** movement: see pp130-131.

Equalisation (EQ) An effect that changes the relative volume of the frequencies in a recording, for an individual track, instrument, or a whole mix. An EQ unit is made of a number of filters, which increase or decrease the volume of audible frequencies from bass to treble.

Extended chord A triad with notes added to it, such as a 7th, 9th, 11th or 13th: see example p198.

Fado Portuguese traditional sung ballad: see full description on p314.

False relation A simultaneous or adjacent occurrence in different parts of a note in its natural form and its sharpened or flattened form, e.g.:

Simultaneous false relation:

Adjacent false relation:

Falsetto Male singing in a high treble or unbroken voice, in the same range as a soprano or alto.

Fermata A pause.

Fill In pop music, a mini instrumental solo between the phrases of a song; the term is usually used with the name of the instrument playing, e.g. drum fill.

Flutter-tonguing A technique on wind instruments of rolling an 'r' while blowing, that creates a trill-like sound, more common in 20th-century classical music.

Four-on-the-floor Bass drum of a drum kit, playing on every crotchet in a $\frac{4}{4}$ bar, common in disco music of the 1970s.

Foursquare A passage of four 4-bar phrases. It is a less sophisticated version of **periodic phrasing** where there is a clear hierarchy of 2-bar, 4-bar and 8-bar pairings.

Fragmentation A compositional technique of breaking down a theme into its constituent motifs and repeating and developing them.

Free jazz An alternative term for **avant-garde jazz**.

French 6th An augmented chord containing the root, major 3rd, augmented 4th and augmented 6th.

Fugue, fugal A contrapuntal musical form in which a main theme is taken up and developed by each part in turn.

Functional harmony A term sometimes used to describe standard tonal harmony in which primary and secondary triads are used with a sense of hierarchy and direction, and chromatic inflexions are understood in terms conventions such as **secondary dominant 7ths**.

Funk Dance music from the 1960s onwards, with a strong emphasis on the rhythmic groove provided by the drum and bass, with rich extended chords.

Fusion A synthesis of two or more contrasting (and unrelated) styles.

German 6th An augmented 6th chord containing the root, major 3rd, perfect 5th and augmented 6th.

Glissando A compositional technique requiring the pitch to slide from one note to another: see also **portamento**.

Golpe de Caja From Spanish, meaning 'hit on the box'. In tango, an instruction to string players to hit the box part of the instrument. This can be done in a variety of ways, such as thumb knuckles or palm, each creating a different sound. More likely on the double bass, but also possible on the violin.

Groove A jazz term for the rhythmic 'feel' of a piece of music.

Guajeo Cuban ostinato melody, usually found in the piano part, often made up of arpeggiated chords played in syncopated patterns.

Habanera rhythm Traditional dance rhythm of Cuban and South American music: see example on p306.

Hard bop A subgenre of jazz, developed from bebop, with hard, funky rhythms and blues influence.

Harmonic rhythm The rate at which the harmony changes in a piece of music.

Harmonic series On many instruments these are the notes which occur 'naturally', due to the way a string vibrates or the air vibrates in a brass instrument to create certain pitches. See p124 as it applies to Baroque trumpet music.

Harmonics On string instruments, including harp and guitar, a very high, pure sound produced by placing a finger on a string very lightly before plucking or bowing.

Harmon mute A **wah-wah mute** for brass instruments.

Hemiola A rhythmic device in which two groups of three beats (*strong-weak-weak, strong-weak-weak*) are performed as three groups of two (*strong-weak, strong-weak, strong-weak*).

Hitchcock chord A B♭ minor major 7th chord:

Homophony, homophonic A musical texture in which all parts (melody and accompaniment) move in similar rhythm creating a chordal effect.

Hook A repeated, catchy **motif** in jazz and pop music.

House music Electronic dance music dating from the 1980s onwards, typically with a strong drum beat, synthesisers, and syncopated cymbals.

Interval The distance between two pitches: count the letter names between the notes including the first and last, so C to G is a 5th. See also **compound interval**.

Inversion (of a chord) A chord is inverted when a note other than the root is in the bass (e.g. chord V). In first inversion the 3rd is in the bass (Vb); in second inversion the 5th is in the bass (Vc). The chord of the dominant 7th can be written in third inversion (V^7d).

Inversion (of a melody) When the intervals in a melody stay the same, but the pitch moves in the opposite direction, e.g. ascends instead of descending. The result is akin to a mirror image of the melodic **contour**.

Inverted pedal See the explanation for **Pedal note**; an inverted pedal note sounds higher than the harmonies beneath it, instead of lower.

Ionian The standard major scale: see example p339.

Italian 6th An augmented chord containing the root, major 3rd and augmented 6th.

Kumbengo An ostinato pattern in kora playing.

Latigo Spanish for 'whip', a type of glissando in tango music. It is played fast, ascending or descending, to mimic the sound of a whip (as used by Argentine gauchos).

Latin rhythm Music of South America and Cuba is characterised by syncopated rhythms and beats of unequal length, e.g. 3 + 3 + 2.

Legato Played smoothly, without breaks between the notes.

Leitmotif A recurring fragment of music that represents a specific character, event or emotion.

Lombardic rhythm A type of syncopation where the short rhythmic value note is accented, also known as Lombard rhythm: see also **Scotch snap**.

Looping A technique in electroacoustic music and sound production in which a short passage of sound material (the loop) is repeated to create **ostinato** patterns. Loops can be created in many ways, including sampler, synthesiser, sequencer, drum machine, and computer.

Lydian mode A major scale with an augmented 4th: see example p214.

Mambo rhythm A dance style of Cuban origin, typically with a syncopated rhythm on the claves comprising two halves (either of which can start the pattern):

Marcato Marked, or accented playing.

Melisma A series of melodic notes sung to the same syllable.

Mickey-mousing A technique in film music of synchronising the accompanying music directly to action on screen. The term is derived from early Walt Disney films.

Middle 8 The central, contrasting section of a song, in pop and jazz music, also called the bridge, or B section in an AABA song form. Often, but not always, 8 bars long.

Milonga A type of tango dance: see p306.

Mixolydian Major scale with a flattened 7th: see example p339.

Mode, modal, modality An alternative series of scales to the diatonic major and minor scales, often used in traditional music.

Modulation The process of changing key midway through a piece.

Monophony, monophonic Music consisting of a single unaccompanied melody line.

Mordent A melodic ornament: see examples on p105.

Moritat A ballad telling a dark or sad story, often of murder, sung by a Cantastoria (a story-teller singer in the tradition of a strolling minstrel).

Motif, motivic A short, distinctive musical idea: see also **leitmotif**.

Motor rhythm An insistently repeating short rhythmic pattern that conveys an almost mechanical, unstoppable quality, a typical example being two semiquavers plus a quaver, a pattern found in both Bach (e.g. Brandenburg Concerto No. 3) and Shostakovich (e.g. Symphony No. 5).

Motown A record label in Detroit, USA, that produced distinctive African-American music: a type of soul music with a pop influence.

Mute Device attached to an instrument to soften the tone and produce a different timbre, for string and brass instruments; see **con sordino.**

Neapolitan chord Major chord based on the lowered supertonic (second note) of the scale. Most commonly it appears in a minor key and in first inversion, when it becomes a **Neapolitan 6th**, so in the key of E minor, this is a chord of F major in first inversion. Romantic period composers first began to use it in root position, then preface it with its own **secondary dominant 7th**, and then explore using it in a major key. The chord usually resolves to the dominant.

Neapolitan key The key found a semitone higher than the tonic key.

Non-functional harmony Harmony where the chord progressions do not follow the needs (functions) of standard harmony: **see functional harmony**. In non-functional harmony chords are used for their inherent 'colour' rather than for their customary progressive function.

Non-harmony note A note outside of the harmony with which it is sounding, so usually dissonant.

Note of anticipation A non-harmony note which is approached by step from the note before, and then stays the same as the harmony changes for the following melodic note: essentially it is a note from the next chord played early.

Nuevo tango Modern style of tango music, introducing new instruments such as saxophone and electric guitar; strongly associated with Astor Piazzolla.

Ondes Martenot An early electronic instrument invented in 1928, played with a keyboard, with a wavering sound. The instrument's most famous role is in Messiaen's *Turangalîla Symphony*.

Open-5th chord A chord containing only the root and 5th, with the 3rd missing. See also **bare 5ths** and **power chord**.

Organ stops A stop on a pipe organ activates a set of pipes; changing stops varies the timbre of the instrument, an interpretative skill called registration. Every organ is unique in this regard. Among specific categories of stop are:

- Open diapasons and Principals: the main set of metal pipes
- Stopped diapasons and Flutes: softer, wooden pipes
- 'Strings': combinations of soft pipes slightly detuned to create a soft 'shimmer' effect
- Mutations: stops that add harmonics to the main note (e.g. the 12th)
- Mixtures: collections of mutations that add 'sparkle' to the sound
- Reeds: pipes that imitate orchestral instruments ranging from quiet oboes and clarinets, to loud trumpets and trombones
- Tremulant: a stop that does not change the pipes being used but creates a vibrato effect

Orquesta típica Spanish name for an instrumental ensemble that plays tango music, typically comprising violin(s), bandoneon(s), double bass and piano.

Ostinato A rhythmic, melodic or harmonic pattern repeated many times in succession (similar to a riff in pop music).

Overdrive Electric guitar effect of distortion, caused by clipping the signal, adding sustain, and compressing the sound.

Panning In music technology, altering the left and right distribution of the sound.

Parallel 3rds A texture where a melodic line is simultaneously played (doubled) a 3rd higher or lower, thus creating a consonant richness.

Parallel harmony The parallel movement of two or more lines often producing chords with an identical intervallic structure.

Passing note A non-harmony note placed between and connecting two harmony notes, each of which are usually a 3rd apart. Passing notes are usually unaccented (on the half beat, or second and fourth quarter beats), but can be accented (on the beat, with no accent symbol required).

Pedalling Use of the sustaining pedal on a piano, which changes the articulation and sonority of the music.

Pedal note A sustained or regularly repeated note, usually heard in the bass, while the harmony above changes between various chords. Usually the pedal note is the tonic or dominant.

Pentatonic scale A scale of only five notes. The most well-known is formed by the black notes of the piano (C♯, E♭, F♯, G♯, B♭) and is anhemitonic, meaning that there are no semitones included (only tones and minor 3rds); alternatively, the pentatonic scale of C, E, F, G, B is hemitonic, as it has a semitone between E and F.

Periodic phrasing Music, typically of the Classical period, in which the melodic phrase is structured in pairs of 2-bar mini-phrases making pairs of 4-bar phrases, making pairs of longer 8-bar phrases, and then 16-bar phrases, and so on.

Phasing A technique used in minimalist composition where the same melodic or rhythmic idea is layered at marginally different tempos.

Phrygian mode Minor key with a flattened second note, a scale with a dark character: see example p216.

Pitch-bend A short slide up or down to the main note.

Pizzicato An instruction for string players to pluck the string instead of using the bow.

Plainsong An unaccompanied single melody line used in early Western church music; characteristically with a fairly free rhythm and a relatively narrow range of pitches.

Polarised Texture common in Baroque music where high-pitched instruments are accompanied by a bass continuo, without instruments included in the middle range. More recently, polarised texture is often used in film music as it portrays an expansiveness (e.g. for a landscape scene) and allows dialogue to be clearly heard spoken in mid-register.

Polyphony, polyphonic A musical texture where two or more parts move independently of one another.

Popular Song Form A common structure in songs in music theatre and popular music, in which there are four phrases where the first, second and fourth are related to give a pattern of AABA: see also **32-bar song form**.

Portamento A performing technique of sliding from one pitch to another, often associated with singing: see **glissando**.

Power chord In pop and rock music, a chord that consists of the root and the 5th, especially on electric guitars and often used with distortion: see **open 5th chord**.

Primary triads Chords I, IV and V in any key, so called because they are of a primary importance in establishing the tonality of a composition.

Protest song A song written to create social change, e.g. raise awareness of political injustice.

Push rhythm A rhythm that anticipates the beat, often entering a quaver earlier than expected, and sometimes tied to the first note of the bar to heighten the effect.

R&B Short for rhythm and blues, a style of music developed in the United States primarily by African Americans, soulful in mood, and often with improvisation and vocal **melismas** to embellish the melody line.

Raga A scale pattern or melodic motif used as the basis for melodic improvisation in Indian classical music.

Ragtime A style of music developed in the 1890s onwards, characterised by a syncopated melody line and regularly accented accompaniment, and usually played on the piano.

Rasgueado Guitar technique of precise, rapid strumming patterns, typical of flamenco music.

Recitative A type of vocal music where the words are the important element, and are usually sung in free time and in normal speech rhythm. Common in opera, it allows the singers to tell the story between the main arias, with minimal accompaniment. See p162 for a detailed explanation.

Relative major/minor A pair of keys which share the same key signature, one major and one minor: for example, the relative minor of F major is D minor, and the relative major of D minor is F major.

Resolution The release of tension in music as the harmony moves from a discord to a concord, or point of tonal stability.

Retrograde An extract of music played backwards: see example p241.

Riff In jazz, pop and rock, a short, catchy melodic or rhythmic idea repeated throughout a song.

Rip In jazz, a quick upwards glissando to a note.

Ritenuto Immediately slowing down.

Ritornello The main structural form for concerto movements in the late Baroque era. The term is also used to name the orchestral section heard at the opening and returns in various keys throughout a movement, punctuated by vocal solos (**episodes**). The ritornello may be repeated whole, or in part, or with variations. See pp130-131.

Rondo A musical structure popular in the Classical period in which a main melody alternates with a contrasting section (ABACA).

Root position A triad with its fundamental note in the bass line.

Rubato An interpretative performance technique, often associated with Romantic music, where some nuanced flexibility of rhythm is used (both holding back and pushing on) to create expressive affect.

Salsa Cuban dance music fused with North American jazz styles.

Sample, Sampling Taking an extract from a pre-existing piece and reusing it in another composition.

Scale Eight notes, making up all the notes in a key. The degrees of the scale have the following names:

- I Tonic
- II Supertonic (i.e. above the tonic)
- IIII Mediant (i.e. halfway to the dominant)
- IV Subdominant (i.e. the 5th below the tonic)
- V Dominant (i.e. the most dominant overtone to the tonic)
- VI Submediant (i.e. halfway to the subdominant when descending)
- VII Leading note (i.e. leading to the tonic)
- VIII Tonic

Scat singing Improvised music used in jazz, in which meaningless syllables are produced, often imitating the sounds of instruments such as the trumpet. Often associated with Louis Armstrong.

Scotch snap A two-note pattern in dotted rhythm (*short-long*), producing a distinctive effect: see also **Lombardic rhythm**.

Secondary dominant 7th A dominant triad which resolves to a chord that is not the tonic, often the dominant of the dominant, V^7 of V.

Secondary triad Chords ii, iii, vi and sometimes vii in any key, i.e. excluding those which are primary chords.

Sequence (in melody) The immediate repetition of a **motif** or phrase in the same instrumental or vocal part but at a different pitch.

Simple time A metre in which the main beat can be subdivided into two. The opposite of **Compound time**.

Simultaneous quodlibet A composition combining several different pre-existing melodies all heard at the same time, often light-hearted in manner.

Sirena Spanish for 'siren', a slow, moody glissando played with double-stopping on the violin, usually descending in pitch.

Smear In jazz, a loud, possibly coarse, slide away from a note.

Son A musical form, or type of song, originating from Cuba, with a distinctive clave rhythm pattern, and where the only accompaniment is percussion or rhythmic instruments.

Sonata form The most common structure for the first movement (and sometimes other movements) of compositions in the Classical style, comprising exposition, development and recapitulation.

Sotto voce Meaning literally 'under the voice', an indication that a hushed or whispered performance is required.

Staccato Short, detached playing, with gaps between the notes.

Stride playing In piano music, similar to ragtime, involving wide left-hand leaps between the bass notes and the corresponding chords.

Stringendo Tempo direction for getting faster.

Strophic A song where each verse is set to the same music.

Substitution chord A complex chord which functions in the same way as the simple chord it replaces.

Sul ponticello Direction to a string player to bow very close to the bridge, producing a whistling tone.

Sul tasto Direction to a string player to bow or pluck the strings over the fingerboard, producing a gentler tone.

Sus4 chord Major or minor chord where the 3rd is omitted and replaced with a 4th, creating an open sound without the 3rd and a dissonance between the 4th and 5th.

Suspension A note from a previous chord is carried over to the following chord, creating dissonance, before resolving. There are four categories: three are understood in terms of the interval above the bass (4-3, 7-6, 9-8), and the fourth is where the suspended note is in the bass.

Swell pedal On a pipe organ, a means of creating crescendo and diminuendo without changing stops (timbre).

Swing In jazz and blues style, the first quaver of a pair will often be played slightly longer than the second one.

Syllabic Vocal music in which each syllable of the lyrics is sung to a single note: see also **melisma**.

Sympathetic strings Also called resonance strings, these are auxiliary strings on an instrument which vibrate when the main strings are being played, providing a halo of sound around the note that is being played.

Syncopation The effect created when accented notes are sounded off the beat or on weak beats.

Synthesiser An electronic device with a keyboard that allows the player to add digital effects and to manipulate the sounds produced.

Tala Rhythmic patterns used in Indian music.

Tambor In tango, a form of pizzicato that causes the string to rebound off your finger creating an unpitched drum-like sound.

Tempo The speed of music, often indicated by a tempo marking at the beginning of a piece or passage of music.

Tenuto From the Italian 'to hold', this direction indicates the player should hold a note slightly longer than written, often for emphasis.

Ternary form A musical structure of three sections with similar outer sections and a contrasting central one (ABA). Usually the B section is in a contrasting key to the A sections. Can also be described as arch form.

Tessitura The average range of an instrumental, or more usually a vocal, piece. It is worthy of remark if a piece is written high or low in the range of the instrument or voice performing it.

Through-composed A song where each verse is set to contrasting music.

Tierce de Picardie A major tonic chord used to end a piece of music in a minor key.

Tonal The use of standard major and minor keys. Not all music is tonal: see also **modal** and **atonal.**

Tremolando A musical effect created by the rapid repetition of a single note, usually associated with string instruments.

Triad, triadic A melody based on the notes of the triad: the root, 3rd and 5th above it. A triad can be major, minor, diminished or augmented.

Trill An ornament: a fast oscillation with the note above or below the given note.

Trio sonata texture A piece written usually for two high-pitched instruments such as violin or flute, with a **basso continuo**, without middle-range instruments.

Tritone An interval of an augmented 4th (or diminished 5th), so called because an alternative way of counting it is as an interval of three tones. It so happens that this is exactly half an octave.

Tritone substitution Common in jazz, a chord where a dominant 7th chord is replaced by another dominant 7th chord whose root is a tritone away: see example on p282.

Turn A melodic ornament: see example on p105.

Una corda The soft pedal on a piano, so that only one string plays rather than three.

Underscore Music that is played under dialogue in a film score.

Unison Two or more people performing the same note or melody; in a choir when everyone is singing the same melody, even though the men are singing an octave lower than the women.

Vamp bar A bar or bars of music repeated to keep the music in time with the action on stage.

Verse-chorus form Simple song form common in pop music, alternating verses and chorus which contrast with one another.

Vibrato A performing technique where the pitch of a note slightly wavers to give the sound greater warmth and resonance.

Wah-wah mute An effect when a brass player alternately applies and removes a mute; on an electric guitar when the player controls output from the amplifier with a pedal.

Walking bass Common in both Baroque music and 20th century jazz and blues, a bass part with a regular rhythm throughout a piece, akin to feet walking.

Whole-tone scale A scale where there is a whole tone between all the notes, with no semitones as there would be in a conventional scale.

Word-painting Music written to reflect the meaning of the words, e.g. ascending when the words mention climbing a mountain.

ACKNOWLEDGEMENTS

Music credits

Rhinegold Education is grateful to the following publishers for permission to use printed music excerpts from their publications.

A Whiter Shade Of Pale, words & music by Matthew Fisher, Keith Reid & Gary Brooker. © Copyright 1967 Onward Music Limited. All Rights Reserved. International Copyright Secured.

Superstition, words & music by Stevie Wonder. © Copyright 1972 Jobete Music Company Incorporated, USA/Black Bull Music Incorporated, USA. EMI Music Publishing Limited. All Rights Reserved. International Copyright Secured.

Big Yellow Taxi, words & music by Joni Mitchell. © Copyright 1970 (Renewed) Crazy Crow Music, USA. Sony/ATV Music Publishing. All Rights Reserved. International Copyright Secured.

Psycho, music by Bernard Herrmann. © Copyright 1960 Sony/ATV Melody. Famous Music Corporation. All Rights Reserved. International Copyright Secured.

Aerith's Theme (From 'Final Fantasy VII'), music by Nobuo Uematsu. © Copyright 1997 Square Enix Co. Limited. Warner Chappell Music Ltd. All Rights Reserved. International Copyright Secured.

Vamo Alla Flamenco (From 'Final Fantasy IX'), music by Nobuo Uematsu. © Copyright 2000 Square Enix Co. Limited. Warner Chappell Music Ltd. All Rights Reserved. International Copyright Secured.

The Threepenny Opera, words by Bertolt Brecht, music by Kurt Weill. © Copyright 1928 European American Music Corporation/Universal Edition AG (Wien). Universal Edition (London) Ltd. All Rights Reserved. International Copyright Secured.

St. Louis Blues, words & music by W.C. Handy. © Copyright 1914 Francis Day & Hunter Limited. All Rights Reserved. International Copyright Secured.

Muskrat Ramble, words & music by Edward Ory. © Copyright 1926 Slick Tongue Ory Music. Bug Music Limited. All Rights Reserved. International Copyright Secured.

West End Blues, words & music by Clarence Williams & Joe 'King' Oliver. © Copyright 1928 Henrees Music Co. All Rights Reserved. International Copyright Secured.

The Mooche, words by Irving Mills, music by Duke Ellington & Irving Mills. © Copyright 1943 EMI Mills Music Incorporated. Lafleur Music Limited. All Rights Reserved. International Copyright Secured.

Ko Ko, words & music by Duke Ellington. © Copyright Robbins Music Corporation, USA. EMI United Partnership Limited. All Rights Reserved. International Copyright Secured.

Ko Ko, words & music by Charlie Parker. © Copyright 1945 Screen Gems-EMI Music Limited. All Rights Reserved. International Copyright Secured.

A Night In Tunisia, music by Dizzy Gillespie & Frank Paparelli. © Copyright 1944 Universal Music Corporation. Universal/MCA Music Limited. All Rights Reserved. International Copyright Secured.

Bird Of Paradise, Music by Charlie Parker. © Copyright 1947 MCA Duchess Music Corporation. Universal/MCA Music Limited. All Rights Reserved. International Copyright Secured.

So What, music by Miles Davis. © Copyright 1959 Jazz Horn Music Corporation, USA. Kobalt Music Publishing Limited. All Rights Reserved. International Copyright Secured.

(Cross The) Heartland, words & music by Pat Metheny & Lyle Mays. © Copyright 1979 Pat Meth Music Corporation, USA/Lyle Mays Music, USA. Kobalt Music Publishing Limited. All Rights Reserved. International Copyright Secured.

Libertango, Music by Astor Piazzolla. © Copyright 1975 by Edizioni Curci S.r.l. Eaton Music Limited for UK and EIRE. All Rights Reserved. International Copyright Secured.

Milonga Del Angel, music by Astor Piazzolla. © Copyright 1987 Lagos Editorial. Warner/Chappell Overseas Holdings Limited. All Rights Reserved. International Copyright Secured.

Swarna Jayanti (traditional), Arranged by Ravi Shankar. © Copyright 2000 St Rose Music Publishing Co/Anourag Music Publishing. Chester Music Limited. All Rights Reserved. International Copyright Secured.

Prayer In Passing, music by Ravi Shankar. © Copyright St Rose Music Publishing Co/ Anourag Music Publishing. Chester Music Limited. All Rights Reserved. International Copyright Secured.

Loucura, words by Joaquim Brito, music by Julio Sousa. © Copyright 2001 Universal Music Publishing MGB Brasil LTDA. Universal Music Publishing MGB Limited. All Rights Reserved. International Copyright Secured.

Retrato, words by Tiago Machado & Eugenio Andrade, music by Tiago Machado. © Copyright World Connection BV. Barking Green Music Limited/Eugenio de Andrade. All Rights Reserved. International Copyright Secured.

New York Girls (traditional), Arranged by Jonathan Boden & John Spiers. © Copyright 2010 Faber Music Limited. All Rights Reserved. International Copyright Secured.

Symphony No. 5, music by Dmitri Shostakovich. © Copyright 1939 Boosey & Hawkes Music Publishers Ltd. All Rights Reserved. International Copyright Secured.

Piano Concerto No. 2 In F Major, Op.102, music by Dmitri Shostakovich. © Copyright 1957 Anglo-Soviet Music Press Limited. All Rights Reserved. International Copyright Secured.

String Quartet No. 8 In C Minor, Op.110, music by Dmitri Shostakovich. © Copyright 1960 Boosey & Hawkes Music Publishers Ltd. All Rights Reserved. International Copyright Secured.

Symphony No. 1 In F Minor, Op.10, music by Dmitri Shostakovich. © Copyright 1925 Boosey & Hawkes Music Publishers Ltd. All Rights Reserved. International Copyright Secured.

Suite For Jazz Orchestra No. 2, music by Dmitri Shostakovich. © Copyright 1938 Boosey & Hawkes Music Publishers Ltd. All Rights Reserved. International Copyright Secured.

Instants Defunts De Preludes, music by Oliver Messiaen. © Copyright 1929 Durand Editions. G Ricordi & Company (London) Limited. All Rights Reserved. International Copyright Secured.

L'ascension, Part 1, music by Olivier Messiaen. © Copyright 1933 Alphonse Leduc Editions Musicales. All Rights Reserved. International Copyright Secured.

Turangalila Symphonie, music by Olivier Messiaen. © Copyright 1946 Durand Editions. G Ricordi & Company (London) Limited. All Rights Reserved. International Copyright Secured.

Music For Eighteen Musicians, music by Steve Reich. © Copyright 1978 Hendon Music Limited. All Rights Reserved. International Copyright Secured.

Different Trains, music by Steve Reich. © Copyright 1988 Hendon Music Limited. All Rights Reserved. International Copyright Secured.

O Radiant Dawn, music by James MacMillan. © Copyright 2008 Boosey & Hawkes Music Publishers Ltd. All Rights Reserved. International Copyright Secured.

Seraph, music by James MacMillan. © Copyright 2010 Boosey & Hawkes Music Publishers Ltd. All Rights Reserved. International Copyright Secured.

Picture credits:
Alamy: 16 (Heritage Image Partnership Ltd), 32 (OJO Images Ltd), 41 (Tetra images), 43 (KAKIMAGE), 84 (Hero Images Inc), 88 (MBI), 130 (GRANT ROONEY PREMIUM), 140 (Olaf Doering), 161 (ITAR-TASS Photo), 203 (RooM the Agency), 208 (Photo: Edd Westmacott), 218, 221, 292 (AF archive), 238 (ZUMA Press inc), 251 (Geraint Lewis), 270 (Pictorial Press Ltd), 281 (Everett Collection Historical), 295 (CTK), 278 (GL Archive), 298 (Jeff Morgan 02), 300 (Jeff Morgan 04), 303 (Guido Schiefer), 304 (Pablo Caridad), 307 (Jeff Gilbert), 310 (imageBROKER), 314 (Gonçalo Silva), 318 (WENN Ltd); ArenaPAL: 244, 261 (Nigel Norrington), 257 (Johan Persson), 268 (Marilyn Kingwill), 328 (Sputnik Images); Bridgeman Art Library: 327 above left (Private Collection), 327 above right (Private Collection / Photo © Christie's Images / © Succession Picasso/DACS, London 2017), 327 below left (© Ellsworth Kelly, courtesy Ellsworth Kelly Studio Archive, USA), 327 below right (© Jack Vettriano Publishing Ltd); M.C. Escher's 'Day and Night' © 2016 The M.C. Escher Company – The Netherlands. All rights reserved. www.mcescher.com: 20; Jeffrey Herman: 349; iStock: 90, 94; National Portrait Gallery, London: 122; Rex Features / Shutterstock: 194 (Frank Micelotta), 210 (ZUMA), 234 (Everett), 240 (Sadaka Edmond / SIPA), 324 (Dan Callister), 338 (Roger-Viollet); Hans van der Woerd: 352.